Implied Licences in Copyright Law

Implied Licences in Copyright Law

POORNA MYSOOR
Leverhulme Trust Early Career Fellow
Faculty of Law, University of Oxford

OXFORD
UNIVERSITY PRESS

OXFORD
UNIVERSITY PRESS

Great Clarendon Street, Oxford, OX2 6DP,
United Kingdom

Oxford University Press is a department of the University of Oxford.
It furthers the University's objective of excellence in research, scholarship,
and education by publishing worldwide. Oxford is a registered trade mark of
Oxford University Press in the UK and in certain other countries

First Edition published in 2021

Impression: 1

Published in the United States of America by Oxford University Press
198 Madison Avenue, New York, NY 10016, United States of America

British Library Cataloguing in Publication Data

Data available

Library of Congress Control Number: 2020947861

ISBN 978–0–19–885819–5

DOI: 10.1093/oso/9780198858195.001.0001

Printed and bound by
CPI Group (UK) Ltd, Croydon, CR0 4YY

For my father

Foreword

Many systems of laws, including state constitutions, operate with an underpinning of unspoken conventions or assumptions. The rationale for this is usually a combination of considerations of economy and efficiency—too many rules can impede the conduct of everyday life—and there is also the understandable desire to have a flexibility that will enable new cases to be resolved promptly without the need to engage in fresh law-making. Copyright laws provide a paradigmatic instance of this phenomenon: there are specific rules prescribing the exclusive rights to be granted to copyright owners, the limits on these rights in both substantive and temporal terms, and their enforcement. But there are many usages of protected works and subject matter not covered by the rules: while strictly infringing, users would mostly be surprised that this is so and, indeed, mostly assume that this is not the case. This is not a matter where guidance for national laws is to be found at the international level in the treaties to which the vast majority of countries are now bound, such as the Berne Convention, the WIPO Internet Treaties, or the TRIPs Agreement.

It is within the gaps between rights and uses that the device of the implied licence comes into play. In common law systems, at least, this flows from judicial decisions rendered on a case-by-case basis, although it is also true that in some instances it is assumed that an implied licence applies even in the absence of any court finding. For common lawyers, this may represent the genius of their legal tradition where judicial decisions in areas not directly covered by statute proceed incrementally by way of analogical reasoning and, over time, develop a body of case law that provides either binding or persuasive precedents for future courts to apply. Such developments, however, take time, particularly as the circumstances and uses to be addressed are themselves in flux and in the process of rapid evolution. This is no surprise to those involved in copyright law and practice: technological change and development are part of everyday life. It should also be no surprise that the case law concerned with implied copyright licences presents, at first sight, as a somewhat amorphous and disorganised body of jurisprudence that lacks the coherence that one finds in other, longer established common law areas such as the tort of negligence or the law of contract.

Providing a systematic study of this aspect of copyright law is the subject of this monograph by Dr Poorna Mysoor, and one that has been long overdue. She provides here an analytical framework for the examination of implied copyright licences in common law systems, with the object of formulating a workable methodology for courts to apply in future cases. For understandable reasons, her work is confined to common law jurisdictions, apart from the USA (the latter presents its own peculiarities), while the position under civil law systems is clearly a promising subject for future investigations of a comparative kind. But even within common law systems such as the UK, Australia, and Canada, the body of material to be examined is large, and the distillation of clear principles is not always easy—judges have to decide the cases before them, and frequently do not have the time or the need to spell out the analytical framework within which they are making those decisions. In this regard, Dr Mysoor's monograph will be invaluable in providing that framework and in making sense of the cases.

Beginning with the adoption of Wesley Hohfeld's classification of rights and duties, privileges and no-rights, Dr Mysoor divides implied copyright licences into bare and contractual licences, which becomes of particular relevance in the context of revocability. She then investigates the various bases for implication: the consent of the copyright owner to the use in question, the role of custom and, most controversially, the role of policy. She then carefully examines how these matters have been dealt with in the case law. In relation to the first, it becomes clear that the issue of consent is better understood as an inquiry into the knowledge of the copyright owner of what was contemplated at the time the copyright work was made available (the 'positive act', in Hohfeldian terms) and the effect of the copyright owner's subsequent conduct in relation to this (the 'neutral act', in Hohfeldian terms). In this regard, she argues that analogies drawn from implication of contractual terms (business efficacy and necessity) are not necessarily appropriate in the copyright licence context. In the second case of implication arising through custom, she examines the scope for this in various areas of copyright uses, noting that implication here becomes non-consensual in relation to the individual copyright owner or, rather, consent is imputed on the basis of a collective consent that has developed through the consistent and uniform practice of the relevant copyright community. This has particular resonance in the age of the internet, where it is often said that there are now well established customs of usage, although the challenges of proving custom will be far from straightforward.

In the third instance, that of policy-based implied licences, Dr Mysoor confronts a complex and often unwieldly beast, yet it is one that judges in several of the jurisdictions studied have embraced in differing ways. A clear methodology for implying licences in these cases, in the absence of some specific statutory limitation or exception, is required, and here Dr Mysoor deploys the three-step test (relevant to all of the common law systems studied by her, as a result of their international obligations) as a useful guide, as well as pointing to the application of fundamental rights under the European Convention on Human Rights in the particular case of the UK. Her analysis is crisp and well informed, and there is much food for thought here, as there is a fine line between judges providing workable solutions to practical problems or becoming judicial legislators. In her concluding chapters, Dr Mysoor then applies her analytical framework to three particular issues in the online environment: browsing, linking, and indexing.

There is much in this monograph to engage, challenge, and instruct the reader. Implied copyright licences provide the lubricant that oils the everyday usage of copyright materials, yet the theoretical bases for implication have never been systematically analysed. Dr Mysoor has done just that, and provides an important contribution to our understanding of the way in which courts in a common law jurisdiction can facilitate the smoother working of the copyright system. She is to be congratulated on her achievement.

Sam Ricketson
Emeritus Professor of Law
Melbourne Law School
2 October 2020

Preface

The monograph is derived from my DPhil thesis submitted in April 2017. Since the time of submitting my thesis, the topic has grown on me and I have grown with it. My engagement with this topic has been enriched by every audience to whom I had the privilege to present. Although my core arguments and conclusions have remained the same, my approach to these arguments and the manner of presenting them to a wider audience has undergone significant changes.

When this topic was suggested to me in 2012 for a doctoral thesis, I had imagined that I would be writing a law and technology thesis. Implied licence seemed to be an interesting topic because of its application to the internet. However, starting a doctorate in Oxford on this topic made all the difference to the way I understood this topic. I soon realised that the internet is only an illustration of the application of implied licences. For implied licences to provide any meaningful support to judicial reasoning, one must understand what a 'licence' is, what one means by 'implying' a licence and finally, how one may go about implying a copyright licence. This brought me close to not only the private law subjects of contract law and land law, but also to private law methodology and values—the fine balance between guidance and flexibility, the strenghts and pitfalls of certainty, the idea of fairness, to name a few. The exposure to private law was a defining moment in my journey towards building my research profile and honing my niche at the intersection of private law and intellectual property law. This is my first monograph arising from this niche.

Characteristically, the audience for private law is different from the audience for intellectual property law. This monograph tries to address both these audiences. The underlying private law concepts will be immediately familiar to private lawyers, whereas their application to copyright law may speak to intellectual property lawyers more. This is the beginning of a conversation where an effort is made to more closely integrate copyright law with private law.

Acknowledgements

This work would not have been possible without the mentorship and continued encouragement of my doctoral supervisor, Professor Graeme Dinwoodie. For this, I will always be grateful. I thank Professor John Cartwright for his patience, empathy, and time in reading my earlier drafts and giving me detailed comments. I am grateful for all the feedback and guidance I have received from Professor Dev Gangjee and Professor Robert Burrell at the Law Faculty at Oxford.

I am deeply indebted to the Leverhulme Trust for supporting the completion of this monograph. The research visits made possible by the Trust during my Early Career Fellowship deepened my engagement with this topic and remarkably transformed the way I presented this book. I am deeply thankful to Professor Sam Ricketson and Professor Megan Richardson for their generosity with their time and for the helpful discussion we had when I was a Visiting Fellow at the Intellectual Property Research Centre of Australia in 2019. Many thanks are also owed to Professor Elise Bant and Professor Andrew Christie, whose comments were particularly helpful. I am also grateful to Professor David Tan and the EW Barker Centre for Business Law for hosting me at the Law Faculty, National University of Singapore. The discussions I had with Professor David Tan, Professor Wee Loon Loy, Professor James Penner, and Professor Umakanth Varottil were engaging and incisive. I am thankful to Professor Kung Chung Liu for inviting me to Singapore Management University to present my work to an enthusiastic private law audience. My particular thanks go to Professor Tham Chee Ho, who took time to discuss the finer aspects of private law with me, and to Professor David Llewelyn for his insightful comments. I am also grateful to Dr Pascale Chapdelaine for her generous invitation for me to visit Windsor Law School, Ontario. I learnt a great deal presenting to the audience at the LTEC Lab. Many thanks to Professor David Vaver for taking time to discuss and share Canadian copyright law resources with me. Many thanks also to Professor Lionel Bently for inviting me to present at CIPIL and to Dr Henning Grosse Ruse-Khan for his helpful suggestions. The feedback I received from the audience was influential in shaping my work. I extend my gratitude also to The Queen's College, Oxford, for offering me a 'home' during my postdoctoral fellowship and to Professor Nicholas Bamforth for his support, encouragement, and friendship.

My special thanks to Jyothsna Gurumurthy for all her hard work, diligence, and excellent research assistance. This work was completed during the worst of the pandemic of 2020 when the Bodleian Law Library had been shut for months. Even through these difficult times, the unwavering support lent by the Bodleian

Law Library staff speaks volumes for their excellence and dedication. I would like to make a special mention of the help I received from Katherine Jackson, Margaret Watson and the Bodleian Law Librarian, Helen Garner. Many thanks also to my dear friends Dr Pascal Kesseli, a computer scientist, and Kalpana Sivabala, for her help with EU law. A big thank you to all my private law and IP law students who constantly challenge me and enrich my research.

Lastly, but most importantly, I cannot thank my parents enough for always believing in me, and Anup for looking after me.

Table of Contents

PART II: RATIONALISING CONCEPTUAL FRAMEWORKS WITHIN COPYRIGHT DOCTRINE

List of Figures

List of Abbreviations

A1P1	Article 1, Protocol 1, ECHR
ACA	Australian Copyright Act 1968
ACEA	Association of Consulting Engineers Australia
ALAI	Association Litteraire et Artistique Internationale
BC	Berne Convention for the Protection of Literary and Artistic Works
BL	British Leyland
CAPAC	Composers, Authors and Publishers Association of Canada
CCA	Canadian Copyright Act 1985 Officially, The Copyright Act RSC 1985 c. C-42
CDPA	Copyright, Designs and Patents Act 1988 (UK)
CFREU	Charter of Fundamental Rights of the European Union
CJEU	Court of Justice of the European Union
CMRRA	Canadian Musical Rights Reproduction Association
CMS	Clearsprings Management
CRA	Consumer Rights Act 2015 (UK)
ECHR	European Convention on Human Rights
ECtHR	European Court of Human Rights
EEA	European Economic Area
Exit Day	Implementation Period Completion Day As defined in s 39(1) of the European Union (Withdrawal Agreement) Act 2020, which is 31 December 2020.
HKCO	Hong Kong Copyright Ordinance (Cap 528) 1997
HRA	Human Rights Act 1998 (UK)
Infosoc Directive	Directive 2001/29/EC on the harmonisation of certain aspects of copyright and related rights in the information society
ISP	internet service provider
MSDS	material safety data sheets
NLA	Newspaper Licensing Agency Ltd
PRCA	Public Relations Consultants Association
RIBA	Royal Institute of British Architects
SCA	Singapore Copyright Act 1987
SCI	Service Corporation International
SGA	Sale of Goods Act 1979 (UK)
SLE	statutory limitations or exceptions
TPM	technological protection measure
TRIPs	WTO Agreement on Trade-Related Aspects of Intellectual Property Rights

UCTA	Unfair Contract Terms Act 1977 (UK)
URL	uniform resource locator
WCT	WIPO Copyright Treaty
WEUL	web end user licence
WIPO	World Intellectual Property Organization
WTO	World Trade Organization

Table of Cases

UNITED KINGDOM

COURT OF JUSTICE OF THE EUROPEAN UNION

EUROPEAN COURT OF HUMAN RIGHTS

AUSTRALIA

CANADA

GERMANY

IRELAND

NEW ZEALAND

SINGAPORE

UNITED STATES

WTO PANEL REPORT

Table of Statutes and Treaties

AUSTRALIA

CANADA

HONG KONG

SINGAPORE

EUROPEAN UNION

INTERNATIONAL TREATIES AND INSTRUMENTS

Introduction

Copyright confers exclusive rights on copyright owners to perform certain acts in relation to their work. A person infringes copyright if she performs any of these acts in relation to a copyright work without 'the licence of the owner of the copyright'.[1] That means, if a person wants to use a copyright work such as a journal article, by exercising one of the acts restricted to the copyright owner, say copying, to avoid infringement the user will need a licence from the copyright owner, which often takes the form of a prior express licence. Alternatively, the user's actions must be covered by one of the statutory limitations or exceptions (SLEs). The SLEs address specific instances of permitted use of copyright works to achieve specific policy goals. For example, if the user wants to reproduce parts of a journal article for criticism, then such use may be permitted under the statutory provisions for fair dealing for this purpose, and therefore, may not amount to infringement. If, however, a certain use is not authorised by either an express licence of the copyright owner or by the SLEs, it does not always amount to an infringement. It may be possible for courts to *imply* a copyright licence to cover such use. Implied licences, which span the spectrum between express licences at one end and the SLEs at the other, are the focus of this monograph.

There are several advantages in focusing on implied licences, when neither express licences nor SLEs cover the use in question. Not insisting on express licence of the copyright owner will enable a court to hold the conduct of the copyright owner to account more astutely to imply a licence. As for the SLEs, the list of specific instances of permitted use in many jurisdictions is exhaustive. Implied licences, in contrast, respond to the facts and circumstances of each case, and not to only a predetermined list of scenarios. When implied, licences have the potential to respond to a broader range of scenarios than the SLEs. Further, the SLEs draw legitimacy from a legislative process, which can be slow moving. The SLEs can be rigid not only in their scope, but also in their inability to cover newer uses. The strength of implied licences, on the other hand, lies in their flexibility to address a diverse set of circumstances. This may prove particularly useful in resolving issues arising from the interaction of copyright with new technologies. Armed with this flexibility and

[1] Copyright, Design and Patents Act 1988 (CDPA), s 16(2); Australian Copyright Act 1968 (ACA), s 36(1). The Canadian Copyright Act 1985 (CCA), s 27(1) says it is without the 'consent' of the owner of the copyright. Chapter 2 below addresses the distinction between consent and licence, as understood in this work.

Implied Licences in Copyright Law. Poorna Mysoor, Oxford University Press (2021). © Poorna Mysoor.
DOI: 10.1093/oso/9780198858195.003.0001

the ability to respond in a case-specific manner, implied licences can bring about a better balance among different stakeholders within the copyright system.

One must acknowledge that there are other ways in which copyright balance may be achieved, and that implied licences are not suggested as a solution to the exclusion of these other means. The other means include interpreting the SLEs broadly or interpreting the exclusive rights narrowly, depending on the circumstances. This may be possible more readily in jurisdictions like Canada than in jurisdictions like the EU, where the SLEs are required to be interpreted narrowly and a high level of protection is guaranteed for rightholders.[2] In any event, these methods could be constrained by the language of the statute defining the right or the exception. A court may take liberties to read into an exclusive right the considerations that are not apparent from the language of the relevant statute, such as in the case of the CJEU's interpretation of the right of communication to the public. This could compromise doctrinal clarity.

The implied licence approach, in contrast, focuses on the infringement itself, rather than the exclusive right or the SLE. It recognises that there are two components that constitute an infringement—the exercise of the exclusive right and such exercise being without the (express or implied) licence. One must admit to the exercise of an exclusive right before an argument on implied licence can be raised. Admitting to the exercise of a right, however, is not admitting to infringement—one still needs to show the absence of licence. By making these licences do the heavy lifting as opposed to the exclusive right, one can achieve a consistent interpretation of the exclusive right at an objective level. This can enable a court take into account only considerations that inform the exercise of the right, and utilise the considerations outside of it to inform whether a licence may be implied to respond to infringement. This approach is particularly useful in relation to the exercise of the right of communication to the public, which tends to be given inconsistent interpretation depending on the desired outcome. Therefore, it is worth exploring whether implied licences can respond better to an alleged act of infringement than other methods can.

Despite the advantages, implied licences have not been studied systematically. Courts in some jurisdictions, notably in the United States and Germany, have engaged with implied licences in dealing with copyright issues on the internet.[3] Courts in the UK, Australia, Canada, and a few other common law jurisdictions have also actively considered implying copyright licences in response to copyright infringement, but mostly in the offline environment. A review of the existing case

[2] More recently, however, the CJEU has recognised that exceptions may also need to be interpreted broadly. See Case C-469/17 *Funke Medien v Bundesrepublik* ECLI:EU:C:2019:623; Case C-516/17 *Spiegel Online v Volker Beck* ECLI:EU:C:2019:625; and Case C-476/17 *Pelham v Ralf Hütter* ECLI:EU:C:2019:624, decided together on 29 July 2019.

[3] *Field v Google*, 412 F Supp 2d 1106; decisions in Google Image Search cases (*Vorschaubilder I and II*) of the German Federal Supreme Court.

law, however, does not reveal a consistent methodology of implying copyright licences. Even if the judges claim that there is a method, the method does not remain consistent or transparent in subsequent cases of similar kind. As a result, uncertainty surrounds the implication of copyright licences. This might explain why in the UK, in *Newspaper Licensing Agency v Meltwater Holdings BV*, a case on the legality of internet browsing, Proudman J stated that she was taken to no authority on implied licence,[4] although implied licences could have been helpful in addressing the issues.

Some of the hesitation the courts have in engaging with implied licences lies in the very nature of 'implication' as a process. Implication in any area of law is contentious because of the apparent discretion it gives the courts as to what is to be implied. To guide the exercise of such discretion, courts try to formulate principles of implication; for example, those for implying a term into a contract or implying an easement. There are, however, no established principles that govern implying a copyright licence. If a copyright licence is implied into a contract, then the rules of implying a term into a contract may be applied. However, this assumes that these rules are unproblematic and overstates their usefulness. Further, a copyright licence may not always be implied into a contact but may be implied as a bare licence. In these circumstances, principles from contract law could be a misfit. There is a need to invest in a distinct methodology for implying copyright licences. This can also ensure that licences are not implied indiscriminately, undermining the rights of the copyright owner; nor are they implied conservatively, denying the users of socially beneficial uses. The methodology should focus on a transparent way of implying copyright licences, so that the methodology offers guidance to future cases, in addition to rationalising the existing case law. This is what the monograph aims to achieve, so that implied licences are more readily accepted than they have been within the copyright discourse.

One may wonder whether the existing literature may have already addressed implied licences and the methodology. Some of the leading textbooks in the UK and Australia on copyright are helpful in bringing to the fore, in differing degrees of detail, cases in which the courts have had an opportunity to consider implying a copyright licence. These textbook accounts are largely descriptive and serve as a good compendium of cases.[5] Others mention briefly a possibility of implying a copyright licence.[6] Although some scholars discuss terms implied in fact and terms implied by law into a contract,[7] they do not explain how this may impact implying

[4] [2010] EWHC 3099 [100] (Ch).

[5] Gillian Davies, Nicholas Caddick, and Gwilym Harbottle, *Copinger and Skone James on Copyright* (17th edn, Sweet & Maxwell 2016) paras 5-244 ff; Mary Vitoria and others, *Laddie, Prescott and Vitoria Modern Law of Copyright* (5th edn, LexisNexis 2018) paras 13.15 ff; Sam Ricketson, Megan Richardson, Mark Davison, and Vicki Huang, Intellectual Property (6th edn, Lexis Nexis 2019) 510-519.

[6] William Cornish, David Llewelyn, and Tanya Aplin, *Intellectual Property* (9th edn, Sweet & Maxwell 2019) para 13-013.

[7] Lionel Bently and others, *Intellectual Property Law* (5th edn, OUP 2018) 312–13.

a copyright licence. Scholars have also discussed the application of implied licences to specific issues, such as making sense of Google Image Search decisions under German law[8] or in explaining copyright exhaustion.[9] Although this literature has its relevance, it does not examine the bigger picture to ascertain how we may bring certainty into the way implied copyright licences evolve.

What we need is not another descriptive work that brings these cases together, but a predictive and analytical work to guide the future direction of this doctrine. This is why this work focuses on developing a methodology for implying copyright licences. For such methodology to be credible, one must demonstrate a teleologically sound rationale and a cogent internal logic. A robust conceptual foundation not only leads to a better understanding of the existing doctrine, but also helps steer the evolution of the future doctrine. Therefore, the conceptual foundation of the methodology is guided by property theory, copyright theory, and analytical jurisprudence. It also draws inspiration from contract law in developing the manner of implying a copyright licence, learning from its shortcomings. Once the foundation is laid, the monograph builds over it inductively using the existing case law, so that the methodology not only stays close to the issues litigated thus far, but also attempts to give a meaningful projection to the future.

By bringing considerations outside copyright law and copyright theory into the conceptual foundation of the methodology, an attempt is made to enhance objectivity and neutrality, so that the methodology does not favour one stakeholder to the exclusion of the others. Copyright users form a disparate group, ranging from record companies and film production houses to individual internet end users, who may not approach a court to defend their ability to access content on the internet. Copyright owners also form a disparate group, ranging from commercially successful authors, record companies, and film producers to up-and-coming struggling authors. For implied licences to produce meaningful results for all parties concerned and to maintain credibility, the methodology must remain neutral. An important reason for focusing on making the methodology transparent is that it helps all stakeholders to see what it takes for implying a copyright licence, so that each can present their arguments accordingly.

The existence of licence, express or implied, negates copyright infringement. In this sense, implied licences are a denial of an element of the copyright owner's cause of action.[10] As regards the burden of proof, a copyright owner as the claimant bears the initial burden of proving that the user engaged in a restricted act without

[8] Tanya Pihlajarinne, 'Setting the Limits for the Implied License in Copyright and Linking Discourse: the European Perspective' (2012) 43(6) IIC 700.

[9] Reto M Hilty, "'Exhaustion" in the Digital Age' in Irene Calboli and Edward Lee (eds), *Research Handbook on Intellectual Property Exhaustion and Parallel Imports* (Edward Elgar Publishing 2016).

[10] James Goudkamp and Donal Nolan, *Winfield & Jolowicz on Tort* (20th edn, Sweet & Maxwell 2020) para 26-007. Authors regard consent and implied consent as a denial of the tort of trespass, as opposed to a defence. ibid para 26-008.

the licence of the copyright owner. The extent to which the copyright owner must also address the possibility of implying copyright licence raises further issues. Likewise, a user may approach the court claiming that the copyright owner has made groundless threats of infringement, relying on the possibility of implying a licence to counter infringement,[11] and so issues of burden of proof arise again. This issue is revisited in the Final Remarks at the end of this work, once the breadth of implied licences is demonstrated.

Jurisdictions Covered

Implied licence considered here is predominantly a common law doctrine in that it is up to the courts to formulate the manner of implying a licence, rather than the statute. Additionally, this monograph draws on common law relating to property and contract. The main footprint covered in this work jurisdictionally is UK law as far as copyright law is concerned and English law as far as the underlying principles drawn from contract and property law are concerned. This work also features other common law countries such as Australia, Canada, Singapore, and Hong Kong in differing degrees of detail. The choice of these jurisdictions is also based on the fact that these jurisdictions have modelled their basic copyright statute directly or indirectly on one of the erstwhile versions of UK copyright statutes—Australia and Singapore on the UK Copyright Act 1956, Canada on the UK Copyright Act 1911, and Hong Kong on the Copyright, Designs and Patents Act 1988 (CDPA). However, these jurisdictions have substantially amended their statutes and have added muscle to the bare bones of the statute with rich case law. This work does not cover US law, although the United States is a common law jurisdiction, as US law has historically charted a different route. Further, the experts in US law are already exploring implied copyright licences, both doctrinally[12] and conceptually.[13]

This work does recognise that, as far as UK is concerned, copyright is not a matter of common law alone, at least until the Exit Day.[14] Therefore, this work also features the relevant EU law and, in particular, the CJEU's jurisprudence on the harmonised aspects of UK copyright law. However, this work does not explore the possibility of a doctrine of implied licence in the continental European jurisdictions, individually or collectively. To a limited extent, the idea of implied consent

[11] A prominent example being *Concrete Pty Ltd v Parramatta Design & Development Pty Ltd* [2006] HCA 55.

[12] Examples include John Sieman, 'Using the Implied Licence to Inject Common Sense into Digital Copyright' (2007) 85 NCL Rev 885, 906; Orit Fischman Afori, 'Implied Licence: An Emerging New Standard in Copyright Law' (2009) 25 Santa Clara Computer & High Tech LJ 275, 291.

[13] Christopher Newman, '"What Exactly Are You Implying?": the Elusive Nature of the Implied Copyright Licence' (2013–14) 32 Cardozo Arts & Ent LJ 501.

[14] Exit Day is the IP Completion Day under the EU (Withdrawal Agreement) Act 2020, s 39, which is 31 December 2020 at 11 pm.

has been recognised under the French[15] and German law.[16] Whether there is sufficient basis in the law of the continental jurisdictions to cover the entire range of implied licences considered here is not a question that this work addresses. This monograph is intended as the start of a conversation to which this author welcomes experts in continental jurisdictions to add, if they find analogies that respond to their respective legal systems. This work is a study in comparative law only within the common law jurisdictions named above. It is an attempt to provide depth in what this work covers, without spreading the analysis too thin by addressing disparate legal traditions.

Words, Meanings, and Scope

In this book, unless otherwise stated, the word 'work' is used universally to refer not only to authorial works, but also to entrepreneurial works. Although both the Australian Copyright Act 1968 (ACA) and the Canadian Copyright Act 1985 (CCA) distinguish between authorial works and entrepreneurial works, this book adopts the approach of the CDPA for simplicity. The CDPA makes a distinction between a 'work' and a 'copyright work' in that a work is that which answers the description of the kind enumerated in the CDPA, whereas a copyright work is a work in which copyright subsists. In this monograph, since copyright subsistence is not the central issue, but rather the infringement and a response to it are, the words 'work' and 'copyright work' are used interchangeably.

The term 'copyright owner' is adopted as a universal term to refer to authors, those who produce entrepreneurial works, and those who are for the time being the owners of copyright—such as assignees of copyright interest, unless the context requires otherwise. The word 'use' of a copyright work means the kind of use of copyright that engages one or more of the exclusive rights. In many places, the term 'user' or 'copyright user' is adopted as an abbreviation to mean the user of a copyright work in this sense.

The scope of this monograph extends only to economic rights and not to moral rights. The predominant reason for this is to keep the discussion focused on one type of rights and manage the diversity of arguments within it. Moreover, economic rights are litigated more extensively than moral rights, lending more opportunity for courts to consider implying licences. In general, the holder of moral rights can consent to certain acts which would otherwise be an infringement. While under the CDPA an implied consent appears to be possible, under the ACA the consent

[15] Case C-301/15 *Mark Soulier v Premier Ministre* ECLI:EU:C:2016:878, to the extent that the reference arose from French courts interpreting French law in the light of EU directives.

[16] Google Image Search cases (*Vorschaubilder I and II*) of the German Federal Supreme Court.

must be in writing.[17] Waiver of moral rights is also recognised in copyright statutes, which normally requires writing.[18] Whether the whole range of implied licences for economic rights discussed here might also apply to moral rights is a question for exploration in a separate work.

The Structure of the Monograph

The monograph is divided into three parts: Part I lays down the conceptual foundation for the methodology for implying copyright licences and proposes frameworks that guide implying copyright licences in different scenarios; Part II goes on to analyse and rationalise the existing case law on implied copyright licences in the light of the frameworks developed in Part I; and Part III applies the learnings from Part I and Part II to address copyright issues on the internet as an illustration of the usefulness of implied copyright licences. It is hoped that this division will help audiences interested in different aspects of implied licences—be it conceptual, doctrinal, or application of implied licences, to access the respective parts readily.

Part I

This part provides the conceptual foundation on which the rest of the monograph is organised. For it to offer a meaningful support for the methodology, it must address the following three questions. First, what kind of legal relationship is a copyright licence? Secondly, on what bases can copyright licences be implied? And, thirdly, how does one go about implying a copyright licence once the basis is known?

Chapter 1 explores the answer to the first question. In unpacking the legal relationship that a copyright licence is, one must first understand what a 'licence' is, because the reliability of the doctrine of implied licence depends on the coherence of the concept of licence. The most widely used definition of a licence (derived from land law) as that which makes an action lawful without which the action would be unlawful,[19] reflects the universality of a licence, but it sheds little light on the constituents of a licence. If one is unsure what constitutes an express licence, how is one to identify an implied licence? Copyright law does not shed any light on the constituents of a licence either. Therefore, the monograph turns to Hohfeldian analytics to identify the constituents of a licence that hold good regardless of the

[17] CDPA, s 87(1) and (4), which may permit implied consent. But see ACA, ss 195AW(2) and 195AWA(2).

[18] CDPA, s 87(2) requires writing and CCA, s 14.1(4) is less clear on writing.

[19] *Thomas v Sorrell* (1672) Vaugh 330, 351.

diversity of circumstances in which licences arise. The identification of constituents of a licence also helps understand the kind of transaction that a licence is. It helps to demonstrate that a licence is not in itself a contract, although a licence can be partly or wholly the consideration that moves from one party to another. This facilitates the distinction between a bare licence and a contractual licence. The distinction is important because a licence within a contract must be assessed as part of the bargain, and therefore different considerations go into implying a licence into a contract than if one were to imply a bare licence.

Chapter 2 explores the second question above, namely the bases on which copyright licences can be implied. It begins by looking at analogies in other areas of private law dealing with implication. The most elaborate doctrine of implication are the rules of implication of a term into a contract—implied in fact, implied by custom, and implied by law. These are known to private law as sources of private and public ordering, which apply as much to the actions of persons vis-à-vis other persons (such as entering into a contract) as they do to the actions of persons vis-à-vis persons in relation to property (such as granting a licence). It follows that these also form the basis on which express copyright licences arise. The bases for implying copyright licences must be the same as the bases for express copyright licences to arise. This way, the exercise of the discretion that the courts have in implying copyright licences is made more transparent and predictable, fostering legitimacy and coherence in the process. Accordingly, the bases for implying copyright licences are: the consent of the copyright owner (consent-based); an established usage in a trade or an industry (custom-based); and state intervention to achieve policy objectives (policy-based). Each of these types of licences can be further classified into bare and contractual licences.

Categorising licences this way will be of no help if we are unable to determine how one is to go about actually implying a copyright licence, ie the methodology of implying. Therefore, Chapter 3 goes on to propose frameworks under each category, which help to assess the facts and circumstances and determine whether a licence must be implied and, if yes, the scope of the licence. Given that the advantage of implied licences is their flexibility, any rigid set of rules governing the implication could strike at the heart of such flexibility. Therefore, the monograph proposes frameworks as opposed to rigid rules, and seeks to balance guidance and flexibility. These frameworks are developed based on the constituents that each category of licence would need to have, had it been an express licence; and when the express licence is absent, these frameworks indicate how the facts and circumstances can be marshalled, so that one can ascertain whether a licence is to be implied. These frameworks approach bare licences differently from contractual licences. Figure 1 below depicts the methodology envisaged in this monograph.

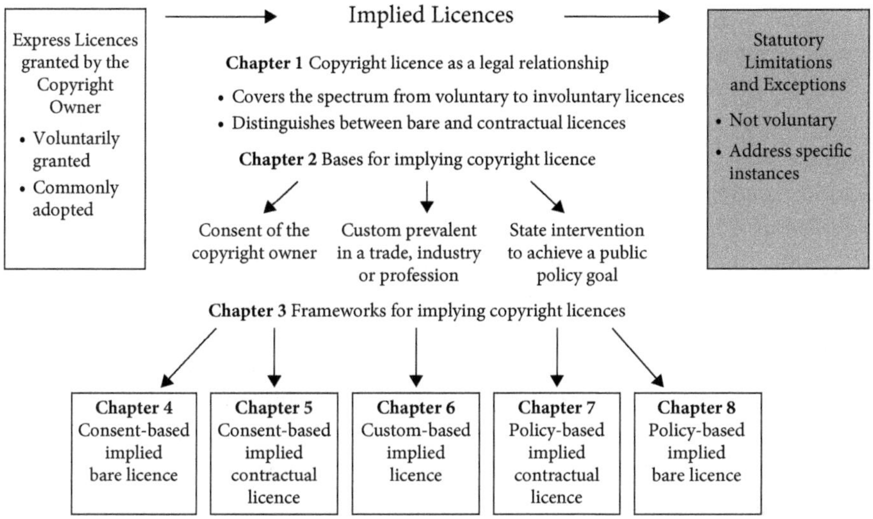

Figure 1 Methodology for implying copyright licences

Part II

Part I puts forward frameworks for implying copyright licences and prepares the ground for Part II to analyse and rationalise the existing case law on implied copyright licences in the light of these frameworks. The chapters in Part II are ordered in such a way as to show the decreasing importance of voluntariness of the copyright owner as one moves towards the SLEs. As shown in Figure 1 above, it covers the spectrum from licences implied based on the consent of the copyright owner representing some voluntariness at one end to licences that are implied based on policy regardless of the consent of the copyright owner. It is possible that in some cases more than one basis for implying copyright licences is explored, demonstrating a connection between the frameworks proposed. This is why each chapter ends with not just conclusions from its own discussions, but also establishes connection with the next.

Chapter 4 deals with consent-based implied bare licences, examining situations where the copyright owner impliedly grants a licence gratuitously, meaning nothing (whether payment or any other form of consideration) flows to the copyright owner in return for the licence. This chapter adopts the framework proposed and analyses the case law by examining the conduct of the copyright owner and her knowledge of the surrounding circumstances. An essential characteristic of consent-based bare licences is that they can be unilaterally revoked or withdrawn. Therefore, this chapter examines whether proprietary estoppel can be deployed in certain cases to declare a bare licence irrevocable.

Chapter 5 deals with consent-based implied contractual licences, which differ from consent-based bare licences in that there is consideration that flows from the licensee in exchange for the licensor undertaking not to revoke the licence, in addition to there being an intention to create legal relations. The existence of a contract provides the structure within which to assess the copyright owner's consent as the basis for implying a licence. This chapter demonstrates that the rules of implication of a term into a contract are less helpful in providing a transparent methodology. Also, they apply generally to any term in a contract, but we are concerned with implying a specific type of term into a contract, namely a copyright licence. Therefore, a separate framework formulated for this purpose is more helpful. To facilitate a systematic analysis, this chapter examines the case law in three broad categories of contractual copyright licences: (i) commissioning contracts; (ii) copyright exploitation contracts; and, briefly, (iii) consumer contracts.

Chapter 6 deals with licences implied by custom. A custom in this context represents the conduct of a community (of members of a trade, profession, industry, or market), as opposed to an individual copyright owner enabling the copyright work to be used in a particular way. So long as the community within which the custom is alleged represents the copyright owner, the community's conduct will be taken as being on behalf of the copyright owner. Once established, a custom does not require validation by a court of law for it to be binding, so that a custom becomes an independent source of power that drives the implication of a copyright licence. Also, once established, a custom can be the basis for implying both a bare licence and a contractual licence, depending on the content of the custom. Therefore, this chapter analyses the case law within a single framework for implying both bare and contractual licences. It builds on the criteria developed by the courts in commercial law to establish a custom (certainty, notoriety, and reasonableness), incorporating factors specific to the copyright context.

Chapter 7 deals with policy-based implied contractual licences, focusing on situations where there is a pre-existing contract and a copyright licence is implied into it to achieve policy objectives. There is some voluntariness to the conduct of the copyright owner in entering into the contract. However, the copyright licence is implied into the contract to achieve a policy objective regardless of the consent of the copyright owner. The framework for implication underlying this chapter is inspired by the rules of implying a term by law into a contract, but made more transparent to acknowledge the role of policy as the basis of implication and the need for the policy to be identified. The chapter examines instances where such implication has been found necessary based on the specific policies they set out to achieve—such as facilitation of trade, the right to repair, health and safety policies at the workplace, and so on.

Chapter 8 deals with policy-based implied bare licences. Unlike Chapter 7, there is no contract in existence and no voluntariness on the part of the copyright owner, and indeed no prior relationship between the parties. Historically, English common law has recognised an open-ended power of the courts to restrict or prevent copyright enforcement in the public interest, which has been acknowledged under section 171(3) of the CDPA. This chapter considers how a successful invocation of this power implies a bare licence to achieve policy goals. Although there is no statutory equivalent of this provision in other common law jurisdictions considered here, this chapter explores if the power was nevertheless exercised by the courts based on their inherent powers. Since policy-based implied bare licences produce the same effect on copyright owners as the SLEs, the framework for implying this type of licence draws inspiration from the three-step test and the fundamental rights regime.

Part III

A significant part the content on the internet is protected by copyright. Therefore, it is of deep concern not only to the copyright owners, but to many stakeholders who are users of this content for various purposes including business, social, and personal, as to how the law balances their competing interests. Utilising the conceptual foundation in Part I and doctrinal analysis in Part II, the monograph moves on to Part III to illustrate the application of implied licences to the internet to address some of the challenges. It focuses on UK and, to the extent relevant, CJEU decisions, which raise copyright infringement issues in relation to browsing, hyperlinking, and indexing copyright works. These are some of the most basic actions on the internet but raise some of the most complex issues on the internet.

Chapter 9 provides the essential connection between the conclusions from chapters in Part II and the internet. This chapter begins by classifying between content on the internet that has been placed by or with the copyright owner's consent and that without. In the former category, it also examines the consequences of placing terms of use in relation to the content on the internet. This classification is essential because it lays the common structure and foundation to determine which bases of implying a copyright licence apply to address browsing, hyperlinking, and indexing in each of the successive chapters.

Chapter 10 deals with browsing. Browsing refers to simply viewing the content on the internet and includes streaming if the content has sound or video elements to it. It engages the right of reproduction, and the UK has tried to address this by way of the temporary copying exception under section 28A of the CDPA. This chapter examines its efficacy and how implied licence may offer a more coherent response.

Chapter 11 deals with hyperlinking. Hyperlinking enables establishing links between different webpages and is critical to enhancing the efficacy of the internet. Although scholars are still divided, courts have held that hyperlinking engages the right of communication to the public. However, the approach adopted by the CJEU suffers from inconsistencies. This chapter explores if implied licence can again provide a more coherent response.

Chapter 12 deals with indexing. Indexing is typically engaged by internet service providers of different kinds such as search engines, content aggregators, and online platform providers, including social media. Indexing simply tries to achieve greater accessibility of the content on the internet; however, it may engage the right of reproduction and the right of communication to the public. This chapter explains how courts have tried to deal with this issue and argues for a greater role of implied licences to address the issues of copyright infringement.

In conclusion, the monograph consolidates the advantages of implied licences not only in the offline, but especially in the online world. The monograph acknowledges that express words can override implied licences, but also explains why it is not a significant limitation on the usefulness of implied licence, arguing that implied licence can and will continue to play a significant role in copyright law. It also highlights how implied licences have the potential to play a greater role after the Exit Day.

PART I
CONCEPTUAL FOUNDATION

> [T]he chameleon-hued term, 'license' ... may be said to be a word of convenient and seductive obscurity; ...[1]

The complexity of licences captured in these graphic words of Wesley Newcomb Hohfeld extends to copyright licences. Indeed, the complexity deepens when a licence is not granted expressly but must be implied. Consider the following scenarios involving copyright works:

(a) A has been invited to sing in a rock band. B helps A as a friend, by writing the lyrics of a song and gives them to A.[2] A assigns the lyrics to C, a member of the band. Can A do this?
(b) A engages B, an architect, for a fee, to draw the architectural plans to build a house.[3] B draws the plans and gives them to A. A pays B the fee, and then engages another architect C, to build the house based on the same plans. Can A do this?
(c) A, the publisher of a newspaper, publishes a story incorporating certain quotes from an interview first published in a competing newspaper B, arguing that this is what newspapers 'normally do'.[4] Can A do this?
(d) A, a repair service provider, makes spare parts to order, knowing that the copyright in the design of the spare parts belongs to B, but does so without B's permission.[5] Can A do this?
(e) A provides a hyperlink on her website to external content online, knowing that the content to which the link leads infringes B's copyright.[6] Can A do this?

As these examples relate to diverse circumstances, it may be difficult to see a common theme running through them. To begin with, it is unclear whether all of

[1] Wesley Newcomb Hohfeld, 'Faulty Analysis in Easement and Licence Cases' (1917) 27 Yale LJ 66, 92.
[2] *Banks v CBS Music Ltd* [1996] EMLR 440.
[3] *Blair v Osborne* [1971] 1 All ER 468.
[4] *Express Newspapers plc v News (UK) Ltd* [1990] 3 All ER 376.
[5] *Solar Thomson Engineering Co Ltd v Barton* [1977] RPC 537.
[6] Case C-160/15 *GS Media BV v Sanoma Media Netherlands BV* ECLI:EU:C:2016:644.

these scenarios even present a case involving a 'licence'. We do not know what constitutes a licence, for us to identify the constituents in each of the scenarios above. In some scenarios like (c), (d), and (e) above, B, the copyright owner, does not appear to have consented to the actions of A. This raises the question of whether a licence can arise in the absence of consent. There is no express grant in any of the scenarios. If a licence is to be implied, we will need a way to ascertain how far implied licence can extend. For us to address all these issues, there must be a method for implying copyright licences that accommodates the diversity of circumstances in which licences arise, as illustrated above.

This part begins the complex pursuit of finding a methodology for implying copyright licences by, first, analysing copyright licence as a legal relationship in Chapter 1, which provides the conceptual rationale for separating bare licences from contractual licences; secondly, by analysing the bases for implying a copyright licence in Chapter 2, which lends conceptual support to three bases for implying a copyright licence—consent, custom, and policy; and, thirdly, proposing frameworks for channelling the facts and circumstances for implying copyright licences that arise under different bases, in Chapter 3, which together form the methodology for implying copyright licences in a more transparent and predictable fashion.

1
Copyright Licence as a Legal Relationship

Before exploring the kind of legal relationship that 'copyright licence' is, one must have an understanding of what a 'licence' is.[7] One of the most extensive and influential analyses of licences in private law can be found in land law. Although copyright is a different kind of property from land, it is possible to extend the analogy of licences in relation to land to copyright licences at a conceptual level. Indeed, copyright law has tried unsuccessfully to deviate from the land law notion of licences. Section 1 deals with this discussion. Section 2 moves on to copyright law on licences. Copyright law speaks of licences that are consensually granted by the copyright owner and those that the copyright owner is compelled by law to grant. However, doctrinal influences on the understanding of licences both in land law and in copyright law mask the true nature of a licence as such, preventing its constituents from being ascertained. This necessitates an exploration of a licence on its own within analytical jurisprudence to help identify the constituents of a licence, which is dealt with in Section 3. These findings provide conceptual support to the diverse range of circumstances under which licences arise. Analysing the nature of a licence as a legal relationship reveals how a licence is distinguishable from contract, thereby giving the first line of classification between bare and contractual licences.

1. Land Law on Licences

Most of land law on licences is common law. Land law relies on *Thomas v Sorrell*,[8] a seventeenth century authority, for its understanding of a licence, although the facts of this case had nothing to do with land as such. The claimant, Thomas, acting on behalf of the Crown, demanded payment from the defendant, Sorrell, on the basis that the defendant sold wine in a parish without a licence, as required by the relevant statute at the time. Sorrell's defence was that he did have a licence granted by the Crown. While describing what a licence is, Vaughan J said: 'A dispensation or licence properly passeth no interest, nor alters or transfers property in any thing, but only makes an action lawful, which without it had been unlawful.'[9] This

[7] The dictionary meaning of licence is 'a permit from an authority to own or use something, do a particular thing, or carry on a trade'. See https://www.lexico.com/definition/licence accessed 5 March 2020.
[8] *Thomas v Sorrell* (1672) Vaugh 330.
[9] ibid 351.

Implied Licences in Copyright Law. Poorna Mysoor, Oxford University Press (2021). © Poorna Mysoor.
DOI: 10.1093/oso/9780198858195.003.0002

statement explains licences at their most generic level and shows their universality, since a dispensation can arise in a variety of circumstances beyond property law.

Thomas contextualised to land law means that a licence is a '*personal* permission to use land belonging to another such that, without the permission, the use would amount to a trespass'.[10] It can only be enforced against the person who grants it. It does not 'run with the land' and cannot be enforced against purchasers or other transferees of the land over which it exists. A licensee is normally unable to sue for trespass or nuisance in her own right. Only a person who has a property interest in land can bring these actions. Although a licensee in exclusive possession of the land might be able to sue in her own right, it may only be under certain circumstances.[11] Scholars have argued that it is necessary for licences to be conceptualised as non-proprietary in order to accommodate the diverse informal and transient uses of land, such as inviting someone home for dinner. It can hardly be said that the person attending the dinner thereby acquires a property interest in land. Legal property interests normally require formalities for their creation,[12] which is too burdensome for transient and informal uses of land. Further, in land law, there is a closed list of property interests (*numerus clausus*), and licences are not among them.[13] For these reasons, land law places licence in a 'residuary category', and conceptualises it as 'any right to enter land that does not fit into one of the recognised property categories'.[14]

One may draw an analogy between implying an easement and implying a licence. Before implying an easement, a court is required to ascertain whether the facts are sufficient to establish an easement (such as the existence of the dominant tenement, the servient tenement, and so on).[15] This presupposes that we understand what constitutes an easement. Similarly, before a licence is to be implied, a court will be required to ascertain whether the facts are sufficient to establish a licence, which requires that we know what constitutes a licence. Land law has invested extensively in what constitutes property interests within *numerus clausus* (such as easements), but has found little reason to explore what constitutes a licence, which is residuary and outside *numerus clausus*. If one wants to explore licences not for what it is not, but for what it is, then land law offers little help.

[10] Martin Dixon, *Modern Land Law* (11th edn, Routledge 2018) para 9.2 (emphasis in the original); see also *King v David Allen* [1916] 2 AC 54, 60, 62.

[11] Roger Smith, *Property Law* (9th edn, Pearson 2017) 502–503; see also *Hunter v Canary Wharf* [1997] AC 665.

[12] Peter Birks, 'Before We Begin: Five Keys to Land Law' in Susan Bright and James Dewar (eds), *Land Law Themes and Perspectives* (OUP 1998) 482.

[13] Law of Property Act 1925, s 1(1)–(3).

[14] Smith (n 5) 481.

[15] Dixon (n 4) para 7.2.

2. Copyright Law on Licences

Unlike land law, the law on copyright licences is more significantly statutory. The current statute in the UK, the Copyright, Designs and Patents Act 1988 (CDPA), provides on the one hand that an infringement is the doing of a restricted act 'without the *licence* of the owner of the copyright'.[16] The Canadian Copyright Act 1985 (CCA), on the other hand, defines infringement as the doing of a restricted act 'without the *consent* of the owner of the copyright'.[17] However, the CDPA also refers to 'consent' while defining the infringement of performers' rights and the Australian Copyright Act 1968 (ACA) uses the word 'authority' in a similar context.[18] Consent is a defence to the infringement of moral rights. This begs the question of whether 'licence', 'consent', and 'authority' are all interchangeable.

The word licence may also be used to mean the 'transaction' of licence, since licensing is one of the most important ways available to copyright owners to exploit their work. Although licensing at an individual level is prevalent, it is also common for copyright owners to opt for collective management of their rights by membership organisations called collecting societies or licensing bodies under section 116(2) of the CDPA.[19] As assignees of copyright or as agents of copyright owners, these organisations negotiate, grant, and manage licences to commercial as well as end-users, by way of licensing schemes. In this context, section 116(3) of the CDPA describes a copyright licence for the purpose of a licensing scheme as 'a licence to do, or authorise the doing of, any of the acts restricted by copyright'.[20] While this explains what a copyright licence does, it takes the meaning of a licence as a given. The CCA does not use the word licence in relation to collective management of rights, but uses the word 'agreement' under section 67(3) to refer to essentially the same sort of relationship where royalties are collected for the use of the rights managed by the respective collecting society. These statutes, including the CCA, go on to confer jurisdiction on the Copyright Tribunal or the Copyright Board to assess reasonableness of the licences granted by the licensing bodies to the users.[21] Assuming that consent refers to what a copyright owner voluntarily gives, a licence granted by a licensing body may not be wholly consensual to the extent that the

[16] Copyright, Designs and Patents Act 1988 (CDPA), ss 16(2), 22, 23, and 24 (emphasis added). See also the Australian Copyright Act 1968 (ACA), ss 36(1), 37(1), 38(1), and 101(1), 102(1), and 103(1); the Singapore Copyright Act 1987 (SCA), ss 31(1), 32, 33, 103(1), 104(1), and 105(1); and the Hong Kong Copyright Ordinance (Cap 528) 1997 (HKCO), ss 22(2), 30, 31(1), and 32(1).

[17] Canadian Copyright Act 1985 (CCA), s 27(1).

[18] CDPA, s 182; ACA, s 248G.

[19] ACA, ss 136, 137, and 148–162; SCA, ss 149, 150, and 156A–170; HKCO, ss 145–168; CCA, ss 6776.

[20] ACA, s 136(1); SCA, s 149(1); HKCO, s 145(2).

[21] CDPA, ss 118(3), 119(3), and 120(3) in relation to licences granted under licensing schemes and ss 125(3), 126(4), and 127(3) in relation to licences granted outside licensing schemes. Similar provisions can be seen in the ACA, ss 149–153. Under the CCA, the royalties fixed under the agreements mentioned above are subject to the jurisdiction of the Copyright Tribunal under ss 70, 71, and 76.

Copyright Tribunal may vary the terms of the licence to make them reasonable, even if the copyright owners had not consented to them.[22] Despite being not based on copyright owners' consent the statute continues to refer to them as licences. Therefore, these statutes convey that consent is not synonymous with licence and there must be more to licences than consent.

We saw above that in land law a licence is non-proprietary. In copyright law, the statute imbues copyright licences with characteristics that appear to make them proprietary. Unlike licences in relation to land, copyright licences bind successors in title generally or those who take with the knowledge of a pre-existing licence.[23] In addition, exclusive licensees have the same rights against successors in title as the grantors of their licence.[24] An exclusive licensee has, except against the copyright owner, the same rights and remedies in respect of matters occurring after the grant of the licence as if the licence had been an assignment. Her rights and remedies are concurrent with those of the copyright owner.[25] An exclusive licensee can obtain a preliminary injunction in an action for infringement in respect of which she has concurrent right of action, without joining the copyright owner; but must join the copyright owner for any final orders.[26] While an exclusive licence must be in writing and signed by or on behalf of the copyright owner, no writing is required for a non-exclusive licence.[27] A non-exclusive licensee can sue in her own name if authorised to do so by the copyright owner in writing, but must join the copyright owner as a co-claimant or as a co-defendant.[28] These provisions seem to suggest that a copyright licence ought to be treated differently from a licence in land. Unlike land, since copyright is an intangible property created by statute, the statute also provides for separate rules that enable dealing in this intangible property, either by way of licence or by assignment. However, commentators and judges insist that neither non-exclusive licences nor exclusive licences are interests in property, and that the rights that licensees have are only statutory.[29] In *CBS United Kingdom*

[22] See ch 2 below for more discussion on non-voluntary licences.

[23] CDPA, s 90(4); ACA, s 196(4); SCA, s 194(4); HKCO, s 101(4). Under the CCA, a copyright owner 'may grant any interest in the right by licence' under s 13(4), raising the possibility that it may be referring to a property interest.

[24] CDPA, s 92(2); HKCO, s 103(2).

[25] CDPA, s 101(1) and (2); ACA, ss 119(a) and (b); SCA, s 123; HKCO, ss 112(1) and (2). CCA, s 13(7) states that 'a grant of an exclusive licence in a copyright constitutes the grant of an interest in the copyright by licence', indicating a possibility that proprietary remedies may be open also to exclusive licensees.

[26] CDPA, s 102; ACA, s 120; SCA, s 124; HKCO, s 113.

[27] CDPA, s 92(1); ACA, s 10(1); HKCO, s 103(1). Under CCA, s 13(4) it appeared that all licences needed to be in writing. However, the judicial interpretation since the inclusion of s 13(7) in 1985 has been that only a licence which is an interest in copyright, such as an exclusive licence, needs to be in writing.

[28] CDPA, s 101A(1)–(5). Gillian Davies, Nicholas Caddick, and Gwilym Harbottle, *Copinger and Skone James on Copyright* (17th edn, Sweet & Maxwell 2016) paras [5-219]–[5-223]. There are no corresponding provisions in any of the CCA, ACA, SCA, or HKCO.

[29] ibid paras [5-204], [5-213]; Lionel Bently and others, *Intellectual Property Law* (5th edn, OUP 2018) 308–309; Mary Vitoria and others, *The Modern Law of Copyright and Designs, vol 1* (5th edn, Lexis Nexis 2018) para [13.2].

Ltd v Charmdale Record Distributors Ltd, Browne-Wilkinson J described the right of an exclusive licensee to sue as 'purely procedural'.[30] He insisted that, despite the provision binding successors in title, the copyright legislation continues to maintain the distinction between a licensee and assignee.

Regardless of the proprietary nature of licences, it might help to extend the residuary characterisation of land licences to copyright licences. A licence would then be everything that is not an assignment. This would be *Thomas* stated in the copyright context—a licence is everything that makes the doing of a restricted act legal, without which it would be an infringement. This helps explain why a copyright licence can be both consensual and non-consensual as described in the statutes. However, if the definition of a licence such as in *Thomas* was sufficient for our purposes, then in copyright law the statutory limitations or exceptions (SLEs) would be licences too. If it was sufficient to understand licences as mere permissions, then the SLEs also permit use of a work, whereas copyright statutes use the language of licences only in relation to compulsory and statutory licences, and not the SLEs in general. This means that there must be more to licences that we need to understand, beyond the land law conception. We, therefore, need a way of understanding a licence on its own to ascertain its nature and its constituents. This leads us to analytical jurisprudence to understand the linguistic and logical elucidation of the concept of licence itself, independent of the doctrinal influences.

3. Hohfeldian Analytics and Licences

Analytical jurisprudence fills the gap left by the inadequate conception of licences in doctrinal disciplines, for our purposes. The effort is to distil the concept of licence to the common denominator of licences that arise under any facts and circumstances. Once the constituents are identified at this level of generality, the concept of licence can be refocused in relation to copyright, in order to identify the attendant characteristics of copyright licences. Hohfeld made one of the best efforts to analyse a licence to reveal its constituents,[31] as the paragraphs below elucidate.

Hohfeld's concern was to clarify the most basic legal conceptions ordinarily used in judicial reasoning, and to urge a more careful and conscious use of these conceptions.[32] To begin with, Hohfeld spoke of eight fundamental legal conceptions,

[30] [1981] 1 Ch 91, 98. This decision dealt with the UK Copyright Act 1956, ss 19 and 36(4).

[31] Many scholars have applied the Hohfeldian framework to licences in various contexts. Examples include Albert J Harno, 'The Revocability of Licences as Applied to Property in Land' (1919) 7 Ky LJ 1, 2; Charles Clark, 'Licences in Real Property Law' (1921) 21 Colum L Rev 757; Hugh Breaky, 'Properties of Copyright' in H R Howe (ed), *Concepts of Property in Intellectual Property* (CUP 2013) 152–55; Ben McFarlane, Nicholas Hopkins, and Sarah Nield, *Land Law Text, Cases and Materials* (3rd edn, OUP 2015) 698–99; Christopher Newman, 'A License Is not a "Contract not to Sue": Disentangling Property and Contract in the Law of Copyright Licenses' (2013) 98 Iowa L Rev 1101, 1108.

[32] Wesley Newcomb Hohfeld, 'Some Fundamental Legal Conceptions as Applied in Judicial Reasoning' (1913–14) 23 Yale LJ 16, 20.

which can be arranged as four jural correlatives between themselves, namely right-duty, privilege-no right, power-liability and immunity-disability. If one person has a right, it creates a corresponding duty in another person as its jural correlative; and, if one person has a privilege, it creates a corresponding no-right in another person. And so on for other correlatives.[33]

To Hohfeld, a licence is 'a generic term to indicate a group of operative facts required to create a particular privilege'.[34] Where a privilege is created in one person, there is a corresponding no-right created in someone else. Therefore, in the Hohfeldian conception of a licence one must understand the following three aspects—privilege, no-right, and operative facts.

(a) Privilege

Hohfeld does not define what he means by privilege, but conceptualises it as the negative of duty. He gives a range of circumstances where privilege could arise—such as privileged communications and the privilege against self-incrimination. For Hohfeld, another way of understanding privilege is to think of it as liberty, which again captures the state of being *free* of owing any duty.[35]

If we were to take the example of *Thomas*, Sorrell owed a duty not to sell wine within the parish, which was extinguished by the crown's dispensation granting him a privilege to sell the wine. In the context of land, if P owns a house with a garden, all members of the public have a duty not to enter P's land. However, if P grants a licence to a member of the public, Q, to enter his garden for a garden party, Q's duty otherwise not to enter P's property is transformed into a privilege to enter the property.[36] Similarly, when copyright subsists in a novel A has authored, all members of the public have a duty not to make copies of the novel. If A consents to a member of the public, B, copying the novel, then B's duty not to interfere with A's copyright is transformed into a privilege to make copies of A's novel.

(b) No-right

The jural correlative of a privilege or liberty is 'no-right' in the person granting the privilege.[37] Hohfeld does admit that this is perhaps an unhappy expression,

[33] ibid 30–32.
[34] ibid 44.
[35] ibid 36, 39.
[36] A similar example can be seen in Wesley Newcomb Hohfeld, 'Fundamental Legal Conceptions as Applied in Judicial Reasoning' (1916–17) 26 Yale LJ 710, 743, where he refers to the grant of a privilege as extinguishing the duty of non-interference.
[37] Hohfeld, 'Some Fundamental Legal Conceptions as Applied in Judicial Reasoning' (n 26) 32–33.

and that there is really 'no single term available' to express this fundamental legal conception.[38] The state of having no-right, as the name suggests, is the opposite of having a right. Where a person would otherwise have had a right to prevent a particular action, when such person creates a privilege, the right she had turns into a 'no-right'.

Going back to *Thomas*, once the crown grants the privilege to Sorrell, the crown will then have no-right to stop Sorrell from selling the wine. Similarly, in the example above, if P, the owner of the house, invites Q for the garden party, P has 'no-right' to stop Q from entering the land, so long as P allows the licence to continue. P's right to prevent Q from entering her land has been replaced by a no-right. Similarly, in the copyright example above, once A, the copyright owner, consents to B copying the book, A has 'no-right' to stop B from making copies of A's book, so long as the licence continues.

(c) Operative facts

For Hohfeld, operative facts 'are those which ... suffice to change legal relations, that is, either to create a new relation, or to extinguish an old one, or to perform both of these functions simultaneously'.[39] In relation to a licence, the change captured by the operative facts is from duty-right to privilege-no right.

In *Thomas*, Sorrell had a duty not to sell wine and the crown had the corresponding right to stop him from selling it. But with a dispensation from the crown, Sorrell's duty was replaced by a privilege to sell wine, with the crown having no-right to stop him, owing to the operative facts that established the existence of a permission from the crown. In a licence in relation to property, in the examples above, the facts that lead to P, the landowner, granting Q the privilege to enter P's land (in place of Q having a duty not to enter), are what Hohfeld calls the operative facts. These facts could be the existence of a letter of invitation or a telephone call or, indeed, any conduct that indicates P's consent. Similarly, in the copyright example, A's granting to B a privilege to copy A's novel could be evidenced by a document to that effect or by A's conduct, either of which would be operative facts.

4. Copyright Licences and Hohfeldian Analysis

The above discussion reveals that Hohfeldian analysis is broad enough to bestow licences with a certain universality, confirming that licences exist outside what is

[38] ibid 33.

[39] ibid 25. Hohfeld distinguishes an operative fact from an evidential fact, 'which, on being ascertained, affords some logical basis—not conclusive—for inferring some other fact'. See ibid 27.

traditionally understood in property law. For our purposes, Hohfeldian analysis is particularly helpful in understanding copyright licences, and specifically implied copyright licences, and their characteristics.

(a) Licence as a group of facts

Hohfeld regards a licence as a 'group of facts' required to create a privilege. In other words, to ascertain the existence of a licence, a court must find the group of facts of a particular description. This is Hohfeld's way of distilling a licence to the lowest common denominator. This provides flexibility to accommodate the diverse facts and circumstances under which licences arise, so long as the facts meet the relevant description (namely those that create privilege). For example, a landowner's invitation to her friend for dinner—which is voluntarily granted by a landowner—is as much a licence as a driving licence issued to a person by a government authority which grants the privilege to drive a motor vehicle on the streets. In both cases, the operative facts capture the extinguishment of duty not to enter someone else's land or the duty not to drive on the streets, replacing them with a privilege. Thus, licences arise not only when they are voluntarily granted by a property owner but also when the state decides to grant them.[40] This lends conceptual support to the copyright statutes which use the language of licence beyond that granted by the copyright owner.

Conceptualising a licence as a group of facts of a specific description is particularly beneficial in implying a copyright licence, since implication is an ex post assessment of the facts and circumstances by a court, to ascertain whether a particular use is covered by an implied licence or amounts to infringement. A court must have some guidance while it navigates through these facts and circumstances and finds those that support a licence. Applying the land law conception that a licence is that which makes lawful what is otherwise unlawful provides no guidance as to what these relevant facts are. Conceptualising a licence as a group of facts of a particular description, therefore, guides the court to look for facts of that description, namely those that give rise to a privilege-no right relation. This also helps in identifying the relevant facts leading to a licence amidst other facts which may give rise to other jural relations.

Operative facts are 'facts', and a 'fact' means something that actually exists as an aspect of reality. It can be an actual or alleged event or circumstance, as distinguished from its legal effect, consequence, or interpretation.[41] This helps an

[40] An analogy can be drawn from the Occupiers' Liability Act 1957, s 2(6), which states that 'persons who enter premises for any purpose in the exercise of a right conferred by law are to be treated as permitted by the occupier to be there for that purpose, whether they in fact have his permission or not'.

[41] *Black's Law Dictionary* (11th edn, Thomson Reuters 2019).

important distinction being made between facts and law. All SLEs permit the doing of a restricted act, because in the absence of these statutory provisions the users would have owed a duty not to engage in these acts. In other words, the SLEs are legal provisions which 'create privilege', satisfying a part of Hohfeldian conception of a licence. However, the SLEs do not create licences because, as statutory provisions, they are statements of law and not statements of fact. One may argue that the fact of an SLE's existence in the statute is itself a fact that brings about the required change in the jural relation, and therefore an SLE itself is a licence. However, this erodes the distinction between fact and law, since all statutory provisions can be argued to exist, and thus all statutes will become facts. Therefore, to the extent that the SLEs are not in themselves facts, distinguishes them from licences.[42] This further helps to clarify the domain of concern in this monograph.

(b) Bare licences and contractual licences

Conceptualising a licence only as facts does not deprive it of the ability to be a legal relationship on its own. It is possible that the only jural relation in a legal relationship is that of privilege-no right, as in the case where P invites Q to a garden party on P's land. The underlying operative facts in this legal relationship only point to a licence. Instead of a complex set of jural relations, in this case only privilege-no right relationship exists. In this case, therefore, both the operative facts that point to a licence and the overall legal relationship are the same. In order to distinguish the legal relationship from the underlying operative facts, courts and scholars refer to this legal relationship as a 'bare licence' or a 'mere licence'.[43]

Hohfeld lamented that much of the difficulty in understanding the concept of licence could be eliminated if we confine the term licence to those operative facts which lead to privilege. He says, instead, the term licence is unhelpfully used in practice by courts and commentators to cover not only more complex groups of operative facts, but also the other jural relations flowing from such complex facts.[44] The existence of the relevant operative facts, therefore, reveals the existence of a licence, but says nothing about the overall legal relationship within which it exists, if the legal relationship has a combination of other jural relations. If the operative facts point to certain rights and duties *in addition* to those leading to privilege and no-right, then the resulting legal relationship as a whole should not be called a licence under Hohfeld's scheme, although a licence is incorporated within such legal relationship.

[42] See ch 2 below for further arguments on the distinction between SLEs and compulsory licences.

[43] Clark (n 25) 762.

[44] Wesley Newcomb Hohfeld, 'Faulty Analysis in Easement and Licence Cases' (1917) 27 Yale LJ 66, 92, n 49.

For example, suppose P is an antique collector who holds an exhibition open to the public on her land, but charges a certain entrance fee. Once a member of the public, Q, pays the entrance fee, P has a duty to let Q in, and Q has a corresponding right to enter the land. There is the fact of permission here, which would have given rise to a licence. But there are also other operative facts which should give rise to different fundamental legal conceptions and jural relations. One such is when the permission is in exchange for a valuable consideration, it gives rise to a right and a duty as stated above. If we call this more encompassing relationship a licence, we will be mistakenly coming to the conclusion that a licence must also give rise to rights and duties. In the same example, instead of selling tickets, if P invites a friend, Q, to come to her land to take a look at the collection, then P has granted Q permission to enter her land, but neither of them has rights or duties over each other. There are no operative facts that warrant the existence of rights or duties, such as exchange of consideration. Even though this is a licence—a bare licence at that—one might make the mistake of not regarding it so, if one believes that a licence must create rights and duties.

Thus, by identifying privilege-no right as the jural relation in a licence, Hohfeld distinguishes licences from other legal relationships, such as a contract. This helps to establish that a licence is not in itself a contract. Some scholars suggest that a bare licence is itself 'a contract not to sue'.[45] Supporters of this idea argue that the grant of the licence itself gives the licensee the *right* to use the property. It is difficult to see how this is correct. From a Hohfeldian perspective, a right to use property must place a corresponding duty on the licensor to let the licensee use the property. However, a licensor as the property owner has no *duty* to let anyone use the property, but has a power to let someone use her property if that person so wishes. A right not to be sued places no corresponding duty on the licensor not to sue,[46] because a licensor (of a bare licence) as a property owner has the power to withdraw the licence granted. Once withdrawn, nothing can stop the property owner from suing a person who uses the property after the withdrawal of the licence.

A contract differs from a bare licence also in the way it is formed. Courts and commentators generally agree that the following are required for the formation of a contract:

- offer, which is an expression of what each party to the agreement must do or refrain from doing and the willingness of the offeror to be bound;

[45] See Newman (n 25) for a discussion in the US context.

[46] ibid 1130; see also Bently and others (n 23) 309, where the authors opine that 'a bare licensee acquires the right not to be sued in relation to the acts set out in the licence . . .'.

- acceptance, which is an expression of willingness to contract on exact terms of the offer;
- intention to create legal relations;
- supported by consideration; and
- fulfilling the formalities, if any.[47]

Although consideration is one of the most controversial requirements of contract formation, it suffices to state here that an exchange is essential for a contract (not contained in a deed) to come into existence.[48] Even without the support of Hohfeld, it is difficult to see how a bare licence can be a contract because both the right not to be sued and the consequent ability to use the property are consideration that flow from the licensor to the licensee; no consideration flows from the licensee to the licensor.

A licence, although not a contract in itself, can arise within a contract. A property owner can provide property rights in their totality or a privilege in relation to property as consideration in exchange for something else that the property owner values—payment or some other obligation being owed. Thus, a contract may be employed to sell all rights to a property or to license the use of the property when consideration of some form flows from the person with whom the contract is made.[49] In the example above of P's antique collection, P's objective is to earn money from letting people see her collection. P exchanges a licence to enter her land in consideration for payment for an entrance ticket. Therefore, where consideration flows in return for a licence, we refer to it as a contractual licence. A contractual licence has elements of both a contract and a licence.

While a licence within a contract presupposes that the parties are already in a contractual relationship, with a bare licence no relationship, contractual or otherwise, may exist between the parties. It is also possible for a copyright owner to grant a bare licence to the public at large, and not to a specific person. For example, a creative commons licence is a bare licence by the adoption of which a copyright owner can provide access to her work to any member of the public who wants to use the work on the terms of the chosen creative commons licence.[50] Thus, bare licences have the potential of throwing open the ability of the courts to find a licence even between strangers.

[47] Patrick Atiyah and Stephen Smith, *Atiyah's Introduction to the Law of Contract* (6th edn, Clarendon Press 2005) 93; Jack Beatson, Andrew Burrows, and John Cartwright, *Anson's Law of Contract* (30th edn, OUP 2016) 31 ff.

[48] In unilateral agreements, which are in the form of, say, a reward for finding a lost article, the requirement of consideration may appear superfluous. See Beatson, Burrows, and Cartwright (n 41) 48.

[49] Newman (n 25) 1103.

[50] https://creativecommons.org/licenses/ accessed 8 June 2020.

(c) Licence as an immunity—an alternative conception

Some scholars believe that a licence is better described as an immunity from being sued. Their argument is that when a person who otherwise may be sued for engaging in certain activity under section 16(2), CDPA is given a licence to engage in that activity, the person acquires an immunity from being sued for breach of that duty. This can be an alternative conception of a licence. Immunity is not the same as a right. Hohfeld defines immunity as freedom from the exercise of power by another as regards a legal relation.[51] Once a licence is granted, for the duration of the licence the copyright owner loses the power to sue the licensee because of the change in the legal relation with the licensee to privilege-no right, although the copyright owner may still retain the power to withdraw the licence at will if it is a bare licence. In this sense, the difference between a licence as a privilege and a licence as an immunity lies in the perspective adopted, in that the latter speaks of the consequence for a copyright owner of granting a licence, and the former reveals what a licensee can do substantively.

If the facts reveal the existence of a privilege, then immunity will be the consequence. This means that if the facts reveal the substantive content of a licence which specifies what it is that the licensee can engage in, it gives the licensee the privilege to engage in these acts. A licence has both an enabling function and a disabling function. While the privilege enables the doing of an act which is otherwise prevented by a duty, the no-right disables the grantor of the licence from asserting the corresponding right. A consequence of the grantor not asserting the right is that the licensee acquires an immunity from being sued for infringement, indicating a disability on the part of the grantor. The copyright owner has the ability to ensure that the licensee keeps to the scope of the licence if the licensee does engage in the activity so permitted. In other words, if the licensee exceeds the scope of the licence, the duty owed to the copyright owner is triggered, giving the copyright owner the ability to enforce the corresponding right. The immunity that the licensee enjoys is contingent upon and a consequence of the licensee staying within the scope of the licence. On this view, the immunity-disability relationship may be regarded as the flip side of the licence because of its dependence on the substantive content of the licence which only privilege-no right relationship can shed light on. This conception is not outside the Hohfeldian conception, but only a complement to it.

Licence as an immunity has an additional connotation in copyright law. It may also happen that, even if there is copyright infringement, a user might gain immunity from the copyright being enforced by the courts. In this sense, immunity is not a consequence of the copyright owner not being able to sue, but a consequence

[51] Hohfeld, 'Some Fundamental Legal Conceptions as Applied in Judicial Reasoning' (n 26) 55.

of not being able to enforce copyright even if the copyright owner can sue for infringement. When an immunity arises in these situations, it is possible to find a licence underlying it. This takes the conception of a licence as an immunity a step further in that even when a licence is not granted by the copyright owner, a licence may arise as a result of a court's denial of enforcement of copyright. Whether this perspective may be adopted depends on the facts and circumstances presented, as explained below.

The facts and circumstances of certain cases may reveal an infringement because the copyright owner has not granted a licence. But the facts may also reveal reasons why the court must prevent or restrict the enforcement of copyright, if there are public interest considerations.[52] This may happen in many ways including when a court denies an injunction if it is convinced of overwhelming reasons to do so, since an injunction is a discretionary remedy. One might read this purely as an immunity being granted to the user by the denial of enforcement of copyright. This monograph, however, recognises this as a licence by adopting the conception of licence as an immunity. The court order granting immunity against the enforcement of a particular use of copyright work comes with an enabling function permitting that particular use. In Hohfeldian terms, behind the immunity from being sued for doing a thing is a privilege to do that thing; behind the disability of the copyright owner in being able to secure a remedy for the breach of a duty lies no-right to stop the breach of that duty. Therefore, even in situations where the apparent relationship is of immunity-disability, the deeper relationship of privilege-no right can be taken into account to support implying a licence.[53] This will typically be a bare licence since it is unlikely that there will be any relationship between the parties other than as a copyright owner and the infringer.

Both these conceptions are useful in developing the methodology for implying a copyright licence. This is not to say that licence as an immunity is contrary to Hohfeldian conception. As explained above, the Hohfeldian notion of a licence as a privilege can be used when the facts reveal a privilege and immunity is a consequence. However, even when the facts reveal immunity, Hohfeldian analytics can be used to show how a licence may be implied because there will be an underlying privilege.

5. Conclusions and Connections

This chapter has explored the legal relationship that a copyright licence is. Since land law and copyright law both have their own influence on the way a licence

[52] Cases of this kind are discussed in ch 8 below in the context of the power of the courts to restrict or prevent the enforcement of copyright under s 171(3) of the CDPA.

[53] There may also be situations where an immunity does not have an underlying privilege, for example, an immunity from paying taxes. This monograph is not concerned with those situations.

is understood, in order to understand licence independent of the doctrinal influences, this chapter has looked to analytical jurisprudence to shed light on not only the constituents of a licence but also its characteristics. Hohfeldian analytics conceptualise a licence as a group of operative facts that create a privilege, and also assists in analysing licence as an immunity. This generalised concept not only helps the first line of classification between bare licences and contractual licences, but also helps to explain other characteristics of a copyright licence.

Having addressed the question as to what a copyright licence is, let us now move to the question as to how a copyright licence arises. In Hohfeldian terms, a licence arises when there is a change in jural relations from right-duty to privilege-no right. We need to explore the question of what brings about such change. After all, such change does not happen without an explanation; there must be something that drives and justifies the change. In Hohfeldian terms, the fundamental legal conception that can bring about such change is 'power'.[54] For example, P, a police officer exercising her power of arrest extinguishes the arrested person's right not to be physically restrained and changes it to a disability. Even without Hohfeldian jargon, one can see how a licence can only be granted by a person who has the power to grant it. Thus, the exercise of power by the relevant government authority extinguishes the duty of a person not to drive on the streets, replacing it with a licence to drive upon satisfaction of certain conditions. The operative facts, therefore, describe the exercise of such power. While being able to identify operative facts is a good start to ascertaining if there is a licence within a legal relationship, it would bring greater predictability to the methodology if the licences were classified based on the sources of power that bring about these licences. This is because licences arising based on the exercise of different sources of power behave differently. This leads us to Chapter 2, which explores what these different sources of power are and the characteristics of a copyright licence arising from each of these different sources as the basis.

[54] Hohfeld, 'Some Fundamental Legal Conceptions as Applied in Judicial Reasoning' (n 26) 44–45.

2
Bases for Copyright Licences to be Implied

To Hohfeld, a licence arises when the duty-right relation is extinguished to create a privilege-no right relation, or when an immunity-disability relation reveals an underlying privilege-no right relation. Extinguishing a legal relation or creating a new legal relation requires the exercise of power. In other words, the sources of such power become the bases for a licence to arise.

Copyright law imposes an obligation on the world at large to exclude oneself from exercising any of the acts restricted to the copyright owner.[1] This in rem obligation may be extinguished, and a privilege granted in its place giving rise to a licence permitting the use of the copyright work. Such change of legal relation must be based on the exercise of power. In exploring the powers that form the basis of copyright licences, express copyright licences are easier to analyse than implied copyright licences, as express licences are more readily discernible from copyright law. Thus, when one examines the manner in which express copyright licences arise, one notes that the sources of power that can achieve this are: (i) the copyright owner's own volition in extinguishing the duty of exclusion owed to her and replacing it with a privilege; (ii) a community recognising a particular use of copyright work as a custom with the force of law, and thereby extinguishing the duty of exclusion and replacing it with a use privilege; and (iii) the law extinguishing the duty of exclusion, and replacing it with a privilege to use copyright works in a particular way, in order to achieve a public policy objective. How copyright law lends itself to these bases is addressed in Section 1 below.

Can these be the bases also for implying copyright licences? To answer this question, one must know, to begin with, what it means to 'imply' in the legal sense of the term in a given context. Thereafter, one can address the question as to whether the bases identified above in relation to express copyright licences can legitimately be the bases for engaging in this process of implication of copyright licences. This is not only a logical way to derive this methodology, but also a way to allay fears of unguided discretion in implying copyright licences because: first, the process of implication will be guided by the legally recognised notion of implication. In this vein, one may recall that the bases for implying a term into a contract closely mirror the bases in copyright law mentioned above. Secondly, the sources of power that are known in copyright law to give rise to express licences will be invoked also

[1] See eg Copyright, Designs and Patents Act 1988 (CDPA), s 16.

Implied Licences in Copyright Law. Poorna Mysoor, Oxford University Press (2021). © Poorna Mysoor.
DOI: 10.1093/oso/9780198858195.003.0003

to imply copyright licences. This ensures that the legitimacy that supports the bases for express licences can likewise support implied licences. This makes the methodology for implying copyright licences reliable and robust. This is discussed in Section 2 below.

The reason for arriving at the classification as to the bases of implying copyright licence is to assess an important characteristic of licences under each basis, namely revocability. This is addressed in Section 3 below.

1. Sources of Power as the Bases for Express Licences

This section begins by exploring the extent to which the copyright statutes refer to consent of the copyright owner as being the basis for a copyright licence to arise and the difference between consent and licence as far as this monograph is concerned. As a matter of general commercial law, a custom may also act as a source to grant a licence. Therefore, a licence could also arise from the action or inaction of the community of which the copyright owner is a member. Copyright statutes empower the state (generally an administrative authority) to grant compulsory and statutory licences in furtherance of public policy. Each of these sources is discussed below.

(a) Copyright owner's power to consent

Copyright statutes in jurisdictions such as the UK and Australia state, on the one hand, that it is an infringement for a person to engage in a restrictive act without the 'licence of the owner of the copyright'.[2] The Canadian Copyright Act 1985 (CCA), on the other hand, uses the words 'consent of the owner of the copyright' in the same context.[3] A question arises whether licence and consent refer to the same thing. An ordinary reading of the words 'licence of the owner of the copyright' refers to a licence that arises from the copyright owner's volition. Such volition to enable the use of the copyright work can be referred to as 'consent'. In this sense, the Canadian, the UK, and the Australian statutes are referring to the same thing, but the word licence is a more appropriate use of the term here. A licence is a more general concept and consent is one of the bases on which a licence arises. This is because a licence can also arise on other bases, as one may see in subsections (b) and (c) below.

But what is it that enables a copyright owner to act out of their volition in relation to a copyright wok? In other words, what is the source of power of the copyright owner that enables her to consent? Property theory offers a credible explanation,

[2] See eg ibid s 16(2); Australian Copyright Act 1968 (ACA), s 36(1).
[3] Canadian Copyright Act 1985 (CCA), s 27(1).

since the ability to consent arises from the powers of ownership. This presupposes that copyright is a property right and that the owner of the copyright has the power to consent.

The use of the phrase 'the owner of the copyright' is widespread in copyright statutes across jurisdictions. This in itself should mean that copyright is proprietary in nature. Some statutes like the CDPA state upfront that copyright is a property right, and others state this in relation to assignability of copyright.[4] Even if the copyright statutes in other jurisdictions like Canada are not as unequivocal as this,[5] it is clear that copyright does place *in rem* obligations on the rest of the world to exclude themselves from performing certain acts that are restricted only to the copyright owner, in relation to copyright works.[6] The statutes also allow the copyright owner to alienate her rights.[7] Therefore, the theories that define property based on excludability[8] and alienability[9] should apply similarly to copyright.

However, some scholars are sceptical about regarding copyright as property. The lack of tangibility of copyright,[10] and the resulting inability of copyright to be the subject of conversion,[11] are among the reasons cited. It is outside the scope of this monograph to establish why, despite being intangible, copyright is a property right. It suffices to say that the prevailing notion is that property refers to the rights 'between persons' in relation to a thing, and not to the 'thing' itself.[12] Therefore, the tangibility or intangibility of the 'thing' should not matter, so long as a structure of exclusionary rights can be built in relation to the 'thing'. Whether one looks to Rahmatian's notion of 'dematerialised property'[13] or Spence's exclusionary rights themselves as the object of protection,[14] there are good arguments to explain why copyright is a property right.[15] Regarding the issue of inability of copyright to be 'converted', commentators now acknowledge that this in itself is not determinative of whether a subject matter is property, as a subject matter can serve as property for some purposes and not for others.[16] They classify personal property into intangible property as a residual category which encompasses all that remains of personal

[4] CDPA, s 1(1); ACA, s 196(1).

[5] The CCA does not specifically say that copyright is a form of personal property.

[6] CDPA, ss 3–8.

[7] ibid s 90.

[8] Thomas Merrill, 'Property and the Right to Exclude' (1998) 77 Neb L Rev 730.

[9] Michael Bridge, *Personal Property Law* (OUP 2015) 2.

[10] Ben McFarlane, *The Structure of Property Law* (Hart Publishing 2008) 132–34.

[11] Simon Douglas, 'Kuwait Airways Corporation v Iraqi Airways Company' in Simon Douglas, Robin Hickey, and Emma Waring (eds), *Landmark Cases in Property Law* (Hart Publishing 2013) 212–13.

[12] Felix S Cohen, 'Dialogue on Private Property' (1954) 9(2) Rutgers L Rev 357.

[13] Andreas Rahmatian, *Copyright and Creativity* (Edward Elgar Publishing 2011) 5–21. See also Hugh Breaky, 'Properties of Copyright' in Helena Howe and Jonathan Griffiths (eds), *Concepts of Property in Intellectual Property Law* (CUP 2013) 137, for another conceptualisation of copyright as property.

[14] Michael Spence, *Intellectual Property* (OUP 2007) 15–16.

[15] See also Henry Smith, 'Property as the Law of Things' (2012) 125 Harv L Rev 1691, 1703.

[16] Bridge (n 9) 15–16.

property after tangibles are removed. Thus, the spectrum of personal property is arguably broad enough to accommodate copyright,[17] and therefore, property is no longer only that which can be converted.

With the ability to exclude the rest of the world from the protected subject matter comes the ability to use or authorise the use of the protected subject matter, short of complete transfer of ownership. One must be able to establish the powers of the owner beyond exclusion and alienation, to ascertain whether she can also consent to someone else using her property. In his discussion on the powers of ownership, or what he calls the 'incidents of ownership', Honoré includes the right to use and the right to manage, among others.[18] While Honoré conceived of the 'use' in the right to use as 'the owner's personal use and enjoyment of the thing owned', the right to manage is:

> the right to decide how and by whom the thing owned shall be used. This right depends, legally, on a cluster of powers, chiefly powers of licensing acts which would otherwise be unlawful and powers of contracting: the power to admit others to one's land, to permit others to use one's things, to define the limit of such permission, and to contract effectively in regard to the use (in the literal sense) and exploitation of the thing owned.[19]

Whether Honoré's incidents of ownership can be regarded as a complete enumeration of property rights is beyond the scope of this book. But Honoré's is one of the most authoritative works that provides a possible list of powers that the owner of property may be able to exercise.[20] An incident of using the property is to authorise the use of the property, by voluntarily consenting to its use by another person, at the property owner's discretion. Such consent is, therefore, the exercise of ownership powers to grant a licence.

Notwithstanding their scepticism, the scholars who disagree that copyright is a property right do acknowledge that copyright does impose *in rem* duties on the rest of the world similar to tangible property.[21] They must do so, because the statutes across jurisdictions are clear about imposing this obligation, as stated above. In vindication of Honoré's incidents of ownership, there are legal provisions in copyright statutes that enable the copyright owner voluntarily to extinguish the duty owed to her and replace it with a privilege permitting the user to perform a restricted act.[22] Additionally, statutes across jurisdictions also enable copyright

[17] ibid 10–16.

[18] Antony M Honoré, 'Ownership' in Anthony Gordon Guest (ed), *Oxford Essays in Jurisprudence* (Clarendon Press 1961) 107, 112–24.

[19] ibid 116.

[20] Honoré did not, however, regard the absence of one of the incidents as necessarily precluding the existence of property. See ibid 124–28.

[21] Simon Douglas and Ben McFarlane, 'Defining Property Rights' in James Penner and Henry E Smith (eds), *Philosophical Foundations of Property Law* (OUP 2013) 240.

[22] See eg CDPA, s 90.

owners to become members of collecting societies and to authorise collecting societies to grant licences through licensing schemes, as explained in Chapter 1 above. Thus, consent of the copyright owner has both conceptual and doctrinal support to be the basis for granting a copyright licence.

When the source is consent of the copyright owner, a licence will conventionally be regarded as express if it is in writing or in spoken words. The fact that the copyright owner signs a licence agreement is an operative fact, since the signed agreement brings about the required change in jural relations from right-duty to privilege-no right. If the licence is in spoken words, facts establishing that the relevant words were spoken become the operative facts. These operative facts make up a consent-based express licence.

(b) An established custom

The words without the licence or consent 'of the owner of the copyright' in the CDPA, the ACA, and the CCA should not be taken as meaning that a licence that arises from the volition of a copyright owner is the only way to avoid infringement. It only means that it is one of the ways. Other ways in which to avoid infringement have been legitimately recognised, one of which is to show the existence of a custom. Historically, a custom referred to a particular rule which had existed from 'time immemorial' in a particular locality, and governed like the local law, even if inconsistent with the general common law of the realm.[23] A usage, however, referred to a particular course of dealing or conduct generally adopted by persons engaged in a particular trade, business, or profession, which is so notorious that persons operating within such trade, business, or profession are taken to have intended to follow it.[24] The significance of a custom in the historical or classical sense is receding.[25] Only usages are relevant in this monograph. Most commentators use the terms customs and usages interchangeably,[26] although technically, the reference is made only to usages. These terms are used interchangeably also in this monograph to mean usages.

A custom in this sense refers to the 'repeated voluntary interactions among parties from the relevant groups'.[27] Customs are created and maintained with 'the general approval and approbation of all the parties within the group'.[28] A custom

[23] *Halsbury's Laws, vol 32* (5th edn, LexisNexis 2019) para 5.

[24] ibid paras 50–51.

[25] ibid paras 1, 41, 45. Examples include manorial customs, ecclesiastical customs, and the like, which have now been abolished by the Law of Property Act 1925.

[26] Gerard McMeel, *The Construction of Contracts: Interpretation, Implication, and Rectification* (3rd edn, OUP 2017) para 12.02.

[27] Richard Epstein, 'Some Reflections on Custom in the IP Universe' (2007) 93 Va L Rev Brief 223, 224.

[28] Richard Epstein, 'International News Service v Associated Press: Custom and Law as Sources of Property Rights in News' (1992) 78 Va L Rev 85, 86, 88.

embodies the conduct or a practice of a community which is formed and maintained by repeated engagement of such conduct or practice by the members of the community.[29] For custom to be counted as being on behalf of the copyright owner, it is essential for the community to be representative of the copyright owner.[30] For example, a journalist operating within the newspaper industry is taken to have intended to follow the customs in that industry, since customs are formed and maintained within the newspaper industry with the collective engagement of its members, such as the journalists.

A custom has an independent power to bind actors within a trade, business, or profession, which comes with the members engaging in the custom voluntarily, repeatedly, consistently and universally. Thus, a custom does not require a court ruling for its establishment, although its subsistence can be challenged or confirmed in a court.[31] Once established, a custom has the power to regulate the conduct of the members of the trade, business, or profession to which it relates, thereby changing their legal relations. Such change of legal relations can be from right-duty in relation to property, such as copyright, to privilege-no right, since it is conceivable for certain practices permitting certain uses of copyright works to have become customs. Such change may also be possible from a power-liability relation to an immunity-disability relation because of the consistent non-enforcement of copyright, underlying which there may be a privilege-no right relation. Commentators speak of many industry specific customs that form the basis of a copyright licence,[32] confirming customs as a source of power for these copyright licences to arise. Therefore, customs can be the basis for a copyright licence to arise.

If a practice has not yet reached the stage of being recognised as binding, it will remain a trade practice. These practices would be insufficient to change the legal relations from right-duty to privilege-no right. However, trade practices can provide evidence for the background in which a contract is to be performed.[33]

A licence based on a custom, and indeed the custom itself, are rarely stated in express terms. However, copyright owners may come together to identify the customary practices specific to that industry in the form of best practices, spelling out the acts permitted in relation to copyright works.[34] These could be called

[29] Jennifer Rothman, 'Copyright, Custom and Lessons from the Common Law' in Shyamakrishna Balganesh (ed), *Intellectual Property and Common Law* (CUP 2013) 243.

[30] Jennifer Rothman, 'The Questionable Use of Custom in Intellectual Property' (2007) 93 Va L Rev 1899, 1974.

[31] *Cunliffe-Owen v Teacher and Greenwood* [1967] 1 WLR 1421, 1438.

[32] Gillian Davies, Nicholas Caddick, and Gwilym Harbottle, *Copinger and Skone James on Copyright* (17th edn, Sweet & Maxwell 2016) para 5-225; see also Mary Vitoria and others, *Laddie, Prescott and Vitoria: Modern Law of Copyright* (5th edn, LexisNexis 2018) para 13.15 for examples.

[33] Richard Austen-Baker, *Implied Terms in English Contract Law* (2nd edn, Edward Elgar Publishing 2017) para [5.01]. See ch 5 below for further discussion on trade practices in relation to consent-based implied contractual licences.

[34] As regards user groups getting organised to create practices of their own see generally Patricia Aufderheide and Peter Jaszi, *Reclaiming Fair Use: How to Put Balance Back in Copyright* (University of Chicago Press 2011).

custom-based express licences. In these cases, if the existence of the custom underlying the licence is challenged, the facts and circumstances establishing the custom will be the operative facts, as these bring about the required change in the jural relations.

(c) State intervention for public policy reasons

As argued above, the words without the licence or consent 'of the owner of the copyright' in the copyright statutes do not enumerate an exhaustive list of bases on which copyright licences arise. As observed in Chapter 1, copyright statutes also use the language of licence to those beyond what a copyright owner grants, to which the conceptual support can be provided by Hohfeldian notion of a licence.

It may seem obvious that since copyright is a creature of statute, the statute can also empower different organs of the state to restrict the enforcement of copyright. That said, a more fundamental question would be what legitimises the intervention of the state in a person's enjoyment of property in the first place. Even though property theory recognises that the copyright owner has power to do as she pleases with her copyright, such power is not absolute. The Blackstonian notion of 'absolute despotic dominium' does not exist in relation to any form of property in modern times, much less copyright. Harris argued that the ownership of property is subject to 'property-limitation rules', which he describes as those that prima facie subtract ownership powers and privileges.[35] He states that these rules presuppose that certain property interests must be restricted or reallocated. Although the examples he gives are more in the nature of rules on nuisance,[36] this idea could apply more broadly to situations where the state can intervene with the use of property for policy reasons. Copyright statutes across jurisdictions empower the state (normally an administrative authority) to compel a copyright owner to grant a licence for public policy reasons.

It is essential at this stage to understand what a policy is and what its confines are. 'Policy' is one of the ways in which the legal rules derive their justification or rationale. There are many definitions of 'public policy' or 'policy' for short. One such is the collective rules, principles, or approaches to problems that promote the general good.[37] When policy considerations are taken into account, the enquiry is broadened beyond the considerations of the parties to a transaction or a dispute, extending to the considerations of social, economic, or community welfare. Policy has a wide remit and it would help to state what is excluded from, rather than attempt to enumerate what is included. It may help to exclude from the conception

[35] James W Harris, *Property and Justice* (OUP 2002) 90.
[36] ibid 5, 90–91.
[37] *Black's Law Dictionary* (11th edn, Thomson Reuters 2019).

of policy the considerations that only concern certainty, coherence, or consistency in law, and those that relate only to doing justice between the parties, as opposed to being directed at the community welfare.[38] By the same token, it would also help to exclude considerations that bring reasonableness and fairness. This is because these considerations also inform the issues involving parties to a transaction or a dispute, and therefore, are not considerations that set apart a policy on its own. Of course, a policy must also be reasonable, must do justice, and must be coherent and consistent, but a policy does much more than achieving these goals. A policy's broader welfare focus, be it social, economic, or community oriented, separates it from other bases being considered here. The term 'public interest' perhaps comes closest to expressing the focus of a policy.[39]

In our pursuit of finding the bases for express copyright licences, it helps to assess the provisions of copyright statutes that effectuate policy considerations and empower an administrative authority to support the grant of a licence. One of the important objectives of copyright legislation is to balance the competing interests of different stakeholders, including the copyright owner and users of copyright content. In this vein, copyright statutes across jurisdictions provide for interventions to compel a copyright owner to issue what are normally called compulsory and statutory licences, to achieve certain policy objectives, on the condition that a licence fee is paid for such use. Compulsory licences are those that compel a copyright owner to grant a licence to enable a particular use of the work, but the licence fee is negotiable; statutory licences are those that compel a copyright owner to grant a licence, but the licence fee is fixed by the state. Together, these are called non-voluntary licences because of the irrelevance of the copyright owner's consent as the driving force behind the grant of the licence.[40]

The following takes the example of the compulsory licences in the UK and demonstrates the underlying policy considerations. Under the CDPA, commentators identify nine instances where compulsory licences could be issued.[41] Some examples include the power of the secretary of state to 'treat as licensed' lending right in relation to certain works under section 66; a recording company may be compelled to license the relevant sound recordings for broadcasting under section 135A; licences that the competition authority may order in exercise of its powers to curtail anti-competitive practices under section 144. Short of granting a compulsory licence, the CDPA also has instances where the state intervenes through the Copyright Tribunal established with wide powers of assessing the reasonableness

[38] Andrew Robertson, 'Constraints on Policy-based Reasoning in Private Law' in Andrew Robertson and Tang Hang Wu (eds), *The Goals of Private Law* (Hart Publishing 2009) 261–68.

[39] Public interest is defined as the general welfare of a populace considered as warranting recognition and protection. See *Black's Law Dictionary* (n 37).

[40] Davies, Caddick, and Harbottle (n 32) para 28-02. For Australian law see Mark Davison, Ann Louise Monotti, and Leanne Wiseman, *Australian Intellectual Property Law* (3rd edn, CUP 2016) para 8.2.2.3.

[41] Davies, Caddick, and Harbottle (n 32) para 28-03. One of them (CDPA, s 73) was repealed in 2017.

of royalties and equitable remuneration, even if a licence emanates from the voluntary consent of the licensor.[42] Similar powers of an administrative body such as Copyright Tribunal can be seen also under Australian and Canadian laws.[43] The public policy underlying these provisions includes social or welfare considerations like making a work available or available on affordable terms; or economic considerations like discouraging anti-competitive behaviour, and so on.[44] These are clearly considerations beyond the parties to the transaction or dispute, and in the domain of fostering community welfare. With the aim of achieving these policy objectives, the state exercises its administrative powers which can replace the duty owed by the users with a privilege. Therefore, the power of the state is a legitimate source of power recognised as the basis for these licences to arise.

As regards state intervention as the source, the statutory provision that empowers the state to grant a compulsory licence is a statement of law, as opposed to a fact. However, the existence of the provision alone does not bring about the required change in the jural relations. In furtherance of such statutory provision, the relevant authority (normally the Copyright Tribunal) will have to consider submissions from the prospective licensee as to the facts such as the scarcity of the relevant copyright work, the price at which it is available, and the like. Assessing these facts, the relevant authority issues an order for compulsory licence. All these facts become operative facts, since these facts bring about the required change in the jural relations. And since the statutory provisions embody the particular policy goals to be achieved, to this extent, compulsory licences can be regarded as policy-based express licences.

It is important to establish why statutory limitations or exceptions (SLEs) are not licences, whereas compulsory licences are, according to the conception of licence adopted here. The SLEs permit uses of copyright works even without the users approaching a court seeking such permission. Some SLEs like fair dealing do grant a discretion to the courts to interpret what is fair, but it does not stop the users from using copyright works for criticism and the like. In this sense, on the one hand, the SLEs behave more like statutory rules that enable users pre-emptively to take refuge in non-infringing actions. On the other hand, there is no compulsory licence without the relevant authority granting one, because the relevant authority has a discretion to grant it. Only upon the exercise of such discretion is a privilege created. All the facts that go into the exercise of the discretion become the operative facts, making a compulsory licence a licence in the Hohfeldian sense.

Another important point of distinction between SLEs and compulsory licences is that SLEs have in some jurisdictions been regarded as 'user rights'. The Canadian copyright law is in the forefront of this jurisprudence, with the Canadian Supreme

[42] CDPA, ss 143, 145, 149.
[43] ACA, Pt VI and CCA, Pt VII and Pt VII.1.
[44] Davies, Caddick, and Harbottle (n 32) para 28-07.

Court in *CCH v Law Society* holding that an SLE is not a limitation, exception, exemption, defence, or a loophole, but a right inherent in the balance that the Copyright Act strikes between owners and users.[45] Whether SLEs are truly rights in the Hohfeldian sense is arguable. In particular, does the law impose a corresponding duty on copyright owners to honour the uses envisaged under the SLEs? To answer this, users must be able to approach a court for a remedy if they are deprived of their exercise of the SLEs by the copyright owners.[46] It is arguable that a copyright user can potentially approach the court seeking a declaration of non-infringement as the remedy. Therefore, one can argue that SLEs are more likely to be closer to being rights in the Hohfeldian sense than privileges, thus distinguishing them further from compulsory licences.

2. Express Licences to Implied Licences

The purpose of identifying the sources of power to grant *express* copyright licences is to explore whether normatively, the same sources could be invoked for *implying* a copyright licence. This depends, first, on what we understand by the process of implying in private law; and, secondly, on how the process of implication is connected with the sources that give rise to licences.

Let us consider the first question as to the legal meaning of 'implication'. In the context of contract law, judges have taken the opportunity to clarify what the process of implication is. The Supreme Court's decision in *Marks & Spencer v BNP Paribas*[47] is one of the most recent authorities on the point. In this case, Lord Neuberger spoke of construing the words used by the parties in the contract and implying additional words not expressly used by the parties as two distinct process in understanding the scope and meaning of contract. He states that the process of implication should not be classified as a part of the process of interpretation. He points out that when certain words are to be implied into a contract, these words would not have existed in the contract to be construed like the express words. Further, the courts do not turn to the process of implication until the express words have been construed, although they might revisit the express terms once the terms to be implied become known.[48] Quoting Lord Bingham with approval, he holds that the process of implication involves:

> [a] different and altogether more ambitious undertaking: the interpolation of terms to deal with matters for which, *ex hypothesi*, the parties themselves have

[45] [2004] 1 SCR 339 [48], quoting Professor David Vaver.
[46] Pascale Chapdelaine, *Copyright Users' Rights* (OUP 2017) 58 ff.
[47] [2015] UKSC 72.
[48] ibid [26]–[28].

> made no provision. It is because the implication of terms is so potentially intrusive that the law imposes strict constraints on the exercise of this extraordinary power.[49]

The idea of implication also exists outside contract law in other areas of private law, such as implied periodic tenancies, implied easements, and even implied licences in land law.[50] These iterations drive home the point that, at its core, implication is a legal tool that involves incorporating something that does not exist in express words.

Normally, one implies a term or an easement into a pre-existing relationship such as a contract or a conveyance. However, this is not necessarily the case. For example, a court implies a periodic tenancy based on the parties' ongoing conduct, rather than into a pre-existing relationship such as a contract or a conveyance or a lease. In situations of this kind, even if a transaction does not amount to a lease (say because the term of the lease is uncertain), but if the parties continue to conduct themselves as if there is a lease (say by paying and receiving rent), then such conduct can give rise to an implied periodic tenancy. Implied licences in land law normally arise as bare licences, also discernible from conduct and circumstances. For example, the absence of a locked gate or some kind of warning notice implies a licence to any member of the public to enter the premises to enquire whether she may be admitted or can perform some other act on land such as delivering milk, for example.[51] Here, there is no pre-existing contract or transaction between the occupier and members of the public; but the occupier's conduct of not securing the gate and the surrounding circumstances give rise to the bare licence. In this sense, the bare licence is a stand-alone transaction implied into the particular situation.

The process of implication, therefore, does not require a pre-existing transaction providing the boundaries or background for implication. This gives an extraordinary discretion to the courts and such discretion ought to be guided. There must be some basis for the process of implication to be triggered. The examples given above appear to convey that the basis for implying could be the conduct of the persons concerned and the surrounding circumstances. These examples appear to suggest that the process of implication is very similar to the process of inferring from the conduct and surrounding circumstances. Assuming that the conduct is volitional, this might mean that the only basis for implying is what the parties concerned have voluntarily engaged in. But this does not appear to be the case in contract law, where non-volitional basis does exist which drives implication of a term.

[49] ibid [29]. The original text in *Philips Electronique v British Sky Broadcasting* [1995] EMLR 472, 481.

[50] Kevin Gray and Susan Francis Gray, *Elements of Land Law* (5th edn, OUP 2008) paras 4.2.51–4.2.60, 5.2.20–5.2.53, 10.2.11.

[51] *Holden v White* [1982] QB 679, 687.

Scholars have identified three bases for a term being implied into a contract:[52] (i) the factual basis of the parties' own conduct and words used in the contract in the light of the surrounding circumstances, in order to give effect to the unexpressed joint intention of the parties.[53] The term so implied is normally referred to as a term 'implied in fact'; (ii) a custom or a usage established within a trade, business, or profession, which may have to be read as part of a contract, or become the basis for implying a term into a contract;[54] and (iii) a term may be implied into a contract as a matter of law, regardless of the intention of the parties, to achieve a policy objective. These are called terms implied by law. Such terms can be a derived from statutory provision[55] or a common law ruling[56] which may be read into all contracts of a particular kind. *Marks & Spencer* acknowledges terms implied in fact and terms implied by law,[57] but not terms implied by custom. Although some scholars regard custom as part of implication by law, it provides greater analytical clarity to separate it as an independent basis of implication, given the plethora of cases in maritime and insurance law that rely on customs in those industries. The bases of implication are contentious for various reasons. In implied in fact cases, the elusive nature of the intention of the parties makes it difficult to be ascertained at an objective level, questioning the method of implication. The erosion of freedom of contract is cited in strong opposition to implying a term by law, questioning the very legitimacy of this basis for implication. Nevertheless, this aaspect of contract law is helpful not least because contract law is one of the few areas of private law which has given detailed attention to the process of implication and the bases of implication.[58]

Our concern in this monograph is licences, which, as we saw in Chapter 1 above, can be a stand-alone relationship and do not necessarily arise within a contract. Then the question is—can we draw an analogy between the bases that drive implying a term in a contract and bases that drive implying a copyright licence? The bases in contract law that drive implication of a term draw their legitimacy from the sources of power that give rise to obligations in private law in general. In private law, obligations can be imposed on a person when the person voluntarily accepts them in an effort towards private ordering; and when the state intervenes through the mechanism of law imposing obligations in an effort towards public

[52] See generally, McMeel (n 26).

[53] *Marks & Spencer v BNP Paribas* (n 47) [16].

[54] *Cunliffe-Owen v Teacher and Greenwood* (n 31).

[55] UK Sale of Goods Act 1978, ss 12–14.

[56] *Liverpool City Council v Irwin* [1976] UKHL 1, for terms implied into all leases of a particular kind.

[57] *Marks & Spencer v BNP Paribas* (n 47) [15] (Lord Neuberger), quoting Lady Hale with approval in *Geys v Société Générale* [2013] 1 AC 523.

[58] In case of implied easements, case law regards all implication to be based on the intention of the parties discernible from their conduct and the circumstances. This is despite the fact that arguments of policy not to sterilise land could potentially form the basis for implying an easement of necessity. *Nickerson v Barraclough* [1981] Ch 426, 440. Therefore, one cannot look to implied easements for clarity on the bases of implication.

ordering to achieve a policy objective. In addition, it is also possible for an obligation to arise from a custom established within a trade, profession, or industry, when the custom has attained the force of law. To the extent that customs have origin in community norms, they represent private ordering; to the extent that customs can attain the force of law, they may also represent public ordering. The sources of power for obligations to arise are, therefore, a person's own volition, an established custom, and the state intervention through law to achieve a policy objective. These mirror the sources of power for copyright licences to arise, as mentioned above, namely: the copyright owner's volition; a custom in the industry; and state intervention to achieve a policy objective. This stands to reason because the sources of power must remain the same whether the conduct being regulated is between persons as in a contract or between persons in relation to property such as copyright. Courts cannot invent new sources of power, as these are well-recognised sources of private and public ordering in private law. Confining the courts to these powers as the basis of implication brings legitimacy to the otherwise controversial process of implication.

Some might argue that 'implying' in the true sense of the term can only be based on the volitional conduct of the parties concerned, since this mirrors most closely the ordinary meaning of implying.[59] They might insist that implied by custom and implied by policy are not truly 'implied' terms, but rather, 'imputed' or 'imposed' terms. As demonstrated above, contract law does regard custom and policy as additional bases and the courts continue to regard the process as 'implication', demonstrating that the legal meaning of implication goes beyond the ordinary meaning of implication. It is legitimate for courts to engage in the process of 'interpolation', as Lord Bingham calls it, even when the bases for doing so do not necessarily arise from volitional conduct of the parties. Accordingly, there should be no reason why the same terminology of 'implication' cannot be used also in relation to copyright licences when the bases for implication are custom or policy.

Therefore, courts can imply a copyright licence either because of the copyright owner's consent or because of a custom, or because the state intervenes for a policy reason to imply a licence. One may recall that the first level of classification of licences between bare licences and contractual licences was established in Chapter 1. In this chapter, the next level of classification is copyright licences that are implied based on consent, custom, and policy. When these levels of classification meet, there could be two types of licences under each basis—consent-based implied bare licence and contractual licence, custom-based implied bare licence and contractual licence, and policy-based implied bare licence and contractual licence. It is worth noting that this monograph uses the terms 'consent-based' instead of 'implied in

[59] The *Oxford English Dictionary* meaning of imply is 'to involve or comprise as a necessary logical consequence; to involve the truth or existence of (something not expressly asserted or maintained)'.

fact' and 'policy-based' instead of implied by law, so that the true source of implication is made transparent.

Before we develop the methodology of implication further, we may pause here to note that this classification helps identify one of the most important characteristics of licences, namely, revocability of licences, as discussed in the section below.

3. Revocability of Licences under Each Basis

Revocation does not amount to breach in the contractual sense, which may entitle the innocent party to elect to terminate the contract and seek damages. Revocation is a unilateral act and has no adverse consequences for the person revoking, as it only amounts to a withdrawal of the licence once it is granted. Revocability is a function of the basis on which a licence is granted and whether it is a bare or a contractual licence. Revocability of a licence affects its durability, and therefore, it is important to understand the circumstances in which a licence is revocable.

If a licence is the result of the exercise of the power of ownership to consent for the property to be used by another person, and if it is a bare licence, then it can be taken back as it was given, upon giving reasonable notice.[60] When a permission is granted as a unilateral exercise of the powers of ownership, as in the case of a bare licence, the owner of the property is not obliged to ensure the continuance of the permission. This rule is consistent with the Hohfeldian analysis. Hohfeld conceptualises property ownership as an aggregate of rights, privileges, powers, and immunities. To Hohfeld, power is 'one's affirmative "control" over a given legal relation as against another'.[61] The result of such control is that there is a choice whether to exercise a specific power, and when the power is exercised, it can be taken back. In a consent-based bare licence which only has privilege-no right relation, there is simply no duty on the part of the licensor to continue the permission granted. As such, the licensor of a bare licence who grants or is implied on the basis of her free will, is free to revoke the licence at will.

However, a licence being the result of the exercise of ownership powers to consent does not mean that it is always revocable. If the licence is a contractual licence within which a consent-based licence has been granted, a licensee can negotiate for the licensor not to exercise her powers of revocation. We saw in Chapter 1 that a licence can be granted in exchange for consideration in a contract, for value, or for some other benefit. Under these circumstances, a duty is imposed on the licensor not to revoke the licence at will. In this sense, a contract is often used as a tool to render a licence irrevocable, making it different from a bare licence. For example, P,

[60] Jonathan Hill, 'Termination of Bare Licences' (2001) 60 CLJ 89, 98.

[61] Wesley Newcomb Hohfeld, 'Some Fundamental Legal Conceptions as Applied in Judicial Reasoning' (1913–14) 23 Yale LJ 16, 55.

an architect, draws the architectural plans of a house for Q for a fee. The fee Q pays is in exchange for the privilege of using P's plans to build a building. By accepting the fee, P places himself under a duty not to revoke Q's licence to use the plans.

Although consent-based bare licences are revocable, there is an additional situation where they can become irrevocable. This happens when the law imposes a disability on the property owner from revoking the licence. This occurs in cases of proprietary estoppel where the licensee, relying on the licence, changes her position to her detriment in such a way that the law will impose on the licensor a disability from revoking the licence, and a corresponding immunity from revocation in the licensee. Proprietary estoppel is used as the basis for rendering a bare licence irrevocable, or revocable only prospectively. Therefore, it is important for a copyright owner to know when the licence she grants might become irrevocable, so that she can take steps to prevent such irrevocability.[62]

In contrast, if the owner did not exercise her power of ownership, but instead was compelled by the state to issue the licence or a licence was implied by the state to achieve a policy objective, then it follows that the owner cannot exercise her powers of ownership to take back the licence. This is the case regardless of whether the licence is a bare licence or a contractual licence. In this scenario, the power in the Hohfeldian sense is exercised by the state to achieve a policy goal. When the state exercises this power to compel the issuance of a licence or implies a licence, it creates a corresponding liability in the property owner.[63] To Hohfeld, liability is a state of being bound or obliged.[64] Therefore, where the source of the licence is the property owner's liability in the sense of being bound to issue a licence or a court implying a licence for public policy reasons, such licence cannot be revoked by the copyright owner at will.[65] What may be possible in a contractual setting, however, is to *ex ante* override the possibility of implying a licence by an express provision where the law does not prohibit such a term, so that an *ex post* revocability issue does not arise. In the absence of an express term, the copyright owner will have to face irrevocability of a policy-based implied licence.

When a licence is implied based on a custom, the power in the Hohfeldian sense exists in the binding nature that a custom has attained owing to its certainty, notoriety, and reasonableness. A custom is rooted in the conduct of a community representing the copyright owner. The content of this power is to compel the relevant behaviour, namely permitting a particular use of the copyright work, in order to

[62] See ch 4, section 3 below for a discussion on proprietary estoppel in copyright cases.
[63] The jural correlative of power is liability. See Hohfeld (n 61) 44.
[64] ibid 53.
[65] There is no direct authority on revocability of compulsory licences. But it is in the 'compulsory' nature of the licence that such unilateral revocation is not possible. See eg Davies, Caddick, and Harbottle (n 32) para 28-02, where the authors regard an order of the court compelling the copyright owner to issue a compulsory licence as changing property rules to liability rules. It is possible that if the state ordering the issuance of a compulsory licence specifies the term of such licence, such licence will end by effluxion of time.

meet the reasonable expectation that the custom will be followed. This power also creates a corresponding liability in the property owner to continue the licence, and therefore, such a licence cannot be revoked by the copyright owner at will, regardless of whether it is a bare or a contractual licence.[66]

4. Conclusions and Connections

Having conceptualised a licence as a group of operative facts, this chapter has sought to identify these facts by first classifying the sources of power that enable the grant of an express copyright licences. The sources identified were: ownership power to consent to a use; a custom; and the state intervention. It argued that the same sources must apply also for implying a copyright licence. It went on to clarify an important characteristic of licences under each source, namely revocability.

The classification of implied copyright licences that has been made possible by Chapters 1 and 2 is consent-based, custom-based; and policy-based implied licences and bare and contractual licences under each of those three categories. While this classification is helpful in a methodical study of implied copyright licences, it is insufficient as a predictive tool to show how one may go about implying a copyright licence. Further suggestion of frameworks is necessary to guide the manner of implying a copyright licence in a transparent way.

Implied copyright licences are the same as express copyright licences, except that in implied licences the existence and terms of licence are to be discerned from factors other than the expressed terms. Analysing express licences closely leads us to the categories of operative facts necessary to imply copyright licences. These broad categories support the frameworks that are proposed in this monograph for implying copyright licences, which in turn leads us to Chapter 3.

66 There is no case law in the UK specifically addressing this point. However, if a licence granted by custom could be taken back by the copyright owner at will, it would go against the binding nature of a custom.

3

Frameworks for Implying Copyright Licences

At a conceptual level, a licence remains the same whether it exists expressly or impliedly, since the jural relation of privilege-no right does not change. The operative facts differ. In express licences, it is more certain how one must go about establishing the operative facts when each of the powers to consent, of establishing a custom, and of state intervention, are exercised, as discussed in Chapter 2 above. In implied licences, by definition, there are no express terms, although we know that these are the very powers we must invoke to imply a licence. Consider the following corresponding to each source of power.

In relation to consent-based express licences, if we want to ascertain, for example, whether an author, P, has given consent for her novel to be made into a feature film, we look at the operative facts that P has signed the licence agreement with the film producer. If a licence is to be implied, however, by definition, express terms will be absent. We will have to ascertain consent based on the conduct of the copyright owner and other circumstances, which will together form operative facts. We need a systematic way of finding these operative facts.

In a custom-based express licence, for example, when a person writes a comment on an online newspaper article, the custom prevalent in the industry that the newspaper has a licence to retain a copy of such comment may be embodied in the newspaper's terms of use online. We look for the operative facts that establish such embodiment in the terms of use. If a licence is to be implied, however, by definition such terms of use will be absent. The user may have to establish the existence of a custom to this effect, to convince the court to imply a licence. The facts and circumstances that go into establishing the custom will be the operative facts. We again need a systematic way of finding these facts.

In relation to policy-based express licences, for example, the policy that the state should provide access to certain copyright works on reasonable terms is embodied in the statute. Based on this statute, a person may approach the relevant authority for an order compelling the copyright owner to issue a licence. We look for the operative facts that the authority issued such an order in the exercise of its powers. If a licence is to be implied based on a policy, however, by definition, there is no express embodiment of such policy in the statute. If a user wants the court to compel the issuance of such licence, the user must convince the court that it has powers validly to enforce such policy. If convinced, the court will exercise such power considering

Implied Licences in Copyright Law. Poorna Mysoor, Oxford University Press (2021). © Poorna Mysoor.
DOI: 10.1093/oso/9780198858195.003.0004

all the facts and circumstances, which will become the operative facts. We again need a systematic way of identifying these facts.

This chapter proposes discrete but related frameworks systematically to identify the operative facts that underlie an implied copyright licence. These frameworks have been developed by analysing what constitutes express licences, to propose a set of criteria to marshal operative facts resulting from the exercise of each source of power. Faced with an infringement, when a court has only facts and circumstances of a case before it, these criteria become a guide to assess whether the facts and circumstances support implying a licence. These criteria are not proposed as rigid requirements which would deny implied licences of their much-valued flexibility. It is also possible that the same scenario lends itself to implying a licence on more than one basis. The objective in identifying these criteria is to make the process of implication transparent. This chapter explains why the specific criteria have been chosen and their normative relevance, for each source of power.

A licence can arise as a bare licence or as a contractual licence. This distinction influences to varying degrees the frameworks proposed and the methodology adopted for implying a licence under the respective sources. While such variations result in different chapters being devoted to bare and contractual licences in relation to consent-based and policy-based implied licences, the distinction is less relevant for custom-based implied licences, as discussed below.

1. Consent of the Copyright Owner

Establishing consent is key to implying a licence based on such consent. Consent freely given is a state of mind which is objectively assessed based on the conduct of the copyright owner and the surrounding circumstances, all of which present themselves as facts.[1] The consent of relevance here is the conduct of the copyright owner in enabling the licensee to use the copyright work. It is not sufficient to focus only on the conduct of the copyright owner. Since we are interested in the voluntary conduct of the copyright owner, the focus here is on the conduct that the copyright owner that she knowingly engages in. Therefore, the knowledge of the copyright owner as to the circumstances that drive her conduct is also equally important.[2] Accordingly, the operative facts that lead to consent can be broadly channelled between those that reveal the copyright owner's conduct and those that reveal the copyright owner's knowledge. The framework below proposes criteria to marshal the operative facts that establish consent, in the absence of any express

[1] James Goudkamp and Donal Nolan, *Winfield and Jolowicz on Tort* (20th edn, Sweet & Maxwell 2020) para 26-009.

[2] Hugh Collins, *The Law of Contract* (4th edn, LexisNexis 2003) 130, where he states that it may be possible to imply consent to a contract by reference to 'the conduct and the *knowledge* of the ... party' (emphasis added).

terms indicating the copyright owner's consent. Once we have a framework to establish consent, we can adapt it to a bare licence and a contractual licence.

In the discussion of the Hohfeldian conception of licence above, it was explained that the world at large owes a duty to the copyright owner not to interfere with her exclusive rights. Any transformation of such duty into privilege must be at the instance of and attributable to the conduct of the copyright owner, when consent is invoked for implying a licence. Such duty owed by the world at large cannot be negated by the copyright owner's inaction.[3] Inaction alone cannot be the conduct revealing the state of mind required for consent. If there is no overt act, it is not certain what might be in the copyright owner's mind. There must be some overt conduct on the part of the copyright owner that signals that the duty has transformed to a privilege to use the copyright work. For our purposes here, we can call such overt conduct the 'positive act'. The copyright owner must engage in the positive act to signal that the copyright work is available for use, enabling another person to use it. The positive act thus results in a privilege being created in another person (licensee) to use the work. For example, if P is a songwriter, P *handing* a piece of paper on which P's song is written, to a person A to sing it, will be a positive act.

The positive act is an essential, but not the only conduct. Since a privilege is granted owing to the copyright owner's power to consent, it can be taken back at any time.[4] To complete the act of consenting, having enabled the work to be used, the copyright owner must stand back when the licensee goes ahead to use the work. In the discussion above on no-right in the Hohfeldian conception of a licence, the duality of privilege-no right relation that underlies a licence shows that there are two parts to showing a licence: one that involves enabling and another that involves standing back. While the conduct of enabling is captured within the positive act, the conduct of standing back is captured within what can be called the 'neutral act'. The neutral act is therefore the manifestation of no-right.

The neutral act as a conduct of the copyright owner is as much a reflection of the state of mind of consenting as is the positive act. While the positive act signals the *creation* of a privilege, the neutral act signals the *continuance* of the privilege. Although the neutral act does involve a level of inaction, the inaction does not signal the creation, but only the continuance of the licence. A neutral act does not mean that the licensor acts negatively, because a negative act signals the privilege coming to an end. As long as the neutral act continues, the licence continues, thereby adequately covering the entire span of the state of mind from its inception to its end.

[3] Mere inaction is insufficient to transform the duty into privilege, unless there is a case for adverse possession. However, the UK copyright law does not recognise adverse possession according to *Fisher v Brooker* [2009] UKHL 41 [78] (Lord Neuberger).

[4] So long as the copyright owner has not placed himself under the duty not to revoke, as in the case of a contract.

The neutral act maintains the status quo, such that where a copyright owner enables her work to be used by the licensee, she maintains the status quo for a length of time by not asserting her copyright. The neutral act may continue indefinitely, making the privilege continue accordingly; or it may become a negative act, ending the licence.[5] In this sense, the continuation of the neutral act accounts for the duration of the implied licence. There can be long periods of inaction on the part of the copyright owner—in one particular case, 38 years.[6] It cannot be that the positive act of enabling a copyright work for use itself continues for 38 years. There must be something else in a licence that explains it. For Hohfeld, the copyright owner exercising no-right in relation to the work for 38 years, having created the privilege, explains it.

The neutral act can be absolute in that it allows all consequences of the positive act to ensue; or it can be partial in that only certain selective consequences of the positive act ensue. A positive act by nature cannot be partial. A person cannot partially give a piece of paper with lyrics on it. However, having given the work, the copyright owner can do something that conveys that she does not wish for all consequences of the positive act to ensue. She can select the parts of her copyright work that can be used or specify the uses that can be made of the work. In this sense, the neutral act is the conduct that controls the extent of the effect of the positive act. A partial neutral act may result in a partially express licence, if it spells out what the user can and cannot do. This is particularly manifest in the case of implied licences on the internet. A copyright owner placing her content on the internet is a positive act. Leaving the content there and standing back is the neutral act with its full effect. However, if the copyright owner places certain terms of use on the internet, then the neutral act of standing back becomes partial, since only some of the consequences of the positive act of placing the content on the internet ensue.[7] One must be sensitive to the neutral act for, otherwise, one might conclude that the copyright owner has consented to a wider use of the copyright work than the copyright owner intended.

The copyright owner's ability to exercise her powers of ownership to consent requires that she knows what she is consenting to.[8] This is what makes her exercise of the power to consent voluntary. Hohfeld does not specifically speak of knowledge as Hohfeld's work was focused on licences in general, and not only those that arise because of consent. However, it is possible to fit knowledge within the Hohfeldian operative facts together with the positive and the neutral acts. This is because the

[5] An example of a negative act is issuing a notice to stop the use of the copyright work. See ch 4, section 2 below for a discussion on this point.

[6] *Fisher v Brooker* (n 3).

[7] See ch 9, section 1 below.

[8] See generally Simon Lee, 'Towards a Jurisprudence of Consent' in John Eekelaar and John Bell (eds), *Oxford Essays in Jurisprudence* (3rd Series Clarendon Press 1987) 199, 213, for a discussion on the importance of knowledge in relation to informed consent in medical law.

positive and the neutral acts cannot take place in vacuum. The state of affairs which the engaging in the positive and the neutral acts will bring about, must be within the knowledge of the copyright owner. In general, the extent of knowledge of the licensor determines the extent to which the licence may extend. One may also characterise the knowledge of the copyright owner as what is within the reasonable expectation of the copyright owner, when engaging in the positive and the neutral act.

Accordingly, the framework establishing consent is:

- the positive act by the copyright owner;
- the neutral act by the copyright owner; and
- the knowledge of the copyright owner.

The first two criteria correspond to the conduct of consenting, and the third criterion captures the state of mind of the copyright owner. Each of these ingredients must be objectively assessed. This means that, although the focus is the conduct of the copyright owner in enabling and staying back, it is assessed based on what a reasonable person in the position of the licensee would understand the conduct to mean. This is so even if subjectively the copyright owner did not intend to engage in such conduct. The knowledge of the copyright owner being ascertained objectively means that the courts are required to be particularly mindful of the matters that ought reasonably to have been within the copyright owner's knowledge, so that the reasonable expectations of the other contracting party are met.[9] Such objective assessment is prevalent in English contract law, which regards it as irrelevant to delve into a person's subjective mind. There is, therefore, no reason to depart from it in relation to copyright licences.

The implication of licence follows the criteria mentioned above with necessary changes as explained below, because the existence of a contract impacts each criterion of the framework. But the broad category of the criteria remains the same because consent continues to drive the implication of the licence.

(a) Consent-based implied bare licence

Chapter 1 explained that a bare licence can be an independent legal relationship. It was also explained that a bare licence has nothing more than a privilege-no right relationship. Since our concern here is a consent-based implied bare licence, the framework that establishes consent would adequately provide for a framework that supports a consent-based implied bare licence. However, when a copyright owner

[9] Johan Steyn, 'Contract law: fulfilling the reasonable expectations of honest men' [1997] 113 LQR 433, 441.

engages in the positive and the neutral act, i.e., gives her work to someone without stating anything, a question arises as to why it should not be regarded as the copyright owner giving away or assigning her copyright in the work as a gift. Apart from the fact that an assignment of copyright requires writing,[10] as a matter of personal property law, a gift is not readily assumed upon delivery, unless there are facts to support an intention to transfer the property by way of a gift.[11] If no such facts are discernible, then we can proceed on the basis that the copyright owner consented to license the use of the work, and not that she alienated the copyright in the work. Therefore, the positive and neutral acts count towards a licence, rather than a gift.

As to the knowledge of the copyright owner, to provide greater transparency further components can be identified. These components capture some of the defining characteristics of bare licences such as the knowledge of the copyright owner as to:

- her authorship of the work and resulting ownership of copyright; this reflects the ease with which bare licences come into existence without the copyright owner realising the full consequences of her conduct, impacting the copyright owner's voluntariness;
- the gratuitous nature of the transaction, reflecting the lack of consideration in a bare licence that sets it apart from a contractual licence; and
- the surrounding circumstances, which capture any other relevant facts and circumstance, including the foreseeable consequences of engaging in the positive and the neutral act.

These are more fully explored in Chapter 4 below.

(b) Consent-based implied contractual licences

An implied contractual licence has elements of both a contract and a licence. Contract provides the structure, which is one of willing parties coming together to achieve an objective. For the purpose of developing the framework, let us suppose the existence of a concluded contract, or that the existence of a contract is not at issue. What is at issue is whether a consent-based licence may be implied into this contract and, if yes, what is its scope. There are general principles for implying a term into a contract (such as business efficacy and the officious bystander tests), where a court tries to determine the unexpressed joint intention of the parties.

[10] CDPA, s 90(3); ACA, s 196(3); CCA, s 13(4); SCA, s 194(3); HKCO, s 101(3).

[11] William Swadling, 'Property' in Andrew Burrows (ed), *English Private Law* (3rd edn, OUP 2013) paras 4-460–4-461. The concept of delivery in this context is distinctly a tangible property concept. However, since a copyright work must be recorded before copyright can subsist in jurisdictions like the UK, giving access to such record is roughly analogous to delivery.

These tests, however, are not applied here because these tests do not make the actual method of implication sufficiently transparent. Also, the term being implied is a specific type of term, i.e., a consent-based licence, and therefore, the framework for ascertaining the existence of consent for implying a licence discussed above is more appropriate, rather than the general principles.

Let us take the example of an executory contract such as a commissioning contract, for a clearer explanation. Let us say Q engages P, an artist, to create a painting, for a fee. In the language of contract law, Q offers to undertake to pay the fee to P if P creates the portrait, and P accepts it by undertaking to create the painting for Q.[12] The undertaking to create and hand over the painting is the consideration that flows from P to Q, in return for Q's undertaking to pay.[13] Let us assume that neither party says anything about copyright. Assuming all other requirements of a contract are met,[14] with these mutual undertakings, a contract comes into existence. The contract is performed where P creates the portrait and hands it to Q, in return for the fee. Since the agreement between P and Q is silent on copyright, in case of a dispute, a court will have to ascertain whether P undertook to assign the copyright in the portrait or to license the copyright for it to be used. Let us see how the framework for establishing consent can be adapted for the contractual context.

The positive and neutral acts are subsumed into the performance of the contract when the actual handing over of the work takes place. The positive act can be conditional on providing consideration, such as paying a fee. In other words, a copyright owner can undertake to part with a work only in return for payment. For example, P might agree to create the painting, but might negotiate for the painting to be handed over only upon an advance payment. In such a case, handing the portrait over is the positive act, which is conditional on the negotiated payment. If the positive act is not conditional (if there is no advance payment, for example), the neutral act will be conditional. Having enabled the use of the work by engaging in the positive act, the copyright owner standing back and letting the work be used may be subject to the licensee providing consideration, which in the example above is the payment. Since the conduct of positive and neutral acts is the same whether an assignment or a licence is to be implied, how do we know which of these is to be implied?

[12] Patrick S Atiyah and Stephen Smith, *Atiyah's Introduction to the Law of Contract* (6th edn, Clarendon Press 2005) 36, 50. Atiyah and Smith define an offer as a proposal by the offeror to undertake to do something or abstain from doing something, provided that the offeree will also undertake to do or abstain from doing something. The offeree, by accepting the offer, creates mutual undertakings. See also Jack Beatson, Andrew Burrows, and John Cartwright, *Anson's Law of Contract* (30th edn, OUP 2016) 1, 2, 35, where the authors describe a contract in terms of mutual promises, rather than undertakings.

[13] In executory contracts of this nature, consideration lies in the mutual undertakings given in exchange for each other. Atiyah and Smith (n 12) 107.

[14] These include the capacity to enter into the contract, intention to create legal relations, and any formality stipulated by law. Atiyah and Smith (n 12) 93.

The default position of licence that exists in relation to handing over an item of property free of charge does not extend to the contractual context because the handing over of the property is in exchange for something of value. Having received value for the work being parted with, whether the copyright owner intended to assign or license the copyright work is a function of the knowledge of the copyright owner as to a range of factors. Accordingly, the components of the knowledge of the copyright owner are:

- whether the counterparty has a prior proprietary interest, discernible from the nature of the copyright work, the nature of the relationship between the parties, the nature of the transaction surrounding the copyright licence, and so on;
- of the terms of the bargain, including the price agreed, the purpose for which the work will be used, and so on; and
- of the surrounding circumstances of the transaction, which include circumstances peculiar to a particular industry, trade, or profession.

The facts and circumstances that need to be within the knowledge of a copyright owner can differ between different types of contract, such as commissioning contracts that may have mutually negotiated bespoke terms, copyright exploitation contracts that may have standard terms, and consumer contracts, which typically always have standard terms. All these factors are more fully discussed in Chapter 5 below.

2. An Established Custom

A custom can also be a source of implying a licence. The practice underlying the custom can originate from copyright owners consenting to a certain practice within their trade, consistently and notoriously, so much so that the actors within that trade begin to recognise such practice as binding. Or, more controversially, the practice can originate from the copyright owner not objecting to a particular use of her works and refraining from enforcing her rights. The continued engagement in such practice within the trade will reach a point where the practice will become binding also on a copyright owner. This is the point where the practice is established as a custom. Applying the framework for consent in Section 1 above will be inadequate, because the specific knowledge of the copyright owner is not a necessary component for establishing a custom; inappropriate if custom did not originate from the act of consenting, but rather from the act of refraining. Therefore, the framework one needs here should address not the conduct of the copyright owner and her state of mind, but the practice of the community and manner in which the knowledge of the practice can be imputed to the copyright owner. The ability to impute knowledge of a practice comes from the practice being clearly identifiable, consistent, universally followed, and so on. In other words, these are the criteria that establish such practice as a custom.

The criteria for establishing a custom already exists in contract law[15] since, historically, contract law has had a greater engagement with customs.[16] Since customs perform the same function here as in contract law, which is to impute knowledge of the custom to the contracting parties, the same criteria apply also for establishing a custom for implying a copyright licence. The following are the criteria for establishing a custom, as generally agreed by scholars and judges in the common law jurisdictions.[17]

- certainty;
- notoriety;
- reasonableness;
- not contrary to law; and
- recognised as binding

A more detailed discussion follows in Chapter 6 below. Scholars of copyright law, especially in the US, have further refined the criteria for the recognition of a custom within the copyright context, keeping in mind the ability of the more powerful players in copyright industries to create and maintain practices that are to their sole advantage, and to the disadvantage of the less powerful players like the end-users.[18] Accordingly, Chapter 6 further refines the main criteria above, and discusses the case law on custom-based implied copyright licences, in the light of the main and the refined criteria. These licences can arise as bare or contractual licences, depending on the content of the custom. However, the issue of concern is often the very existence of a custom, rather than the bare or contractual nature of the licence. Therefore, both bare and contractual licences are dealt with together in Chapter 6 below.

3. State Intervention to Achieve a Policy Goal

As discussed in Chapter 2 above, just as it is possible for the state to intervene for policy reasons and order a copyright owner to issue a compulsory licence, it should

15 Gerard McMeel, *The Construction of Contracts: Interpretation, Implication, and Rectification* (3rd edn, OUP 2017) paras 12.11, 12.13.

16 Sir Johan Steyn, 'Written Contracts: To What Extent May Evidence Control Language?' (1988) 41 CLP 23, 26.

17 McMeel (n 15) para 12.11; Beatson, Burrows, and Cartwright (n 3) 169.

18 Jennifer Rothman, 'Copyright, Custom and Lessons from the Common Law' in Shyam Balganesh (ed), *Intellectual Property and Common Law* (CUP 2013).

be possible for the state to intervene for public policy reasons to *imply* a licence. The first issue we must tackle is whether courts can legitimately engage in identifying and giving effect to policy.[19] Legitimacy of this kind is less of an issue in relation to consent because courts can rely on what they see as the voluntary conduct of the copyright owner as the basis for implying a copyright licence. This is also less of an issue in relation to custom because courts have themselves accepted that it does not require a court ruling for a custom to be established, confirming the legitimacy of a custom on its own as a basis for implying a copyright licence. However, it is an issue in case of policy because legislature and not the judiciary is the constitutionally legitimate repository of power to formulate policies and embody them in legislative enactments.

Indeed, there are scholars who argue that courts giving effect to policy considerations exceed their judicial role and act improperly in their legislative capacity.[20] In response, there are those who argue that policy considerations have a legitimate role to play in private law decision-making, because that is the way common law has historically developed.[21] A large part of private law in many jurisdictions of the Commonwealth is made up of common law—a source of law that is judge-made.[22] Examples include a significant part of tort law, contract law, and property law, where for centuries courts have weighed policy considerations and steered the law in a particular direction, with little or no legislative intervention. The legitimacy of common law as a source of law is so well settled in private law that scholars in public law rely on such legitimacy likewise to support judicial review of administrative actions.[23] Courts therefore making policy choices and steering the direction of the law to achieve those objectives is not a novel phenomenon. On the contrary, it is a legitimate source from which a significant part of private law and administrative law have developed. As such, there is no reason to shield copyright law from the courts' exercise of this jurisdiction over identifying and giving effect to policies.

Even if the courts are able to engage in identifying and giving effect to policy, can they make a policy objective the reason for denying a copyright owner her property rights? One may argue that the jurisdiction to deny property right rests with the legislature. And, to the extent that policy objectives balancing the interests of other stakeholders need to be incorporated within the copyright regime, the legislature has spoken through compulsory licences and statutory limitations or exceptions (SLEs). The legislature having thus spoken excludes courts from having a role to

[19] Policy has the same meaning ascribed to it as in ch 2, section 1(c) above.

[20] See eg Robert Stephens, *Torts and Rights* (OUP 2007) 312–14.

[21] See eg Andrew Robertson, 'Constraints on Policy-Based Reasoning in Private Law' in Andrew Robertson and Tang Hang Wu (eds), *The Goals of Private Law* (Hart Publishing 2009) 261, 279–80.

[22] John Bell, 'Sources of Law' in Andrew Burrows (ed), *English Private Law* (3rd edn, OUP 2013) para [1.21].

[23] See eg Paul Craig, *UK, EU and Global Administrative Law: Foundations and Challenges* (CUP 2015) 125–53. Craig further argues that this does not in any way challenge parliamentary supremacy because it is open to Parliament to affirm or alter the course of common law at any point.

play in denying the property right of copyright owners. This may be the case where a statute regards the SLEs to represent an exhaustive incorporation of all policy considerations of relevance to copyright (such as in EU copyright law). This means that no new exception embodying a new policy outside those already captured by the existing exceptions is permitted.

Given all these constraints, how do we create a legitimate role for the judiciary when dealing with the property right of the copyright owner? Applying Hohfeldian analytics one may see that the SLEs operate as rights granted to users or, at the very least, as privileges (that do not give rise to a licence because they are statements of law and not of fact), whereas compulsory licences operate more as privileges. In both these cases, the legislature provides the required legitimacy in taking away a property right such as copyright and replaces it with a duty or no-right. It is unlikely that a court can derive legitimacy to deny copyright as a property right by directly changing the property right to a no-right and the duty of the user to privilege, providing policy reasons as the basis. Some consensual basis stemming from the copyright owner, even if to a limited extent, appears necessary. However, if there is no such consensual basis at all, then a court is unlikely to have the legitimacy to target the right-duty relation directly, leaving it with the more indirect route through immunity-disability.

This brings us to the distinction between a policy-based implied contractual licence and a policy-based implied bare licence. In a policy-based contractual licence, the existence of a contract brings about an element of voluntariness on the part of the copyright owner in entering into the contract with another person in relation to the copyright work. For the consideration already given in the contract from the user to the copyright owner, the court implies a licence in favour of the user not because the copyright owner consented to it, but because the courts need to achieve a policy objective. The voluntariness that comes with a contract already in existence, even if to a limited extent, provides the legitimacy for the licence to take the form of a privilege that a court implies in favour of the user. In other words, by way of implying a licence courts compel a (property) right and duty relationship to be replaced by a no-right and privilege relationship for policy considerations, but within a contractual context. We need to develop a framework that recognises the contractual setting but makes way for policy as the basis for implying a licence.

In contrast, in a policy-based implied bare licence a contract is absent and, therefore, no consideration moves from the licensee to the copyright owner in exchange for this licence. Therefore, the legitimacy attached to the voluntariness that a pre-existing contract provides is absent. Under these circumstances, it is unlikely that courts can imply a licence derived from privilege. Instead, it may be possible to explore whether a licence derived from immunity can be implied. The court will then not be interfering with the property right directly, but will only deny the enforcement of such rights. As it is certainly within the powers of the courts to enforce a right and grant remedies, here the court uses its powers to prevent or restrict enforcement of copyright, including by withholding remedies in the public interest. The courts already have a discretion in the grant of equitable remedies like injunctions. Although there is an overlap, a court's powers are wider in that the court is empowered to refuse whatever it takes to enforce copyright, to give effect to a countervailing public interest. We need a framework that recognises the background constraints and guides the exercise of this power of the judiciary.

The above discussion reveals that the courts can not only engage legitimately in identifying and giving effect to policy, but can also make the policy a basis for implying a copyright licence. Given that the existence of a contract makes a significant difference to the approach adopted, policy-based implied contractual licences are considered separately from policy-based implied bare licences, as follows.

(a) Policy-based implied contractual licences

In contract law, although the tests for implying a term in fact are also controversial, courts generally try to find legitimacy on the basis that they only give effect to the unexpressed joint intention of the parties, and that it is the contracting parties, and not the courts, that make the contract. Underlying this manner of implication is the ideal of freedom of contract. However, freedom of contract is an ideal rarely realised in practice and the process of contract formation cannot be relied upon to ensure that contract terms will be fair or efficient.[24] Therefore, at common law, courts also imply a term by law into a contract even if the term does not represent the joint unexpressed intention of the parties, to achieve policy objectives that are broader and beyond the parties' concerns.[25]

It is not always possible to depend on the legislature to make provision for implying terms into a contract because courts are closer to the reality of the circumstances requiring terms to be implied on a case-by-case basis, which the generalised view of a legislature might miss. Phang argues that even if statutes are the 'purest' source of terms implied by law, courts act as a 'testing ground' for implying terms by law, and assist 'in the gradual (and ultimate) shift toward the legislative implication of terms'.[26] Some scholars might want to see the statutory embodiment of terms which the courts had originally implied by law as the legislature placing a restriction on the general powers of the courts. However, a more constructive way to view this is as a vindication of the courts' decisions. The legislative provisions do bring certainty to litigants in relation to the terms specifically codified. But these provisions should not be read as a prohibition on the courts' discretion to rise to

24 Atiyah and Smith (n 12) 156, 162.

25 In *Liverpool City Council v Irvin* [1977] AC 239, 253–54, Lord Wilberforce described implying terms under different circumstances as shades in a spectrum, reinforcing a view that the courts find it an extension of their judicial function to imply terms not grounded in the intention of the parties.

26 Andrew Phang, 'Implied Terms Revisited' [1990] JBL 394, 410–11.

newer occasions to imply terms as the circumstances demand. It is possible for this cyclical process to take place also in the copyright context where courts imply a copyright licence and then the legislature enacts a provision capturing the licence.

Although there is common law recognition of courts giving effect to a policy, in their methodology of implying a term by law courts do not make it clear how they engage with policy. In general, courts imply a term by law into all contracts of a particular type, so long as it is necessary to imply the term, such that the term implied becomes a default rule. This promotes certainty by implying the term into all contracts of a particular type and encourages courts not to interfere with the freedom of contract by inserting new terms on a case-by-case basis into every contract which is challenged. However, the methodology is not transparent because it does not shed light on *how* the particular type of contract is to be identified and *why* it is necessary to imply a term. Clearly, it is a policy reason that unites the type of contract and necessitates the implication of the term. Therefore, the methodology needs to be reframed to make it more transparent as to what the court is doing—i.e., giving effect to a policy. The following framework is suggested:

- identifying the policy objectives underlying the term sought to be implied into the contract;
- ascertaining the type to which the contract at issue belongs such that the policy objective influences a common incident shared by all contracts of that type; and
- implying the term if it is necessary, meaning that it is the only way in which the court can address the policy reasons.

A more detailed discussion on the inadequacies of the existing framework and how the above framework has been arrived can be found in Chapter 7 below.

(b) Policy-based implied bare licences

The first step towards developing a methodology is to find the source of power that enables the courts to deny enforcement of copyright. Section 171(3) of the Copyright, Designs and Patents Act 1988 (CDPA) states that: 'Nothing in this Part affects any rule of law preventing or restricting the enforcement of copyright, on grounds of *public interest* or otherwise' (emphasis added). Public interest is broader than public policy and, for our purposes, subsumes public policy in that all those considerations that are outside of the copyright owner and those that inform the welfare and community interests can be termed public interest.[27] This

[27] *Black's Law Dictionary* defines public interest as '(1) the general welfare of a populace considered as warranting recognition and protection, and (2) something in which the public as a whole has a stake; esp., an interest that justifies governmental regulation'.

provision is included under the savings provisions under the sub-heading 'Rights and privileges under other enactments or the common law', meaning that all laws that prevent or restrict the enforcement of copyright in the public interest, whether statutory or judge-made, continue to apply. Based on the legislative history of this provision and consistently followed common law authority, scholars have argued that there is such a judge-made rule.[28] In the exercise of this power, if a court decides to prevent or restrict the enforcement of copyright, the user acquires an immunity from having to stop the use of the work that is causing infringement, replacing the power of copyright owner to enforce copyright with a disability. Behind the immunity from having to stop engaging in certain use is the privilege to engage in such use. As explained in Section 4(c) of Chapter 1 above, this is how a licence derived from immunity comes into existence. Thus, a court's decision exercising the power under section 171(3) can become a policy-based implied bare licence, with the facts going into the decision-making as the operative facts.

This power of the courts does not owe its origin to the statute; indeed, it is a common law power which the statute confirms and reinforces under section 171(3). Therefore, the absence of an equivalent provision in other jurisdictions is not fatal to recognising this power. Canada, for example, has a philosophy of taking public interest considerations into account in resolving intellectual property disputes.[29] Indeed, the Canadian copyright jurisprudence goes further to declare that all intellectual property exists not only for the owners, but primarily in the interest and for the protection of the public.[30] Scholars in Canada therefore acknowledge that the Canadian law accommodates this power, while judges and scholars in Australia consider the existence of such powers under Australian law doubtful.[31] However, the power of the courts to prevent or restrict copyright enforcement is very narrow. Unlike in policy-based implied contractual licences, the court's rulings in case of policy-based bare licences do not apply to all transactions of a particular kind, but only operate on a case-by-case basis. This is to ensure that, by the exercise of this power, the judiciary does not take on the role of the legislature by laying down broad-based general principles of law. The exercise of this power does not interfere with the relevant work gaining copyright protection, but only prevents or restricts copyright enforcement in the particular case, including by addressing the remedies granted, which in any event is the court's domain. On this basis, one may argue the possibility of this power being exercised also by the courts of other jurisdictions.

It is important to drive home the exceptionality of this power. Otherwise, a court may be asked to save every case which falls short of meeting the requirements of one or more of the SLEs in the name of the public interest. This may render

[28] Although many of these cases only concern interim remedies, Burrell argues that 'they are part of a wider picture which shows that the courts were clearly moving toward the recognition of such a defence'. Robert Burrell, 'Defending the Public Interest' (2000) 22 EIPR 394, 402.

[29] *Théberge v Galerie d'Art du Petit Champlain Inc* [2002] 2 SCR 336 [30]–[31].

[30] David Vaver, *Intellectual Property Law* (2nd edn, Irwin Law 2011) 14. Vaver takes examples also from patent law and argues for a discourse closely informed by the public interest.

[31] See Gummow J's observations obiter in *Collier Constructions v Foskett* (1990) 97 ALR 460, 471–74.

pointless the legislative provisions of SLEs. Therefore, the public interest must be of such gravity that it is not captured within any of the SLEs. Any concerns one may have that there may be floodgate of litigation to give a wide reading to public interest can be addressed by driving home the exceptional nature of the circumstances that trigger this power.

Even if we confine the application of the public interest defence to exceptional cases, the exercise of this power still needs to be guided. From a methodological viewpoint, it makes sense to provide a framework within which this power is exercised. To the extent that there is no voluntariness on the part of the copyright owner in the user being able to enjoy this licence, one may argue that policy-based implied bare licences behave like the SLEs. That this power may be triggered when no other SLE can address a scenario also lends credence to the argument that it may behave like an SLE, although the exercise of this power primarily grants immunity and only indirectly gives rise to a privilege. While scholars call this power a 'public interest defence', there is no consensus on whether it should be treated as an SLE. Calling it a defence stands to reason because, like all SLEs, the evidential burden in this regard rests on the copyright user. If it is to be treated as an additional SLE, then the matter becomes fraught with additional complications since EU law dictates a closed list of SLEs. One may argue that this is only stated in recital 32, which is not as such transposed into UK law, and therefore is not part of retained 'EU derived domestic legislation' under section 2 of the European Union (Withdrawal) Act 2018. However, to the extent that the closed list is borne out by the case law of the Court of Justice of the European Union (CJEU) before the Exit Day, will continue to apply to the UK unless the Supreme Court decides to depart from it.[32] It may also be noted that the EU and the UK concluded their negotiations on the Trade and Cooperation Agreement a few days before the Exit Day. This Agreement was approved by the European Council (OJ L444) in time for it to provisionally take effect after the Exit Day. Part Two, Heading One (Trade), Title V of this Agreement deals with Intellectual Property, within which Chapter 2, Section 1 deals with copyright. Article IP.15 deals with the limitations and exceptions to copyright. It is noteworthy that this provision only reinforces the three-step test and does not mandate that the UK should maintain a closed list of the SLEs. Further, under the Agreement, the CJEU does not have an ongoing supervisory jurisdiction to ensure compliance of the UK domestic law with EU law.

Nevertheless, it makes sense to subject the court's power to imply a policy-based bare licence to the same kind of regulation as all other SLEs. Article 5(5) of the Infosoc Directive requires that the SLEs in Articles 5(1) to 5(4) be made available by the Member States only in (i) certain special cases which (ii) do not conflict with the normal exploitation of the copyright work and (iii) do not unreasonably

[32] Exit Date is referred to as the IP (Implementation Period) completion date, which is defined in European Union (Withdrawal Agreement) Act 2020, s 39(1) as 31 December 2020 at 11.00 pm UK time. Sections 6(4)(a) and 5(5), read with s 7 of the European Union (Withdrawal) Act, 2018 state that after the Exit Date, the Supreme Court can depart from the CJEU decisions given before the Exit Day.

prejudice the legitimate interests of the copyright owner. This is commonly referred to as the 'three-step test'. The test is also a guideline enshrined in the Berne Convention, and so is equally applicable to countries like Australia and Canada. Although the test is not transposed into the national statutes, compliance with the test by the courts can provide the required guidelines for the exercise of this power. If the exercise of this power satisfies the three-step test, then a policy-based bare licence can be implied.

There is significant scholarly opinion that the three-step test was not formulated with copyright users in mind and that it is heavily biased in favour of copyright owners. It must be acknowledged that the test embodies the three internationally accepted criteria to guide derogation from the exclusive rights, which presuppose copyright protection as the norm. But one may argue that when we have a concept as general as the public interest representing the interests of other stakeholders, guidelines that are drawn from the rights perspective might provide the appropriate counterbalance. One may also wish to ensure the exceptionality of the public interest defence by the application of three-step test. Arguably, the test does have its flexibilities within which to weigh the public interest in order to arrive at a just and fair conclusion.[33]

However, it might happen in certain cases that public interest is of such fundamental significance that even with its flexibilities, the rights-based approach of the three-step test is incapable of accommodating public interest. In this situation, one will have to turn to the fundamental rights regime as the basis for implying a policy-based licence. This is because the three-step test originated within the copyright context and operates as a response to copyright infringement. The fundamental rights regime, in contrast, is clearly not limited to the copyright context, but has much broader application. The fundamental rights regime is an important constitutional source to guide state action. Most liberal democracies have their own fundamental rights regime with their own methodology for application which can be pressed into service. Some scholars believe that when a case meets the three-step test, normally it leads to a result that is compliant with the fundamental rights regime, because the considerations factored within the balancing exercise undertaken in the third step are akin to those under the fundamental rights regime.[34] However, even if a case does not comply with the three-step test, a court can still proceed to examine it for compliance with the fundamental rights regime. Thus, if a court complies with the fundamental rights regime, even if it does not comply with the three-step test, the public interest defence can be still be successfully raised. Accordingly, the framework consists of the following:

[33] Christophe Geiger, Daniel Gervais, and Martin Senftleben, 'The Three-step Test Revisited: How to Use the Test's Flexibility in National Copyright Law' (2013) PIJIP Research Paper no 2013-04, 4–7; Martin Senftleben, 'The International Three-step Test A Model Provision for EC Fair Use Legislation' (2010) 1 JIPITEC 67, para 46.

[34] Geiger, Gervais, and Senftleben (n 33) 24.

- To ascertain whether a court in implying a policy-based bare licence is satisfied that it confined the licence to
  - special cases which
  - do not conflict with a normal exploitation of the copyright work and
  - do not unreasonably prejudice the legitimate interests of the copyright owner.
- Alternatively, a policy-based bare licence could be implied on the strength of the fundamental human rights regime.

Chapter 8 below discusses in greater detail the suitability of this framework for adoption by the courts, and analyses case law on policy-based implied bare licences in the light of this framework. To demonstrate the fundamental rights regime, it takes UK law as an example.

4. Conclusions and Connections

This chapter has analysed the aspects that are present in express copyright licences through the prism of the Hohfeldian conception of licence to develop frameworks to guide the implication of copyright licences under different bases. The significance of a licence being conceptualised as a group of facts may be reinforced here. What this chapter did is to indicate the criteria based on which to marshal facts to ascertain if a licence can be implied and, if so, its scope. These criteria serve as the building blocks for the frameworks proposed in this chapter.

The next part, Part II, will analyse the case law in the light of the frameworks proposed in this chapter and demonstrate how the frameworks can enable a methodical and transparent way of implying copyright licences. The chapters in Part II each focus on the frameworks suggested for each of the bases for implying a copyright licence, considering further in separate chapters, bare or contractual licences, as necessary.

PART II

RATIONALISING CONCEPTUAL FRAMEWORKS WITHIN COPYRIGHT DOCTRINE

Part I above proposed frameworks for implying copyright licences. The effort in Part II will be to rationalise the existing doctrine in the light of these frameworks. By rationalising what is meant here is analysing the doctrine in the light of the frameworks proposed to ascertain the rationale behind the findings of the court. The outcome of these cases may not necessarily change; however, one needs to map the reasoning of the court if these cases are to support the implication of copyright licences in future cases. This is achieved by channelling the facts and circumstances of the cases into the criteria identified by the frameworks to make the courts' reasoning transparent and the analysis methodical. The case law considered in this Part is predominantly from the UK, but cases from Australia and Canada are also discussed.

The framework for implying consent-based bare licences considered in Chapter 4 essentially tracks the conduct of the copyright owner and her knowledge. The framework may come across as intuitive, but conceptual reasoning is necessary. Parallels can be drawn with the intuitive concepts of offer and acceptance in contract formation, where these steps are necessary for a methodical appreciation of the legal relationship that has come into existence. Since the courts' reasoning for implying a copyright licence does not reveal consistency nor a systematic way of assessing the facts, the framework proposed here tries to fill that gap.

One may wonder why the principles of contract law for implying a term in fact could not have been used for consent-based implied contractual licences in Chapter 5. It is because the tests of business efficacy and officious bystander do not make transparent the reasoning adopted by the judges. Judges can achieve a great deal in the name of business efficacy, which only serves to bypass the essential steps leading to their conclusions. On the contrary, the framework proposed not only makes their reasoning methodical and transparent, but also serves as a bespoke framework for implying a consent-based implied contractual copyright licence, as opposed to generally any term in a contract.

Custom-based implied licences fill the middle ground between consent-based and policy-based licences. Customs in the copyright context exist more in the practice of a community than in the case law. The copyright cases where a custom is successfully established are few, given the volume of evidence required to establish it. Judges as much as litigants ought to know what it takes to establish a custom, so that a licence may be implied on its basis. Chapter 6 addresses this. Therefore, rationalisation in this context means applying the main and the refined criteria to complete the reasoning in copyright cases and arriving at conclusions that are logical and doctrinally well-supported.

It is very important for the policy to be demarcated and its role appreciated in policy-based implied contractual licences. Although the framework proposed closely follows the one applied in contract for implying a term by law, it gives the place of importance to identifying the policy driving the implication. This, it is argued, is what distinguishes a term implied in fact and a term implied by law in a contractual context. In relation to copyright licences, proposing markedly different framework for implying a policy-based contractual licence from a consent-based contractual licence, Chapter 7 tries to clear up the confusion surrounding the methodology to be applied.

The peculiarity of policy-based implied bare licence is that, because of the absence of a contractual relationship between the parties, one may observe that strangers come to benefit from an implied licence. This is acceptable only because the implication is firmly grounded in the public interest. The frameworks proposed here, namely the three-step test and the fundamental rights regime both already exist in the copyright discourse. However, courts in the UK have not yet considered the application of the three-step test to those cases where denial of copyright enforcement was sought in the public interest, although courts have considered applying the fundamental rights regime. Chapter 8 demonstrates how the seemingly unregulated power of the courts can be regulated by the application of the three-step test in addition to the fundamental rights regime, when evaluating whether public interest justifies the denial of copyright enforcement.

The purpose of grouping these chapters under Part II is also to demonstrate the entire spectrum of bases that can be used to imply copyright licences. While consent captures only those considerations that surround the copyright owner, as we move away from it, larger considerations of the community are considered in custom, leading finally to policy, where only considerations of public welfare are considered.

4
Consent-based Implied Bare Licences

This chapter will consider licences where no terms are expressly stated and no consideration flows back to the copyright owner in return for the licence, either payment or otherwise. These are called bare licences. In Hohfeldian terms, the operative facts considered here are those that point to the existence of consent, which lead to a privilege-no right relationship, and no other, such as rights or duties.[1] The modern relevance of a consent-based implied bare licence lies in its application to the copyright work placed on the internet by its owner or with the owner's consent.[2]

There are several reasons why a bare licence may arise, other than in casual or friendly circumstances. First, the copyright owner might not realise that a copyright work has come into existence; secondly, even if she does realise it, she might not realise her own entitlement to it; thirdly, even if the copyright owner does realise her entitlement, she might not claim a share in the ownership owing to, inter alia, the lack of bargaining power to assert her entitlement. Fourthly, even if the copyright owner has the bargaining power and does enter into a negotiation, the negotiations may fail, but the counterparty continues to use the copyright work in question. These factors could influence the very existence of consent. These considerations must fit within any framework of analysis of the case law.

However, when one examines the existing case law, a 'rule' which the courts acknowledge they must follow when implying a copyright licence is to consider all facts and circumstances.[3] Clearly, this is too general and gives no guidance at all as to how the courts come to the conclusions they do on consent. In some other cases, courts use by analogy the contract law tests of implying a term, namely business efficacy and obviousness tests.[4] As discussed in the next chapter below, these tests are unfortunately so opaque that it is difficult to ascertain the considerations that go into their assessment. Even if the courts discuss generally the conduct of the copyright owner that implies consent, it is not clear how such

[1] A group of operative facts that create privilege is a licence, in Wesley Newcomb Hohfeld, 'Some Fundamental Legal Conceptions as Applied in Judicial Reasoning' (1913–14) 23 Yale LJ 16, 44.
[2] See ch 9, section 1 below.
[3] *Banks v CBS Songs Ltd* [1996] EMLR 440, 499.
[4] *Trumpet Software v OzEmail Pty Ltd* (1996) 34 IPR 481, 500.

Implied Licences in Copyright Law. Poorna Mysoor, Oxford University Press (2021). © Poorna Mysoor.
DOI: 10.1093/oso/9780198858195.003.0005

conduct could be identified in future cases. Even when the courts discuss the state of mind of the copyright owner, there is no systematic analysis of the aspects of the knowledge one must look for. This not only results in uncertainty and a hesitation to imply licences in newer scenarios, but may prevent the courts from being mindful of the manner in which copyright owners are positioned within an industry.

Rationalising the case law in the light of the framework for implying consent-based bare copyright licence makes transparent the factors that constitute consent and enables their critical evaluation. It was explained in Chapter 3 that consent is a combination of the conduct of the copyright owner and her knowledge of the circumstances. The conduct that creates a privilege-no right relationship is the positive act (facilitating access to the work to be used) and the neutral act (refraining from interfering with such use), both of which must be engaged in, with the knowledge of the circumstances. Accordingly, Section 1 analyses the case law in the light of these criteria. Of course, the courts do not use the terminology of the framework, namely the positive act and the neutral act. However, from the general discussion of evidence, it is possible to identify facts that could otherwise make up the positive and the neutral acts. A similar analysis can help identify the knowledge of the copyright owner. In some cases, the process of rationalisation also helps reveal any unsoundness in the courts' reasoning, so that suggestions as to ways to set them right may be put forward.

Section 2 deals with the revocability of bare licences. A consent-based bare licence can be revoked, since the ability to grant such a licence and to revoke it (upon reasonable notice) both originate from the powers of the copyright owner. However, there are situations where these licences cannot be revoked, and the courts have ascribed proprietary estoppel as the reason for irrevocability. This is discussed in Section 3 below. This author has provided a detailed analysis of proprietary estoppel in copyright law elsewhere.[5] This section provides an overview of the case law, advocating the application of proprietary estoppel in a manner more adapted to the needs of copyright law, so that it can lead to fairer results.

1. Establishing Consent to Imply a Bare Licence

Chapter 3 identified the framework for implying a consent-based licence as including the positive act, the neutral act, and the knowledge of the copyright owner. For bare licences, the third criterion splits into several sub-ingredients. Let us examine each of these criteria in the light of the case law.

[5] Poorna Mysoor, 'Proprietary Estoppel and Copyright Law' (2018) 29 King's LJ 470.

(a) The positive act

Chapter 3 explained that the positive act is the act of enabling the copyright work to be used by the licensee. In the absence of an express grant, one must start with an 'overt conduct' on part of the copyright owner that indicates her state of mind to consent. Mere inaction is insufficient.

The cases concerning consent-based implied bare licences discussed in this chapter are not cases of mere inaction. The copyright owner does engage in an overt act and, therefore, in most cases there is no discussion on the importance of such overt act to prove consent. However, in cases where there is no overt act of whatever kind, courts have normally refused to recognise a licence. The Australian High Court decision in *Interstate Parcel v Time-Life International*[6] is perhaps the most explicit in this regard. It was argued here that the lack of restriction by an overseas copyright owner on the importation of certain magazines into Australia was sufficient to amount to a licence to import these magazines. The court rejected this argument, and held that a 'positive licence' would be required, which may not be express, but implied where 'a copyright owner overseas sells copyright articles in commercial quantities to a purchaser in Australia'.[7] Thus, in this case, the selling of commercial quantities of copyright articles to an Australian purchaser could have been regarded as the positive act. In its absence, there was no licence.

Since the case law in the UK is more tacit in its acceptance of the fact that without the positive act, a copyright owner cannot demonstrate her consent, this section makes explicit the act or the series of acts that represent the positive act. The objective is to make transparent the need for the positive act, so that in future, a court does not erroneously conclude that consent exists even where there is no positive act. The manifestation of a positive act depends on the nature of the work and the medium in which it is created. If it is a literary or dramatic work, handing over the piece of paper on which it is written or is printed would be a positive act. If it is a musical work, the positive act may manifest in taking part in the recording. Normally, the conduct of creating the work precedes the positive act, but may not in itself be sufficient to be the positive act. The positive act is a conduct noticeable in addition to the process of creation, evident either from a physical handling of the work or from the circumstances that enable the work to be accessed or used.

One may begin illustrating it with *Banks v CBS Songs Ltd*.[8] In this case, Banks, the claimant, was acquainted with Khan, a machinist, when he told her that he had

[6] (1977) 138 CLR 534.

[7] ibid 556–57 (emphasis added). The judge was speaking of the Australian Copyright Act 1968 (ACA), s 37. This was confirmed again in *Computermate Products v Ozi-Soft* (1988) 83 ALR 492, 498, where it was held that silence as to a restriction is not sufficient to grant a freedom from restriction. In neither of these cases was there a grant of a bare licence, as the alleged licensee had paid for the purchase of the copyright articles. However, the licence, if implied, would have been consent-based. For a discussion on how these licences are contractual see ch 5 below.

[8] [1996] EMLR 440.

an opportunity to sing for the rock group UB40. Banks claimed that Khan had asked her to 'come up' with some words. However, Khan claimed that he himself wrote the words with the lead singer of UB40, Campbell, one of the defendants. Thus, not only was Banks' authorship in dispute, but also that she gave the lyrics to Khan. Regarding authorship, based on the verbal and documentary evidence before the court, it was held that Banks composed the lyrics.[9] But this is only the process of creation. If Banks had stopped at this, no consent could have been inferred. From the available evidence, the court concluded that Banks gave the lyrics, typed on a piece of paper, to Khan.[10] This act of 'giving' the lyrics to Khan is Banks enabling Khan to use the work, and therefore represents the positive act. The court, of course, did not call it a positive act, but took evidence on it, and concluded in fact that Banks gave the song to Khan, contrary to Khan's version.

In *Brighton v Jones*,[11] Brighton, the claimant was going to direct a play called *Stones in his Pockets*, which Jones, the defendant, was going to write, for a production company Brighton owned. Apprehending that Jones had not started writing the script, Brighton wrote a draft of the opening scene and sent it to Jones to 'kick-start' Jones' playwriting.[12] Brighton's act of writing the opening scene alone would not have been sufficient to count towards her consent. The act of sending the draft is the positive act of concern here. The court stated that Brighton 'sent the script with an implied licence to use it'.[13] However, this makes it appear as if the act of sending was external to the implied licence, and does not clarify how the licence came to be implied in the first place. A better way to understand this is to regard the act of sending as part of the conduct based on which a licence could be implied. Separating the positive act thus shows how consent comes into play, enabling a licence to be implied based on it when other criteria are met.

In *Tumber v Independent Television News Ltd (ITN)*,[14] a poem that Tumber, the claimant, had written had gained fame for being the longest love poem ever written, which attracted the defendant television news company's attention. ITN's employee telephoned Tumber and told him that she wanted to write an article for ITN's website carrying an interview about him and his work. Tumber agreed and over the phone the employee also asked him to send his poem to her. Tumber emailed the poem to her. ITN argued that him sending the poem to her amounted to his implied licence for the poem also to appear on ITN's website together with the interview. Tumber applied to the court to strike out this defence, arguing that his 'silence' cannot be taken as consent.[15] However, all it takes for the positive act

[9] ibid 443, 448.
[10] ibid 448.
[11] [2004] EWHC 1157 (Ch).
[12] ibid [21].
[13] ibid [72].
[14] [2017] EWHC 3093 (IPEC).
[15] ibid [1]–[3], [11]. This case is also discussed in relation to custom-based licences in ch 4, section 3(a) below.

is the copyright owner's conduct, even if no particular words are said. Therefore, it is possible to regard Tumber's initial act of sending the poem as the positive act. Whether this was sufficient to amount to consent must be assessed based on other factors such as neutral act and knowledge of the copyright owner discussed below.

In case of musical works, as discussed in the three cases below, the positive act may lie in giving access to the sheet music, or in the copyright owner's performing in a recording studio. There is no discussion of the act of participation in these cases, as the copyright owner in each case admits to taking part in the recordings. The main issues in each case are the scope of the licence and its revocability, which are addressed later in this chapter.

In *Godfrey v Lees*,[16] Godfrey, the claimant, was acquainted with the members of a band by the name of Barclay James Harvest, but was not part of the band himself. Godfrey participated in the rehearsals by sometimes playing the piano, arranging, or conducting the orchestra for the songs that the band recorded or played in concerts.[17] Among these, Godfrey's original contribution lay in his orchestral arrangement linking orchestral sequences and passages to the songs,[18] which was presumably in the form of sheet music. Thus, Godfrey giving access to his orchestral arrangement, whether in a recording or a live performance, is the positive act.

In *Beckingham v Hodgens*,[19] the claimant Valentino was hired as a session violinist to record a song called *Young at Heart* by a band called The Bluebells. Valentino composed the solo violin part in the song, during the rehearsals, or what are commonly known in the music industry as jamming sessions.[20] Even if Valentino created the solo part, if he had not taken part in the recording, it would have been difficult to establish his consent. Therefore, the positive act was the taking part in the recording.

Similarly, in *Fisher v Brooker*,[21] Fisher, the claimant, who joined the band Procol Harum, rehearsed with the band for the song *Whiter Shade of Pale*, and composed an original organ solo during the jamming sessions, as a prelude and interlude to the song.[22] In addition to rehearsing with the band, Fisher also played the organ in the recording session. The act of participating in the recording was the act that amounted to the positive act.

There is a common practice in the music industry for the session musicians to sign a consent form, such as the one signed by Valentino in *Beckingham*.[23] The contents of the consent form are not clear from the decision in *Beckingham*, except

16 [1995] EMLR 307.
17 ibid 315–16.
18 ibid 326–29.
19 [2002] EWHC 2143 (Ch).
20 ibid [5].
21 [2006] EWHC 3239 (Ch).
22 ibid [32].
23 *Beckingham v Hodgens* (n 19) [55] (Ch). Also referred to in the appellate court's decision in [2003] EWCA Civ 143.

that by signing the consent form Valentino gave consent for his 'performance' to be used in the recording. It appears, therefore, that this is all the consent form was meant to do—consent to the recording of his live performance at the studio,[24] as opposed to the use of his original composition. A session musician is not expected to contribute to the composition of music, but only to play the music composed by someone else. Where a session musician does compose a copyright work in his own right, as in the cases of *Beckingham* and *Fisher*, their performers' rights must be distinguished from their rights as the author of the original music they create. The signing of the consent form is not the positive act of concern here, since it does not concern the copyright in the composition.

It may so happen that the copyright owner begins negotiating a contract and provides access for her work to be used while the negotiations continue, as happened in the Australian case, *Tamawood Ltd v Habitare Developments*.[25] Here, Tamawood, a builder, entered into negotiations with Habitare, a developer, to develop a certain site. While the negotiations continued, Tamawood prepared certain drawings and provided access to these drawings for Habitare to apply for development consent from the relevant authorities.[26] This act of providing access to the drawings accounted for the positive act.

A similar situation arose in anther Australian case, *Rebeschini v Miles Laboratories*,[27] where the claimant, an advertising agent of the defendant, hit upon the idea of a clutch purse to hold the equipment manufactured by the defendant. While in discussion with the defendant, the claimant made iterations of the design and handed over the final design with photographs of a prototype.[28] On the face of it, this can amount to a positive act. However, other constituents also need to be examined before one can ascertain whether consent has been established.

If the negotiations for a licence break down, but the copyright owner has made the relevant work otherwise accessible, does provision of such access count as the positive act? One may query this in relation to *Trumpet Software v OzEmail*.[29] Here, Trumpet had provided Trumpet Winsocksoftware for download online on a shareware basis, which is a form of software marketing which gives the user an opportunity to evaluate the product, enabling her to try before she buys, free of charge. Accordingly, Trumpet's software described it as shareware for a 30-day trial, reserving all rights in copyright and stating that no sale of the software on its own or together with other software was permitted. Users who wished to acquire the software after trial were required to forward a registration fee to Trumpet.[30] Let

[24] Copyright, Designs and Patents Act 1988 (CDPA), s 182.
[25] [2013] FCA 410 (Federal Court of Australia).
[26] ibid [96]. These facts were unchallenged on appeal to the Full Court, reported at (2015) 112 IPR 439.
[27] (1982) 1 IPR 159 (Supreme Court of Victoria).
[28] ibid 162–63.
[29] (1996) 34 IPR 481 (Federal Court of Australia).
[30] ibid 485.

us call this the general licence. The defendant, OzEmail, an ISP, had approached Trumpet to distribute Trumpet Winsock software free of charge on diskettes, together with a personal computing magazine. This was OzEmail's attempt to obtain a specific licence for its activity. Trumpet informed OzEmail that he would only permit a version of Trumpet software to be used if it was time-locked (a technological protection measure). Although Trumpet agreed to provide a time-locked version, it never did so. This, therefore, cannot be regarded as a positive act, and therefore, the specific licence never materialised. However, OzEmail subsequently asked Trumpet if it could instead use the version currently available on a shareware basis. Trumpet refused to permit this.[31] Even if the software was otherwise accessible freely, Trumpet's clear refusal for what OzEmail proposed to do with it indicates that there was never a positive act even as far as the general licence was concerned. The initial act of Trumpet making available its software as shareware is a positive act only to those who wanted to try it according to its terms. It could have been a positive act for OzEmail if all it wanted to do was to try it like it was intended to. In this sense, one might say that the positive act was conditional.

The positive act is by no means a complete grant of licence. It is only a part—albeit a significant part—of the conduct that conveys consent. For the act of consenting to be complete, having enabled the use of the work, the copyright owner must stand back while the work is used, which takes us to the neutral act.

(b) The neutral act

The neutral act follows the positive act closely and is the other part of the conduct representing consent. The neutral act is the inaction or refraining from doing something which will alter the effect of the positive act. Courts provide discussion on this to different degrees, but identifying the facts making up the neutral act is necessary to make transparent the reason why an implied licence continues for the length of time that it does.

In *Brighton*, as explained above, Brighton had sent a draft opening script to Jones to kick-start Jones' playwriting, and that act of sending the draft amounted to the positive act. Brighton's inaction to stop Jones from using the draft is the neutral act of relevance here. By this neutral act, Brighton conveyed that she did not object to Jones using the draft in her playwriting. The inaction was absolute in that Jones could use the draft in any manner that was within Brighton's knowledge. Although the judge did not use the word inaction, he referred to the lack of an effort on Brighton's part to revoke the licence as the reason why the implied licence

[31] ibid 487–88.

continued, allowing Jones to use the draft also in rewriting the play a few years later for another production house.[32]

The judge further pointed out that if Brighton had wished to limit the use of the draft opening script by Jones, she could have included a covering letter when sending it to Jones, laying down the restrictions placed on its use.[33] This would have made the neutral act partial in that Brighton could have specified the actions she objected to, resulting in an express licence allowing only some of the consequences of the positive act to take effect. Had there been restrictions that the draft could only be used for a play with Brighton's production company, Jones may have chosen to ignore the draft altogether, in order to free her work of Brighton's contribution.

Also, in *Banks*, *Beckingham*, *Godfrey*, and *Fisher*, the neutral act was absolute. In none of these cases did the copyright owners restrict the use of their copyright works. The neutral act in each of these cases conveyed that the copyright owners did not object to their copyright works being used. As explained in Chapter 3 above, so long as the neutral act continues, meaning so long as the copyright owner takes no action, the licence continues. The neutral act continued for five years in *Brighton*, nine years in *Beckingham*, 14 years in *Godfrey*, and 38 years in *Fisher*. The moment the neutral act changes to a negative act, i.e., the inaction changes to an action to stop the use of the work, the bare licence is revoked. It might also happen in certain cases that the neutral act is relied on by the licensee to her detriment, leading to a claim of proprietary estoppel, preventing the copyright owner from revoking the licence. Revocability of bare licences is discussed in Section 2 below.

A good example of a conditional neutral act is *Tamawood*. Here, as noted above, the copyright owner, Tamawood, had provided access to its drawings to the defendant developer to obtain development consent, but on the condition that Tamawood should be retained as the builder. Although no written contract ever came into existence, this condition was sufficiently clear in the evidence.[34] This meant that Tamawood would stand by and allow its plans to be used to obtain development consent only if, subsequently, Tamawood was engaged as the builder.

A conditional neutral act is also clear from *Rebeschini*. Here, having sent the design and the photographs of the prototype, Rebeschini then sent a 12-page recommendation on marketing the defendant's equipment with the claimant's packaging design. This document began with the premise that the claimant created and shared the packaging design based on his belief that there was a mutual understanding to give the advertising contract to the claimant if the defendant went ahead to market the product.[35] This document, although called a recommendation, showed that

[32] *Brighton v Jones* (n 11) [73], [77].
[33] ibid [76].
[34] *Tamawood Ltd v Habitare Developments* (n 25) [102]–[104], [139]. These findings were confirmed on appeal. See (2015) 112 IPR 439 [131]–[132].
[35] *Rebeschini v Miles Laboratories* (n 27) 163 (Murphy J).

having shared the designs for the clutch purse, the claimant had put the defendant on notice that he was not going to stand back and let the defendant use the design in disregard of the document.

Also, in *Trumpet*, it would have been a conditional neutral act if Trumpet had provided the time-locked software to OzEmail for distribution upon successful negotiations of the specific licence. It would have meant that Trumpet standing back when the software is used is conditional on the technological protection measure being honoured. However, Trumpet never supplied a time-locked version,[36] and the specific licence never materialised. But as far as the general licence is concerned, Trumpet continued to make the shareware version available. However, in the light of Trumpet's specific refusal for OzEmail to use the shareware version as it pleased negates the possibility that there could have been a neutral act in relation to the general licence. The continued availability of the software as shareware was a neutral act only to those who complied with shareware trial terms. In this sense, one might say that the neutral act was also conditional.

Perhaps the shortest neutral act was in *Tumber*. Having sent the email with his poem to ITN's employee, Tumber found that once the article featuring his interview appeared on ITN's website, subsequently ITN also uploaded a copy of Tumber's poem on its website. The very next day, Tumber wrote an email to ITN protesting the publication of his poem on ITN's website. ITN did take the poem down, but the website had already had many visitors. ITN argued that Tumber could have told its employee on the phone if he objected to the poem being published, which would have confined the use of the work by ITN only to prepare for the interview.[37] Whether the lack of any condition attached to his sending of the poem gave ITN an implied licence depends on the knowledge or reasonable expectation of Tumber.

For a copyright owner to decide how much of the effect of the positive act she wants to ensue, she must know the state of affairs that wil be brought about by her positive and neutral acts. The positive and the neutral acts are, therefore, inexorably linked to what the copyright owner knows about the surrounding circumstances, which brings us to the section below.

(c) The knowledge of the copyright owner

No one can consent without knowing what one is consenting to.[38] In an express licence, the copyright owner will have articulated what it is that she is consenting to. In an implied licence, the knowledge of the copyright owner of the overall

[36] *Trumpet Software v OzEmail Pty Ltd* (n 4) 487–88.

[37] *Tumber v Independent Television News Ltd* (n 14) [2], [7].

[38] Simon Lee, 'Towards a Jurisprudence of Consent' in John Eekelaar and John Bell (eds), *Oxford Essays in Jurisprudence* (3rd Series, Clarendon Press 1987) 212.

circumstances in which she is consenting is to be assessed. To bring greater clarity, the following three aspects to assess the knowledge of the copyright owner are proposed: first, the realisation of the authorship of the work; secondly, the realisation that the work will be used gratuitously; and, thirdly, the knowledge of the foreseeable consequences of engaging in the positive and neutral acts, and of any other surrounding circumstances which influence the uses to which the copyright work may be put.

The knowledge of these aspects should be assessed objectively. An objective assessment does not mean that knowledge is to be imputed to the copyright owner. Imputation of knowledge may only be permissible of a practice that has become a custom in a custom-based licence.[39] If no such custom exists, and the knowledge of the circumstances is unreasonably imputed to the copyright owner, the resulting consent and its ability to act as the basis for implying a licence both become weaker.

(i) Realisation of authorship of the work

Authorship in this context is a mixed question of law and fact: first, a person being an author as a matter of law; and, secondly, the person realising that she is an author as a matter of fact. The author of a copyright work is its first owner.[40] Chapter 2 above discussed that the exercise of the ownership powers is one of the sources for granting a copyright licence. Ownership connects a lawful licence with the owner. If such connection did not exist, there would be no difference between a person lawfully giving permission and a person authorising the use of certain content she herself is not authorised to use (thereby infringing its copyright). For example, in *Banks*, if Banks gave a song to Khan that she did not write or had no rights to, we might still be able to speak of a positive act of handing over the song and the neutral act of standing back when Khan used the song. But it will not give rise to a licence because she does not own the song and cannot, therefore, exercise the powers of ownership to grant a licence.

Many cases considered in this chapter involve joint authorship, which brings its own challenges. A work of joint authorship is produced by the collaboration of two or more authors in which the contribution of one author is not distinct from that of the other(s).[41] The Copyright, Designs and Patents Act 1988 (CDPA) states that where a copyright work is owned by more than one person jointly, any provision requiring the licence of the copyright owner requires the licence of all of them.[42]

39 See ch 6 below.

40 CDPA, s 11(1). However, a copyright owner may not always be the author, but an assignee from the author. When an author as the first owner of copyright assigns her copyright interest, the assignee will have the same rights as the author in relation to the assigned interest. A common example is when the copyright owner assigns her copyright to a collecting society. Assignment is usually an arm's-length transaction where both parties are likely to realise what is being assigned. The issues as to the realisation of the ownership of the copyright work arises more in the context of an author, as the case law shows, than in the context of an assignee.

41 CDPA, s 10(1).

42 ibid s 173(2).

Therefore, the requirement of a licence of the copyright owner to avoid infringement,[43] requires a licence of all the joint authors, if the work is of joint authorship. Such licence can be an express or an implied licence. Therefore, joint authorship must be established first, before the issue of implied licence can be addressed.

A detailed account of when a person becomes eligible to be a joint author is outside the scope of this chapter.[44] For our purposes, the rules of joint authorship can be summarised as follows: the collaborator must make some contribution towards the creation of the work; such contribution must be significant, but not necessarily to the same extent as others; but the contribution must be original.[45] However, copyright rules of authorship in general, and joint authorship in particular, are complex and contentious. It is not surprising, therefore, that the copyright owner does not realise that her actions have given rise to a copyright work. Even if a person is regarded as an author as a matter of law, if the author fails to realise her authorship as a matter of fact, she will be unable to have the required state of mind to consent for her work to be used. Courts do sometimes mention the copyright owner's lack of knowledge of copyright entitlement. However, they do not necessarily recognise it to be an impediment to the finding of consent, based on an objective assessment of the circumstances.

A good example of the issues presented in this regard is *Brighton*.[46] In this case, as stated above, Brighton was the director of a play which Jones was going to write. Brighton's first claim was for joint authorship based on her contribution as a director during rehearsals, and the second claim was based on her authorship of the draft opening script that she sent to Jones. The judge observed that it had not occurred to Brighton to claim her joint authorship until she approached the court. But Brighton's lack of knowledge did not matter because the judge dismissed her claims of joint authorship as a matter of law. However, it is possible that Brighton did not articulate her authorship also in relation to her second claim, i.e., of the draft script she sent to Jones, until she sought legal advice. The judge does not acknowledge this in the judgment, although he records that Brighton had been 'hurt' by the way her 'contribution' to the play had not been recognised.[47] Brighton sending the script was completely unsolicited, and Jones stated in her evidence that she did not need it. However, Jones used whatever she could of the draft, out of deference to Brighton, in creating the script for the play.[48]

It is difficult to conjecture exactly what Brighton thought her relationship was with the draft script she sent to Jones. Being the director of the play Jones was

43 See eg ibid s 16(2).

44 For a detailed discussion and critique of joint and collective authorship see Daniela Simone, *Copyright and Collective Authorship* (CUP 2019).

45 Gillian Davies, Nicholas Caddick, and Gwilym Harbottle, *Copinger and Skone James on Copyright* (17th edn, Sweet & Maxwell 2016) para 4-47.

46 *Brighton v Jones* (n 11).

47 ibid [28].

48 ibid [21], [61].

going to write, Brighton may have thought that she was sending some notes, to which she may have felt a proprietary attachment since these were expressed in her own words. This may explain why she felt that she had contributed to the play beyond her role as a director, for which she expected to be acknowledged. Although Brighton did not subjectively articulate in terms of copyright, objectively assessed, she had a sense of proprietary attachment. However, this issue was neither raised nor discussed in the judgment. The court only held that Brighton had impliedly licensed her work.

The issue is particularly troublesome in case of joint authorship. The plaintiff in many of the cases considered below is in a creative collaboration with others, for example a music band. The plaintiff is normally a background musician or takes on a support role, as opposed to a lead role in the process of creation, and is normally unaware of the significance of her contribution towards the creation of the work.

In *Barrett v Universal Island Records Ltd*,[49] the claimants, the Barrett brothers, were each a base guitarist and a percussionist with the well-known reggae musician, Bob Marley. The Barrett brothers were not signatories to the key agreements entered into by Marley with the defendant record company (Island), having always depended on Marley to deal with the business aspects of the band. The issue was whether the Barrett brothers had impliedly licensed their copyright to Island by participating in the recording. The Barrett brothers claimed that they did not realise that they were also entitled to copyright as joint authors when the songs were being created.[50] The court held that they were not session musicians, as they were always part of the band, being paid by Marley during his lifetime, and from his estate after his death. They were also paid for record sales, and one of them was recognised as a co-author of some of the songs recorded. The court therefore held that the Barrett brothers may not have known as little about their copyright entitlement as they claimed,[51] and went on to conclude that the Barrett brothers had impliedly licensed their copyright to Island.

In *Godfrey*, Godfrey was not a member of the band, but played the piano for them and arranged the music for many of the songs. The court found that owing to the 'free and easy' lifestyle they led and the informal nature of the relationship between the band members, it is unlikely that Godfrey or any member of the band realised at the time of recording that Godfrey could be entitled to copyright.[52] However, Godfrey had persuaded the band to acknowledge him on the albums as the 'resident musical director' or as the 'conductor and musical director'.[53] In addition, Godfrey asserted that there was an agreement to share the profits with him,[54]

49 [2006] EWHC 1009 (Ch).

50 ibid [18], [207], [214], [229].

51 ibid [60], [207], [208], [259]. Since the claimants were paid as authors, the implied licence at issue was not a bare licence, but a contractual licence.

52 *Godfrey v Lees* (n 16) 330–31.

53 ibid 330.

54 ibid 322–24.

although the court found the evidence too lean to support a concluded agreement with the other members of the band.[55] These facts revealed that Godfrey may have known about his rights to some degree, even if he did not articulate it as copyright.

Thus, the courts have generally tended to favour the view that the licensor does not need to articulate clearly that a copyright work has come into existence. It may be sufficient if the copyright owner has a sense of proprietary attachment to the work created, objectively assessed. This could be as simple as knowingly creating something. Courts have set the threshold of this knowledge low. Ideally, one might wish to insist on the full articulation of copyright, so that a state of mind necessary for consent can be decisively formed. However, there are practical considerations. A copyright owner can allege lack of articulation of her copyright entitlement, if only to defeat a licence being implied. In a joint authorship situation, if the other authors have gone ahead to licence the work of joint authorship, the lack of implied licence from one joint author who unscrupulously claims lack of knowledge of copyright ownership might have the effect of annulling those licences. Imposing a low threshold of knowledge of copyright entitlement might avoid such opportunistic behaviour. However, signalling that there is a need for such realisation of entitlement to copyright is essential, even if the threshold for such realisation is set low for pragmatic reasons. Otherwise, the copyright owner's conduct (positive and neutral acts) could result in consequences of which she had no knowledge.

(ii) Realisation of gratuitous nature

This aspect of the licensor's knowledge is important because a bare licence, by definition, is gratuitous. If a licence is in exchange for consideration, then it is not a bare licence, but a contractual licence. In some cases, a copyright owner might want to give away the work out of friendship. In some others, it may be that because the copyright owner does not realise that a copyright work has come into existence, she may not bargain for a fee. However, sometimes, even if she realises that a copyright work has come into existence, she might not have the bargaining power to negotiate. Sometimes, even if she negotiates, she might not be able to prove that a contract came into existence, as opposed to a bare licence. Therefore, the facts and circumstances of relevance here are: the nature of the relationship (informal, friendly); whether the copyright owner gives her work upon request or unsolicited; whether a bargain was negotiated and can be proved.

Let us begin with cases where the nature of the relationship itself points to the permission being gratuitous, such as a friend helping another friend. In *Banks*, as stated above, Banks had been acquainted with Khan, who told her that he had an opportunity to sing with the rock group UB40, and asked her to come up with some lyrics.[56] Banks' evidence also reveals that she considered Khan as someone

[55] ibid 325.
[56] *Banks v CBS Songs Ltd* (n 3) 442–43.

who could 'barely read or write' English, and therefore, agreed to write a song for him. The other factors that may have acted on Banks' mind could be that Khan, being a machinist by profession, had been approached by a well-known rock group to perform for them, recognising his singing talent.[57] Banks might have wanted to 'help' a friend break through into the world of pop music. These facts show that Banks meant to give permission to Khan to use the lyrics of her song, without anything else being evident from her words or actions as to her expectation of any form of return. The court does not sufficiently underscore the importance of the relationship. Instead of Khan, suppose Campbell, the lead singer of UB40, had approached Banks to write the song. Then, presumably owing to the lack of friendship with Campbell, Banks may have acted differently, and made it apparent that she was not giving the lyrics away for nothing.

A privilege could become gratuitous also in a commercial relationship, as happened in *Brighton*, where circumstances other than the nature of the relationship must be considered. In this case, as stated above, Brighton was the director of a play that Jones was going to write.[58] Brighton and Jones had worked together for many years on theatrical plays for various production houses. As stated above, apprehending that Jones was taking longer than expected to write the play, Brighton sent a draft to Jones consisting of about 11 pages of narrative of the opening scene, with the view to 'kick-start' Jones' writing of the play.[59] Although Jones claimed that she did not need such help from Brighton, owing to their long-standing collaboration on theatrical plays and since Brighton was going to direct the play, Jones did read the draft and used what she could. Brighton had sent the draft opening script to Jones unsolicited, and Jones' evidence revealed that she had neither asked for it, nor had she needed it.[60] Brighton did not dispute this in her evidence. Indeed, Brighton was not paid for writing the opening scene, based on which the court acknowledged the permission as being gratuitous.

It could also happen that both the relationship and the circumstances point to a possibility that the copyright owner could have bargained for her permission being in exchange for value. This normally happens when artists collaborate to produce a work of joint authorship. Normally, the part played by the chief composer or songwriter is uncontroversial. However, the part played by performers who bring in an instrumental backing to a song, or arrange the music for a song tends to be controversial. Their lack of confidence as to their contribution to the creative process reduces their bargaining power, particularly for up-and-coming artists. Assuming that joint authorship of these artists is proved, the question is whether they should be taken to have impliedly licensed their work gratuitously.[61]

[57] ibid.
[58] *Brighton v Jones* (n 11) [2], [12].
[59] ibid [12]–[13], [21], [60].
[60] ibid [61], [75].
[61] See generally Richard Arnold, 'Reflections on "The Triumph of Music": Copyrights and Performers' Rights in Music' (2010) 2 IPQ 153.

One of the leading examples is *Beckingham*, where Valentino, the claimant, was hired as a session violinist to record a song.[62] However, Valentino claimed that he had not merely performed music, but had composed the solo violin part in the song.[63] He further claimed that he had discussed with his manager the possibility of being regarded as a co-author of the song, but was told that if he made such a claim 'he would get a reputation as a troublemaker when he was trying to make a career as a musician'.[64] Thus, Valentino made no claim at that stage, making his permission gratuitous.

Similarly, in *Fisher*, Fisher had composed the organ solo for a song that went on to acquire 'something approaching a cult status' according to the trial judge.[65] However, when Fisher raised his claim for joint ownership in 1967 when the song had just been recorded, he was met with a rebuff.[66] His evidence further reveals that he feared that if he persisted with the claim, he would be asked to 'say goodbye to a career in . . . the number one pop group'.[67] As such, Fisher made no claim at that stage, making the permission gratuitous.

In *Godfrey*, apart from claiming joint authorship, Godfrey also claimed that there was a common understanding and an express agreement that he would be given a share in the profits the band earned.[68] However, the court found that after leaving the band Godfrey had made no effort to claim joint ownership of the relevant songs, nor his share, except on two occasions as to which the evidence was too sparse to come to a sensible conclusion. The court found that Godfrey was neither able to prove the common understanding he claimed to have existed nor the express agreement for sharing profits.[69] Therefore, even if a copyright owner claims that she did not give unilateral consent, but made an offer, if there is insufficient evidence to show that it was treated as an offer, and was accepted on its terms, no contract can come into existence.

It may so happen that there is a protracted negotiation between the parties, but a contract is never concluded, as in *Tamawood*. Here, as stated above, Tamawood provided access to Habitare to apply for development consent. The evidence revealed that it was in the very business model of Tamawood not to charge a fee for the plans, but instead absorb its costs with a view to make its profit by building according to the plans. Tamawood was a building business and not a design

[62] *Beckingham v Hodgens* (n 19) [5].

[63] ibid.

[64] ibid [57]. This fact was further confirmed by the Court of Appeal, where Parker LJ noted that the advice Valentino had received was that 'his share of such royalties would be eaten up by legal costs and that to make a claim might affect his developing career as a session musician'. See [2003] EWCA Civ 143 [28].

[65] [2006] EWHC 3239 [3] (Ch). This sentence was quoted again in his decision by Lord Neuberger before the House of Lords in *Fisher v Brooker* [2009] UKHL 41 [29] (HL).

[66] [2006] EWHC 3239 [57] (Ch).

[67] [2009] UKHL 41 [35] (HL).

[68] *Godfrey v Lees* (n 16) 311–12.

[69] ibid 317–19, 322–25.

house, and did not sell its plans as such. Therefore, no consideration flowed to Tamawood.[70] Similarly, in *Trumpet*, it was in the very nature of shareware as a software marketing method that the software so distributed would be free of charge during the trial period, and thus, the licence provided would be a bare licence.

In *Rebeschini*, negotiations were relatively short. Here, as stated above, the claimant had sent his drawings for the clutch purse and had followed it up with a recommendation for marketing it, conveying his belief that he would be given the advertising contract. There was no further discussion of the document, but the claimant had been led to believe that the defendant was going to spend a substantial amount on marketing the product, which would translate into a substantial advertising contract for the claimant. Further, the cost of preparing the prototype and of taking photographs of the prototypes had been paid for by the defendant, encouraging the claimant's belief.[71] These made it clear to the court that the claimant did not envisage his designs being used free of charge. The cumulative effect was that the court refused to imply a bare licence and held the defendant's actions to be an infringement of the claimant's copyright.

If, however, there are mutual undertakings as to the permission being in exchange for payment or other consideration, then the mere fact of no consideration being forthcoming does not make the licence a bare licence. It is still enforced as a contractual licence, since the contract would have come into existence. Accordingly, in *Concrete Pty Ltd v Paramatta Designs* an argument for a licence to use architectural plans to be regarded a bare licence (and therefore revocable) because no fee was paid, failed.[72] This is because a contract had been concluded with the required undertakings on consideration, placing immediate obligations on the parties. The licensor in such cases will be able to sue for damages for non-performance of the contractual licence.

The receipt of any payment at all by the copyright owner does not convert the bare licence into a contract. If the copyright owner was paid not in recognition as a co-author, but for the services rendered as a performer (session musician), then such consideration does not support the permission given to use the property, but only the rendering of services. The element of originality distinguishes a service from a copyright work. The following cases illustrate this point.

In *Beckingham*, Valentino was in fact paid a sum of £75 for playing as a session musician.[73] Hodgens, the defendant, had composed the song and had written a part of the background score. To the extent that Valentino played the music composed by Hodgens, it represents the payment for the services rendered, and not for any original work created by Valentino. The service contract should be separated

[70] *Tamawood Ltd v Habitare Developments* (n 25) [102]–[104], [137]. These findings were affirmed on appeal. See (2015) 112 IPR 439 [131]–[137].

[71] *Rebeschini v Miles Laboratories* (n 27) 163.

[72] (2006) 231 ALR 663 [82]–[84].

[73] *Beckingham v Hodgens* (n 19) [55].

from the bare licence, even though both arise from Valentino's playing of the violin. There was a completed contract in relation to the services rendered so far as the non-original part of the music was concerned. In relation to the original part of the music and the property right in it, only a gratuitous licence arose, as Valentino had expressly stated to the defendants that he was not going to make a claim to be compensated.[74]

In *Godfrey*, Godfrey had been paid as a performer for his services. The evidence showed that the payment averaged only a few pounds a week and Godfrey had been paid £100 by the band's manager.[75] As stated above, Godfrey was never part of the band. Only a part of the work he had done for the band gained him copyright protection. The payment he received was only in exchange for the services he had rendered. It had been argued in this case that the amount paid to Godfrey was indeed sufficient compensation for a licence of his property rights in the works for which he had established himself to be a joint author. However, the judge rejected this and found that the evidence of such payment was 'too slender', and in any event did not cover payment for Godfrey's contribution to the copyright works in question.[76] Godfrey's inability to prove a concluded contract, together with the fact that no payment had been made for his share in copyright, made his licence gratuitous.

(iii) Knowledge of the consequences

The assessment here is of the knowledge of the foreseeable consequences of engaging in the positive and neutral acts. In practice, implication is an ex post assessment of copyright infringement. Therefore, instead of assessing in the abstract the scope of the implied licence, one may look at the alleged infringing acts of the defendant and ascertain if based on the knowledge of the claimant as to the consequences of their conduct, the claimant could have authorised those acts. In this sense, the assessment of this aspect of the knowledge influences the scope of the licence.

Banks is a good starting point because the licence was sought to be implied in a non-commercial context. The assessment here is of what Banks knew before engaging in the positive act of handing over the paper with the song written on it. Like all the other cases being considered here, there was no agreement between Banks and Khan regarding the use of the lyrics or any compensation.[77] There was no relationship between Banks and Campbell—friendly or commercial. All Banks knew was that the song she wrote would be sung by Khan with the band UB40. Let us see how this knowledge influenced the use to which the copyright work could be put.

[74] ibid [57].
[75] *Godfrey v Lees* (n 16) 316.
[76] ibid 329–30.
[77] *Banks v CBS Songs Ltd* (n 3) 449.

Khan took the lyrics to Campbell and had the latter make some changes. Since Banks knew all along that the objective was to turn the lyrics she had given to Khan into a song to be sung with UB40, Harman J held that if she had been asked whether changes could be made to suit the band's music and singing styles, she would have readily agreed.[78] Therefore, Khan had Banks' consent to adapt the lyrics into a song. However, it was not Khan who made the changes, but Campbell. Could Banks' licence to adapt to Khan be sub-licenced to Campbell? Collaboration is in the very nature of the way a band functions, and therefore this should have been within Banks' knowledge. Although Harman J did not articulate it in these terms, it is possible that the implied licence to adapt in favour of Khan could be sub-licensed to Campbell. In any event, Khan assigned the copyright in the song to UB40, for which he received a consideration of £10,000, because Khan's version of the facts was that he had written the lyrics himself, and that he had found the lyrics Banks gave him not suitable.[79] On that basis, there should be no difficulty for Campbell to adapt the song. However, once Khan sold the rights to the lyrics to UB40, UB40 went on to perform the song without Khan.

The first question is whether Banks assigned her copyright in the lyrics, and did not licence it; and, secondly, if she granted a licence, did it extend to someone else performing the lyrics, and not Khan. Harman J concluded that Banks had not intended, nor could it be implied that she was making an outright gift of copyright in the lyrics, on the basis that no 'reasonable bystander' could regard the handing over of the lyrics as an assignment.[80] There is no further discussion of why a reasonable bystander would not regard it as an assignment. As a matter of personal property law, Banks is required to have intended the gift. To the extent that she could reasonably foresee, Banks' own knowledge of the way the lyrics would be used simply did not extend to a possibility of her not having any rights over the lyrics in future. Therefore, it was only a licence.

Harman J held further that when Banks gave the piece of paper with lyrics on it to Khan, it was only for Khan's personal benefit to sing with UB40. At that time, Banks did not have in her mind, nor did Khan indicate the possibility, that the lyrics could be used for a different person singing with UB40. As such, the implied licence only extended to Khan being able to perform the lyrics, and not for it to be sub-licensed for someone else to perform. Banks had no communication with Campbell. As such, there was no question of her granting an implied licence to him or UB40, which Harman J did recognise.[81] As such, UB40 had no rights to perform the lyrics or to exploit them in any other manner, either by way of a licence from Banks, a sub-licence from Khan, or an assignment from Khan.

[78] ibid 450.

[79] Note that there was no issue of whether Banks assigned or licensed her lyrics, as Khan simply claimed that Banks never wrote the lyrics.

[80] *Banks v CBS Songs Ltd* (n 3) 450.

[81] ibid 450–51.

If the relationship between a licensor and a licensee is commercial or in their professional capacity, the implied licence in some cases can be sub-licensed to parties other than the original parties to the implied licence. In *Banks*, since the relationship was informal and friendly, Khan was not able to use the lyrics if he was not himself performing the song with UB40. On the contrary, the result was different in *Brighton* since Jones and Brighton were in a commercial relationship.

In *Brighton*, Brighton sent the draft opening script to Jones to use it in her writing of the play. Brighton had claimed that there was a separate copyright that she owned in the draft, which was incorporated in Jones' script of the play. Brighton accepted that she not only knew that the draft could be used by Jones, but it was indeed the purpose of her sending it to Jones.[82] The original version of the play was staged in 1996. However, Jones rewrote the play in 1999 and released it through a different production company and a different director, which became a big success throughout the English-speaking world. Brighton claimed that Jones had no implied licence from her to use the draft to rewrite the 1999 script nor to exploit the 1999 script with other production companies.[83]

To assess Brighton's knowledge, we must examine the relationship Brighton and Jones had under the commissioning agreement. Oddly, Brighton revealed in her evidence that she was not aware that written agreements were required for Doublejoint to engage Jones, or indeed that one was actually entered into.[84] But her subjective lack of knowledge (or refusal to get involved) did not affect an objective conclusion that as the owner of Doublejoint, Brighton should have known that these agreements had been entered into, as the discussion below will reveal.

Under the agreement, Jones was required to stage the play with Brighton's production company (Doublejoint) for nine months. Jones understood this, rightly according to Park J, to mean that she was a 'free agent' to do as she pleased with the play script after this period. In addition, the commissioning agreement between Jones and Doublejoint stated that if Jones chose to stage the play with any other production company after Doublejoint, she had to acknowledge Doublejoint as the original production company and had to share a certain percentage of the profits for a period of five years.[85]

These clauses in the agreement go to show that Doublejoint, and hence Brighton, had envisaged Jones staging the play for other production companies. Both Brighton and Jones knew that Jones was not exclusively tied either to Brighton or to Doublejoint indefinitely. Park J, therefore, rejected Brighton's claim on the basis that the implied licence granted by Brighton to prepare the 1996 version of the script was still in existence and continued until Jones wrote the 1999

82 *Brighton v Jones* (n 11) [4], [21], [69].
83 ibid [5], [26], [72].
84 ibid [18].
85 ibid [16(ii)–(iv)], [25].

script.[86] Therefore, Brighton impliedly licensed Jones to adapt the dramatic work in the draft into a play, and to exploit the play in whatever manner Jones pleased, including having the play performed in public. This right to perform the play publicly incorporating the script could be sub-licensed, given the provisions of the commissioning agreement.

In *Brighton*, Jones had the benefit of the express terms of the commissioning agreement in order to assess what ought to have been in Brighton's knowledge. In certain other cases, for example when musicians collaborate in a band, either as session musicians or as members of the band, there may be no express terms to rely on. The mere taking part in a recording knowing that a record will be produced of it or giving access to sheet music knowing that it will be performed appears to make the implied licence granted extend to all reasonable exploitation of the work. This appears to be the case in *Beckingham*, *Godfrey*, and *Fisher*. In *Beckingham*, the judge noted that there was an 'implied gratuitous licence for Mr Hodgens to *exploit* the copyright in "the Work" '.[87] Similarly, in *Godfrey*, the judge simply said the implied licence was granted for the 'exploitation' of the work.[88] Similarly, in *Fisher*, Blackburne J also held that Fisher had granted a gratuitous implied licence to exploit the work at issue.[89]

The meaning of the term 'exploitation' is not clear. In these cases, exploitation could mean deriving income from all reasonable uses of the recording, such as mechanical rights (i.e., reproducing the record to make copies for sale), public performance of the record, and live public performance of the songs.[90] But it might not include making an audio-visual music video of the song, unless the copyright owners also participated in the making of such music video. Within the framework proposed here, however, exploitation can only mean what is within the knowledge of the copyright owner based on what she can reasonably foresee. The court should not impute the knowledge in the abstract of technological innovation.

This issue was briefly discussed in *Barrett*. The judge found that, at the time when the recordings were made, the chief means of reproduction were vinyl records and cassettes. The judge also found that the agreement which Marley had signed in 1974 envisaged that the recordings could be reproduced by 'other means'.[91] The Barrett brothers had depended on Marley to enter into all business transactions, and accepted whatever amount he paid without objection. The Barrett brothers were held not to be parties to this agreement, but it appears from the judgment that the Barrett brothers were imputed with knowledge of the agreement. They

86 ibid [72].

87 *Beckingham v Hodgens* (n 19) [64] (emphasis added).

88 *Godfrey v Lees* (n 16) 331.

89 [2006] EWHC 3239 (Ch) [94].

90 See *Barrett v Universal Island Records Ltd* (n 49) [37] for a summary of the principal sources of income of the artists in that case.

91 ibid [360].

were held to have impliedly licensed their copyright to the recording company. Accordingly, the court held that this included reproducing by means of CDs and DVDs 'as a more technologically advanced means of reproducing the same work in essentially the same form' and, therefore, did not require a fresh licence.[92]

This holding is problematic. Even if the Barrett brothers were imputed with the knowledge of the agreement, the agreement itself was signed in 1974—a time when CDs and DVDs did not exist. Further, CDs and DVDs do not essentially reproduce the songs in 'the same form', as the judge claims. As technological advancements, they transform an analogue copy of the recording into a digital copy. A digital copy can easily be uploaded on the internet, reaching an unprecedented audience, potentially also increasing the risk of unauthorised copying to a significant degree. It is unreasonable to hold that merely because the agreement provided for the recordings to be reproduced by other means, the Barrett brothers had within their knowledge or contemplation in 1974 such a drastically different technology posing such different challenges. Therefore, the scope of an implied licence cannot extend to technologically more advanced media and media not yet invented, since the copyright owner's knowledge may not extend to these technologies at the time that the implied licence arises. A more nuanced assessment of the knowledge of the copyright owner is required here for consent to be a legitimate basis for implying a licence.

In *Tamawood*, the only consequence that Tamawood was aware of when it provided access to its plans to Habitare was that they would be used for obtaining the required building approvals. It was not within the knowledge or expectation of Tamawood that the plans could be used for building if the permissions were given, without engaging Tamawood as the builders. Although Tamawood agreed that a licence could be implied to this limited extent, it could not go further.[93] This meant that the only way Habitare could proceed with the development was to engage another architect to draw up the plans and get a new building approval.

In *Trumpet*, as explained above, Trumpet's actions never amounted to a positive or a neutral act as far as the specific or general licence was concerned. Trumpet had always maintained that OzEmail could not use the shareware version of the software for distribution in diskette form with a computer magazine, even if free of charge. Technically, one can say that Trumpet was aware or ought reasonably to have expected that the shareware version could still be used by OzEmail since it was accessible online. However, Trumpet can and did rely on the honesty of those who operate in the business to respect each other's expectations. Since the shareware version had been available before and for a different audience and purpose, namely

[92] ibid [229], [360]. This case is not discussed in detail here since the implied licence was not gratuitous but contractual, as the Barrett brothers had been paid as co-authors.

[93] *Tamawood Ltd v Habitare Developments* (n 25) [96], [140], reconfirmed on appeal at (2015) 112 IPR 439 [135].

end users, Trumpet was not obliged to take this version offline simply because of the possibility that OzEmail would use it otherwise. On this basis, OzEmail never had any specific or general licence and OzEmail's distribution of the shareware version was an infringement, even if it distributed it again as shareware.

But this was not the court's finding. The court held that Trumpet's refusal revoked any licence (more on revocation below). If this meant that it revoked both the general and the specific licence, then OzEmail's actions should clearly have been an infringement. However, the court still went on to consider the alternative argument that the general licence permitted commercial distribution of software as shareware, since the objective is to reach a greater number of users. It considered evidence from both sides to ascertain whether there were any practices that had become a custom in relation to the ability of distributors like OzEmail to distribute shareware. Having rejected the possibility of a custom,[94] the court was still informed by the evidence of trade practices. Further, the court applied the business efficacy and obviousness test by analogy to ascertain the licence that may be implied based on Trumpet's distribution of its software as shareware (the general licence in our analysis). It concluded that OzEmail using the software for its own commercial benefit and distributing other software with Trumpet software was not opposed to business efficacy. But the modifications that OzEmail had made to the software before distribution was outside the scope of the shareware licence. Such modifications, the court held, had potential ill-effects on Trumpet's business and, therefore, OzEmail was liable for infringement to this limited extent.[95]

Even if one were to assume that OzEmail may have had the benefit of the general licence, business efficacy might not explain the scope of the licence with sufficient clarity. Instead, assessing what was within the knowledge or reasonable expectation of the copyright owner as to the use that could be made of the software is more appropriate to arrive at the scope of the consent-based implied licence, if any. The evidence on the existence of a custom in this regard having failed, it was all the more important to consider this case as a purely consent-based implied licence. When the purpose of shareware is for end-users to evaluate the efficacy of the software during the trial period, it would be wholly outside Trumpet's knowledge or expectation that an end user would produce copies of the software in commercial quantities, much less gain commercial advantage by distributing it in commercial quantities, even if free of charge. The express terms of copyright notice had stated that the software should not be distributed with any other software on sale. Although OzEmail did not offer it for sale, it included other software with Trumpet's. This must be a violation of the term in spirit since this must be considered together with Trumpet's specific refusal to OzEmail to use the shareware for mass distribution. It is also unlikely to have been within Trumpet's knowledge

[94] A possible custom in this regard is discussed in ch 5 below.
[95] *Trumpet Software v OzEmail Pty Ltd* (n 4) 498–500.

or expectation that its software would be distributed with other software. Similarly, it would be beyond Trumpet's knowledge that the end users would alter or adapt the software during the trial period. While the court was correct on this last point, making copies in bulk quantities and making commercial use of shareware software should have been an additional reason why OzEmail's actions went beyond the shareware licence. This is likely to have affected the quantum of damages Trumpet received.

This highlights that if the court was vigilant as to the conduct that leads to a licence, it would have noticed the distinction between the specific and the general licence, and that there was no conduct supporting either. If the court had understood the scope of the licence to be a function of the knowledge or the expectation of the copyright owner, as opposed to an underlying trade practice, it would not have held the infringement to have been so minor. This analysis could have a potential impact on the cases concerning implied licences on the internet.

Finally, in *Tumber*, ITN argued that Tumber handing over the poem knowing that it was a journalist who had requested a copy of his poem on behalf of ITN who was going to write about him and his work meant that he consented to it being published with the article.[96] But the same facts can mean to Tumber that the employee being the one who would interview him on his work, at the very least, needs to know what is in the work for her to ask relevant questions. If her article quoted lines from his poem, it could have been saved by fair dealing. However, publishing the entire poem was beyond what Tumber had in his reasonable expectation. ITN argued that whether Tumber consented could turn on what might be revealed during the trial as the exact conversation between them. Although this does seem persuasive, the court found that ITN had neither pleaded this nor indicated that any evidence was forthcoming in that regard. Accordingly, the court struck out the consent-based implied licence defence.[97]

2. Revocation of Bare Licences

Revocation is different from termination, although judges and commentators use these terms interchangeably.[98] Any contract can be terminated at will, but consequences follow for the person terminating, if such termination is not according to the terms of the contract. An option to terminate a contract may also arise in response to a repudiation, but termination in this matter must follow the rules of repudiation. However, revocation is an eventuality without such consequences for the person revoking. In this sense, we can only speak of revocation in relation to

96 *Tumber v Independent Television News Ltd Plc* (n 14) [7].
97 ibid [12]–[13].
98 See generally Jonathan Hill, 'Termination of Bare Licences' [2001] CLJ 89.

bare licences.[99] As discussed in Chapter 2(1)(a) above, to permit the use of one's property is one of the incidents of ownership. Such power can be exercised by the owner at will. When such permission is unilateral, there is no duty on part of the copyright owner to continue the permission. As such, the copyright owner is free to withdraw what had been given, upon giving reasonable notice.

Revoking an implied licence in this context means that the implied licence in gratuitous form comes to an end, and therefore all uses of the work should be stopped. If the licensee intends to use the work beyond revocation, she must negotiate with the licensor for a new licence. If the negotiations are successful, a new contractual licence will normally come into existence, depending on whether the copyright owner seeks any consideration to flow from the licensee. The copyright owner is also required to give reasonable notice to the bare licensee before revocation takes effect.[100] Thus, the revocation of the bare licence can only operate prospectively.

As stated above, turning the neutral act into a negative act results in the revocation of a bare licence. In each case discussed above where a bare licence could be implied, the licensor at some point had tried to revoke the permission given. The act of revocation can sometimes take the form of a letter before action, demanding the cessation of the use of the copyright work. If there is no letter before action, the fact of the licensor approaching the court revokes the bare licence. Sometimes, it might take the form of a verbal exchange well before commencing such action, which might be factually controversial to prove .

In *Tamawood*, as stated above, the court had concluded that Habitare did enjoy an implied licence to the limited extent of applying for planning permission. Any further use of the plans was conditional on Tamawood being appointed as the builders for the project. Thus, the conduct of Habitare in engaging someone other than Tamawood to build according to the plans Tamawood had prepared ended the licence Habitare had.[101] The court observed that it would not be for Tamawood to revoke as it would be unaware when Habitare might appoint new builders, and therefore it was Habitare's actions that revoked the licence, not Tamawood's.

In *Trumpet*, as argued above, the specific or the general licence were never granted and, therefore, there should have been nothing to revoke. However, OzEmail argued that the shareware licence granted to the public at large could never be revoked. The court disagreed and held that Trumpet could revoke the shareware licence and had in fact done so when it sent a letter to that effect.[102] As

[99] In *Ng v Clyde Securities* [1976] 1 NSWLR 443, it was held that in a contractual licence, if the licence fee is only partly paid, the copyright owner cannot revoke the licence. He must bring an action for an unpaid sum. See also *Gruzman v Percy Marks* (1989) 16 IPR 87, 90, for the consequences of repudiation by the licensee.

[100] Hill (n 98) 98.

[101] *Tamawood Ltd v Habitare Developments* (n 25) [149], reconfirmed in (2015) 112 IPR 439 [136].

[102] *Trumpet Software v OzEmail Pty Ltd* (n 4) 498.

argued above, the correct view would have been to regard this letter as denying consent for a licence to arise in the first place; if the court preferred an interpretation that a licence did exist, then it could be revoked in this way. In principle, it is possible that even if the software was available to the public at large, since it is a bare licence, nothing stopped Trumpet from revoking the shareware licence to the extent that it related to OzEmail.

Beckingham is a case where the date of revocation was controversial. In this case, the song with Valentino's violin piece was a reasonable success when it was released, but a bigger success later in 1993.[103] The trial judge concluded on the facts that in 1993, there was a conversation between Valentino and Hodgens, where Hodgens had told Valentino that he would 'see him alright'. Valentino had replied saying that if he did not do so, he would 'go to law this time'. Upon Valentino's further enquiries thereafter, Hodgens responded that he had not yet received any royalties.[104] There are several points for consideration here. First, once the defendant establishes an implied licence, the burden shifts back to the claimant/copyright owner to prove that it was revoked. Secondly, the colloquial usage of words such as 'see him alright' or 'go to law' must be considered in the context in which they were spoken. Thirdly, if the licensee wants to challenge revocation and put forward her own version of events, the burden shifts back again to her to prove her claim, and often the assessment tends to be the words of the claimant against those of the defendant. That is indeed what happened in *Beckingham*, where at the appellate stage it was argued unsuccessfully that the trial judge came to an incorrect conclusion that Valentino's version was truthful.[105]

In most other cases, the act of revocation is largely uncontroversial. In *Banks*, the claimant approaching the court revoked the licence. In *Brighton*,[106] and in *Fisher*,[107] it was the letter before action. In *Godfrey*, Godfrey also issued a letter before action in an attempt to revoke any implied licence he may have granted;[108] however, the court held that the implied licence was not revocable, which brings us to the next issue.

3. Irrevocability: Proprietary Estoppel

A licence continues so long as the neutral act continues—meaning that the conduct of the copyright owner in standing by continues when the licensee proceeds

[103] *Beckingham v Hodgens* (n 19) [59].
[104] ibid.
[105] [2003] EWCA Civ 143 [17], [19].
[106] A letter before action dated 7 November 2001 revoked the gratuitous licence. *Brighton v Jones* (n 11) [73].
[107] [2009] UKHL 41 [45].
[108] *Godfrey v Lees* (n 16) 319–21.

to use the copyright work. While the neutral act continues, the licensee might change his position, relying on the continuation of the neutral act, such that when the neutral act stops and the act of revocation begins, the licensee suffers a detriment. This might give rise to proprietary estoppel, preventing the copyright owner from revoking the bare licence. In the Hohfeldian sense, the power of the copyright owner freely to grant and revoke a permission transforms to a disability, giving rise to a corresponding immunity to the licensee from revocation, owing to a set of new operative facts.[109] Finding these operative facts is the challenge in these cases.

Since the doctrine of proprietary estoppel traces its origin to land law, copyright cases that have applied proprietary estoppel have sometimes expressly and sometimes tacitly relied on the principles of land law.[110] As argued in detail elsewhere, this has given rise to two problems.[111] First, courts have analysed copyright cases without the awareness of the specific context of copyright cases. In land law, it is said that in its very origin the doctrine of proprietary estoppel was conceptualised in order to correct reliance loss,[112] and the belief is that the parties who rely on the conduct of a landowner need protection. The roles are reversed in many copyright cases—it is not the person relying on copyright owner's conduct but the copyright owners themselves who might need protection. Given the evident lack of bargaining power of copyright owners including Fisher, Godfrey, and Valentino, as reflected in Section 1 above, it must be considered whether the lead singers and songwriters in a band (who are estoppel claimants) should be protected from reliance loss, or copyright owners like Fisher, Godfrey, and Valentino against the high-handed treatment of the estoppel claimants. Secondly, the uncertainties and incoherence that surround the historical development and current understanding of proprietary estoppel in land law have likewise prevailed in copyright cases. These also need to be addressed.

(a) Proprietary estoppel in land law

Broadly stated, one of the objectives of proprietary estoppel is to promote conscientiousness in dealings in land.[113] Rights are created in land in an informal way based on an expectation of 'proprietary entitlement',[114] since these rights do not arise

[109] For jural correlatives and opposites see Hohfeld (n 1) 30.

[110] While *Godfrey v Lees* (n 16) refers to land law authorities on estoppel, *Brighton v Jones* (n 11) does not.

[111] Mysoor (n 5).

[112] Simon Gardner and Emily McKenzie, *An Introduction to Land Law* (4th edn, Hart Publishing 2015) 159.

[113] Kevn Gray and Susan Francis Gray, *Elements of Land Law* (5th edn, OUP 2009) para 9.2.2.

[114] ibid para 9.2.1. However, it is possible that, sometimes, instead of a proprietary interest, the court grants monetary compensation to the person successfully claiming proprietary estoppel. See *Jennings v Rice* [2002] EWCA Civ 159.

from the property owner's intentional transfer of a property interest nor is there a contract or formalities to that effect.[115] These rights arise in order to protect the claimant from the detriment that might result from her reliance on a commitment made to her by the landowner.[116] The conduct on the part of the estoppel claimant is to act in reliance of a commitment made to her to her detriment. However, the exact conduct required on the part of the landowner that would be sufficient for the claimant to place a detrimental reliance is anything but certain. It is common to understand proprietary estoppel as a three-part test, with reliance and detriment as the second and third parts. It is the problems caused by the first part, namely the conduct of the landowner, which is of bigger concern here.

Historically, when one reviews the cases on proprietary estoppel, one may notice a wide variety of conduct on part of the landowner that the courts have found to have induced detrimental reliance. It ranges from standing by and taking no action to an active representation or repeated promise of future conduct.[117] While a court might regard the active making of a representation or a promise a conscious action of the landowner, a court should be slow to regard inaction as inducing detrimental reliance. This is because the landowner might not even realise that she was required to act or that her inaction was being detrimentally relied on by another person. Thus, before finding a detrimental reliance on an inaction, a court must ask why there was an inaction. *Willmott v Barber*,[118] an early case on proprietary estoppel, shed light on this. These cases can be broadly classified as acquiescence-type cases. *Willmott* required that, before the inaction of a landowner can be relied on by a claimant, it must be shown that the claimant acted under a mistake as to her rights. Further, it must be proved that the landowner had the knowledge not only of this mistake but also of landowner's own right which is contrary to that of the claimant. If despite having this knowledge the landowner simply stands by when the claimant, relying on the landowner's inaction incurs detriment, then the landowner by his inaction is deemed to have acquiesced in the rights of the claimant and the landowner cannot assert her contrary rights.

Not all estoppel cases involve mistake on the claimant's part and inaction on the landowner's part. As stated above, sometimes a representation made by the landowner as to a certain state of affairs or a promise by the landowner of future conduct may be relied on by the claimant to her detriment. Instead of recognising the diversity of conduct inducing detrimental reliance, *Taylors Fashions Ltd v Liverpool Victoria Trustees Co Ltd*[119] held that all proprietary estoppel cases are bound by

[115] Ben McFarlane, *The Structure of Property law* (Hart Publishing 2008) 445.

[116] In land law, it is normally the claimant of the suit who asserts proprietary estoppel, and in the copyright cases discussed here it is asserted by the defendant to deny infringement. However, it is conceivable for proprietary estoppel to be claimed by the claimant in an action for a declaration of non-infringement. The term property owner is used as a shorthand for the holder of a freehold or a leasehold title.

[117] See generally Ben McFarlane, *The Law of Proprietary Estoppel* (OUP 2014).

[118] (1880) 15 Ch D 96.

[119] [1982] QB 133 (Ch).

a unifying principle of unconscionability. The nuanced approach to cases of acquiescence was lost in this historical development. Further, the Supreme Court in *Thorner v Major* reinforced *Taylors Fashions* in unifying all kinds of conduct inducing detrimental reliance—be it acquiescence or representation cases—all within a single criterion of assurances.[120] With this, a separate and a more detailed enquiry into acquiescence cases as opposed to representation or promise cases was rendered unnecessary, so long as there was detrimental reliance.[121] Even if one were to repose confidence in the assessment of unconscionability to set right any flaws in the assessment of other criteria, unconscionability is often a subjective yardstick of the judge concerned. It makes the judge's reasoning neither methodical nor transparent. *Willmott* may have lost its favour with land law because the number of cases in land law on acquiescence in the last few decades has been few. At the very least, there should be a difference in the way the inaction of the property owner is treated from cases where a specific action leads to detrimental reliance.

As regards reliance, even if the conduct of the landowner is not the only reason for reliance, it must be a primary reason. Any relaxation of this rule is normally only possible in close family relationships and domestic as opposed to commercial contexts where reliance is more difficult to prove.[122] As regards detriment, *Taylors Fashions* held that detriment should be such that it owes its result to the reliance placed.[123] Unconscionability plays an important role in assessing each ingredient.[124] The following paragraphs explore how these principles were applied in copyright cases.

(b) Proprietary estoppel in copyright cases

Copyright cases raise acquiescence-type scenarios. In the copyright context, it is still common for a person deeply engaged in a creative process not to realise her entitlement to copyright (as in *Brighton*). Given the complicated and unintuitive nature of rules of originality and joint authorship, it is unsurprising that a person whose only occupation is art is unaware of or is mistaken about these rules. Even if a person becomes aware of these rules, she might not be able to dispel mistaken beliefs without legal advice or approaching a court. Therefore, losing nuance in the assessment of proprietary estoppel in copyright cases could lead to unfair results. For these reasons, even if *Willmott* may be less relevant in land law, we need to

120 [2009] UKHL 18 [55].

121 Some scholars commend the unifying approach. Elizabeth Cooke, *The Modern Law of Estoppel* (OUP 2000) 60–65; Piers Feltham and others, *Spencer Bower: Reliance Based Estoppel* (5th edn, Bloomsbury 2017) paras 1.104–1.106.

122 An example of relaxed approach to reliance is *Wayling v Jones* (1993) 69 P & CR 170 (CA).

123 *Taylors Fashions Ltd v Liverpool Victoria Trustees Co Ltd* (n 119) 156–57.

124 *Cobbe v Yeoman's Row* [2008] UKHL 55 [92].

resurrect it for copyright cases. More than in land law, it matters in copyright law that the acquiescence is recognised as a separate type from other types.

Applying *Willmott*, it will be shown in the following paragraphs that the court was incorrect in holding Godfrey's implied licence irrevocable and that, although *Fisher* and *Beckingham* were decided correctly, these cases can help refine *Willmott* requirements further to suit copyright cases. In none of these cases, however, was a reference to *Willmott* made. Indeed, the court in these cases did not explain with any level of precision what is required of the copyright owner to trigger detrimental reliance by the licensee. Further, the assessment of reliance and the consequent detriment was also problematic in these cases.

(i) Assessment of acquiescence

It is unfortunate that judges in copyright cases maintain that acquiescence adds nothing to proprietary estoppel.[125] Therefore, we must establish why copyright cases present acquiescence-type cases. To begin with, it is the belief that the implied licence will continue that induces reliance and the consequent detriment. This means that the conduct of concern here is the one that enables the continuance of the licence. The discussion above reveals that, while the positive act—an action—connotes the beginning of the licence, the neutral act—an inaction—continues it. It cannot be that the positive act in itself induces detrimental reliance. In *Godfrey*, if the conduct required was an action, then Godfrey providing access to the music he had arranged would be sufficient, together with the detrimental reliance of Lees and others, for proprietary estoppel to be established. It cannot be said that providing such access in itself represented to Lees and others that Godfrey was not going to assert his copyright entitlement in future. Otherwise, the positive act, such as taking part in a recording in *Beckingham* and *Fisher*, alone would lead to an irrevocable implied bare licence, which is an unjust outcome for copyright owners. Therefore, it is not the copyright owner's action that must be considered. It must therefore be the continuance of the neutral act that brings about detrimental reliance. The neutral act and reliance are closely related in that the longer the neutral act, the greater the likelihood of reliance. Therefore, it must be the inaction that underlies the conduct of the copyright owner to establish proprietary estoppel, and such proprietary estoppel must be of the acquiescence type.

The next step is to demonstrate how *Willmott* can help copyright cases. *Willmott* requires that, before inaction on the part of the copyright owner makes him lose a part of his ownership powers,[126] one must enquire what caused the inaction. The cause of such inaction may well be that the copyright owner was unaware of her

[125] *Fisher v Brooker* [2009] UKHL 41 [62] (Lord Neuberger). But see [2008] EWCA Civ 287 [55].

[126] By inaction, a copyright owner can only lose a part of her ownership powers, and not the ownership in its entirety such as in adverse possession. A person cannot acquire copyright by adverse possession. See *Fisher v Brooker* [2009] UKHL 41 [78] (Lord Neuberger).

rights. As discussed above, the framework for implying a consent-based bare licence does incorporate assessment of knowledge of the circumstances, of which realisation of ownership is a part. However, what is required in establishing proprietary estoppel is the knowledge of the copyright owner as to the mistake on the part of the licensee as to her rights, in addition to the realisation of the copyright owner's own rights. Therefore, the low threshold of the copyright owner's knowledge as to her own rights normally found sufficient in implying a licence will not be sufficient to establish proprietary estoppel. This stands to reason because the consequences of proprietary estoppel are more drastic in making a copyright owner lose a part of her powers of copyright ownership irrevocably.

The contention in *Godfrey* was that Godfrey stood by for 14 years, which made Lees and others rely on the continuation of the implied licence. Applying *Willmott* to *Godfrey*, one must assess whether Godfrey knew that Lees and the others were under a mistaken belief as to their entitlements, and that his own copyright entitlement was inconsistent with theirs. As discussed above, Godfrey had a vague sense of his rights, reflected in his insistence on the existence of a profit sharing agreement, and that his contribution be recognised in the albums.[127] When Godfrey became aware that he could have copyright ownership as an arranger, he tried to convince Lees and the other band members of his rights. They insisted on believing that only the composer of the song becomes a copyright owner, and not the arranger. This led Godfrey not to assert his copyright claim. The only option open to Godfrey to convince Lees and the others that they were mistaken was to take legal action. Thus, although Godfrey had not fully articulated his knowledge of his own copyright entitlement and whether the rights of Lees and the others were contrary to his own, he was still held to be estopped from revoking his licence.

In *Fisher*, Fisher had let 38 years pass which, by objective standards, should have made Brooker and the others believe that Fisher would not raise his rights. Fisher always knew of his own rights that were contrary to the rights asserted by Brooker and the others. Brooker and the other band members were not under any mistake as to their rights—they knew Fisher had his rights of authorship. However, what Brooker and the others may have been mistaken about may have been that Fisher would never revoke the implied licence, since Fisher had let 38 years pass by. Although Fisher was aware of this mistake and of his own intention to assert his authorship being contrary to the defendants' rights, it was still held that Fisher was not estopped from asserting his rights. This is because Fisher had indeed raised the issue of his authorship in the song on many occasions, but was met with a rebuff, warning him that he might stymie his career by being a trouble-maker.[128] Therefore, it was not sufficient to know of his own rights. Indeed, Fisher should

[127] *Godfrey v Lees* (n 16) 330–31.
[128] [2006] EWHC 3239 [57], [70] (Ch).

have been able to assert his own rights. This is a requirement that may be added to the *Willmott* framework to adapt it to the copyright context.

Similarly, in *Beckingham*, Valentino only made a claim to his copyright about nine years later, which by objective standards may have led Hodgens to believe that Valentino might not assert his rights. Valentino was aware of his own rights and also of Hodgens' mistaken belief that Valentino would never raise his own rights that were contrary to Hodgens'. However, the court still held that Valentino was not estopped from asserting his own rights.[129] This is again because Valentino had been prevented from asserting his rights because he had been bullied into not creating any trouble. Given the high likelihood of inequalities in the copyright context, the requirement that the copyright owner should not only know of her rights, but also be able to assert them, should be added to the *Willmott* framework.

(ii) Influence of unconscionability

As regards reliance, in *Fisher* the court held that Brooker and the band could not have relied on a belief that Fisher would never assert his rights, given that Fisher had been forced not to assert his rights. As for detriment, the court noted that Fisher's contribution was significant. The song was an instant success. Its fame only grew over the years. The first eight bars of music, of which Fisher was the author, had been so successful that it was being independently exploited, such as for ringtones of mobile phones.[130] This appears to be also why the judges held that there was no detriment caused; but on the contrary the band members were financially very handsomely rewarded, including with what would otherwise have been Fisher's share. The court held that it was clear from the evidence that it was not solely because of the efforts put in by the other members of the band in promoting the song that it became successful.[131] Thus, in *Fisher* the other band members rode on the initial success of the song attributable largely to Fisher's contribution.[132] As such, in *Fisher* it was held that the defendants were unable to establish detriment, and therefore their claim to estoppel failed.

Again, in *Beckingham*, as far as reliance was concerned, the court noted that there was no reason for the defendants to believe that no claim would be made, since Valentino had informed the band that he knew of his rights and was not going to assert them. As regards detriment, the success of the song was fortuitous in being featured in Volkswagen's TV advertisement in 1993.[133] The band had broken up long before 1993 and, therefore, the success of the song was not attributable to the efforts of the remaining members of the band labouring to promote the band. The court found that, after the success of the song in 1993, it was fully open

[129] *Beckingham v Hodgens* (n 19) [65].
[130] [2006] EWHC 3239 [3] (Ch).
[131] ibid [76].
[132] ibid [77].
[133] *Beckingham v Hodgens* (n 19) [66].

for Valentino to change his mind and assert his ownership. As such, the claim to estoppel failed.

In *Godfrey*, the claim to estoppel succeeded. As regards reliance, as stated above, since Godfrey's engagement with the songs was largely as an arranger of the music, the defendants had assumed that Godfrey had no copyright. The court held that the defendants' incorrect belief that Godfrey did not have copyright is not relevant here. The fact that Godfrey allowed them to believe it and did not do anything to change it is the relevant fact.[134] The only way to change the defendants' belief was to initiate legal proceedings and Godfrey had taken a pragmatic view that there was no point in going to the court unless the songs were successful. Godfrey avoiding expensive copyright litigation could not have itself been taken as inducing reliance. As in *Fisher* and *Beckingham*, it should have made Lees and the other band members not labour under the belief that Godfrey would never assert his rights, since they were put on notice that Godfrey had realised that he had copyright in the songs. Fisher and Valentino also avoided expensive copyright litigation for many years, but that was not regarded as inducing the defendants in those cases into a belief that their claims would never be raised.

In *Godfrey*, the court also erred in its assessment of the detriment as a consequence of reliance. The songs at issue were not an immediate success. After Godfrey left the band, it took the remaining members of the band many years to make the songs popular by giving many live performances, which Lees and the others claimed to be a loss-making and expensive affair. The court noted that, through the years of their hard work to earn popularity and recognition, Godfrey was completely absent.[135] Therefore, the detriment in Godfrey's case was the financial outlay and the physical efforts Lees and the other band members had put in. This assessment is problematic. In *Godfrey*, even if the remaining members of the band believed that Godfrey would not assert his rights, they would have incurred the expenditure and invested time and effort to promote the song regardless. In other words, it was not their reliance on Godfrey not making a claim for his share in the copyright that prompted them to promote their songs and incur consequent expenditure. Godfrey's not claiming his rights was not even the primary reason for the rest of the band's reliance. They would have acted in the same way in any event, as that is what bands do—promote their songs. The court erred in concluding that Lees and the other members of the band had relied on Godfrey not making a copyright claim and, therefore, suffered detriment.

The commercial success of the song should not be the criterion for the courts to consider whether there was a detrimental reliance, even in *Fisher* and *Beckingham*. It should have been the same reasoning here as argued in relation to *Godfrey*, that the band members would have gone ahead to expend effort and money to promote

[134] *Godfrey v Lees* (n 16) 333–34.
[135] ibid 334–45.

the song anyway. This has the potential of setting a precedent that in a joint authorship scenario, only if a joint author's contribution is spectacular, will a court hold that the remaining members of the band did not suffer detriment. If they needed to spend money and effort to promote the song, then the court is likely to hold that there is a detrimental reliance, despite the fact that they would have expended the money and effort anyway, and not in reliance of a co-author's lack of assertion of copyright ownership.

The assessment of unconscionability can tip the balance in some cases. In *Godfrey*, the court strongly supported the approach in *Taylors Fashions*,[136] and accordingly, the court's assessment was based entirely on unconscionability caused to Lees and others owing to their detrimental reliance. As a person who arranged music for these songs, Godfrey could not have done more than writing those arrangements. He was not part of the band and, therefore, his efforts in making the song a success would necessarily be different. When the songs did become a success, it would have been to some extent also because of Godfrey's arrangement of the music, which the other members of the band had used, without having to pay anything to Godfrey. Given that the court addressed none of these issues beneficial to Godfrey to this level of detail, the decision may have been influenced by the judge's subjective bias over who suffered greater unconscionability.

This is exactly the danger commentators have warned of—the subjectivity in the assessment of unconscionability. Instead of depending on unconscionability as the sole yardstick to assess proprietary estoppel, a more nuanced approach as recommended here may be followed to avoid a miscarriage of justice.

(iii) Remedies and estoppel licences

In the implied licence context, a successful claim of proprietary estoppel will lead to the implied licence being held irrevocable. An example of this is *Godfrey*. Godfrey had asked for a declaration as a joint author of the works in issue, in addition to a share of profits. Although the judge held Godfrey to have been entitled to copyright ownership in those works, he simply dismissed the suit by ruling that he was estopped from asserting his claims against the defendants. Technically, it is still possible that if someone other than the defendants in that case sought to perform the songs Godfrey had arranged (for example, for a cover version), then Godfrey's consent would still be necessary (together with that of the other joint authors), for which he could charge a fee.

The licence that the defendants in that case enjoyed are sometimes called estoppel licences because, unlike other bare licences, these have become irrevocable, although they are not contractual licences. However, for the purpose of this chapter, a clearer analysis would be to regard irrevocability as a remedy that results

[136] ibid 333.

from a successful claim of proprietary estoppel in the case of bare licences, rather than re-characterising bare licences as estoppel licences.

If the claim for proprietary estoppel fails, then the implied licence becomes revocable, but only prospectively. This means that an act already performed while the implied licence was in existence is protected (a licence acted upon).[137] For example, in *Brighton*, it was held that Brighton could revoke her implied licence,[138] but only prospectively. Jones had entered into commitments, including licensing Jones' script to other production houses. The court held that it would now be unconscionable to compel Jones to reopen all of those licences, and to have to account for all the profits allegedly owed to Brighton.[139] However, it was not because of unconscionability that these licences could not be reopened, but rather because they were entered into when the implied licence was in force. A declaration of ownership which Brighton had sought was granted, allowing Brighton to revoke her implied licence prospectively, with Jones having to renegotiate with Brighton if Jones wished to exploit the play in the future.[140] This was the case also with *Fisher* and *Beckingham* in that they were not allowed to reopen the licences already entered into or seek compensation for the exploitation of the work when their implied licences were still in force.

Since in many cases a licence is implied based on a low threshold of the copyright owner's knowledge of her entitlement, as argued above, it is reasonable not to rely on this knowledge to deprive her of a part of her copyright interest by making an implied licence irrevocable. A court should therefore be slow in holding an implied licence irrevocable. It is acknowledged that the ability of copyright owners to revoke their implied licence affects the other joint authors and record companies which have their own copyright interests based on authorial works. However, if such revocation is only prospective, it does not cause a great deal of disruption to these stakeholders. On the contrary, it makes the future exploitation of the works more inclusive. This gives an opportunity to struggling copyright owners to end a gratuitous implied licence and negotiate a contractual licence.

4. Conclusions and Connections

This chapter began rationalising the case law on consent-based implied bare licences with the framework proposed in Chapter 3. In the process, it has demonstrated that even if in some cases the positive act and the neutral act are

137 Stuart Bridge, Elizabeth Cooke, and Martin Dixon, *Megarry and Wade: The Law of Real Property* (9th edn, Sweet & Maxwell 2019) para 15-041; see also *Armstrong v Sheppard & Short Ltd* [1959] 2 QB 384, 399.

138 *Brighton v Jones* (n 11) [77].

139 ibid [79].

140 ibid [60], [96].

uncontroversial, it helps to appreciate that they exist, and to identify the facts that represent these acts. The discussion on the knowledge of the circumstances identified nuances that are essential to connect the conduct of consenting to the state of mind. The chapter went on to discuss proprietary estoppel to underscore further the need for an analytical framework for revocability of implied bare licences.

In *Godfrey*, if Godfrey had been able to establish a profit-sharing agreement with the band, he would have been able to claim damages for lost profits. What does it take for a licence to become a contractual licence? This brings us to Chapter 5, which deals with consent-based implied contractual licences. Being consent based, as in bare licences, contractual licences also have an identifiable positive and the neutral act. However, the components of the knowledge of the copyright owner vary, such as from knowing that the licence is gratuitous to knowing that the licence is in exchange for consideration, as discussed below.

In *Trumpet*, if OzEmail had been successful in establishing a custom, a licence could have been implied based on such custom to benefit OzEmail. Trumpet's express words may have limited such implied licence. But what does it take to establish a custom? This is discussed in Chapter 6 below.

5
Consent-based Implied Contractual Licences

A copyright owner may consent to her work being used gratuitously or in exchange for value. Chapter 4 above dealt with implied gratuitous (bare) licences. This chapter will deal with the copyright owner consenting to her work being used in exchange for value, where the consent is not in express terms raising the issue whether a consent-based copyright licence must be implied into the contract. We saw that the only jural relation in a bare licence is that of privilege and no-right. A contractual licence, on the contrary, has rights and duties in addition to privilege and no-right.[1] One of the duties of the copyright owner is not to revoke the licence at will, and the licensee has a corresponding right against revocation. Further, the sanctity of a contract demands that the parties keep to their bargain, and do not renege on their contractual obligations.[2] The modern significance of implied contractual licences lies in their application to copyright content placed online by or with the consent of the copyright owner, and is subject to terms of use that amount to a contract.[3]

From a contract law perspective, in situations of this kind courts try to ascertain the terms that the parties 'intended' to include, even though they did not do so expressly.[4] They maintain 'the classical view that it is the parties, and not the courts, who determine the content of contract'.[5] Since one of the core objectives of contract law is to give effect to the intentions of the parties to transact or cooperate with each other,[6] courts have formulated the following tests or approaches to assess the unexpressed joint intention objectively. The tests approach the issue from three different, but overlapping perspectives, and are controversial. Much of the case law on implied contractual copyright licences also applies these tests.

[1] A group of operative facts that create a privilege is a licence, in Hohfeldian terms. See Wesley Newcomb Hohfeld, 'Some Fundamental Legal Conceptions as Applied in Judicial Reasoning' (1913–14) 23 Yale LJ 16, 44. See also ch 1, section 3 above.

[2] Jack Beatson, Andrew Burrows, and John Cartwright, *Anson's Law of Contract* (30th edn, OUP 2016) 8.

[3] See ch 9, section 1 below.

[4] Hugh Collins, *The Law of Contract* (4th edn, LexisNexis 2003) 222.

[5] Patrick Atiyah and Stephen Smith, *Atiyah's Introduction to the Law of Contract* (6th edn, Clarendon Press 2005) 156.

[6] Gerard McMeel, *The Construction of Contracts: Interpretation, Implication, and Rectification* (3rd edn, OUP 2017) para [1.68].

Implied Licences in Copyright Law. Poorna Mysoor, Oxford University Press (2021). © Poorna Mysoor.
DOI: 10.1093/oso/9780198858195.003.0006

Business efficacy can be described as the commercial purpose of a transaction. When the intention of the parties is not readily discernible, the strategy is to look at the commercial objective that the parties intended to achieve. This test was pioneered in *The Moorcock*, where Bowen LJ held that, in entering into a contract, the parties intended to achieve the commercial objective, and not to frustrate it.[7] In *Marks & Spencer v BNP Paribas*, Lord Neuberger noted that the test of necessity is not that of absolute necessity for business efficacy, but that without the term the contract would lack 'practical or commercial coherence'.[8] However, the business objective of a contract may not always be unified, but divergent or even at cross-purposes between parties, and the reasons why a judge chooses to promote the business efficacy of one party and not the other becomes opaque.[9] Further, business efficacy hides a complex process of reasoning that a court undertakes, blurring the steps leading to the relevant conclusions.

The officious bystander or obviousness test expounded in *Shirlaw v Southern Foundries* applies to cases where the term being implied is 'so obvious that it seemed unnecessary to state it formally'.[10] However, if the term to be implied was so obvious to the parties that its implication went without saying, there would have been no dispute requiring a court to resolve it. This might result in oversimplification and in an inability to demonstrate the true reasons for the court's conclusions. Commentators point out that since 'the officious bystander has not in fact intervened', the courts must resort to other evidence from which to infer the intent of the parties, such as the express terms used and their meaning.[11]

This leads us to the holistic approach adopted by Lord Hoffmann in *Attorney General v Belize*,[12] where he stated that the court must ascertain whether the implication 'would spell out in express words what the instrument, read against the relevant background, would reasonably be understood to mean'.[13] In Lord Hoffmann's own admission, his test is not new, and all tests lead to the same objective, namely to ascertain what the agreement means.[14] In focusing the enquiry on the agreement and the surrounding circumstances, this approach clarifies where one must look to ascertain the term to be implied. Since the search for business efficacy or obviousness can make the court's reasoning opaque, clarifying that the source of any implication must be the agreement within the surrounding circumstances can make the court's reasoning more transparent. In this sense, the holistic approach is not a new test, but brings greater clarity to the other tests. Despite the criticism that

[7] (1889) 14 PD 64, 68 (CA). See also Collins (n 4) 240.
[8] *Marks & Spencer v BNP Paribas* [2015] UKSC 72 [21].
[9] Collins (n 4) 240.
[10] [1939] 2 KB 206, 227, affirmed by the House of Lords in [1940] AC 701. See also Collins (n 4) 222; Atiyah and Smith (n 5) 156.
[11] Collins (n 4) 239.
[12] [2009] UKPC 10.
[13] ibid [21].
[14] ibid [27].

this approach has received,[15] one may see that this approach is more in consonance with the framework proposed in this monograph.

Since the objective of this monograph is to make the method of implying copyright licences methodical and transparent, the opacity of business efficacy and the obviousness tests will be problematic, regardless of their wide acceptance. Further, these are general tests of implying a term into a contract. However, the term being implied here is of a specific type, namely a consent-based implied copyright licence. For a more transparent and specific framework, we can press into service the framework suggested in Chapter 3 for establishing consent, but adapted to the contractual context. Consent, as demonstrated in Chapters 3 and 4, is a combination of conduct and state of mind. While the conduct is analysed based on the positive and the neutral acts, the components of the knowledge of the copyright owner differ between a bare licence and a contractual licence.

Not all contractual licences are alike in the extent of consent implied and the corresponding range of rights permitted to be exercised by the user of the copyright work. Therefore, a further classification of contracts into the following three broadly representative but not exhaustive, types would be necessary. The copyright owner may create a work upon request from another person (commissioner), giving rise to a commissioning contract.[16] Commissioned works owe their existence to the act of commissioning. The commissioned work is created responding to the request of or to the specification of the person commissioning, resulting in a customised work. Given the level of involvement of the commissioner in bringing the commissioned work into existence, the scope of the consent of the copyright owner is wider, even when it is not granted in express terms. The consent to use the work can be as broad as an assignment (complete or partial)[17] or a licence (exclusive or non-exclusive).[18] Two issues arise here: first, whether the term to be implied is in the nature of an assignment or a licence. Upon assessment, if it becomes clear that it is not an assignment, but a licence that must be implied, then the extent of licence can be determined as a second issue. Although this monograph concerns implied licences, it is essential to separate cases of implied assignment from implied licences. This is considered in Section 1.

A person may create a work in her own time and send it to another person to exploit copyright in the work. An example of this is when a musician creates and records a song and sends it to a publisher in the hope of being published.[19] This may be called a copyright exploitation contract, which is considered in Section 2. In

[15] *Marks & Spencer v BNP Paribas* (n 8) reaffirmed the traditional tests of business efficacy and officious bystander, and urged not to regard the holistic test as changing the law. See para [24].

[16] *Blair v Osborne* [1971] 2 QB 78.

[17] Copyright, Designs, and Patents Act 1988 (CDPA), s 90(1) and (2). We can exclude security interest here because the chargee of copyright does not necessarily have the ability to exercise the rights in the work.

[18] CDPA, ss 90(4) and 92.

[19] *Confetti Records v Warner Music UK Ltd* [2003] EWHC 1274 (Ch).

copyright exploitation contracts, copyright works are not created in response to the request of another person. The involvement of the publisher in publishing the work is not comparable to the involvement of a commissioner in having a work created. Nothing stops a publisher from seeking an express assignment. However, if the contract is silent on this issue, the cases where a court might decide to imply an assignment would be very rare. This obliterates the need for a process of implication as in commissioning contracts, resulting only in implied licences coming into existence.

The third category are the contracts that come into existence once the product incorporating a copyright work enter into the mass-market, namely consumer contracts, which are considered in Section 3. Consumer contracts are almost always in standard form, with no direct contractual relationship between the copyright owner and the consumer. Once the products incorporating a copyright work enter into the distribution chain, the sale of such products to a consumer for personal use does not under any circumstances warrant implying an assignment of copyright into the contract of sale. Given that the room for individual negotiation is small, in these cases there is likewise little room for implying a licence beyond the narrow purpose of these contracts.

1. Commissioning Contracts

The author of a work is the first owner of copyright in the work.[20] It follows that when the author is contractually engaged to create a copyright work, the author should continue to remain the first owner of the copyright. However, from the commissioner's perspective, when a commissioner engages a copyright owner to create a work for a purpose, consent in favour of the commissioner to use the work for that purpose must be within the contemplation of the parties at the time of commissioning. In some jurisdictions, the copyright legislation provides for the ownership of the commissioned works which is different from the first ownership rule.[21] However, copyright statutes in many jurisdictions leave it for the parties to decide the ownership of copyright and the consented uses contractually. The following paragraphs rationalise the case law in the light of the framework for ascertaining consent discussed in Chapter 3, capturing the conduct and the state of mind of consenting, but adapted to the contractual context.

[20] CDPA, s 11(1); Australian Copyright Act 1968 (ACA), s 35(2); Hong Kong Copyright Ordinance (Cap 528) 1997 (HKCO), s 13; Singapore Copyright Act 1987 (SCA), s 30(2).

[21] See eg s 15 of the HKCO, which provides that the person who commissions a copyright work will always have an exclusive licence to make all reasonable use of the work contemplated at the time of commissioning, regardless of the provisions of any agreement between them and the copyright owner. See also s 35(5)of the ACA, which treats the commissioner of a photograph commissioned for private or domestic purposes as the owner of the copyright in the photograph.

(a) Positive act

While implying a consent-based bare licence, the difficulty is in ascertaining whether there is consent at all. Therefore, the positive act is crucial in signalling an initial and essential act of consenting. Entering into a commissioning contract, which is an executory contract, is already a consensual act on the part of the copyright owner, whereby they undertake to create and hand over the work to the commissioner. The positive act is in most cases subsumed within the performance of this undertaking and identifying the positive act is normally not difficult, nor controversial in a commissioning contract. This is the case regardless of whether the consent extends to an assignment or a licence. For example, in *Robin Ray v Classic FM*, Ray, the plaintiff, was a writer and a broadcaster of classical music, who was engaged by Classic FM, the defendant, a radio station, to create a document setting out the categorisation of classical music, and to catalogue the music accordingly.[22] The terms of engagement were reduced to writing in a consultancy agreement.[23] Once the contract was signed, Ray created the catalogue and handed to Classic FM. The latter act amounts to positive act. Similarly, it is possible to identify the positive act in all concluded commissioning contracts when the copyright owner performs the contract to give access to the commissioned work once completed.

(b) Neutral act

The neutral act signals the continuance of the consent. As explained in Chapter 3, a neutral act in a contractual context is conditional on consideration being provided, such as payment. Once the copyright owner performs the positive act, for the copyright owner to perform her undertaking to stand back and not interfere with the commissioner's use of the work, the commissioner must perform her undertaking, which is to pay or perform some other obligation undertaken within the bargain. This is the case regardless of whether the agreement is eventually held to be an assignment or a licence. If it is a one-off payment; no issue arises if the payment is made in full. But if the payment is not made in full, then according to the Australian case of *Clyde v Ng*,[24] it is not within the powers of the copyright owner to terminate the copyright licence for non-payment of the fee.[25] The copyright owner can only sue for unpaid sums as a money claim. This is because the contract is based on mutual undertakings that the licence will be given in exchange for an undertaking to pay. If no payment is received, then it goes to performance of the contract, and not

[22] [1998] EWHC Patents 333 [10].
[23] ibid [5], [6].
[24] [1976] 1 NSWLR 443 (Supreme Court of New South Wales).
[25] This case was cited again in *Guzman v Percy Marks* (1989) 16 IPR 87, 89 (Supreme Court of New South Wales), and was held arguable, as it was only an interlocutory stage.

formation. The relief is limited to the part not performed. It is a breach of contract and the copyright owner has the option to accept the breach and sue for the unpaid sum. However, the decision in *Katz v Cytrynbaum* gave a contrary finding.[26] Here, the architect Katz had not been paid, although his fee had been agreed in advance. The court held that it was within Katz's powers to revoke consent for his plans to be used to obtain planning permission, although the relief granted was only damages calculated based on unpaid fees.[27] A better reasoning would have been to regard non-payment as a breach, as argued above.

If the contract is for a recurring payment, missing or stopping the payment can amount to repudiation depending on the circumstances of breach, and the copyright owner can consider herself discharged from the obligations.[28] This means that instead of standing back and letting the work be used, the copyright owner can approach the court to stop the use. By this stage in a commissioning contract, since the copyright owner is likely to have already parted with the work or given access to it to the commissioner, the only way to stop the commissioner from using the work any further is by seeking an injunction.

By the same token, acceptance of a recurring payment amounts to the continuation of implied licence. In the Canadian case of *Pinto v Bronfman Jewish Education Centre*,[29] the plaintiff, Pinto, had been retained by the defendant school to compose, perform, and record music to develop the school's curriculum. The verbal agreement was that Pinto would be paid on an hourly basis for his work and all his expenses reimbursed. The curriculum became successful worldwide, but the relationship between the parties deteriorated and the school terminated the engagement with Pinto. Pinto brought an action claiming that the school had infringed his copyright by reproducing and distributing his work. However, throughout this period, Pinto continued to work for the school and accepted the payments made to him for 14 years, knowing that his works were being used for the school's curriculum.[30] Since the neutral act is conditional upon consideration being given, the acceptance of the consideration with the required knowledge implies continuation of the neutral act.

The neutral act is also conditional on the commissioner acting within the scope of the agreement if the agreement is for partial assignment or a licence, making the neutral act partial in these cases. The condition upon which neutral act is based may be a matter of industry practice, as in *Blair v Osborne*, where Blair, the architect and claimant, informed the commissioning landowner that the Royal Institute of British Architects (RIBA) conditions (as they existed in 1970) applied by handing

26 [1983] BCJ No 2421 (Court of Appeal for British Columbia).
27 ibid [18]–[22].
28 Gillian Davies, Nicholas Caddick, and Gwilym Harbottle, *Copinger and Skone James on Copyright* (17th edn, Sweet & Maxwell 2016) para [5-238].
29 [2013] 115 CPR (4th) 245 (Federal Court of Montreal, Quebec).
30 ibid [29], [163], [168], [182].

the landowner a booklet containing those conditions.[31] If the commissioner acts beyond these terms, the copyright owner can turn the neutral act to a negative act, by approaching the court for injunction. However, the condition on which neutral act depends is not always clear. For example, in *Ray*, once Ray handed the completed catalogue to Classic FM, the latter incorporated it into a software, and successfully used it to air classical music in the UK. Soon, Classic FM also started to exploit the catalogue outside the UK.[32] Ray objected to this as being outside the scope of the agreement and brought an action for injunction to stop Classic FM from using the catalogue outside the UK. The success of Ray's action depended on the interpretation of the agreement.

(c) Knowledge of the copyright owner

The conduct of consenting, namely the positive and the neutral acts, do not take place in vacuum. These actions must be accompanied by the knowledge of the copyright owner. The extent of knowledge corresponds to the extent of consent. This takes us to the section below as to the assessment of the copyright owner's knowledge.

The consent in favour of the commissioner to use the work could be embodied in a non-exclusive licence, an exclusive licence, a partial assignment, or even an assignment of the entire copyright interest,[33] although a partial assignment in practice may not be different from a perpetual exclusive licence.[34] How does one know whether consent of the copyright owner manifests as an assignment or a licence? The answer lies in the assessment of the knowledge of the copyright owner. Where the terms of the commissioning contract are in writing, the parties to the contract are taken to have the knowledge of these terms. However, in many cases, the terms of the commissioning contract are not in writing, in which case the courts go by what is within the knowledge of the copyright owner gained from the parties' conduct, the communication between them, and the surrounding circumstances. Although case law routinely refers to business efficacy and officious bystander tests, it is unclear how these tests assist in arriving at the guidelines. Instead, the following paragraphs argue that methodologically, analysing the knowledge of the copyright owner by applying the criteria set forth below could make the court's reasoning more transparent.

One of the most important factors in cases where an assignment may be implied is that the commissioner has a pre-existing independent proprietary interest in or

[31] *Blair v Osborne* (n 16) 85.
[32] *Robin Ray v Classic FM* [1998] ECC 488 [13].
[33] Davies, Caddick, and Harbottle (n 28) para [5-184].
[34] See eg Australian Federal Court decision in *Wilson v Weiss Art* (1995) 31 IPR 423, 433.

associated with the commissioned work. The knowledge of the copyright owner of the commissioner's interest of this kind provides a more transparent analysis to separate cases where an assignment is to be implied, as opposed to a licence. If an assignment is not to be implied owing to the lack of such proprietary interest in the commissioned work and instead the court decides that a non-exclusive licence must be implied, then we move on to ascertain the uses to which the licence extends. The uses authorised by a licence again turn on the knowledge of the copyright owner. For bare licences, Chapter 4 above identified aspects of the knowledge of the copyright owner,[35] which may be reframed for the contractual context. Normally there is no issue with the knowledge of the copyright owner as to her copyright entitlement, since in many instances, it is because the copyright owner is aware of her entitlement that she demands value in exchange for the copyright licence.[36] What is required to be within the knowledge of the copyright owner is of the bargain itself and the surrounding circumstances, in order to ascertain the scope of the licence. The discussion below begins by separating the cases where implying an assignment is more appropriate and moves on to the cases of implying a licence.

(i) Knowledge of the prior proprietary interest

Historically, until exclusive licences were recognised in the UK by the Copyright Act 1956, many cases had leaned in favour of an assignment, if it was intended that the commissioner must be free to make copies and defend against infringement. Courts had held that under these circumstances, the very act of creating a copyright work in response to a request from a person commissioning could amount to an implied assignment of the author's copyright interest.[37] The decision in *Ray* revisited this historical position,[38] and provided guidelines as to whether an assignment or a licence must be implied.[39]

Before we discuss *Ray*, a technical matter must be considered. An assignment is required to be in writing and signed by the assignor.[40] An implied assignment, by definition, will not be expressed in writing. If an assignment was intended, courts in the UK and Australia normally hold that the legal title to copyright remains with

[35] See ch 4, sections 1(c)(i), (ii), and (iii) above.

[36] See the discussion on *Barrett v Universal Island Records Ltd* [2006] EWHC 1009 (Ch) in ch 4, section 1(c)(i) above, where the claimants' receipt of payments cast a doubt on whether they were truly unaware of their copyright entitlement.

[37] *Massine v de Basil* [1936–45] MCC 233 and *Drabble (Harold) Ltd v Hycolite Manufacturing Co* (1928) MCC (1923–28) 322. Partial assignment was not considered in these cases. See also *Pasterfield v Denham* [1999] FSR 168, 178, a case decided days before *Robin Ray v Classic FM* (n 32), where the court held that an assignment had to be implied, following the line of cases thus far.

[38] *Robin Ray v Classic FM* (n 32) [43], [46].

[39] This case is regarded the *locus classicus* on the law of implied terms in commissioning contracts. See Mary Vitoria and others, *Laddie, Prescott and Vitoria: The Modern Law of Copyright* (5th edn, LexisNexis 2018) 13.19.

[40] CDPA, s 90(3); ACA, s 196(3); CCA, s 13(4).

the author as the first owner, while the equitable title vests with the commissioner.[41] The equitable owner can compel the legal owner to assign the legal ownership in order to perfect the title of the equitable owner.[42] However, in Canada this line of reasoning has not been followed. Therefore, even in cases where assignment may have been implied, owing to the inevitable lack of writing, an irrevocable licence—which need not be in writing—has been implied.[43] In the discussion below, among the UK and Australian cases, some use the language of implied assignment and others rely on the split of equitable and legal ownership.

In *Ray*, Classic FM had started exploiting the catalogue which it had commissioned Robin Ray to create outside the UK, despite Ray's protests, and Ray sued it for infringement. The terms of engagement had been reduced to writing in a consultancy agreement. However, the agreement was silent on copyright. Ray's claim of copyright infringement was on the basis that any implied licence granted under the consultancy agreement only allowed Classic FM to exploit the catalogue within the UK, and any extension abroad had to be specifically permitted. Classic FM in turn claimed that even if Ray was the first author of the catalogue, there was an implied assignment of copyright under the consultancy agreement.[44] The issue was whether there was an implied licence as Ray contended or an implied assignment as Classic FM claimed. Lightman J discussed the authorities on the business efficacy and officious bystander tests, and provided guidelines on how a distinction may be made between implying an assignment and a licence.[45]

Lightman J held that the underlying principle is that a minimalist approach must be followed; if it is necessary to imply a grant, and the necessity can be fulfilled by either a licence or an assignment, then only a licence should be implied. He observed that the cases where only an assignment would be required and an exclusive licence does not suffice would be very rare.[46] He went on to identify a presumably non-exhaustive list of situations where an assignment may be implied as those where the commissioner needs to exclude the copyright owner from 'using' the work in competition with the commissioner. He gave examples of situations where the commissioner intends to sell multiple copies of products incorporating the commissioned work in a market that is free of competition for that product from both the author and third parties; or where the commissioner may provide her prior copyright work for the copyright owner to create a derivative work; or the

[41] Davies, Caddick, and Harbottle (n 28) para [5-179].

[42] *A&M Records Ltd v Video Collection International Ltd* [1995] EMLR 25, 33.

[43] *Silverson v Neon Products Ltd* 1978 Carswell BC 502, [1977] BCJ No 1029 [38]–[39] (Supreme Court of British Columbia). However, Vaver does envisage a role for equity in these situations. See David Vaver, *Intellectual Property Law* (2nd edn, Irwin Law 2011) 138.

[44] *Robin Ray v Classic FM* (n 32) [5], [6], [10]–[13], [15]–[16].

[45] ibid [45(4), (5) and (7)]. Lightman J referred to *Liverpool City Council v Irwin* [1977] AC 239; *Philips Electronique v BSB Ltd* [1995] EMLR 472; and *BP Refinery (Westernport) v Shire of Hastings* (1978) 52 ALJR 20.

[46] *Robin Ray v Classic FM* (n 32) [45(5) and (6)], [46].

employees of the commissioner work together with the copyright owner to create a work of joint authorship.[47]

Although Lightman J only spoke of cases where the copyright owner must be excluded from the 'use' of the work rather than the 'ownership' of the work, he still went on to identify situations where implying an assignment may be warranted. If excluding the copyright owner from 'use' of the work was all that was required, then according to the minimalist approach implying an exclusive licence would be sufficient. Indeed, some cases that followed *Ray* implied an assignment as opposed to a licence. One may argue that the commissioner as an exclusive licensee can use the work in exactly the same way as she would if she were an assignee, given that an exclusive licensee has substantially similar rights and remedies as an assignee.[48] Nevertheless, by choosing an assignment as opposed to an exclusive licence, these cases did not imply into the contract what was the minimum necessary for business efficacy. It will be clear from the discussion below that the minimalist approach is not much of a guideline in deciding when an assignment is necessary; rather, it is the copyright owner being excluded from the ownership of copyright, and not the use.

Although Lightman J did not say it in so many words, what he essentially points to are cases where the commissioner has a prior proprietary interest in the work commissioned, whether it arises out of copyright, trade mark, or patent associated with the commissioned work. In addition to adaptation of a prior copyright work that Lightman J gave as an example, this may happen where the commissioned work becomes a trade mark to be placed on products or services traded by the commissioner; or forms the manufacturing drawings of a product patented by the commissioner. This means that the commissioner's proprietary interest in the commissioned work should be of such a nature that it results in an expectation that the copyright owner be excluded from exercising copyright in the commissioned work. As the discussion below shows, this approach helps explain most, if not all, cases of equitable ownership of copyright. Rather than assessing what is necessary for business efficacy, the specific factors that are or ought reasonably to be within a copyright owner's knowledge are a better gauge for deciding the extent of consent.

In *R Griggs v Evans*,[49] Griggs, the claimant, was the manufacturer of the well-known 'Doc Martens' footwear. Griggs had two different trade marks, which they wished to combine and create a single mark. Griggs also owned copyright in each of these trade marks. Griggs engaged an advertising agency, of which the first defendant, Evans, was a freelance designer. Evans created the combined logo, which was essentially a derivative work of the copyright works in the two trade marks. Once the combined logo was created, Evans assigned it to the second defendant, an

[47] ibid [45(7)(a), (b), and (c)].
[48] CDPA, ss 101 and 102.
[49] [2003] EWHC 2914 (Ch).

Australian shoe company, which was, ostensibly, the claimant's competitor. Both Evans and the second defendant claimed that Evans was the legal and equitable owner of copyright in the combined logo. Griggs approached the court for a declaration that Griggs was the equitable owner of the combined logo. It was common ground that the Australian company took assignment of the combined logo with the actual knowledge of the claim by Griggs.[50]

The High Court found that copyright subsisted in the stylised version of the logo. Having elaborated the principles laid down in *Ray*, the court found that Evans could not be free to assign the copyright in the combined logos. Evans argued that he was not aware of the actual use to which the combined logo was going to be put. The advertising agency he was working for, which later went out of business, only informed him that it was for use on UK point of sale material. Evans argued that had he known that the logo would be used worldwide and more widely than on point of sale material, he would have charged more, claiming that the price did not represent an assignment of his copyright.[51] However, in the court's view, there was no evidence that Evans would have charged more had he known the scope of the use of the work, and that the amount paid to Evans was commensurate with the amount of skill and labour involved in creating the work. The court found that business efficacy demanded in this case that the commissioner needs more than simply a right to use, and this is a clause that is so obvious that it goes without saying. The court also found that the *Ray* principle of excluding the copyright owner from using the work applies here.[52] The Court of Appeal confirmed the trial judge's findings in their entirety, holding that if an officious bystander were to ask whether the author would retain the copyright and the commissioner only a user right, the parties would have replied with an emphatic no.[53]

Commentators believe that an exclusive licence would have sufficed.[54] However, this criticism appears misplaced. The court did consider implying a perpetual exclusive licence, but held that even if such licence behaved similar to an assignment, it would cause Griggs as an exclusive licensee great inconvenience if they had to join Evans in infringement proceedings.[55] This is perhaps not a sufficiently convincing reason, since as an exclusive licensee, Griggs could also add Evans as a defendant, if he did not cooperate.[56] If the joinder of the copyright owner is regarded as inconvenient in all cases, then no exclusive licence can be implied, preferring an implied assignment in all cases. The true reason appears to be that there was a need to exclude Evans from all rights in the work, not merely the right to use.

50 ibid [11]–[14].
51 ibid [18]–[19], [40]–[46].
52 ibid [36]–[37], [48], [51]–[52].
53 [2005] EWCA Civ 11 [10]–[11], [19]–[25].
54 Rebecca Baines, 'Copyright in Commissioned Works: a Cause for Uncertainty' (2005) 27 EIPR 122.
55 *R Griggs v Evans s* (n 49) [58].
56 CDPA, s 102(1). This is the reverse of what was held in *Robin Ray v Classic FM* (n 32) [46].

In assessing this, clearly the most relevant factor that influenced the court's decision was what was within Evans' knowledge, namely that he was given the trade marks of Griggs, over which Griggs had proprietary rights (copyright and trade mark rights).

Indeed, one may go a step further and regard Griggs handing the two logos to Evans as giving rise to an implied contractual copyright licence from Griggs to Evans (through the middleman), with the limited scope of Evans using them to create an adapted work. There could never have been an implied assignment of Griggs' copyright in these two logos to Evans, since the instructions from Griggs were clearly to commission Evans to create a combined logo as an adapted work using the two logos. Once the combined logo was created, since Evans was aware that the ownership of the core of Evans' adapted work belonged to Griggs, Evans' ability to use the adapted work he created was severely curtailed. Although Evans assigning the combined logo to a competitor of Griggs' was exactly the kind of transaction Griggs would want to prevent, Evans would have infringed Griggs' copyright even if he had used the combined logo for any purpose other than to hand it back to Griggs. Since Evans acquired nothing more than initial authorship of the combined logo, it followed that all rights in the combined logo should belong to Griggs, resulting in an implied assignment. It may also be noted that this analysis not only throws light on the true reasoning behind the decision, but demonstrates that the concept of minimalism or business efficacy is nebulous and lacking in transparency.

In *Lucasfilm v Ainsworth*,[57] the defendant, Ainsworth, was asked by a third party to help him create a plastic prototype of a helmet, letting Ainsworth know that it was for a film prop for his client, based on the paintings and a clay mould in which Lucasfilm, the claimant, had acquired copyright. It was common ground that Ainsworth added some of his own features.[58] Once the helmet was made it was approved by Lucasfilm who placed an order with Ainsworth to manufacture a number of such helmets to be used in the film. It became clear to Ainsworth at this stage that it was for Lucasfilm that he had been asked to produce the helmets. After the success of the film, when Ainsworth realised the potential for exploitation of the helmets, he wrote to Lucasfilm that it could exploit the helmet moulds, but nothing came of it. Ainsworth went on to set up his own competing business selling these helmets. Lucasfilm sued Ainsworth, alleging that as part of the commissioning agreement Ainsworth was taken to have assigned his copyright in the design of the helmets.[59] The peculiarity of this case is that the helmet was held not to be a sculpture under UK law becoming eligible, therefore, for protection only as an unregistered design, whose term had expired by the time Ainsworth had begun

57 [2008] EWHC 1878 (Ch).
58 ibid [35]–[36].
59 ibid [84]–[86].

exploitation of the helmets. Both the courts below nevertheless went on to discuss the issue of copyright ownership in the helmet on the basis that it may be eligible for copyright protection outside the UK.[60]

Ainsworth had taken instructions from a middleman, rather than Lucasfilm. When he came to know of it and started a direct relationship with Lucasfilm, the potential for commercial exploitation was not known at that early stage. However, the court stated that even if the licensing prospects could not have been foreseen, the 'appearance and "feel" of the film' was key. As such, the court found that a parallel exploitation of the props could not have been the intention of either party.[61] The court further held that Ainsworth himself was working to render in three dimension what was given to him in two dimension, and therefore would have in any event been unable to exploit the helmets to the exclusion of others who had copyright in the two-dimensional work. Therefore, the court took the view that Ainsworth should have known that the claimant would want full exploitation rights for the work. The court went on to hold that Ainsworth should have known that he would not retain any copyright in them, and that implying an assignment alone makes sense.[62]

Lucasfilm relied on *Ray* principles and the *Griggs* example. Ainsworth had used the copyright work for his own purposes, rather than assigning it to a third party as in *Griggs*. If indeed *Ray*'s minimalist approach had been followed, to prevent Ainsworth from using the work, the court could have implied an exclusive licence, since an exclusive licence prevents even the copyright owner from using the work. However, the court held that an assignment was required. Not only did the court not follow a minimalist approach; it is also unclear how this is supported by business efficacy. Again, what influenced the court was Ainsworth's knowledge of Lucasfilm's rights in the core works based on which he created his adapted work. As in *Griggs*, when Lucasfilm handed the core works to Ainsworth, the implied licence in favour of Ainsworth in those core works extended only to Ainsworth using them to create an adapted work and handing them back to Lucasfilm. Any other use of the adapted work would have infringed the copyright in the core works. So, it did not matter that Ainsworth did not assign the copyright in the masks to a third party, but used it himself for his own business. This use in itself was beyond the implied licence of the core works from Lucasfilm to Ainsworth. Again, Ainsworth's knowledge of the proprietary entitlement of Lucasfilm in the core works required an assignment to be implied.

The proprietary interest of the commissioner must be in existence prior to the commissioning. For example, if a producer in the process of producing a film

[60] ibid [182], confirmed on appeal in [2009] EWCA Civ 1328 [196]. The Supreme Court refused permission to Ainsworth to appeal on this ground. See [2012] 1AC 208 [7].
[61] ibid [189]; [2009] EWCA Civ 1328 [206].
[62] ibid [185], [189]; [2009] EWCA Civ 1328 [207]–[208].

commissions a composer to score music for the film, in the absence of an express agreement, the music may not be impliedly assigned to the producer, although the film producer has a proprietary interest in the film. This is because the film was not a pre-existing work from which the music arose, unlike the pre-existing copyright or trade mark in the cases discussed above. If an assignment were to be so easily implied, film producers need not enter into express agreements at all, taking comfort in copyright in all works they commission being impliedly assigned to them anyway. In *Lucasfilm*, although the film was not in existence as a prior work before the helmet was created, Lucasfilm had acquired copyright in the painting, which was a prior work based on which the helmet was created. An example of a prior interest in film industry is *Hexagon v ABC*, where a person had been commissioned to write the script of the sequel to a film about a fictional character called Alvin Purple. Since Hexagon, the claimant, had been the owner of copyright in the first film about this character, the court proceeded on the assumption that the equitable ownership of the copyright in the script of the sequel belonged to the producer. As such, the scriptwriter could not have used the offcuts of this script to write a television series for ABC, as the equitable ownership in the script—including the offcuts—belonged to Hexagon.[63]

In the Australian case of *Gold Peg v Kovan*, one Mr Smith was the inventor of a cooker, which he wished to sell through a company he controlled called Gold Peg, the applicant herein. Gold Peg had secured a patent for certain aspects of the cooker. Gold Peg had commissioned the respondent, Kovan, to prepare engineering drawings and to manufacture the cookers. However, the commissioning agreement had not been reduced to writing.[64] When the relationship between the applicant and the respondent deteriorated, Kovan went on to manufacture the cookers independently under a different name. Gold Peg approached the court, alleging that Kovan was threatening to infringe its copyright in the engineering drawings, which Gold Peg claimed to have been assigned to it.[65]

The court confirmed the existence of a commissioning agreement. The court further held that Gold Peg would not have been able to maintain its rights exclusively to manufacture its machine if its manufacturer were to assert rights in the drawings against it, and that Kovan would never have been retained by Gold Peg on any other basis. Citing *Ray* and *Griggs* with approval, the court further held that there was a term which was partly oral and can partly be implied as a matter

[63] (1975) 7 ALR 233, 235–37, 257–58. Interestingly, the question as to whether there was copyright in the character of Alvin Purple itself was raised but not answered. See ibid 252.

[64] (2005) FCA 1521 [37], [72], [80] (Federal Court of Australia). A less relevant fact was that Gold Peg had assigned all its intellectual property in the cooker to a Danish company, which had first appointed Kovan to manufacture. Later, Gold Peg obtained a reassignment of all the intellectual property from the Danish company, but continued to engage Kovan to manufacture the cookers. See ibid [38].

[65] Gold Peg also claimed that Kovan was liable for deceptively offering for sale to the persons interested in purchasing the applicant's cooker, a cooker under a different name, under s 52 of the Trade Practices Act 1974. See ibid [50].

of business efficacy, that the copyright in manufacturing drawings based on Gold Peg's drawings or any enhancement in manufacturing drawings created by Kovan would be owned by Gold Peg.[66] In essence, the court found that Kovan agreed to manufacture cookers 'according to the applicant's specifications, to the applicant's order and using the applicant's prior drawings' and any improvements were 'always as agreed by the applicant'.[67] Here, again, instead of business efficacy, a better explanation can be offered by examining what was within the knowledge of Kovan as to the proprietary nature of the interest held by Gold Peg in the work created. The core invention was owned by Gold Peg, together with the copyright in the initial drawings based on which the respondent had created its manufacturing drawings. As argued in relation to *Griggs* and *Lucasfilm*, with such proprietary interest of the applicant at the heart of Kovan's work, Kovan could not have used the work for any purpose other than to complete the work and use it to manufacture cookers according to Gold Peg's orders.

If the prior proprietary interest is not in the nature of a defined property such as copyright, trade mark, or patent, then rules of equity determine copyright ownership. This may appear to interfere with the statutory scheme unreasonably.[68] However, there is nothing in a copyright statute that makes it immune from the application of equitable principles. Since one of the objectives of equity is to promote fairness, it is difficult to see why these rules should be rejected. An example of this is the Australian case of *Intelmail Explorenet v Vardanian*,[69] where the nature of the historical relationship with the copyright owner enabled the commissioner of the work to acquire copyright in the concerned work. Here, Vardanian, the respondent, was an employee of Intelmail, the applicant, and wrote software for Intelmail during his employment and continued to do so after ceasing to be an employee. When the relationship between them deteriorated, Vardanian sued Intelmail for continued use of the software he created after ceasing to be an employee, claiming it infringed his copyright. Intelmail had also brought significant input into the business in terms of hardware design. Based on the close collaboration between the parties in the past and on the dependence and centrality of the software to Intelmail's business, the equitable ownership of the software was held to have vested in Intelmail, with an ability to demand a legal assignment from the respondent.[70] In this case, equity relied on the fact that, historically, Intelmail was the owner of the copyright in the software when Vardanian was an employee, and that

[66] ibid [102]–[104].

[67] ibid [112]. On appeal, the existence and enforceability of the oral agreement with its implied terms was confirmed by the full court. See *Kovan Engineering v Gold Peg* (2006) 234 ALR 241 [52]–[54], [116].

[68] For a criticism of the decisions on commissioning see L Bently and others, *Intellectual Property Law* (5th edn, OUP 2018) 138–39.

[69] (2009) FCA 1018 [60] (Federal Court of Australia).

[70] ibid [65]–[66].

the parties continued to collaborate closely without adverting to copyright ownership issues.[71]

The nature of the transaction can also influence the nature of the relationship.[72] An example is the Australian case of *Andritz Sprout-Bauer v Rowland Engineering*,[73] where the appellant, Andritz, had purchased the rights of manufacture and distribution in Australia of Aqua-Guard technology from Rowland, the respondent distributor in Australia of the technology when Rowland's parent company had gone into liquidation. Having sold the drawings and tools of manufacture, Rowland went on to start an independent business using the manufacturing drawings. The court held that, although there was no clause referring to copyright, a term had to be implied into the contract of sale, assigning the copyright in the drawings.[74] Clearly, in this case the appellant's interest in the copyright works was to acquire them in their entirety and carry on the business, stepping into the shoes of the original proprietor. Having known of the proprietary interest of Andritz, Rowland could not have set up a competing business of its own.[75] The proprietary interest arose out of the fact that Andritz intended to acquire the entire business from Rowland and had stepped into the shoes of Rowland in being the rightful owner of all intellectual property associated with Aqua-guard technology.

Sometimes courts follow the minimalist approach to its logical end and imply an exclusive licence. An example is the copyright owner in collaboration with the commissioner as a partner of a firm, as was the case in *Coward v Phaestos Ltd*.[76] In this case, Coward, the claimant, created a specialised software for use in trading in hedge funds, for a partnership of which he was a partner. Over time, the employees of the partnership had also assisted in the development of the software, but it was common ground that Coward's contribution was significant. He fell out with the partnership, and it was subsequently dissolved, with its assets transferred to one of the defendants. The issue was whether the copyright in the software Coward created had become partnership property, such that Coward had no rights in it; alternatively, that if Coward continued to be the owner, whether there was an implied licence in favour of the successor in title of the partnership, and the scope of such licence.[77] The court held that the copyright in the software had become partnership property. However, the court also considered the alternative argument to hold that, given the centrality of the software to the business, and the need to exclude Coward

[71] Another example of the nature of relationship is *Atelier Eighty Two v Kilnworx* [2015] EWHC 2291 (IPEC) [28]–[31], where the claimant's ownership interest in the defendant prevented it from claiming copyright ownership in a trade mark it had commissioned and paid for, since it always knew that it was for the defendant's use.

[72] See generally Davies, Caddick, and Harbottle (n 28) paras [5-178] ff.

[73] (1993) 28 IPR 29 (Federal Court of Australia).

[74] ibid 38–40.

[75] See *TS & B Retail Systems Pty Ltd v 3Fold Resources Pty Ltd* [2007] FCA 151 (Federal Court of Australia), for a similar example.

[76] [2013] EWHC 1292 (Ch).

[77] ibid [1]–[3], [12]–[13].

from using the software, the implied licence from Coward should be exclusive.[78] Here, the partnership as a business organisation, the speciality of the software, and Coward's own behaviour in relation to the software appear to have influenced the court to imply an exclusive licence.

In *Wrenn v Landamore*,[79] the defendant had been retained to code software to interface with audio equipment that the claimant sold to motor companies through another company the defendant controlled. The defendant had acknowledged in some of the correspondence that the claimant owned the copyright in the software. There was evidence also to show that the defendant had been promised a royalty based on the success of the venture.[80] Dispute arose between the parties and they set up another joint venture company with 50 per cent shareholding in it by each party and assigned the copyright in the software to that company. But the parties reached a deadlock and could not make the joint venture function. The claimant sued for infringement on the basis that it had the equitable ownership of the copyright in the software. The court held that, in view of the parties conduct in entering into the joint venture and to protect the defendant's right to royalties, an implied exclusive licence was the appropriate way forward.[81] The nature of the software and its usefulness to the claimant was found to be such that the defendant had to give claimant the access to the source code. Here, there was no pre-existing proprietary interest in the software which the claimant had. The audio equipment he fitted to cars was not proprietary to him. Therefore, an implied assignment was not required, but only an exclusive licence.

The position in Canada is somewhat different. In *Silverson*, the claimant designed a large sign for a motel, incorporating its trade name, to be displayed on the front of the motel. When the motel wanted more signs to be produced, it employed the defendant to produce them. When the claimant learned about this, he sued the defendant for copyright infringement. Here, since the motel had a pre-existing proprietary interest in the trade name which was being incorporated into the sign, the copyright in the sign should have been impliedly assigned to it, according to the argument here. However, since neither an assignment nor an exclusive licence could be granted without writing under Canadian law, the court held that an irrevocable licence should be implied.[82] The court went further in *Tremblay v Orio Canada*, where there was a document that evidenced assignment, but it was not signed by the assignor. The trial court held that there was no assignment,[83] and there could only be an implied licence. However, the appellate court doubted this

[78] ibid [232], [242], [248]–[249].
[79] [2007] EWHC 1833 (Ch).
[80] ibid [1]–[4], [19].
[81] ibid [22]–[23], [37]. These findings were confirmed by the Court of Appeal in [2008] EWCA Civ 496.
[82] *Silverson v Neon Products Ltd* (n 43) [39], [45].
[83] [2014] 3 FCR 404 [41]–[44] (Federal Court of Montreal).

view and was willing to regard it as an assignment since the agreement showed intention of the parties to assign.[84]

(ii) Knowledge of the bargain

Moving on, if the agreement between the parties does not show prior proprietary interest held by the commissioner, then no assignment will be implied. Instead, a non-exclusive licence may be implied. The question then is what other aspects of the bargain should have been within the copyright owner's knowledge, such that the scope of the licence to be implied can be ascertained. Unlike in bare licences where the copyright owner must know that the licence is gratuitous, in a contractual licence the copyright owner must know that a bargain exists. A bargain in this context simply means the exchange. A person entering into a contract is taken to have the knowledge of the terms of the contract, whether it is in writing or is verbally agreed. One of the most important forms of consideration exchanged for a copyright licence is its economic value reflected in the price paid. The question is, given a specific price, what actions should the copyright owner be taken to have permitted under the licence. Although the price agreed is a good starting point, the bargain must be assessed as a whole.

Let us first complete the story of *Ray*. We noted above that a licence as opposed to an assignment was to be implied. In persuading the court for a wider scope of the licence, Classic FM had argued that, by the time the commissioning project was complete, it had paid Ray £250,000, which it claimed to be substantial enough to imply a licence wider than being limited to the UK.[85] Lightman J observed that, although the amount of fee paid could determine the extent of the implied licence, the parties had not envisaged such significant payment at the time of entering into the agreement; it became a significant amount over time. He relied on recital A of the consultancy agreement between the parties, which stated that Ray's work would be used for enabling Classic FM to carry on its business, namely to broadcast classical music. He interpreted this to extend only to the UK, thereby confining the implied licence only to the UK. He also went on to hold that the licence accordingly was to be limited to what is in the joint contemplation of the parties at the date of the contract, and does not extend to enable the relevant party to take advantage of a new unexpected profitable opportunity.[86]

The recital, however, did not mention that Classic FM carried on business only in the UK. It was clear from a plain reading of the recital that it was only a background statement that Classic FM carried on business in classical music. Lightman J may have meant to say that this is how the parties understood it at the time of entering into the contract, given that the amount to be paid was not known up front.

[84] [2014] 4 FCR 903 [22] (Federal Court of Appeal, Montreal).
[85] *Robin Ray v Classic FM* (n 32) [5].
[86] ibid [45(8)–(9)], [48].

Therefore, Lightman J's assessment was regarding what the parties knew about the bargain. His approach of looking at the agreement as a whole, and not simply at the price paid, was also appropriate. But acknowledging that that was what he was doing would have provided greater clarity. In his eagerness to imply in principle only that which is the minimum required for business efficacy, he failed to provide clear enough reasons on the facts as to why the scope of the agreement was confined to the UK.[87]

The dispute is not always about the price paid, but could also be about the mutual entitlements of the parties to a commissioning contract. Another example is *Wilkinson v London Strategic Health Authority*.[88] Here, Wilkinson, the claimant, was the author of Wilkinson Variant, a methodology of teaching communication skills to nurses while treating cancer patients. The defendant engaged Wilkinson to bring together many such methodologies under one unified programme. As such, a substantial part of the works Wilkinson had authored before entering into this contract, was taken for preparing the course materials for the unified programme under the defendant's auspices. Unlike in *Ray*, the agreement engaging Wilkinson expressly provided that the intellectual property in any new works created owing to this engagement would be owned by the defendant. The agreement with Wilkinson was terminated according to its terms, but the defendant continued to use the material created under the agreement elsewhere, including abroad, and for diseases other than cancer. Wilkinson claimed that the defendant infringed her copyright and that any implied licence did not extend to providing the training in other countries and for other diseases. The defendant claimed that Wilkinson had impliedly assigned her prior works to the defendant to the extent they were incorporated into the new works, and that the defendant was free to exploit the new works.[89]

The court ruled out the implication of an assignment of Wilkinson's prior works, and held that only a licence may be implied.[90] The question arose as to the extent of this implied licence. The court observed that the proper place to consider the scope of the implied licence is the very agreement into which the term is sought to be implied. The court found that the defendant was to have its own copyright in all the new material that was created as a result of this agreement and that at a minimum, any implied licence must not fetter the defendant's exploitation of the rights in the new works.[91] It followed that the defendant could exploit the new works for other diseases, and in other jurisdictions, even if these possibilities were not specifically discussed. In keeping with the express terms, the court held that the implied licence must be irrevocable,[92] royalty

87 ibid [47]–[48].
88 [2012] EWPCC 48.
89 ibid [3]–[6], [56]–[60].
90 ibid [79]–[80], [89]. Note that the defendant had no pre-existing proprietary interest associated with the work.
91 ibid [92].
92 Since it is a contractual licence, it is unsurprising that it is irrevocable.

free,[93] and can be sub-licensed or assigned together with the defendant's copyright. The court also held that if the defendant provided services in competition to Wilkinson, there was nothing in the agreement that could stop it; nor could Wilkinson be stopped from using Wilkinson Variant in any manner.[94]

All these conclusions arose from what the parties had bargained, which was to give the defendant the ownership of copyright in the new works created owing to the collaboration with Wilkinson. Having bargained thus, Wilkinson could not assert her own copyright to hold back the defendant's copyright. In coming to this conclusion, the court declared the implication of the term to be 'reasonable and equitable, necessary to give the contract business efficacy, clear and does not contradict any express term of the contract', more as a conclusion, than in discussion.[95] It is evident that the court was analysing the express terms closely, rather than trying to achieve what was necessary for business efficacy.

When the agreement is not in writing, the court will have to review the evidence of all that was discussed between the parties. Although it is the knowledge of the copyright owner that is the key to deciding how far the licence was authorised, it is also possible for the court to consider what the copyright owner led the other contracting party to believe. In this context it is possible that the court finds the evidence of the counterparty more credible than the copyright owner. This was demonstrated in the Canadian case, *Nicholas v Environmental Systems*.[96] Here, the plaintiff had been engaged to write an assessment report on the defendants' environmental systems. The plaintiff claimed his understanding of the arrangement to be that the report was to be shown to one investor only. The defendant's understanding was that, having paid US$500 to the plaintiff, it was free to copy it and show it to any other investors, although it acknowledged that the copyright would remain with the plaintiff. At the trial, the court found the defendant witness' version of the conversations more credible, as to what the plaintiff led the defendants to believe. Upon a detailed and thorough analysis of the evidence, the court ascertained what the plaintiff knew or ought reasonably to have known the use to which the report would be put. Although the plaintiff had impliedly licensed the use of the report in relation to other investors, it found that placing of the report on a third party website was not within the contemplation of the plaintiff and, to this extent, there was copyright infringement.[97]

In the software industry, questions normally arise as to when the source code of a commissioned software is to be transferred over to the commissioner. Since the

[93] The judge could have held that the fee paid for the creation of the commissioned works also covered the fee for the implied licence of Wilkinson's previous works, and for such implied licence to be sub-licensed and assigned. Royalty-free gives the impression of an implied bare licence, which it was not.

[94] ibid [95]–[96].

[95] ibid [92].

[96] [2010] FCJ No 892 (Federal Court, Toronto).

[97] ibid [31]–[35], [98].

source code gives control over the software in a way that the software can be modified or developed further, potentially permitting more rights to the software to be exercised including adaptation, transfer of the source code could be considered more appropriately in cases where an implied assignment or an implied exclusive licence is found. If the bargain lends itself only an implied non-exclusive licence for use rather than modification, access to the source code is normally not provided. This is confirmed by *Centrestage Management Pty Ltd v Riedle*.[98] Riedle was commissioned to write a program for Centrestage for the latter's client, the Salvation Army. The bargain indicated that Riedle was an independent contractor and not an employee of Centrestage, although the latter exercised some control over his work.[99] The question was the extent of the licence to be implied. Centrestage had claimed that there were defects in the program which required them to have access to the source code. The court found that there were no defects and, additionally, there had been discussions with Riedle that he would provide ongoing maintenance services. Therefore, no source code was transferred.[100] Even if there had been no maintenance services agreed, access to source code is not a normal incident of ordinary use of software. The decision in *Saphena Computing v Allied Technologies* also confirms this.[101] Here, the only reason why the court held that the commissioner had access to the source code was because the copyright owner was in the process of removing the defects in the software it had developed and installed for the commissioner when the relationship between them broke down. It was held that, although the contract was terminated abruptly, it could not have been the intention of the parties that the software would remain with defects. If not for the uniqueness of the facts of this case, the commissioner would not have had access to the source code.

We now move the discussion over to what some textbooks call 'architects' plans' cases,[102] not because of any reasons in law that set these group of cases apart.[103] The plethora of cases is perhaps attributable to landowners, land developers, and firms of architects having the financial wherewithal to litigate, and in many cases up to appellate stages. These cases do raise issues that are specific to this market. For one, the adoption by the parties of the terms of engagement proposed by the

[98] [2007] FMCA 1147 (Federal Magistrates' Court).

[99] ibid [3]–[7], [55].

[100] ibid [60], [67]–[69]. Confirmed on appeal by the Federal Court of Australia in (2008) 77 IPR 550 [72]–[73].

[101] [1995] FSR 616, 637–40. This decision does not disturb the precedents on policy-based rulings on repair.

[102] Davies, Caddick, and Harbottle (n 28) paras 5-241 ff; Sam Ricketson, Megan Richardson, Mark Davison, and Vicki Huang, Intellectual Property (6th edn, Lexis Nexis 2019) 512.

[103] Some Australian authorities regard these as a class of contract where terms are implied by law. See *Devefi Pty Ltd v Mateffy Perl Nagy Pty Ltd* (1993) 113 ALR 225 and *Concrete Pty Ltd v Parramatta Design and Developments Pty Ltd* (2006) 231 ALR 663 [18] (Gummow J), [59] (Crennan and Kerby JJ), and trial judge at [2004] FCA 1312 [136], [298]. A more detailed discussion why this view may be incorrect is in ch 7, section 1 below.

professional bodies of architects and builders such as RIBA in the UK or those of the Association of Consulting Engineers of Australia, can influence the scope of any licence implied.

In *Blair*, certain owners of land had engaged the claimant, an architect, to draw plans to build a house, for a fee. The claimant had informed the owners that his engagement would be governed by the RIBA conditions (as they existed in 1970). The claimant prepared complete plans and submitted them to the local authority for planning permission. Once the planning permission was obtained, the claimant sent the drawings and the certificate to the owners, together with his bill for the work done.[104] The owners paid the bill, but did not engage the plaintiff for further works. Instead, they sold the land to the second defendant. The second defendant in turn engaged the first defendant, another firm of architects, to do the work. The first defendant used the claimant's drawings to obtain building permission, putting in details of its own. The building permission was granted and the buildings were built. The claimant happened to see the completed buildings, and sued the first defendant for using his plans and the second defendant for building according to his plans.[105] The parties did not dispute that the copyright in the plans belonged to the claimant. Two issues arose: first, whether a licence may be implied in favour of the commissioner to use of the plans; and, secondly, whether such licence is assignable to a purchaser of the land in relation to which the plans are drawn and approved by the authorities. Having lost at the first instance, the claimant appealed to the Court of Appeal.

As to the first issue, Lord Denning MR held that, in return for his fee, the architect gives a licence to the owner to use the plans for the building on that site. Although the copyright remains in the architect, so that he can stop anyone else copying his plans, or making a house from them, he cannot stop the commissioner, who employed him from doing work on that site in accordance with the plans.[106] Lord Denning MR relied on the decision of the Supreme Court of New South Wales in *Beck v Montana*, that if not for the commissioning, the copyright work would not exist, and therefore, at the very least, the commissioner must be able to use the work she commissioned.[107] Widgery LJ found that the RIBA terms did not contemplate that the engagement would run its full course at all times. Various stages of services of an architect were clearly envisaged under the RIBA conditions, with a corresponding payment for a specific service. He disagreed with the claimant that the plans could only be used by the defendants so long as the plaintiff was in their continued service, or that the plans came into existence only to get planning permission. Widgery LJ stated that if this argument was correct, it would

[104] *Blair v Osborne* (n 16) 83–85.
[105] ibid 84.
[106] ibid 85.
[107] [1963] FLR 298, 304-305.

allow architects to hold their clients to ransom, which goes against the spirit of the relationship. He concluded that since the claimant had been paid for his services, a licence could be implied, which extended to all purposes for which those plans would normally be used in connection with the constructing the building to which the plans relate.[108]

The effect of the RIBA schedule of fees, according to *Blair*, was that the person engaging an architect would have an implied licence to use the plan depending on the stage up to which the architect is engaged, for activities commensurate with that stage. When the claimant applied for and obtained the planning permission, the claimant receiving the payment at this stage made it possible that if the owners wanted to proceed to use the plans to build, they should have the implied licence necessary to perform all actions to build accordingly, including making copies and issuing them to the builders. Since RIBA conditions did not force a client to engage the same architect throughout, if the owners in *Blair* had themselves engaged another architect after the planning permission was granted, to build according to the approved plans, the implied licence could be sub-licensed to the new architect and any other person who would need it to build. This explains why the owners of the land who had a direct contractual relationship with the claimant enjoyed the implied licence.

As to the second issue of the assignability of the implied licence, Lord Denning MR went on to hold, without giving further reasons, that if the owners sell the site, the implied licence extends to also avail the purchaser. For Lord Denning MR, it followed from the owners having paid the full price for the implied licence, in that even when they sold the land, the purchasers received the benefit of the approved plans. The implied licence that allowed the commissioner to do everything necessary to build according to the plan also allowed it to assign the implied licence to use the plan when the land was sold.[109] This explanation is far from satisfactory, as the price alone cannot determine assignability, if there is nothing else in the bargain to support it. A more complete picture may emerge when one analyses the surrounding circumstances that ought reasonably to have been within the architect's knowledge, as discussed in the next subsection below.

The subsequent case law on architect's plans broadly divide between the same two issues as in *Blair*. The first issue of the implied licence in favour of the commissioner was again brought into focus in *Stovin-Bradford v Volpoint*.[110] However, unlike *Blair*, in this case the claimant agreed to accept a nominal fee for drawing up and applying for the planning permission, which was far less than what he would have been entitled to under the RIBA terms. Also, unlike in *Blair*, the claimant

[108] *Blair v Osborne* (n 16) 86.

[109] ibid 85, as he relied on *Beck v Montana Constructions Pty Ltd* [1963] FLR 298, where the facts were slightly different, as discussed in the next subsection.

[110] [1971] 3 All ER 570.

stated in his invoice that the copyright in the drawings belonged to him, and that his permission would be required for any reproduction of the drawings. Before the planning permission was given, the plaintiff resigned from the project. Although planning permission was refused at the first instance, the defendants had managed to resubmit and obtain it. However, the claimant was unaware of the resubmission and the eventual grant of planning permission. The defendants had used the original part of the claimant's design, which made the claimant sue for copyright infringement.[111]

The RIBA conditions had not been adopted. The defendants contended that *Blair* was a binding authority on the court and that, once the claimant was paid for his services, the defendants were free to use the plans for all purposes for which the plan was prepared. The court disagreed. Lord Denning stated that when the architect charges the full-scale fee for the work done, that fee in the ordinary way must be taken to include permission to use the plans for the building of that very house. He further held that the scale charges for partial services are so fixed that they contain a 'built-in' compensation for the use of the design and drawings right through till the completion of the work. Since the claimant had only charged a nominal fee in addition to stating on his invoice that any reproduction required permission, it meant that he intended the plans not to be used for building purposes. If the defendants wanted to use the plans, then they would have to pay the plaintiff the full RIBA scale charges to have the implied licence to carry out the building works.[112] No licence was implied in the defendants' favour.

It may be questioned whether *Stovin-Bradford* was a case of implied licence at all, because there was an express term as to the need for permission for reproduction which was given effect to, in the light of the payment made. However, even if there was no express term as to copyright, the fact that the architect was not paid according to the scale for the work done, but only a nominal fee, and that he had resigned from the engagement before the planning permission had been granted, could still have supported the argument that there should be no implied licence.[113] While in principle this case reinforces that the bargain as a whole must be considered, and not the price alone, it also drives home the point that there may be cases where a commissioner may end up with no implied licence to use the work at all.

An iteration of the first issue is if the commissioner can benefit from an implied licence, whether such licence extends to altering the plans, which arose in the Canadian case of *Netupsky v Dominion Bridge*.[114] Here, Netupsky was commissioned by an architect acting on behalf of the City of Ottawa to prepare engineering

111 ibid 572–74.
112 On this point, all three judges agreed. See ibid 573–81.
113 ibid 575.
114 [1972] SCR 368 (Supreme Court of Canada).

plans to construct Ottawa Civic Centre, and Dominion was appointed to build for the City of Ottawa. The agreement provided that Netupsky could make alterations to the plan. However, during the course of construction when Dominion requested Netupsky to make alterations to save costs, Netupsky refused to do so, leaving Dominion to make those changes, but without altering the artistic look of the building and proceeding with the construction. When Netupsky was replaced by another company, Netupsky sued Dominion for copyright infringement, stating that Dominion had no right to alter the plans.[115] The Supreme Court pointed out the existence of a provision in the commissioning agreement to permit alteration by Netupsky as an indication that alteration was within the joint contemplation of the parties. On this basis, and owing to the repudiatory breach of Netupsky in refusing to make the alterations, a licence could be implied permitting Dominion to make those alterations and reproduce the altered plans as required to complete the construction.[116]

A similar issue arose in *John Maryon v New Brunswick*,[117] where John Maryon had been engaged to draw the plans by New Brunswick to construct a telecommunications tower. Upon completion of the construction, cracks had begun to appear. Although initially Maryon assured that there was no threat to the strength of the tower, on independent inspection, it was discovered that the tower was under considerable strain. New Brunswick brought an action against Maryon for negligence, among other things. Maryon defended the action by counterclaiming that New Brunswick violated Maryon's copyright in the plans by unauthorisedly altering the tower design.[118] Upon losing before the trial court, Maryon appealed to New Brunswick Court of Appeal, which doubted whether Maryon was the author of the tower's design, as Maryon was only the structural designer. Assuming that Maryon was the author of the tower design, the court relied on *Netupsky* that a term may be implied into the commissioning contract permitting the alteration of the work at issue. The Court further held that Mayron knew that the tower was located in a public place and needed to be safe and perceived to be safe by the public. On this basis, the Court held that a term must be implied to permit alteration of the tower design.[119]

In *Netupsky*, there was an express term of alteration by the copyright owner, which supported the implied term. In *Maryon*, the very subject matter of the project, namely a tall tower in a public place, supported the implied term. However, if none of these factors exists, can the implied licence in favour of the commissioner still extend to alteration of plans? *Hunter v Fitzroy*[120] appears to confirm this,

[115] ibid [2]–[4], [11]–[14].
[116] ibid [20]–21], [26], [28].
[117] 1982 CanLII 2906; (1982) NBJ No 387 (Court of Appeal, New Brunswick).
[118] ibid [2]–[7], [9]–[10].
[119] ibid [151].
[120] [1978] FSR 167.

although it was not a judgment on merits, but only an interlocutory injunction. In this case, the commissioner who engaged the architect had gone into receivership and the site for development had been sold. A different firm of architects had been appointed to complete the work, who substantially changed the plans. The architect sought to stop the construction on the site by way of an injunction. Oliver J held that there was a 'strongly arguable case' that the commissioner had an implied licence to do all the acts in relation to the construction of the building, 'including if necessary the engagement of another architect to modify them'.[121]

As regards the second issue of the assignability of the implied licence, the law of assignment of choses in action recognises the possibility of the benefit of a contract to be assigned if the contract is not for personal services. Therefore, the benefit of an implied licence in the hands of the licensee can also be assigned. However, this does not mean that once a court implies a licence within a contract the court is deemed to have also implied a term enabling the assignment of the implied licence. Whether this additional term enabling assignment may also be implied is again dependent on whether there is a basis for it to be implied.[122] Although consent can be a basis for implying this term,[123] it is more common for assignability or lack thereof to be expressly provided.

Accordingly, the existence of express terms enabling or preventing assignment of the licence, for example those adopted from RIBA conditions, are increasingly being relied on. In the Scottish case of *Muir Dorrans v The Shand Partnership*,[124] the owner of the land was not the one to instruct the claimant, the architect, to prepare plans; instead, it was a developer who was interested in developing the land. However, this developer never proceeded with his plans once the planning permission was obtained. The land was subsequently sold twice over, finally to one of the defendants who started developing the land based on the planning permission obtained. The RIBA conditions in existence at the time of commissioning provided for the scope of the licence as extending only to 'the client', and that the benefits and obligations under the agreement were not assignable by either party without the consent of the other.[125] The defendants relied on *Blair* and *Beck* to argue that, as a matter of principle, the licence was assignable.

Lord Kingarth rightly distinguished the facts of this case from *Blair* and *Beck*, in that there was no contractual relationship between the person commissioning the plans and the person who set about to build in accordance with the plans. The agreement was between the claimant and the first developer. The first developer had not tried to assign the benefit of the agreement, and thus, neither the facts of the

[121] ibid 173.
[122] Michael Bridge and others, *The Law of Personal Property* (2nd edn, Sweet & Maxwell 2018) para 21-010.
[123] A policy can also be the basis for implying a term to this effect. See ch 7, section (1) below.
[124] 2003 Scot (D) 21/12.
[125] ibid [2]–[3]. RIBA Terms 1992, and the specific clauses are cl 2.3.1 and cl 1.4.1, respectively.

case nor the terms of the agreement justified implying a term that the licence was assignable. The RIBA conditions that applied here expressly provided that copyright in the plans stayed with the architect, and defined the extent of the licence given to the client to exclude the assignability of the licence. Therefore, he held that there was no need to imply a term into this agreement.[126] This will increasingly be the case as RIBA conditions are amended to be more comprehensive and architects are encouraged to adopt these conditions to avoid uncertainties later.

For example, in *Devefi v Mateffy Perl Ngay Pty Ltd*,[127] the commissioning agreement between the commissioner and the structural engineer, Mateffy, adopted the 'Guideline Terms of Agreement Between Client and Consulting Engineer for Professional Services' published by the Association of Consulting Engineers Australia (ACEA) in October 1983. The terms clearly provided that the copyright work benefited only the client, i.e., the commissioner, and for non-assignment of any right or obligation under the agreement without a written consent of the other party. When the commissioner went into financial difficulties, it sold the development site to Devefi, without taking Mateffy's consent and without having fully paid Mateffy for its services. Devefi engaged a different company to complete the project. When it came to Mateffy's attention, it sued Devefi. One of the issues was whether a term could be implied making this express licence assignable. It was held that the contract between Mateffy and the commissioner was for providing complex professional services in which 'personal trust and confidence in the exercise of specialised skills' would be of importance to the commissioner; as also the identity of the commissioner to the person providing the service. This, read with the express provision meant that the benefit of the licence could not be assigned to Devefi. On the one hand, the existence of an express provision in the agreement prohibiting assignment should have been sufficient. If, on the other hand, there was no express provision in the agreement preventing assignment, and if the commissioning contract is found to be not for personal services, then it would be assignable if a term to that effect can be implied.[128]

It is still possible that the ACEA or similar terms are not adopted by the parties, as in the celebrated Australian case of *Concrete Pty Ltd v Parramatta Design & Development Pty Ltd*, where there was not even a written contract for commissioning. The issue of assignment also came up in an oblique way. The copyright owner, i.e., the architect Mr Fares, was the sole shareholder and director of his design company, the respondent herein. He set up another company called Landmark Development with one more person, and Landmark entered into a joint venture with another company Toyama Development to purchase and develop particular sites. The joint venture initially developed a site for which the plans were drawn by

[126] ibid [16], [20].
[127] (1993) 113 ALR 225 (Federal Court of Australia).
[128] *JWH Group v Kimpura* [2004] WASC 39 [74]–[75] (Supreme Court of Western Australia).

Parramatta for payment of a fee. However, when another development opportunity arose, Parramatta was again engaged to draw up plans, but the parties to the joint venture together decided that no further payment would be made. This commissioning agreement was not in writing. Development approval was also obtained based on these plans.[129] When the joint venture subsequently went into administration, trustees were appointed to sell the development site and Concrete Pty Ltd, the appellant herein purchased the site. However, in the sale and purchase agreement, it was stated that no warranty was given in relation to the copyright in the plans. Parramatta further refused to grant a licence to Concrete to use its plans, stating that it was not paid for its services. Concrete brought an action for unjustified threat of infringement against Parramatta.[130] While the trial judge held that Concrete benefited from a licence implied by law based on the authority of *Beck* and *Blair*,[131] the full Federal Court held that, since Parramatta had not been paid for its services, no licence could be implied. The Federal Court distinguished *Beck* and *Blair* as cases where the architect had been paid for his professional service, relying on *Stovin-Bradford* to justify why there was no implied licence.[132]

On a further appeal, the High Court of Australia reversed the Federal Court's decision and held that Concrete benefited from an irrevocable implied licence of the plans. Although it was not specifically pleaded, the Court held that it was not a bare licence which could be withdrawn, since the profit that would have been made by the joint venture by the successful sale of the developed land in future was Parramatta's consideration for preparing the drawings.[133] The Court held this to be sufficient consideration not only for Paramatta to draw the plans, but also to support a licence in favour of Concrete. The Court made an assessment of essentially what was within the copyright owner's knowledge—that Parramatta was only a corporate front of the copyright owner, who was also the principal of Landmark, one of the companies in the joint venture holding two-thirds of the share in the development site. The Court rightly held that the copyright owner's motivation in drawing up the plans was to keep the cost of development down and to maximise profit, which would have eventually benefited him upon the sale of the developed land.[134]

A more refined analysis of the implied licence is necessary here. Although the court's findings on consideration supporting the verbal commissioning agreement is correct, the implied licence first benefited the parties to the joint venture, namely Landmark and Toyama and it was irrevocable. However, trustees appointed to carry out the sale did not interrupt this chain, as the beneficial ownership still

[129] (2006) 231 ALR 663 [23]–[27].
[130] ibid [28], [31]–[35].
[131] [2004] FCA 1312 [298].
[132] (2005) 144 FCR 264 [18]–[20].
[133] (2006) 231 ALR 663 [7], [16] (Gummow, ACJ), [95] (Kirby and Crennan JJ).
[134] ibid [23]–[26], [74], [80]–[84] (Kirby and Crennan JJ).

remained with the joint venturers. Indeed, when the trustees were to advertise the auction of the land, both the joint venturers agreed that they could do so disclosing to the prospective purchasers that there was a development consent.[135] It should be noted here that the principal of Parramatta was the same as the principal of one of the joint venturers (Landmark), namely Mr Fares, the architect. His conduct in agreeing to sell the land with the benefit of the development consent makes his knowledge of the bargain quite clear. This knowledge was a sufficient basis for the implied licence in favour of the joint venturers to be assignable. As stated above, this licence was irrevocable, and arose in favour of any person who would become the purchaser. Thus, Concrete came to benefit from the assigned implied licence. And the express refusal of Parramatta to grant a licence to Concrete to use the plans, which occurred subsequent to Concrete benefiting from the assignment of the implied licence, came to have no effect.[136] Nevertheless, as in *Blair*, in addition to the bargain, the surrounding circumstances also need to be considered to bolster the argument, as discussed below.

(iii) Knowledge of the surrounding circumstances

This part focuses on all facts and circumstances within the knowledge of the copyright owner surrounding the bargain, which could include what the parties depose as being within their knowledge. However, if it is an evolved market, the courts might take a view that a copyright owner who operates in such market ought reasonably to have some knowledge of the market and its trade practices.[137] If the product incorporating the copyright work is highly specialised, the product knowledge may also be considered. The effort in the discussion below is to show how a broad array of knowledge may inform the scope of the licence. Therefore, it is difficult to say that the courts only try to do the minimum necessary for business efficacy or that such broad array of knowledge is so obvious that it goes without saying.

Let us begin the discussion with *Beck*, where the knowledge of the copyright owner came into focus. Although both *Blair* and *Stovin-Bradford* rely on the decision in *Beck*, the facts in *Beck* that were different need to be highlighted. The claimant in this case was an architect engaged to prepare plans to build over a piece of land. The claimant was aware that after the planning permission was obtained, the land had been put on auction advertising that fully approved plans were available for inspection. In addition, the purchaser at the auction (first defendant) initially did consult the claimant to have detailed drawings drawn, only to decide not to engage them owing to their fees.[138] The auction went through and the first

[135] ibid [33].
[136] ibid [96]–[97], although the court did not analyse it to the degree of detail provided here.
[137] A trade practice is a practice which has not yet become a custom, but can be considered as background information for a contract. For discussion on licences implied by custom see ch 6 below.
[138] *Beck v Montana Constructions Pty Ltd* (n 109) 299–300.

defendant purchased the land and built on the site according to the approved plans. The claimant then sued for infringement.

The court concluded that there was an implied licence in favour of the previous owner who commissioned the drawings. As to whether such licence was assignable to the subsequent purchasers, the judge stated that when the land owner sold their land and held out to the purchaser that plans had been approved and showed the plans, with the sale of the land, a licence must be implied in favour of the purchaser to use the plans. The judge rightly pointed out that this assumed in the first place that the licence which the original owner of the land held, was itself assignable. The judge, however, did not speak of the specific knowledge of the claimant regarding the sale of the land, although he recorded evidence to this effect. The judge simply concluded that having commissioned the plans and obtained the permission, the original owner of the land should also have the right to assign the use of the plans.[139] Nevertheless, the specific knowledge of the claimant as to the sale of the land is likely to have influenced the judge, making it possible to hold the implied licence assignable to the purchaser from the original owner.

Can a court regard that an architect ought reasonably to know that the land for which she draws plans can be sold by the landowner, it being the nature of the market the architect operates in? The reasoning in *Blair*, that the assignability of the implied licence to the future purchasers of land arises out of the payment of the RIBA scale fee, is incomplete. In particular, if the architect had also been engaged to obtain the planning permission, the architects ought reasonably to know that planning permission increases the value of the land for future purchasers. On this view, the claimant in *Blair* ought reasonably to have had the knowledge that the original landowner would sell the land and that the subsequent owner would have the use of the plans. This may have influenced the decision in *Blair*, although the court did not articulate it expressly.

The market knowledge came out strongly also in *Concrete*. Here, the development consent had been granted for 14 units, and it had been recorded as evidence at the trial that if the consent lapsed, the planning regime had changed such that a permission only for eight units would be possible.[140] This fact must have made the land in that area with unexpired development consent more valuable, which would be behind Mr Fares' agreement for the trustees to sell the land with development consent. The court effectively stopped Mr Fares from benefiting not only from the sale at a high price of the development site as a joint venturer, but also from a remuneration for the plans separately as an architect, ensuring that the profit on the sale of land was the singular compensation for both his capacities.[141]

[139] ibid 300, 303, 305.
[140] (2006) 231 ALR 663 [27].
[141] The decision in *Concrete Pty Ltd v Parramatta Design and Developments Pty Ltd* (n 103) was also based on the fiduciary nature of a joint venturer's role.

Another peculiarity about the market concerning land development is that planning permission runs with the land.[142] It is reasonable to conceive of this principle to be within the knowledge of an architect as part of her profession. In *Concrete*, both the trial judge[143] and the High Court were of the view that the development consent runs with the land.[144] The Australian Environmental Planning and Assessment Act 1979 provided under section 78A that where application for development consent is made under that provision, the authority may grant the consent subject to a condition on the duration of its validity or that the consent will not run with land or both. The relevant authority only imposed a restriction on duration (FIVE years), which meant implicitly that the consent ran with the land.

However, one cannot take this principle too far. Lord Kingarth cautioned against it in *Muir*, where he observed that even though the planning permission runs with the land, a copyright licence to use the plans should not be regarded as similarly attached to the land. If that was the case, an implied licence would also inure to the benefit of any purchaser of the land, regardless of her contractual relationship or the lack thereof, with the architect.[145] In Lord Kingarth's view, *Blair* concluded that the licence was assignable only because it had been assigned when the land was sold. If no such sale had occurred, the use of the plans could not have been assigned, even if the planning permission itself ran with the land.[146] Nevertheless, *Muir* drives home the point that in an appropriate case, the knowledge of the architect that the planning permission runs with the land can be considered.

Another factor the courts can consider is the evidence as to the normal fees a person may charge in the respective industry for the services rendered, in the absence of a standard scale of fees such as RIBA's. In *Ray*, although Lightman J sympathised that £250,000 was perhaps a high price to pay, he held that it did not in itself mean that Classic FM had wider rights in relation to the catalogue Ray created. The court could have sought evidence of what in the industry would be regarded a reasonable fee for the work Ray performed. Evidence of Ray's pay for similar assignments he undertook for other clients may also have been considered. If he was being so clearly overpaid, then the higher fee may have represented wider actions which Classic FM could have engaged in, in respect of the catalogue. Also, the industry practice of a broadcasting organisation engaging consultants like Ray, especially of content that could be of potential interest internationally, could have also been considered to ascertain the scope of the licence for Classic FM.

A good example of a specialised product and the knowledge as to the market in that product is *Clearsprings Management v Businesslinx*.[147] In this case, the

[142] Town and Country Planning Act 1990, s 75, read with the Law of Property Act 1925, s 62.
[143] [2004] FCA 1312 [133].
[144] (2006) 231 ALR 663 [66].
[145] *Muir Dorrans v The Shand Partnership* (n 124) [14].
[146] ibid [20].
[147] [2005] EWHC 1487 (Ch).

claimant (CMS), commissioned the defendant, Businesslinx to create a software for its use in relation to asylum seekers. It was common ground that Businesslinx owned copyright in the software. However, CMS argued on the one hand that Businesslinx had impliedly assigned the copyright in the software it had created to CMS, or at least an exclusive licence for CMS to use. Businesslinx, on the other hand, argued that CMS only had a non-exclusive licence to use the software, and such licence was not assignable, nor could it be sub-licensed.[148] The court found that BL had used its own generic code (an authorial work) to create the software, which Businesslinx must be able to use when working on other third party projects. Assigning the software therefore, would prevent Businesslinx from using this code which it legitimately owned and used even before Businesslinx' engagement by CMS, and therefore, a non-exclusive licence would suffice. The fact that software developers use certain generic code to bring about usual routines and operative procedures in a software was taken to be a trade practice, which provided the background information as to the performance of this contract. On the evidence available, the court held that such trade practice must have been within the knowledge of both parties.[149]

If the market is a highly regulated one with statutory provisions governing its operation, then the question arises whether a licence implied in this scenario is consent-based or policy-based. A good illustration of this are the Australian cases, *Acohs Pty Ltd v RA Bashford*[150] and *Acohs Pty Ltd v Ucorp*.[151] In cases of this type, the persons with whom the commissioner must share the commissioned work and the uses to which the commissioned work may be put are all regulated by law. A licence to enable these uses is implied less because the copyright owner ought reasonably to have known the law, but more because of the policy that support the law. Even though a copyright owner operating within such a highly regulated market ought reasonably to know the regulations, the implication is regardless of the copyright owner's knowledge. Under these circumstances, it is more appropriate to consider this implication based on policy, rather than consent, as discussed in Chapter 7 below.

2. Copyright Exploitation Contracts

The bulk of creative work takes place spontaneously, and not as a result of commissioning. For example, a fiction writer writes a novel in her own time, as her inspiration guides her. But these authors might still wish to exploit their works.

148 ibid [3], [6].
149 ibid [39], [43], [48].
150 (1997) 144 ALR 528.
151 (2012) 287 ALR 403.

They might approach publishers in the respective creative industry,[152] and if negotiations succeed, enter into contracts to exploit their copyrights.[153] Depending on the creative industry, these contracts can take many forms, including licensing or assigning of certain rights in the current works, or of future works for a defined period of time or a defined number of works, and the like.[154] It is more likely than not that in these agreements copyright ownership and any provisions for licensing will be expressly provided. If a licence is to be implied, the framework proposed herein could assist in locating the facts necessary to ascertain its scope.

(a) Positive act

The positive act of enabling the work to be accessed by the publisher may take place in different ways depending on the kind of exploitation contract the copyright owner enters into. If a copyright owner has an ongoing publishing relationship, (e.g., a songwriter) she might send the work as and when it is ready. If the copyright owner is a relatively new entrant into the market, she might simply send the copyright work speculatively, and wait for it to be accepted for publication.[155] If a contract follows, there is normally no issue with sending the work ahead. However, issues sometimes arise as to how the positive act should be construed, especially if the copyright owner wants to take back the work. It does not always follow that when authors send their work speculatively, they necessarily make an offer. They could be making an invitation to offer, which could be responded to by the publisher by making an offer of the terms of publication.

However, in some cases, as in *Confetti Records*, the very sending of the work to the record company came to be regarded as an offer. Here, the claimants (author and a small record label) owned the copyright in the song and the record of *Burnin'*, which had become very popular in their genre of UK garage music. The defendant, a bigger record company, 'discovered' them and wanted to include 'Burnin' in an album that the defendant was going to release. Negotiations ensued, and all the communications and the deal memo setting out the important terms were expressly 'subject to contract'.[156] The deal memo sought the claimants to sign

[152] The term 'publisher' is used in a generic sense here. It includes book publishers, academic journal publishers, newspaper and magazine publishers, music publishers, record companies, film producers, and broadcasters.

[153] It is possible that a publisher might commission a work (eg biographies, translations), which must be assessed as commissioning contracts.

[154] For example, it is more common for music industry to have exclusive songwriter agreements whereby a songwriter assigns her rights in her present and future works; and for recording contracts to require exclusive licences from the artists for their current and future works for a term or by the number of works. See Davies, Caddick, and Harbottle (n 28) paras [26-96], [26-109].

[155] A publisher may insist on a literary agent to submit books. See https://www.penguin.co.uk/company/work-with-us/authors.html accessed 27 July 2020.

[156] *Confetti* (n 19) [1]–[6],[10], [13], [17].

it and return it with the original cleared track. The claimants signed the deal memo, and returned it with the original cleared track as requested, and an invoice for the amount of the advance (£1,500), stating that the invoice was for a non-exclusive licence granted for three years. The defendants went on to use the track in the album and prepared for its release. The claimants had tried to communicate to the defendants subsequently that they wanted to refuse the inclusion of the track in the album, but this communication did not reach the defendant before the album was ready.[157] The question arose as to the effect of the claimants sending the signed deal memo, the cleared original track, and the invoice.

The court held that since the deal memo was expressly subject to contract, signing it and returning it did not bind the claimants. However, the sending of the track and the invoice became an offer by the claimants in a unilateral contract, which could be accepted by performance of the contract by the defendant, which is to include the track in the album.[158] This means that the positive act of sending the track under these circumstances became an offer, the acceptance (by performance) of which created a contract. In this sense, the positive act played a different role from signalling that the initial act of granting a licence had begun, as in bare licences, or being part of the performance of the contract, as in commissioning contracts.

The effect of entering a copyright work in a competition was considered in *Larrikin Music Publishing v EMI Records*.[159] Here, a preliminary question arose as to whether Larrikin was the owner of the copyright in the song *Kookaburra*. Ms Marion Sinclair had written the song (lyrics and the music). The Girl Guide Association of Victoria had announced a competition to enter, among other things, songs. The rules of the competition in this case had said that all material entered in the competition were to become the property of the association. The question was whether, by entering the song knowing this rule, Ms Sinclair had assigned her copyright to the association.[160] However, in *Larrikin*, there was insufficient evidence to show whether Sinclair had entered her song in response to this announcement and whether she had the notice of the rules of the competition.[161] Normally, the announcement of the competition amounts to an invitation to offer. Entering a copyright work into the competition amounts to an offer and performance of the contract on part of the offeror, the acceptance of which gives rise to a contract. Whether the contract addresses copyright in the work entered depends on the terms of the competition and its interpretation in the light of the circumstances, in the absence of an express provision.

157 ibid [17]–[20], [22]–[37].
158 ibid [100], [109].
159 (2009) 179 FCR 169 (Federal Court of Australia).
160 ibid [10]–[15].
161 ibid [109]–[126].

If it is an ongoing arrangement as in *Bowden Brothers v Amalgamated Pictorials*,[162] the copyright owner's conduct could be regarded as an offer. Here, the copyright owner, a freelance photographer, continually supplied a series of photographs in advance for the defendant publisher to choose from, on an arrangement that the defendant would pay for each photograph once published. This arrangement continued until the copyright owner wrote to end the arrangement and stopped supplying photographs. The court held the action of the copyright owner to be an open offer, which, when accepted for publication brought into existence a binding contract. And the copyright owner ending the arrangement had the effect of withdrawing all open offers. Since the defendant continued to use the photographs it had even after such withdrawal, the defendant was held to have infringed copyright in the photographs.[163]

(b) Neutral act

As described in the case of commissioning contracts, the neutral act in copyright exploitation contracts is also conditional on the licensee performing her part of the bargain. This may be a payment or other conditions, as the cases below indicate.

In *Redwood Music Ltd v Chappell Co Ltd*,[164] the author of the song *Zing* had originally assigned the song to a publisher, who had licensed it to the defendant. However, owing to the operation of the section 5(2) proviso of Copyright Act 1911, the assignment to the original publisher had become void, and the copyright had reverted to the heirs of the author. The heirs of the author finally assigned the remaining term of the copyright to the claimants. Seeing that the defendants were continuing to exploit the song even when the copyright had reverted, the claimants sued them for infringement. However, during the period of exploitation, the heirs of the copyright owner continued to accept royalties, knowing that the royalties were for such exploitation. The court therefore held that the acceptance of the royalties meant that the defendants were impliedly licensed to continue their exploitation.[165]

Since the neutral act was conditional on the royalties being paid, accepting royalties meant that the condition had been fulfilled, thereby continuing the neutral act. Further, the heirs of the author had the accompanying knowledge as to what the royalties were for, which enabled the continuance of the implied licence. Therefore, being sensitive to a conditional neutral act can explain the reasons for the court's conclusions.

[162] [1911] 1 Ch 386.
[163] ibid 389–91.
[164] [1982] RPC 109.
[165] ibid 120–23, 128–29.

The neutral act can also be conditional upon something other than a payment. In *Sawkins v Hyperion Records Ltd*,[166] the claimant, Sawkins, had created new editions of the compositions of a 17th century French composer by the name of Lalande. Sawkins had agreed with the conductor of an orchestra which was going to perform it that a record should be produced of it. The conductor had identified the defendant to record the performance. Before the recording took place, Sawkins sent the draft of a recording agreement, detailing his charges to provide the music, and had made it clear to the defendant that he was asserting his copyright and he should be paid royalties. The defendant had refused and never signed the agreement.[167] Having reached a deadlock, the recording session was at risk. Upon the assurance of the conductor, Sawkins allowed the recording to continue, but made it clear on the invoice for his charges that the music should only be used for the recording, and no further use was permitted. He also accepted the recording charges and allowed the recording to proceed, in the hope that the conditions stated in the invoice would be followed. However, the defendant went on to use the recording and released a CD. Sawkins sued for infringement, and the defendant claimed an implied licence, since Sawkins had permitted the recording to take place. The court held that the condition stipulated in the invoice made it clear that there was no licence for any purpose other than for recording, and therefore no implied licence could come into existence.[168]

The point to note here is, initially, the neutral act of standing back when the recording continued was to let the recording continue, but not to let CDs to be created. This made the neutral act partial, in that the neutral act did not continue for anything other than the act of recording itself, such as creating CDs or releasing them without payment. Since the defendant released CDs without payment, no implied licence extended to such act. Being sensitive to the nuances of the neutral act, therefore, makes the reasons given by the court more understandable.

If there are no issues with the positive or the neutral act, the next question is how we may determine the extent of the licence. For the same reason as the commissioning contracts, it is argued here that the framework proposed in Chapter 3 should be applied.

(c) Knowledge of the copyright owner

As in the case of commissioning contracts, in copyright exploitation contracts, the knowledge of the copyright owner of what is in the bargain and its surrounding circumstances must be considered. This knowledge holds the key to the extent of the

[166] [2004] EWHC 1530 (Ch).
[167] ibid [9], [77]–[79].
[168] ibid [80], [82]–[83].

licence granted. However, unlike commissioning contracts, the knowledge of the copyright owner as to the prior proprietary interest of the publisher (the counterparty) is normally not relevant. This is because the publisher does not bring any of its own proprietary elements such as its prior work, trade mark, or patent into the bargain. For the effort put in by the publisher in the music industry, film industry, and broadcasting industry, in any event, it receives a separate recognition as the owner of the respective entrepreneurial work.

In addition, it is very rare that the provision of access to a work in a copyright exploitation agreement will amount to an implied assignment. The example of *Larrikin* may be cited here again. In its bid to defeat the title of Larrikin in the copyright to the song *Kookaburra*, EMI tried to prove that the rules of the competition organised by the Girl Guide Association claiming property in all 'matter' submitted to the competition meant that Sinclair, the author, had impliedly assigned her copyright in the song when she allegedly entered the song in the competition. However, the court held that, even if one were to assume that Sinclair did enter the song in the competition, her signature at the end of the song indicated only her identity as an author and not her assent to an assignment of the copyright.[169] The proper construction of the term was that the word 'matter' only referred to physical property and not intellectual property. Thus, even when there was writing (rules of competition) and signature, the two were not put together to make it an assignment of copyright. It was held that the conduct of Sinclair in printing the song for the association's benefit was insufficient to show an intention to assign her copyright.[170] Such action could only have meant an implied licence to sell copies of her song and use the proceeds of sale for the association's benefit.

In *Grisbrook v MGN Ltd*,[171] the claimant was a freelance photographer, and the defendant was a publisher of many newspapers. There was no written agreement that governed the relationship between them, but the claimant used to supply photographs that he had taken of celebrities and send them to the defendant. The trade practice was that many photographers would submit their photographs, and the relevant editor would choose a photo and publish it. It was up to the photographer who took the photo to see the paper the next day and claim the price, which was typically a standard rate. It was also a trade practice of newspapers that unused photographs would go into a picture library, which the defendant could use in its future publications.[172] However, the defendant placed the back issues of the newspapers carrying the claimant's photographs on its websites, and made them commercially available for purchase by the public. The claimant claimed this to be

[169] *Larrikin Music Publishing v EMI Records* (n 159) [130].

[170] ibid [142]–[143], [155]. These issues were not raised on appeal in *EMI Songs v Larrikin* [2011] FCAFC 47.

[171] [2009] EWHC 2520 (Ch).

[172] ibid [2]–[8].

an infringement of his copyright since his original licence did not extend to the defendant exploiting his photographs in this manner.

The court held that it must be for the defendant to justify, in the absence of express terms, the basis for extending the licence to cover what would otherwise be separate acts of infringement. The court held that, as far as the compilation of the database was concerned, the defendant did have an implied licence to put the claimant's photographs to this use. However, to the extent that the photographs appearing in the back issues of the newspapers were archived and exploited through websites, it amounted to a different kind of operation which was not contemplated at the time when the licence was granted; nor was this manner of exploitation known to the claimant at the time he permitted his photographs to be used in the newspapers. The court therefore concluded that the claimant's copyright was infringed.[173]

Although in *Grisbrook* there was no express agreement, the discussion of the knowledge of the copyright owner as to what is normal exploitation of their work was far more nuanced than in *Barrett*, where there was an express contract. [174] The court in *Grisbrook* did not extend the normal exploitation to simply all forms of exploitation that the newspaper industry is capable of; rather, it limited it to what the copyright owner knew would be normal at the time he granted the licence, keeping in mind the practices of the newspaper industry.

In the Canadian case of *Robertson v Thomson Corp*,[175] a similar issue arose. Robertson, the claimant, a freelance journalist, had written two articles which were published by *Globe*, a newspaper published by the respondent group. Upon publication, *Globe* placed all articles on two of their commercial electronic databases and their subscribers could access these articles by paying a fee. Robertson claimed that this infringed her copyright in her articles. Robertson's complaint was a class action on behalf of all journalists whose articles had been placed on these commercial databases.[176] The respondent moved the trial court for summary dismissal of the suit, but the trial court dismissed respondent's action and held that there were serious issues to be tried. Having lost at both the trial and appellate stage, the respondent appealed to the Supreme Court on the issue of summary dismissal. The Supreme Court held that the databases in issue are altogether different products from daily newspapers, not only in their commercial significance for later research, but also in their format and medium of access. Thus, although the respondents have copyright in the newspaper as a collective work, their copyright does not extend to reproducing individual articles in the collective work in a decontextualised form.[177] The Supreme Court held that the implied licence from the freelance

[173] ibid [65]. The decision was confirmed on appeal in [2010] EWCA Civ 1399.
[174] See ch 4, section 1(c)(iii) above.
[175] 2006 SCC 149.
[176] ibid [11]–[18].
[177] ibid [41], [44], [47].

journalists as authors of their own works only extended to the newspapers publishing them within the format and the medium of a newspaper. If it were to be examined whether this implied licence extended beyond that, it needed to go to trial.[178] If the issue had gone on trial, the trial judge would have sought evidence as to whether the knowledge of the freelancers extended only to their works being published within the newspapers, and not for being incorporated into different formats and media.

In the last few decades, copyright owners have increasingly preferred to have collecting societies manage the exploitation of their rights. This means that a majority of the licences granted to the users of copyright are express licences. Since the collecting societies are also divided based on the rights they manage, implying one right into the licence of another is normally not possible. The celebrated Canadian case of *Bishop v Stevens* is a good example where a licence granted by the Composers, Authors and Publishers Association of Canada (CAPAC) to perform a work did not imply a right to produce ephemeral copies of the work as an incident of broadcast. The broadcaster was required to take a separate reproduction licence from the Canadian Musical Rights Reproduction Association (CMRRA), which is responsible for mechanical rights in musical works.[179] By the same token, a licence for synchronisation from Society for the Reproduction of Rights of Authors, Composers and and Publishers in Canada (SODRAC to a broadcaster does not imply a licence to make incidental copies to facilitate broadcast.[180] These cases indicate a level of disconnect between the copyright owners and the users. In these cases, the scope of licence is more a function of the remit of collecting societies' management, rather than the knowledge of the copyright owner. The upshot is that the copyright owners can let professional managers deal with licences, but the users lose their wriggle room.

3. Consumer Contracts

Consumer contracts considered here are contracts of purchase of products incorporating a copyright work. These contracts normally come into existence after a copyright exploitation contract. The purpose of a copyright owner entering into a copyright exploitation contract is so that the final product incorporating the copyright work (e.g., books or CDs) may be sold in the mass market. A consumer contract is the final contract of sale in this chain between the retailer and the consumer. While both distribution and consumer contracts arise when the products incorporating the works are in the distribution chain, the difference is that a

[178] ibid [57]–[58].
[179] [1990]2 SCR 467.
[180] *Canadian Broadcasting Corp v SODRAC 2003 Inc* [2015] 3 SCR 615.

distributor's business is to sell the product further and the consumer's purchase is outside such business or trade.[181]

The copyright owner in the work incorporated in the products sold reserves to herself all rights in the copyright. Consumer rights have strengthened across jurisdictions in recent times, and the circumstances where a licence may be implied are very limited. The act of sale of the products incorporating the copyright work is the positive act, since this is the act that provides access to the copyright work to the consumers. The positive act in most cases in consumer contracts will not be on part of the copyright owner herself, but by the manufacturer or distributors higher up in the chain who are the licensees or assignees of the relevant copyright. Once the sale is complete, the copyright owner standing back and not interfering with the use of the work is the neutral act. A consumer contract is more often than not a contract of sale in standard form. Therefore, the knowledge of the copyright owner as to the bargain is normally a non-issue. In most cases, the only variable will be the knowledge of the circumstances, which, to a limited extent, can influence the scope of the licence, if at all a licence can be implied.

Consumer contracts provide very little room for implying a licence. However, most uses which consumers need to make of the goods incorporating copyright work do not interfere with the copyright owner's exclusive rights—such as reading a book or listening to music or watching a DVD one buys. When a use does interfere with the exclusive rights, the assessment will be whether a copyright owner, given the circumstances, has it within her knowledge or contemplation that such use can be made.

For example, in *Roberts v Candiware Ltd*,[182] the question was whether the sale of a knitting pattern book entitled its purchasers to use the patterns to make knitwear for commercial purposes. The court held that the purchasers could only use the knitwear designs for personal purposes, and not for commercial purposes.[183] This is not a consumer contract per se, since the defendant used the book for commercial purpose. But if the defendant had been a consumer, namely using the book for personal purposes, she would have benefited from the implied licence. The very purpose of the copyright owner creating a pattern book is for the consumers to implement those patterns, but only for personal use. As such, for this kind of book, implied with it is a licence to the consumers that they can adapt the two-dimensional designs to three-dimensional knitwear. Reproducing the adaptation in commercial quantities is not within the contemplation of the copyright owner, and therefore the implied licence does not extend to such use. This kind of limited licence may extend to any pattern book (e.g., embroidery) or craft book.[184]

[181] See eg the UK Consumer Rights Act 2015, s 2(3), which defines a consumer as an individual acting solely or mainly outside her trade or profession. Section 1(1) extends the Act to goods, services, and digital content.

[182] [1980] FSR 352.

[183] ibid 354–55.

[184] Cf *Brigid Foley Ltd v Ellott* [1982] RPC 433.

Similarly, a question arises whether the sale of a newspaper implies that any consumer purchasing a newspaper can go on to provide a newspaper clipping service (media monitoring service) on a commercial basis. In *De Garis v Neville Jeffress Pidler Pty Ltd*,[185] although the defendant was not labelled as a consumer, the only way the defendant could have gained access to the newspaper was by purchasing a copy of it like all other consumers. The only contract into which the court could have tried to imply a licence was the contract the defendant entered into purportedly as a consumer. Having purchased many newspapers and magazines over time, the defendant had developed a business where it provided newspaper clippings of the subject matter of interest to its clients for a fee. It was held that the defendant had no implied licence to make use of the newspaper articles in this manner. Media monitoring services have prompted much litigation from newspapers that had a free online version in recent times.[186]

4. Conclusions and Connections

This chapter has adapted the framework proposed in Chapter 3 for establishing consent to a contractual context and put forward different factors that need to be considered as part of the knowledge of the copyright owner. It has argued that the tests of business efficacy and the officious bystander are nebulous and opaque, although in many of these cases the courts put forward these tests as the reason behind the implication. It went on to argue that, given the breadth of knowledge of the circumstances that the courts take into account in deciding the scope of the implied licence, it is difficult to say that the courts only try to achieve the minimum necessary for business efficacy, or the most obvious result. It has demonstrated that rationalising the case law under the framework suggested herein by appreciating the various elements of the knowledge of the copyright owner can make these decisions more transparent in showing the actual reasons for the courts to arrive at their conclusions, than a mere assertion of the tests of business efficacy or obviousness. For greater clarity, this chapter has analysed different types of contracts from bespoke commissioning contracts to standard form consumer contracts.

In *Clearsprings*, the court considered the knowledge of a common practice for software developers to retain their right to use their generic code. In *Grisbrook*, the court considered the knowledge of the normal practice of the newspaper industry. However, if these practices are consistently followed, but not within the actual knowledge of the party claimed to be subjected to it, it is only possible to rely on such practice if it has become a custom within the respective industry. This is

[185] (1990) 95 ALR 625.
[186] See eg Meltwater and Retriever Sverige in recent times. See ch 11 below for further discussion.

the focus of Chapter 6 below, where a practice may become an objective standard in an industry, claiming the status of a custom.

Consent-based implied contractual licences consider not only the knowledge of the bargain but also the knowledge of the surrounding circumstances. What if the surrounding circumstances or the peculiarity of a particular market leads to a policy objective which a court wants to give effect to? For example, in *Concrete* it was observed that the land that is subject of an approved development plan should not be allowed to become sterile. To regard consent as the basis for implying a contractual licence here might push the limits of consent. Similarly, in the *Acohs* cases, the need for commissioned works being available to the designated users as a matter of mandatory requirement in a highly regulated market makes the consent of copyright owners to such use irrelevant. Instead, the public policy considerations of health and safety may be more appropriately put forward as the basis for implying a contractual licence. This is discussed in Chapter 7 below.

6

Licences Implied by Custom

This chapter concerns licences implied based on custom.[1] As discussed in Chapter 3 above, a practice, course of dealing, or a line of conduct ('practice') becomes a custom because the members of the relevant trade, business, or profession engage in it voluntarily, repeatedly, consistently, and universally in such a way that they begin to recognise it as binding.[2] Therefore, it is not the court,[3] but the voluntary conduct of a community that gives rise to a custom. The practice of concern for this chapter is the kind that permits the use of copyright work, so that a licence may be implied from it. The modern significance of customs lies in exploring whether there are any customs on the internet now, based on which a licence may be implied for the use of copyright works online.

It is not necessary for a contract to be in existence before a licence based on a custom can be implied into it. There are three ways in which a custom-based licence may be implied the first of which is where there is a pre-existing contract, into which a custom-based licence is implied. This includes cases where there is a concluded contract in relation to a copyright work and, for the consideration received, a licence may be implied to enable the doing of a certain act. An example could be a commissioning contract in a particular industry, say architecture, into which a licence may be implied permitting a specific use of the drawings, if such practice has become a custom.[4] Secondly, where a custom-based licence can be implied on its own as a bare licence. This includes cases where there is no pre-existing contract or any other relationship between the parties, but a licence is nevertheless implied if no consideration is built into the practice underlying the custom. For example, when an academic sends an article to a journal, the usage within the academic publishing trade enables implying a licence in favour of the editor to make copies of the article for peer review.[5] No contract would have come into existence at that stage, and no expectation for this licence to be in exchange of some form of consideration is built into this licence, leading to a bare licence being implied. Thirdly, the content of the custom itself determines whether the licence is a contractual or a bare

[1] The terms custom and usage are used interchangeably. See ch 2, section 1(b) above.

[2] See ch 3, section 2 above. It was also discussed that such binding nature makes a custom a source of power, which can serve as the basis for implying a copyright licence.

[3] *Cunliffe-Owen v Teacher and Greenwood* [1967] 1 WLR 1421, 1438.

[4] In *TS & B Retail Systems Pty Ltd v 3Fold Resources Pty Ltd* [2007] FCA 151 a custom was pleaded to be the basis for implying an assignment, as discussed below.

[5] *Express Newspapers Plc v News (UK) Ltd* [1990] 3 All ER 376 was an example of a bare licence.

Implied Licences in Copyright Law. Poorna Mysoor, Oxford University Press (2021). © Poorna Mysoor.
DOI: 10.1093/oso/9780198858195.003.0007

licence. This includes situations where a practice may have developed, requiring the licence to be always in exchange for consideration; for example, a custom that if a newspaper publishes a freelance photograph already published in another newspaper, it can do so only if it pays a fee to the photographer.[6]

Whether the legal relationship into which a licence is implied goes on to become a bare licence or a contractual licence depends on the content of the custom. In Hohfeldian terms, the content of a custom may give rise to only a privilege and nothing else, which results in a bare licence; if it gives rise to a privilege in addition to duties, then it results in a contractual licence. If the use that has gone on to become a custom is not contingent upon providing consideration (such as in the journal peer review example above) then the transaction would be a bare licence. If the use that has gone on to become a custom is contingent upon consideration being paid or a contract being in existence (such as the commissioning contract and freelance photographer example above) then it would be a contractual licence. The content question is largely governed by how the participants of a particular trade, industry, or profession manifests a particular practice. A range of circumstances organic to the respective trade, industry, or profession may influence the content of the custom, and whether the custom supports a bare licence or a contractual licence.

In all of these cases, what is essential is to establish that the practice permitting the use of a copyright work in question has become a custom. If there is no methodical and transparent way of establishing a custom, then one cannot use it as the basis for implying a copyright licence—bare or contractual. Therefore, what takes greater precedence is the question of identifying the criteria that establish a custom and a framework that incorporates them, rather than the ability to ascertain whether a licence implied is a bare or a contractual licence. Accordingly, this chapter explores the criteria that go into establishing a custom within a single chapter, rather than devoting separate chapters to bare and contractual licences.

The underlying practice which permits the use of a copyright work may or may not be originally based on the consent of the parties. This means that the practice may indicate the conduct necessary for consent (a positive and a neutral act) on the part of the copyright owner, but it is not necessary for it to be so. Practices which are purely based on non-objection of the copyright owner where there may be no positive act giving access to the copyright work can also go on to become customs. This is particularly the case when the public interest is involved in the copyright work concerned being more widely available for use. It is important to note that what is being assessed here is not the individual conduct of the copyright owner, but rather its community effect. Further, if the assessment had been similar to consent-based licences, then the courts would have been required to ascertain

[6] See eg *Allen v Toronto Star Newspapers Ltd* 1995 Carswell Ont 1688; [1995] OJ No 3473, discussed below.

what the copyright owner knew or ought reasonably to have known about the circumstances. However, in this chapter, the courts presume the knowledge of the practice which has become a custom. This is possible because of the broad-based acceptance that a custom attains when it is established.[7] In other words, for courts to be able to ascertain whether such knowledge can be presumed, the custom should first be established. Thus, whether a licence may be implied or not depends less on the individual conduct of the copyright owner and more on the existence of the custom itself. Therefore, the framework for implying a licence based on custom must be different from that for consent-based licences.

Although it does not take a judicial decision to establish a custom, courts have developed criteria for proving the custom when its existence is challenged. Section 1 discusses these criteria, drawing case law from different areas of commercial law that deal with establishing a custom. It may be noted here that the case law largely concerns implying a term into a contract based on a custom. But it would be incorrect to assume that there must be a pre-existing contract before a term based on a custom may be implied, since a custom can also be the basis for implying a bare licence, as explained above. Section 2 contextualises the discussion to copyright law, and addresses the scepticism that certain scholars have expressed as to the ability of stronger players in copyright industries to establish and perpetuate customs to their sole advantage, leading to an imbalance in the application of copyright law. This helps further refine the main criteria to the copyright context. In the light of these criteria, Section 3 goes on to discuss not only cases where a custom was pressed into service before a court as the basis for implying a copyright licence, but also to support the copyright owner's demand for remuneration and generally to regulate the use of copyright works between competitors in different industries. Accordingly, this Section discusses cases that give rise to implied contractual licences, implied bare licences, implied assignments, and implied terms that do not amount to licences. It looks at customs in industries such as news and publishing, therapeutic goods, design and art, and the legal profession, where cases have been litigated.

1. General Principles of Establishing a Custom

Courts are categorical in holding that 'it does not need a court of law to establish a custom. A custom is binding on the parties irrespective of any judicial decision'.[8] Courts further observe that if a custom had to be sanctioned by a court, 'a practice

[7] *Con-Stan Industries v Norwich Winterthur Insurance (Aust) Ltd* (1986) 64 ALR 481, 486 (High Court of Australia); *Marek Machtinger v HOJ Industries Ltd* [1992] 1 SCR 986 (Supreme Court of Canada).

[8] *Kleinwort Benson Ltd v Lincoln City Council* [1999] 2 AC 349, 394; *Goodwin v Roberts* (1875) 1 App Cas 476 (HL).

so obviously universally accepted and acted on as not to be challenged could never be a usage'.[9] However, courts have identified certain criteria to prove the existence of a custom, when parties challenge its existence. The recognition of a custom by a court is valuable in that it is conclusive in establishing the custom.

(a) Criteria for establishing a custom

Cases from the nineteenth to early twentieth centuries, especially in maritime law, have contributed to identifying criteria to establish a custom. These cases continue to be relevant. In this vein, commentators and judges agree that the minimum criteria necessary to establish a custom are that a custom must be certain, notorious, and reasonable.[10] Some commentators also insist that a custom should not be contrary to law and should be recognised as binding.[11] The following paragraphs deal with each of these criteria.

(i) Certainty

Certainty refers to the recurrence of the same pattern of behaviour in such a way that it becomes definable. In *Nelson v Dahl*,[12] the court a particular maritime custom in the Baltic wood trade was in question. Jessel MR recognised that there ought to be uniformity in the practice.[13] More recently, in the leading case of *Cunliffe-Owen v Teacher and Greenwood*, the court had to ascertain the existence of a custom that the declaration of options could not be made by anyone other than a member of a stock exchange. Ungoed-Thomas J ruled that for a custom to be recognised by the courts, 'it must be certain in the sense that the practice is clearly established'.[14] These aspects are related in that if a conduct is repeated uniformly many times, then it becomes more identifiable.

This does not mean that there must be complete uniformity in following the same conduct or a universal acceptance of it. It was recognised by the Australian High Court in *Con-Stan Industries v Norwich Winterthur Insurance (Aust) Ltd* that if a custom is required to be universally accepted, 'such a requirement would always be defeated by the denial by one litigant of the very matter that the other party seeks to prove in the proceedings'.[15] Therefore, in *Sagar v H Ridehalgh & Sons Ltd*, a practice of an employer of a loom making certain deductions in wages for poor

[9] *Cunliffe-Owen v Teacher and Greenwood* (n 3) 1438.

[10] Gerard McMeel, *The Construction of Contracts: Interpretation, Implication, and Rectification* (3rd edn, OUP 2017) para 12.11.

[11] Jack Beatson, Andrew Burrows, and John Cartwright, *Anson's Law of Contract* (30th edn, OUP 2016) 170–71.

[12] (1879) 12 Ch D 568.

[13] ibid 575. See also *Wood v Wood* (1823) 1 C & P 59; Beatson, Burrows, and Cartwright (n 11) 170.

[14] *Cunliffe-Owen v Teacher and Greenwood* (n 3) 1438.

[15] *Con-Stan Industries v Norwich Winterthur Insurance (Aust) Ltd* (n 7) 485.

quality work of its employees had been followed in 85 per cent of the looms in Lancashire.[16] This was held to make the practice sufficiently certain. This was captured in *Anderson v Wadey*,[17] where Darley CJ stated that since a custom is to be inferred from a large number of individual acts, the only way to prove it is by aggregation or multiplication of a great number of instances. He went on to caution that these instances must not be miscellaneous in character, 'but must have a principle of unity running through their variety, and that unity must shew a certain course of business and an established understanding respecting it'.[18]

(ii) Notoriety

Notoriety refers to the extent of knowledge that the members of the relevant community have of the usage. In *Cunliffe-Owen*, Ungoed-Thomas went on to say that a usage must be notorious 'in the sense that it is so well known in the market in which it is alleged to exist, that those who conduct business in that market contract with the usage as an implied term'.[19] This position was reiterated in *Con-Stan Industries* that the custom relied on must be 'so well-known and acquiesced in that everyone making a contract in that situation can reasonably be presumed to have imported that term into the contract'.[20] Notoriety does not mean that the practice in question must be known to the whole world, but the practice must be well known in the context where it applies and be capable of ready ascertainment by any person who proposes to enter into a transaction.[21] The opposite of this means that the notoriety of the custom in a particular market cannot be cited in support of a practice in another market. Accordingly, in *Con-Stan Industries*, the court refused to rely on a well-known practice of marine insurance in the London market in the nineteenth century to support a practice in Australia in the twentieth century.[22]

The actual knowledge of the practice by the party need not be proved, so long as the practice is proved to be notorious.[23] Knowledge of the practice is imputed to the person in such case. Confirming this, Stephen J goes further to say in *Con-Stan Industries* that notoriety thus came to be co-extensive with the issue of presumed knowledge. In his words, a person would be presumed to know of the practice 'if it was of such notoriety that all persons dealing in that sphere could easily ascertain the nature and content' of the practice. Thus, the achievement of sufficient notoriety

[16] [1931] 1 Ch 310, 339.
[17] (1899) 20 LR (NSW) 412, 417–18.
[18] ibid 417–18. He adopted these words from Brown on Customs and Usage. These words were quoted with approval by the Australian High Court in *Majeau Carrying Co Pty Ltd v Costal Rutile Ltd* (1973) 1 ALR 1, 10 (Stephen J).
[19] *Cunliffe-Owen v Teacher and Greenwood* (n 3) 1438; *Nelson v Dahl* (1879) 12 Ch D 568, 575.
[20] *Con-Stan Industries v Norwich Winterthur Insurance (Aust) Ltd* (n 7) 485.
[21] *Strathlorne Steamship Co Ltd v Hugh Bird & Sons Ltd* [1916] SC 134 (HL).
[22] *Con-Stan Industries v Norwich Winterthur Insurance (Aust) Ltd* (n 7) 485.
[23] *Cunliffe-Owen v Teacher and Greenwood* (n 3) 1439; McMeel (n 10) paras 12.21–12.22.

is both a necessary and sufficient condition for the knowledge of a custom to be attributed to a person who was in fact unaware of it.[24]

Underlying such imputation is also the assumption that such person is a member of the concerned community (be it a trade, business, market, or profession). It follows that if the lack of knowledge of a practice is because the relevant person is not a member of that community, then the practice is not binding on such person. As such, in *Gabay v Lloyd*,[25] a certain usage of Lloyd's Coffee House was held not to bind a party who was unaware of it, because he did not effectuate his insurance policies at the Lloyd's House, and was not a member of the community of insurers who did so. The more representative a community is of the person claimed to be bound by its practices, the more likely the practices will be considered notorious, regardless of their actual knowledge. Unlike a consent-based implied licence, the conduct of concern is not of one person, but of the whole community representing such person.

(iii) Reasonableness

A custom must be reasonable.[26] A custom is reasonable if it is fair and proper and is of such kind as to be adopted by 'reasonable, honest, and right-minded men'.[27] A practice is unreasonable if it outrages justice and common sense.[28] Although these are broad and general statements of principle, at a more practical level unreasonable can also mean a practice that favours only one party. When considerable number of participants are part of one side of a particular business, they are likely to establish usages which act in favour of their side of the business. In this regard, it may help to note Brett J's observations in *Robinson v Mallett*:

> So long as they do not infringe some fundamental principle of right and wrong, they may establish such a custom; but if, on dispute before a legal forum, it is found that they are endeavouring to enforce some rule of conduct which is so entirely in favour of their side that it is fundamentally unjust to the other side, the Courts have always determined that such a custom, if sought to be enforced against a person in fact ignorant of it, is unreasonable, contrary to law, and void.[29]

Since reasonableness is a criterion for the very recognition of a practice as a custom, a practice that is unreasonable should not go on to become a custom. In this vein, if a practice is based on non-objection of the members of a trade, rather than their consent to it, then an argument of unreasonableness may be raised for

24 *Con-Stan Industries v Norwich Winterthur Insurance (Aust) Ltd* (n 7) 486.
25 (1825) 107 ER 927, 928.
26 *Nelson v Dahl* (n 19) 575.
27 *Produce Brokers Co Ltd v Olympia Oil & Cake Co Ltd* [1916] 2 KB 296, 297.
28 ibid 301.
29 [1874–74] LR 802, 818.

such practice becoming a custom on the basis that it favours one party unjustly. Under these circumstances, one may have to demonstrate larger community interest that is served by the recognition of the custom, which makes the custom reasonable when the matter is considered in the round.

There is some authority that even if a custom is unreasonable, it is enforceable if the party claiming to be bound by it was aware of it and agreed to it.[30] It is unclear if this is still the law since it is only in *Cunliffe-Owen* that it has been reiterated in modern times.[31] Assuming that the practice must have been notorious to become a custom, it would be strange to require the party for whom the custom is unreasonable to have complied with it. Nevertheless, if it is good law, this is problematic because there is no reason to perpetuate an unreasonable practice, and the awareness of the parties of the practice does not condone its unreasonableness. Further, there may be no opportunity or bargaining power to contract out of a custom .

(iv) Not contrary to law

This takes us to the next immediate question—is reasonable the same as lawful? Some scholars combine the requirement of reasonableness with lawfulness,[32] to the extent that reasonableness may be ingrained within the relevant laws. As stated above, owing to the recognition of 'unreasonable customs' under certain circumstances, a second layer of scrutiny by law is welcome. However, whether an unreasonable custom will also be found unlawful depends on whether there is a statutory or common law rule against the enforcement of such custom. Therefore, if a custom is found to violate a law, it will not be recognised, regardless of the knowledge of it by the parties to the transaction.

Anglo-African Merchants Ltd v Bayley[33] illustrates this point. It concerned a practice of insurance brokers who acted as the agents of the assured at the time of issuing the policy. But if a claim had to be made and the underwriters asked the brokers for a claim assessment report, the brokers would become agents of the underwriters instead. Megaw J doubted the notoriety of the custom. But he went on to state that, even if the custom was well known, it would not be upheld if it contradicted the principle that an agent may not act for two principals at the same time whose interests conflict with each other, unless the agent had the explicit informed consent of both principals.[34] Therefore, it may not have been a good argument on the part of the insurance brokers that the assureds were aware of the custom and, therefore, the custom should be recognised. Since the custom violated a principle of the law of agency, the court might still have not recognised the custom.

[30] *Perry v Barnett* (1885) 15 QBD 388, 393.
[31] *Cunliffe-Owen v Teacher and Greenwood* (n 3) 1439.
[32] McMeel (n 10) paras 12.19–12.20.
[33] [1970] 1 QB 311.
[34] ibid 322–24. See *North and South Trust Co v Berkeley* [1971] 1 WLR 470, 482, 484.

Other than the specific law addressing a situation (such as law of agency in *Anglo-African*), is there a general rule of common law against unreasonableness, unfairness, or unconscionability? If one party takes advantage of the other owing to their unequal bargaining power because of a custom, is there a general law to hold such custom unenforceable? Some commentators argue that there is such a common law rule,[35] although the courts have been reluctant to recognise it as a general rule outside the specific statutory expression.[36] For example, in the UK, the Unfair Contract Terms Act 1977 (UCTA), despite its grand title, does not address all unfair terms, but only the terms in a contract that exclude or restrict liability of one of the contracting parties under certain circumstances.[37] Similar provisions in relation to consumer contracts are separately addressed in the UK Consumer Rights Act 2015.[38] The applicability of these statutes outside a contractual scenario is limited to the exclusion or restriction of liability for negligence in notices that may not form part of a contract.[39] Therefore, in the UK the courts may not have an all-encompassing power to scrutinise customs for unconscionability (and thus, unreasonableness), including in relation to bare licences.

(v) Recognised as binding

The conduct should be shown to have been intended to have a legally binding effect, and the compliance with the conduct must have been the result of a belief in a legal obligation to do so.[40] A custom should be distinguished from a practice which is followed as a grace or a matter of commercial convenience. For example, in *Strathlorne Steamship Co Ltd v Hugh Bird & Sons Ltd*, the question was whether a practice of bulking the grains from their original sacs to large bins, transferring and delivering them in new sacs, was a matter of convenience of ship owners or an established custom. Upon evidence, the court confirmed that it was only a matter of convenience, and that the ship owners could adopt any other practice if found more convenient.[41]

Commentators observe that the clearest way of establishing the binding nature of a custom is to show that it has been enforced in a court, but this does not need to be so, since the courts have ruled that the binding nature of customs is not contingent upon a ruling of the court. It is sufficient for a party to establish that a custom

[35] Patrick Atiyah and Stephen Smith, *Atiyah's Introduction to the Law of Contract* (6th edn, Clarendon Press 2005) 300, 309–13.

[36] *National Westminster Bank Plc v Morgan* [1985] AC 686, 708 (Lord Scarman). Scarman LJ was referring to statutes such as the Consumer Credit Act 1974, and the like, which address unequal bargaining power.

[37] UCTA deals with exclusion clauses relating to liability for negligence (ss 2, 3, 7), breach of terms implied into a contract by statutes such as sale of goods (ss 6, 7) and breach of contract in standard form contracts (s 3).

[38] CRA relates to goods, services and digital content, and includes provisions on exclusion clauses.

[39] UCTA, s 2; CRA, s 57.

[40] Beatson, Burrows, and Cartwright (n 11) 170.

[41] *Strathlorne Steamship Co Ltd v Hugh Bird & Sons Ltd* (n 21) 137.

has been acted upon. In some cases, showing that a custom has been embodied in the code of conduct of a particular business, profession or trade, can be good evidence that the members thereof regard the code as regulating their conduct.[42]

(b) Proof of a custom

Courts insist on strict proof of each criterion, since repeated actions of a community must be proved for its consistency and universality. In *Cunliffe-Owen*, Ungoed-Thomas J noted that proving a custom is a mixed question of law and fact.[43] In *Nelson*, however Jessel MR stated that it is a question of fact and that a custom must be proved like any other term in a contract, except that it will most likely all be oral evidence.[44] While certainty and notoriety are questions of fact, reasonableness and recognition as binding can be mixed questions of fact and law. Not being contrary to law is clearly a question of law.

Since a custom relates to a community, it must be proved by persons familiar with them; typically, the members of the community. In *Nelson* Jessel MR noted that before the trial judge there were any number of witnesses who testified to the existence of a practice and there were even were more number who testified that they had not even heard of such a practice. This resulted in the practice not being recognised as a custom. It must also be noted that the evidence as to a custom is not a matter of opinion of even the most highly qualified experts; it must be of fact.[45] Judges have expressed concern that it is very rare that two witnesses give exactly the same account of a custom. Therefore, in *Tucker v Linger* where the issue was the existence of an agricultural custom Jessel MR noted that the evidence of a custom 'must be collected not from what the witnesses say they think the custom is, but from what was publicly done'.[46]

Gibbs J noted in *Majeau Carrying Co Pty Ltd v Coastal Rutile Ltd* that proving a custom is a difficult burden to discharge.[47] Sometimes the difficulty may also arise from the expense and effort involved. If not proved, however, a practice remains a 'trade practice'. A trade practice is a custom in the making, meaning it has not reached a stage where it is binding. It might assist in establishing the background of a transaction, but cannot be the basis for implication.[48]

42 Beatson, Burrows, and Cartwright (n 11) 170.
43 *Cunliffe-Owen v Teacher and Greenwood* (n 3) 1238.
44 *Nelson v Dahl* (n 19) 576.
45 McMeel (n 10) paras 12.11, 12.13.
46 (1882) 21 Ch D 18, 34.
47 (1973) 1 ALR 1, 3.
48 R Austen-Baker, *Implied Terms in English Contract Law* (2nd edn, Edward Elgar Publishing 2017) para [5.01]. The court accepted trade practices in *Clearsprings Management Ltd v Businesslinx Ltd* [2005] EWHC 1487 (Ch) and *Grisbrook v MGN Ltd* [2009] EWHC 2520 (Ch).

2. Customs in Copyright Law

The previous section dealt with the criteria for proving a custom before a court in commercial law. This section moves over to the specific context of copyright law. Copyright landscape is fraught with vast inequalities amongst its stakeholders, ranging from copyright owners that are large multinational record companies to busking musicians, and users of content such as multinational film producers to individual consumers. If a custom is to be recognised, questions must be asked as to the way it is formed, how the community where it applies is defined and, normatively, what purpose it serves. The possibility of dominant players in the market with the wherewithal to prove a self-serving practice, which is to the detriment of the other stakeholders, as a custom before a court, cannot be ruled out. The way customs are formed and maintained could then perpetuate these self-serving practices. This Section begins by discussing these concerns and analyses the extent to which the criteria identified in Section 1 above address them. To the extent that these concerns are not addressed, the discussion goes on to refine the criteria so that we have a framework for custom-based implied licences specifically suited for the copyright context.

Rothman has provided one of the most detailed analyses of the application of customs to copyright, although in the specific context of US law. Rothman argues from the perspective that in almost every case where the US courts have considered an industry practice, they have used it to reject a defence for infringement or have used it as a basis to find infringement. Very rarely, she says, the US courts have used an industry practice as a defence to copyright infringement.[49] Even if the copyright landscape in the Anglo-Australian context may be markedly different from the US, Rothman's arguments that warn of certain pitfalls in the formation of a custom specifically in the copyright context, are worth considering.

Rothman argues that the courts in the US have given effect to customs indiscriminately, to the benefit of copyright owners, and to the detriment of all other stakeholders. She illustrates this with many examples. One such is the practice prevalent among certain media industries seeking copyright clearance of all content regardless of the specific use being permitted by fair use exception, merely to avoid the risk of litigation.[50] She cites cases where courts take cognisance of this practice, even in cases where fair use exception should have applied.[51] She also gives examples of self-serving guidelines and best practices

[49] Jennifer Rothman, "The Questionable Use of Custom in Intellectual Property' (2007) 93 Va L Rev 1899, 1906.

[50] ibid 1903–904, 1911–16.

[51] She cites *Ringold v Black Entertainment Television* 126 F 3d 70, 73 (2d Cir 1997), among others.

applied by specific industries permitting the use of copyright works under very specific circumstances, in stark contrast to the general wording of the fair use exception, and the courts taking cognisance of those practices.[52] She argues based on these examples that incorporating customs within copyright law does not produce optimal results because they are one-sided, leaning towards the more powerful copyright owners. She also argues that adopting a custom as a means of private ordering should not be preferred over public ordering by law, when there are public policy goals to be achieved.[53] In conclusion, she proposes a normative framework to identify the customs that are worth adopting in copyright law.[54]

Not all of Rothman's concerns in relation to customs hold true before the UK courts, as explained in the following points. First, Rothman's definition of 'custom' is very broad. She includes industry practices, community-developed standards of behaviour, common community practices, and practices dating from time immemorial.[55] As discussed in Section 1 above, the term custom has a technical meaning, and requires a high standard of proof. Therefore, not all that Rothman regards as custom may be a custom under Anglo-Australian law. Many of them might stop at being trade practices qualifying as background evidence, and not a basis to alter legal obligations. Secondly, Rothman points out the need for certainty in identifying a custom,[56] and emphasises that a lack of certainty can lead to opportunistic use of customs. Again, certainty is a key aspect of proving a custom under Anglo-Australian law. Thirdly, built into proving a custom are the requirements that the custom be reasonable and be recognised as binding. Rothman's examples where a practice is one-sided or unduly favouring one party may not pass the reasonableness test, if the person claimed to be bound by it was unaware of it. If a practice is adopted only for the convenience of avoiding litigation, it may not pass the test of being recognised as binding. Thus, Anglo-Australian law has pre-empted some of Rothman's concerns. However, the suggestions Rothman makes to improve the reliability of customs, which are not fully captured by Anglo-Australian law, are discussed below. The factors that Rothman identifies to make customs more acceptable for adoption within copyright law can be distilled to three points. These are proposed here as further refinement of the main criteria discussed in Section 1 above.

[52] Rothman (n 49) 1905–906, 1916–24. See also Richard Epstein, 'International News Service v Associated Press: Custom and Law as Sources of Property Rights in News' (1992) 78 Va L Rev 85, where he disagrees with Rothman as to her examples.

[53] Rothman (n 49) 1907, 1947–67.

[54] ibid 1908, 1967 ff.

[55] ibid 1901, n 1.

[56] ibid 1968.

(a) Motivation

Rothman says that the more normative and aspirational a custom is, the stronger the case for its adoption.[57] She emphasises that if the motivation is merely to avoid litigation, then the case for recognising the practice as a custom should be weak. If the concern is to avoid practices adopted merely for convenience, the requirement of a custom being recognised as binding captures the motivational aspect to some extent. However, normative goals can go much further, and may help to address the issues surrounding 'unreasonable customs' discussed in Section 1(a)(iii) above. It is difficult to see a normative goal that an unreasonable custom might achieve, except maintaining freedom to contract reflected in the parties choosing knowingly to abide by an unreasonable custom. However, if the circumstances show that the parties did not enter the contract freely (such as in standard form contracts), or that there is a significant difference in their bargaining power, then there will be very little normativity in the motivation to support the custom. If an unreasonable custom is being relied on to support implying a bare licence, i.e., there is no consideration in exchange for the licence, aggravating the adverse power relations of the parties, a requirement of normativity might address this imbalance. Even in the absence of a general rule on unconscionability, this criterion may be able to capture unreasonable practices, and prevent them from becoming customs.

(b) Impact of a custom

Rothman argues that the more balanced the allocation of rights, the greater the suitability of the custom in the copyright context.[58] This point returns to the reasonableness requirement in Section 1(a)(iii) above. Given the issue of unreasonable customs, this requirement can serve as an additional pointer to the courts to ensure that the party with weaker bargaining power is not exploited simply because they have the knowledge of the unreasonable practice. Further, one of the objectives of copyright system is to balance the rights of the copyright owners with those of other stakeholders, such as copyright users and the public in general. It should not be possible to recognise a custom that goes against this objective. Therefore, this criterion is also worth incorporating within the copyright context.

[57] ibid 1970.
[58] ibid 1976.

(c) Representative nature

The more the participation of all parties concerned in formulating these practices, the more the strength of a custom.[59] Rothman says that copyright industries are given to ignoring the rights of weaker stakeholders, which can be avoided by requiring a custom to be more representative of all parties concerned. She also cautions against defining the community of operation of a custom too broadly, as potentially the whole world could be a community if a custom relates to popular content.[60] This aspect is addressed to some extent in notoriety, in that the more representative a practice is of the person claimed to be bound, the more the likelihood of a finding of notoriety. But having this factor in mind when assessing notoriety can bring more nuance to the assessment.

3. Custom as the Basis for Implying a Copyright Licence

With the above discussion in mind, we now turn to consider the cases in which courts have had an opportunity to address implying a custom-based copyright licence. It is evident from the discussion below that not in all cases have the litigants been successful in proving a custom, given the expense and effort involved. The discussion below also shows the diversity of circumstances when a custom may be pressed into service, not only by a defendant in support of an implied licence to defend against infringement, but also by a copyright owner to demand payment, restrict use and so on. Further, it is also interesting to note that in some cases customs are not directly in issue, but courts take judicial notice of them.

One of the first issues that arises is that a custom must not violate the law; but a licence by definition makes lawful what would otherwise be unlawful.[61] Does this mean that a custom cannot make legal what would otherwise be unlawful? Could a custom not permit the use of a copyright work, which if not for the custom, be an infringement? The High Court decision in *British Leyland Motor Co Ltd v Armstrong Patent Co Ltd*, raised this issue.[62] The question was whether there is a custom permitting repair service providers to manufacture spare parts in advance of receiving orders. The court held that to recognise a custom to that effect would be to 'permit infringement with impunity'.[63] Some commentators

[59] ibid 1972–75.

[60] Jennifer Rothman, 'Why Custom Cannot Save Copyright's Fair Use Defense' (2008) 93 Va L Rev In Brief 243, 246. However, in principle, it should be possible to define a community broadly, if it can be shown that its participants have consistently followed certain practices. An example is the community of internet users engaging in consistent practices on the internet that can go on to become customs. See ch 9 below.

[61] *Thomas v Sorrell* (1672) Vaugh 330, 351.

[62] [1982] FSR 481.

[63] ibid 493. For the appropriate basis for implying a licence in this context see ch 8, section 1(b) below.

understand this to mean that a custom cannot be relied on in defence of copyright infringement.[64]

This cannot be correct. When it is possible for an individual copyright owner to consent to specific copyright uses, a community of copyright owners can likewise actively consent to or passively not object to a specific use, if all other requirements of establishing a custom are satisfied. Just as one can alter one's powers and privileges by way of private ordering through contracts and licences, one can also subject oneself to the private ordering in a community. Law does not prohibit private ordering. However, what the law does dictate is that in fashioning such private ordering, one cannot violate other laws. As the discussion in Section 1 above reveals, a significant part of commercial law in the late nineteenth and early twentieth centuries was governed by customs. The same appears to be true for copyright industries that were at a nascent stage at the time.[65] The decision in *Springfield v Thame* was based on a prevalent practice where a freelance journalist submitted his story to a newspaper and the newspaper could publish it in return for a payment that was standard in those days.[66] We still rely on some of these practices to this day without questioning. For example, when a person sends a letter to the editor of a newspaper commenting on a matter published in that newspaper, a licence is implied by custom that the editor is permitted to publish the letter in the newspaper. These practices reveal that it is possible for a custom to be the basis for implying a copyright licence, so long as the custom is established in the manner required by the criteria discussed above. We will examine in the following paragraphs certain sector-specific customs.

(a) Newspaper and publishing industry

An example where a newspaper custom was litigated is *Express Newspapers Plc v News (UK) Ltd.*[67] Here, a reporter of the plaintiff newspaper had managed to interview Ms Pamella Bordes, a person in the public eye owing to her relationships with persons in power. The reporter wrote up the story quoting extensively from the interview, which was published the next day. Having read the story in the plaintiff newspaper, the defendant also carried a story quoting extensively from the interview by the plaintiff's reporter. Ten days before the hearing, the defendant published a story based on an interview by its reporter with a member of the royal family, again quoting extensively from the interview. And the plaintiff, having seen the defendant's newspaper, published in its own newspaper a couple of days later

[64] *Halsbury's Laws, vol* 32 (5th edn, LexisNexis 2019) para 51.
[65] Mary Vitoria and others, *Laddie, Prescott and Vitoria: The Modern Law of Copyright* (5th edn, LexisNexis 2018) para [25-15].
[66] (1903) 89 LT 242, 243.
[67] [1990] 3 All ER 376.

its own story, also quoting extensively from the interview by the defendant's reporter. Both parties sued each other in different proceedings.[68] The plaintiff complained of infringement, but defended itself based on a licence implied by custom in the newspaper industry, that a newspaper is allowed to pick up a story published in another newspaper, and publish it in its own words in its newspaper. This may not have been a problem ordinarily since there is no copyright in information. However, the concern was as to the substantial similarity of the story as a whole and of the quoted text from the interview, over which the interviewer claimed copyright based on *Walter v Lane*.[69]

The court noted that upon publication of the defendant's interview with the member of the royal family, many other newspapers had picked up the story and had published it in their own words. Therefore, the court acknowledged that there may be a custom in the newspaper industry to this effect, which could be proved at the trial.[70] However, since the plaintiff had made contradictory claims in these two proceedings, based on the principle that a litigant cannot approbate and reprobate at the same time, the court dismissed the suit summarily.[71] Had the plaintiff not raised these contradictory claims in these proceedings, this case may have gone to trial, where a custom permitting a newspaper to pick up stories and quotes from interviews from other newspapers, may have been established. Such custom could then have become the basis for implying a copyright licence.

It is important to note that this implied licence is a bare licence, since the competing newspapers were not in a contractual relationship. Indeed, neither newspaper engaged in a positive act providing access to their content to the other. This custom has developed based more on non-objection of the parties than on consent to use their copyright works. Such custom, if factually proved to exist with certainty and notoriety, would nevertheless have been regarded as reasonable, because as the court acknowledged, there is a clear public interest in not recognising monopoly in news, so that a wider dissemination of news and information may be achieved. Such non-objection would also not have been against the law because the copyright owner can choose not to assert their right and by doing so, they violate no law. The custom would have satisfied the aspirational motivation because of the public interest in news. It would have balanced the copyright owner's own rights against those of the consumers of news. Applying between actors within newspaper industry, this custom would have stayed true to the need for being representative within the industry.

[68] ibid 377–78.

[69] ibid 380, 383. *Walter v Lane* [1900] AC 539.

[70] ibid 380. The court distinguished *Walter v Steinkopff* [1892] 3 Ch 489, which had held that quoting from other newspaper reports was an unreasonable practice, on the basis that the newspaper industry has changed in the last 100 years and, in any event, that case was not about quoting from the words of an interviewee.

[71] ibid 383–84.

There is, however, an additional issue in this case of the spoken word having its own copyright, which was addressed in this case by declaring *Walter v Lane*[72] to be still good law. The court held that the journalist exercises sufficient effort and skill to record the spoken words, such that an independent copyright comes into existence in the journalist's favour.[73] There is scholarly support to the argument that *Walter v Lane* is no longer good law.[74] Let us assume that it is not, and that the interviewees in both these cases have a copyright in their spoken words coming into existence the moment their words were 'recorded, in writing or otherwise' under s 1(3) of the Copyright, Designs and Patents Act 1988 (CDPA). It would appear from the reading of this decision that there may have been a separate licence implied from the person interviewed in favour of the newspaper, which may arise from another custom in the newspaper industry. This custom may be to the effect that when a person gives an interview to a journalist from a newspaper, the interviewee's copyright in their spoken words is impliedly licensed to the newspaper to be published per se or as part of a story. It is unlikely that there would be an implied assignment by custom from the interviewee in favour of the newspaper that organises the interview, but only a licence, resulting in the interviewee retaining the copyright in the spoken words. If spoken words reported in one newspaper are again quoted in a subsequent newspaper as part of their own story, it would appear that the custom-based implied licence from the author of the spoken words (interviewee) could also extend to the subsequent newspaper, to publish as part of their story. This is a bare licence that can come into existence as the situation arises, rather than tied to the parties who have a contractual relationship. It is possible for a newspaper to arrange with an interviewee that the interview is exclusively published by that newspaper, but it may still not prevent other newspapers from reporting that the interview took place.

This custom might only exist in the newspaper industry and might not be generally applicable in all publishing industries owing to the public interest associated with news. It cannot be extended to literary works in general. A weak attempt was made to claim the existence of a custom in the industry of mock examination papers for medical students. In *Boyapati v Rockefeller Management Corporation*, the claimant was in the business of publishing mock exam papers for medical students. The defendant copied a substantial number of these question and answers.[75] When the claimant sued for copyright infringement, one of the defences put forward by the defendant was that it was common among providers of preparation exams to borrow from other copyright material, without permission or acknowledgement. The court disagreed with the defendant and held it liable for infringement.[76] Apart

[72] [1900] AC 539.
[73] *Express Newspapers Plc v News (UK) Ltd* (n 67) 380–81.
[74] Justine Pila, *The Subject Matter in Intellectual Property* (OUP 2017) 159–61.
[75] [2008] FCA 995 [1]–[5] (Federal Court of Australia).
[76] ibid [50]–[51].

from the fact that no evidence was produced to show the certainty and notoriety of the practice, this practice could never have been held reasonable or recognised as binding. The content of the literary work not being 'news' makes all the difference, although to some extent the exam questions are factual.

These practices within the newspaper industry do not extend to news clipping services. An argument was put forward in *De Garis v Neville Jeffress Pidler Pty Ltd* that it was common practice for newspaper clipping services to copy extracts from published newspapers and make them available to their own readers, but no evidence was produced in support. The court held that even if evidence had been produced of a common practice, it would not be justifiable to reproduce these works without the copyright owner's permission.[77] News clipping services are not in the business of providing news, but in the news archiving business. The public interest associated with provision of news cannot be extended to news archiving services. Therefore, even if there was a practice that was certain and notorious, it would not be reasonable, nor would it be possible to recognise it as binding.

It has long been thought that when a person sends a letter to a newspaper, a bare licence is implied based on a custom in favour of the newspaper to publish the letter. But does this custom extend any writing sent to the newspaper? The question arose in *Tumber v Independent Television News Ltd (ITN)* .[78] Here, the claimant had written a love poem which had gained some publicity and the defendant, ITN, wanted to interview the claimant. Its employee telephoned Tumber and spoke to him about an article being published on the defendant's website about him and his work. The employee also asked for a copy of the poem, which Tumber sent her. An article about the poem appeared on ITN's website, but later ITN also provided a copy of the poem itself on its website. Tumber saw that the poem was also published and complained to the defendant about it the next day. ITN took it down, within which time internet users had already accessed the poem and had also linked to it.[79] Tumber brought an action for copyright infringement against ITN. ITN claimed that it had the benefit of an implied licence both on the basis of consent and custom.[80]

Tumber also brought an application to strike out the defences and for summary judgment. In support of the custom, ITN relied on cases including *De Garis*, and on commentaries that confirmed the existence of a custom in the newspaper industry permitting a newspaper to publish the letter sent to it. On the question of whether this would extend to the poem, ITN argued that there is a sliding scale of when a work will become too long to be published and it is a matter to be explored with evidence. Although Hacon J expressed 'serious doubts' about whether

77 (1990) 95 ALR 625, 635.
78 [2017] EWHC 3093 IPEC)
79 ibid [1]–[4].
80 For discussion on consent-based bare licence see ch 4, sections 1(a), (b), and (c)(iii) above.

an implied licence based on a custom existed in this case, he was not 'in a position to rule it out altogether'.[81]

While Hacon J did recognise the possibility of a custom-based implied licence, one must also ask whether the claimant was in the position of an ordinary newspaper reader who sent a letter to a newspaper about an issue. The fact that Tumber was indeed the subject matter of the news and the interview should have distinguished him sufficiently for this custom not to apply to him. The fact that his work had potential for exploitation unlike a letter written to a newspaper,[82] and the fact that he may have sent it to help the employee prepare for the interview both seem reasonable and relevant. The sliding scale that ITN argued about makes no sense. If the argument was that the longer the work, the weaker the custom justifying the publication of the work, then the poem being the longest love poem ever written should have weakened this custom. In case of a letter addressed to the editor, although technically the editor has the licence to publish whole of the letter regardless of its length, the editor might edit the letter to the relevant publication's editing style. But this does not mean that there is a sliding scale. On the whole, the defence of custom-based implied licence in this case should also have been struck out, even if Hacon J wanted to affirm the existence of a licence to publish a letter sent to the editor based on custom.

Within the newspaper industry, if the work is an artistic work in photographs, the custom is different, as demonstrated by the judgment of the Ontario Court of Justice in *Allen v Toronto Star Newspapers Ltd*, but reversed on appeal. Allen, the claimant, was a freelance professional photographer who was commissioned by a magazine, *Saturday Night*, to take photographs of an eminent politician for the magazine cover. Allen took the photographs and one of them was used as the magazine cover. Once this issue of *Saturday Night* was published, Toronto Star, the defendant newspaper, featured an article about the same politician and reproduced the magazine's cover as a whole. When Allen saw it, he sued Toronto Star for copyright infringement.[83] He argued that the custom in the newspaper industry was that if a newspaper wants to reproduce a photograph that has appeared in another newspaper, the former must pay for it. In other words, the custom claimed in relation to photographs was that there would be an implied licence in favour of subsequent publications to reproduce the photographs so long as it is paid for. Allen produced many witnesses to support this claim. Toronto Star denied the custom and, in the alternative, pleaded fair dealing for newspaper summary. The trial court rejected the fair dealing argument and concluded that a custom indeed exists where the subsequent newspaper must pay for reproduction in its own newspaper of a published photograph.[84]

[81] *Tumber v Independent Television News Ltd* (n 78) [14], [17].
[82] The claimant sold his poems on Amazon. See ibid [27].
[83] *Allen v Toronto Star Newspapers Ltd* (n 6) [2]–[5].
[84] ibid [8]–[16], [34]–[39].

This case seemed to be a triumph of a custom that went through a court trial and was upheld. A line of witnesses had been examined. Although an assessment based on the criteria in Section 1 above had not been specifically carried out, from the evidence presented, it appeared that the custom was certain and notorious. It is reasonable for a copyright owner to expect the reproduction of her work on a commercial scale to be remunerated. In its motivation and impact, the custom seemed to be geared towards empowering the copyright owner—especially the freelancers who do not normally have financial power in comparison to big media companies. This would have been a good example where the content of the custom determined the implied licence to be contractual. However, the appellate court reversed the decision and upheld fair dealing. In a very strange reading of the case, the Court regarded the cover as an independent work in its own right and *Saturday Night* had not objected to its cover's reproduction.[85] This ignored the fact that the cover was a compilation of original works, most significant of which was the photograph. The copyright in the photograph did not merge with that of the cover, but had been retained by Allen. The Court was swayed by the fact that the politician was very much in the news, and therefore the use of the cover was fair dealing as a newspaper summary. The Canadian Copyright Act 1985 (CCA) does not exclude photographs from news reporting, which the CDPA does for exactly this reason.[86] Reporting news often involves reproducing photographs in their entirety, and if that is captured within fair dealing, then an important stream of revenue is lost for the photographers.

While the appellate court in Canada gave the decision on fair dealing, the same year in the UK the High Court decided it in the copyright owner's favour. In *Banier v News Group Newspapers Ltd*, the plaintiff was a well-known photographer, who had taken photos of a member of the royal family.[87] His agent had licensed their publication in a particular newspaper (which licence had been disputed in another proceeding). The defendant newspaper wanted to publish these photographs, but could not establish contact with the plaintiff's agent in time to obtain the licence. The defendant published the photographs anyway. When sued for infringement, the defendant claimed that the practice among newspapers was always to obtain a licence beforehand. However, if it was not possible, given the tight deadlines within which newspapers function, there was a practice among newspapers to publish a photo which had already been published in another newspaper, and obtain a licence later. There was also an expectation to pay a licence fee where appropriate. Lightman J held the practice to be clearly 'unjustified and unlawful'.[88]

[85] 1997 Carswell Ont 4087 [35]–[44].
[86] Copyright, Designs and Patents Act 1988 (CDPA), s 30(2).
[87] [1997] FSR 812, 813–14.
[88] ibid 815.

Although one cannot quarrel with the insistence in this decision on the desirability of taking a prior express licence from a copyright owner, one may sympathise with the tight deadlines that the newspapers work with. The first instance decision in *Allen* strikes the right balance between the financial concerns of freelance photographers and the operational considerations of newspaper industry. As discussed above, the licence being contingent upon payment of a licence fee makes the underlying custom a more balanced one. As discussed above, the custom recognised in *Allen* satisfies the main and the refined criteria for the recognition of customs. Photographs also have newsworthiness. While it is commendable for the CDPA to have excluded photographs from news reporting, the implied licence of the kind in *Allen* would have been a reasonable compromise since the financial interests of the photographer are not harmed. With the *Banier* decision, the existence or the future recognition of a custom like the one recognised in *Allen* may be difficult.

(b) Product information in therapeutic industries

Apart from newspaper industry, the sharing of information between competitors also attracts scrutiny in other industries such as the therapeutic goods industry. The Australian case of *Sanofi-Aventis Australia Pty Ltd v Apotex Pty Ltd*[89] is a good illustration. Apotex registered a generic version of leflunomide on the Australian Register of Therapeutic Goods, to supply it for the treatment of psoriatic arthritis and rheumatoid arthritis. Sanofi-Aventis, the holder of the patent for the originator drug, Arava, saw this as a threat to infringe its patent and brought an action against Apotex. Sanofi also claimed that Apotex had copied the product information for Arava that it had prepared and submitted for approval to the relevant authority. Apotex claimed that there is a custom that enables a generic drug company to copy the product information from the originator company.[90] In support, Apotex produced the affidavit of a solicitor which annexed product information for many drugs for which the originator included Sanofi and those of the generics, to demonstrate that the product information for the generic versions were close copies of the product information of the originator and Sanofi had not complained of copyright infringement in relation to these. Much later in the proceedings, Sanofi produced product information of generic drugs which did not copy the originator product information to the same extent as Apotex had done.[91] The question before the court was whether this practice had become a custom.

89 (2011) 281 ALR 705.
90 ibid [6], [283], [289], [369].
91 ibid [363], [376].

The trial court held that the overall evidence was insufficient to establish a long-standing and industry-wide practice, although the affidavit had revealed that the generic companies often copied from the originator, including product information which suggested such copying by Sanofi-Aventis itself. It observed that in comparison with the total numbers of product information approved, the product information in evidence lacked any meaningful context, and that the evidence did not reveal 'anything more than apparent neutrality by participants in the industry as to the copyright implications of such copying' until the present case. It went on to add that such neutrality alone could not be the basis for discerning that the 'participants in the industry implicitly consented to an industry-wide practice of copying'.[92]

One must accept that the assessment of the judge as to the insufficiency of evidence to demonstrate that the practice was notorious and had been recognised by the participants of the industry as binding. However, if it had been a consent-based implication, one could have agreed with the judge that if there is no positive act, mere neutrality is insufficient for implied licence to be established. However, the judge was considering whether a custom had been established. She discussed no authority that enumerates the requirements of establishing a custom. As discussed above, in principle, there appears to be no reason why neutrality or not taking objection to a certain conduct cannot become a custom if it can be proved that such non-objection as a practice is certain, notorious, and reasonable. *Express Newspapers* is a good example to demonstrate the possibility of a custom based on the non-objection of the copyright owner.

Apotex appealed but the appellate court agreed with the trial court.[93] It confirmed that non-objection to copying and non-assertion of copyright cannot be seen as an agreement on the part of the participants of the industry to let their product information be copied by the generic drug companies. The Court went on to observe that Apotex did not identify any contract into which the custom could be implied. It also noted that Apotex did not establish that customs could apply between competitors. The Court found that a mere non-objection by the copyright owners could not be read as their surrender of the liberty to compete.[94]

The premise that a custom can only be implied into a contract is incorrect. As we have seen above, in *Express Newspapers* the court was willing to accept as a custom the practice of copying reported interviews between newspapers who were not in any contractual relationship. If there was no contract in existence, then a custom can be implied as a bare licence. *Express Newspapers* is also an example of a custom that applies between competitors. If the competitors all belong to the same industry, there is nothing in principle preventing the application of the custom to

[92] ibid [376].
[93] [2012] FCAFC 102 [75] (Keane CJ); [206] (Bennett and Yates JJ).
[94] ibid [77]–[80] (Keane CJ); [202]–[203] (Bennett and Yates JJ).

all of them, again like in the newspaper industry. Indeed, that is the basis on which customs are recognised—that it has been consistently and notoriously observed by the participants, who will most likely be competitors. Assuming there was sufficient evidence to establish certainty and notoriety of this practice, it would have been held reasonable. As in the newspaper industry, there is clear public interest in substantially reproducing the product information, since the authorities have the discretion to ask for safety and efficacy trial results from the generic drug producers if they claim their product information to be different from that of the originator's. This would not only delay the approval process, but also add to the cost of producing generic drugs. Such non-objection would also not be contrary to law because the copyright owner can choose not to object to its work being copied. Further, the compelling public interest argument would also have made the custom aspirational and balanced. It is unfortunate that the shortfall in this case was the evidence produced in support of the custom.

(c) Software industry

In *Clearsprings Management Ltd v Businesslinx Ltd*, the court noted the existence of a common practice in the software industry. The practice was that the developers could retain their ownership to their own generic code which they use to bring about routine commands in a software, and not have to assign rights in it even if the copyright in the commissioned software is assigned.[95] In that case, it was not proved to have become a custom.

An attempt was made in *Trumpet Software v OzEmail Pty Ltd* to establish a custom as to the scope of licence that may be implied in relation to software distributed as shareware. As noted in Chapter 4 above, software distributed as shareware gave a bare licence to an end user to try the software before buying it for a length of time expressly stated on the cover (normally 30 days). After this period, if the user retained the software, she had to register herself as a user and pay a licence fee.[96] The scope of this licence was at issue, with OzEmail claiming that the licence extended to a mass distribution of the software by any other user and Trumpet claiming that it did not. Evidence was led by both Trumpet and OzEmail, but the court found that the evidence revealed opinions of experts, rather than statements of fact. The court held that the evidence on neither side met the high evidentiary requirement to establish a custom. However, the court still took note of the practices of the industry when software is distributed as shareware.[97]

[95] *Clearsprings Management Ltd v Businesslinx Ltd* (n 48).
[96] (1996) 34 IPR 481, 485.
[97] ibid 499–500.

The existence of the distribution mechanism of shareware was not in dispute. It may be that the mere use of the word shareware with the trial period had become a bare licence implied by custom. But who else the bare licence extended to had not yet become a customary practice. Nevertheless, this reinforces the argument above that a custom can support the implication of a bare licence.

(d) Design installations and the art sector

Moving on to other industries, in *TS & B Retail Systems Pty Ltd v 3Fold Resources Pty Ltd* the claimants were in the business of manufacture, supply, and installation of shop fittings including interior fittings, displays, stock presentations, and shelves for retailers. The defendants were previously employed with the claimant. The claimant defaulted on its loans and receivers were appointed to sell its assets. Having realised that their jobs would not survive, the defendants set up their own competing business. The defendants took manufacturing drawings with them from the claimant to assist in their business. The claimant sued them for copyright infringement.[98] One of the defences relied on by the defendants was that the copyright in the drawings was impliedly assigned to the relevant customer for whom the design services were being provided, based on a custom in the trade. The argument was that since the drawings were so specific to the client's needs and configurations that a practice had developed in that industry whereby the copyright owner of the drawings impliedly assigned the copyright in the drawings to the client. The defendant produced an agreement entered into by the claimant with one of its customers in relation to the drawings which were not at issue in these proceedings, in support of the custom. The court ruled that, for a custom to be established, it must be certain and notorious, holding the evidence produced to be insufficient. It went on to point out that the other agreements produced in evidence in the proceedings with other retail outlets showed a vast diversity of terms, and therefore, it was difficult to see a consistent practice in this regard.[99] The practice of assigning copyright in the drawings to the respective client could not have gone on to become a custom because of lack of certainty in that practice. Each arrangement with each client at different points in time was different, lending these to an argument of implied by consent, rather than one by custom.[100]

A customary practice in art industry was at issue in *Danowski v The Henry Moore Foundation*,[101] although not in support of an implied licence, but rather an implied

[98] *TS & B Retail Systems Pty Ltd v 3Fold Resources Pty Ltd* (n 4) [4]–[14].
[99] ibid [148]–[150].
[100] ibid [151]–[157]. The court also considered implied by consent arguments, but held that such licence if it can be implied only extended to isometric drawings and not to manufacturing drawings of the claimant.
[101] [1996] EMLR 364 (CA).

reservation. The well-known British sculptor, Henry Moore, partway through his career, established the defendant, a charitable company limited by guarantee, to which he transferred all his previous works and his copyright in them. He also established a wholly owned subsidiary of the defendant, with which he entered into an employment agreement, and transferred to it all his tools of the trade and work in progress. The employment agreement stated that the company was the owner of copyright in any work Moore created during the course of his employment. After his death, his daughter—who inherited his assets—claimed that, during his lifetime, Moore had retained what are called artist's copies of certain works, as is customary among sculptors to do so. Therefore, this custom should be read into his employment contract. As a result, she claimed that these artist's copies belonged to her, rather than to the defendant.[102]

Nourse LJ relied on the description of the custom of artist's copies from the trial records and described it as follows. When an artist creates a work that can be reproduced (using say a mould for a sculpture, lithograph for a print, etc) the artist can choose to declare it to be limited edition to a purchaser. If the artist does so, then the artist must limit the copies to the number declared. However, this is always subject to the artist's right to make two additional copies for themselves, called artist's copies, for the artist's own purposes. The artist may retain these for future reference, give them for exhibitions, or even sell them. Reviewing the evidence, Nourse LJ held that, although artist's copy convention was a practice amounting to a custom in the art trade applying between the artist and a purchaser of a limited edition work, the evidence did not show that this practice was likewise followed between an employer and an employee. The expert evidence could speak only to the existence of the custom when the artist is self-employed, and any evidence as to the existence of the custom when the artist is employed was only a matter of opinion of the experts. Nourse LJ held such an opinion to be inadequate to support the application of the custom to an employment relationship.[103] He noted that the existence of a general custom in relation to 'a particular part of a trade does not cause it to become a general custom or usage of the trade generally'.[104]

He also went on to hold that, even if the custom was established between an employer and employee, such custom would be inconsistent with the express terms of Moore's employment agreement and its general tenor.[105] By general tenor, Nourse LJ meant the employment agreement expressly vesting copyright with the company, read with the sale of Moore's tools of trade to the company. He held that together these convey that Moore had transferred any artist's copies he had retained of his works to the company. Nourse LJ did not have to consider what was

102 ibid 367–70.
103 ibid 371, 373–75.
104 ibid 375.
105 ibid 376. McCowan LJ and Thorpe LJ also agreed with Nourse LJ's decision. See ibid 376–78.

in the agreement with the purchasers of the limited-edition sculptures, as these agreements would have been entered into by the company of which Moore was an employee, and not by Moore himself. On this basis, the court held that since the company owned copyright in all works Moore created during the course of his employment, if any artists copies were created, those should have belonged to the company, and not to Moore.

The custom was that when a self-employed artist sold their limited-edition work to a buyer, implied into that sale was a reservation for the artist to retain the ownership of two copies of the work. Although the court recognised artist's copy as a custom, it held in effect that by entering into an employment contract Moore had contracted out of this custom. Artist's copy custom emanates not only from the copyright ownership but also the ownership of the physical copies of the work. As the owner of copyright in the works he creates, the artist is free to create any number of copies of his work. As the creator of the works, he also has the knowhow and possibly also the required material for reproducing the work. When the artist declares a work as a limited edition, he places a restriction on his ownership powers in the tangible property. In this case, Moore had transferred his copyright by way of an employment agreement to the company and the work in progress and the tools of the trade from which the materials for the creation of copies of the work came. This indicated to the court that the artist's copies were transferred to the employer. Thus, the custom did not serve as the basis for implying a reservation into the employment agreement retaining the ownership of two copies of limited-edition works.

However, *Danowski* is still a good illustration of how a custom applies in a copyright case, discussing in detail the evidence of the custom at the trial.[106] The motivation behind the custom being to assist the artist's artistic freedom and livelihood is clearly not for mere convenience. By defining the community to which the custom applies as being only the self-employed artists, and not extending it to those in employment, the court did not make the custom too broad based. Thus, the existence and maintenance of this custom stand on a firm footing based on the main and the refined criteria discussed above.

(e) Judicial proceedings and legal documents

There have been instances where courts have acknowledged certain customs being in existence in relation to judicial proceedings and legal documents, although the existence of the custom was not the main issue, nor any evidence presented to prove it. However, these customs are so certain and notorious that

[106] ibid 368. Nourse LJ stated that the trial took 20 days and the trial judge's decision ran to 118 pages.

judges have proceeded to take judicial notice of these customs. Of these, some have been used as a basis to imply a copyright licence. The Canadian case of *Cojocaru v British Columbia Women's Hospital* recognised the practice of judges copying from the pleadings and affidavits to write judgments, so long as the judge applies her mind to the judicial process.[107] The main issue was not copyright. There is clearly no contractual relationship between the lawyers who are copyright owners of these affidavits and summary of arguments, but there is a positive act on the part of the lawyers in submitting these documents to the judges in a proceeding. Thus, a bare licence may be implied based on the custom that judges may reproduce the content of affidavits. In the UK, the use of a copyright work in a judicial proceeding is excluded from copyright infringement under section 45(1) of the CDPA.

In other cases, customs have been relied on not to imply a licence for the use of a copyright work, but to reinforce the copyright owner's ability to reproduce her own work. In the Canadian case of *Pizza Pizza Ltd v Gillespie*,[108] the defendant was in the employ of the claimant and subsequently left the claimant to set up his own business called Chicken Chicken. The claimant alleged that the defendant took with him confidential information, including the franchise agreement, such that a substantial part of the defendant's franchise agreement reproduced the claimant's franchise agreement. There was a possibility that the same law firm may have drafted both the franchise agreements. The court held that the copyright in these agreements belonged to the law firm and there was no assignment of its copyright to either claimant or defendant. If further noted that it was a common practice among lawyers to use agreements as a template to prepare agreements for other clients.[109]

Similarly, in another Canadian authority, *Strother v 3464920 Canada Inc*,[110] the claimant accused the solicitor in a firm of breach of fiduciary duty and conflict of interest, and one of the grounds relied on was that the solicitor had copied from the agreement drafted for the claimant to prepare an agreement for the claimant's competitor. The court observed that 'recycling precedents is the life-blood of corporate law practice'. It further held that a document prepared for one client is part of the lawyer's work product which could be reused any number of times so long as confidential information had not been disclosed. It held further that 'the practice of law would be hopelessly inefficient and costly for clients if transactional documents had to be reinvented rather than customized'.[111]

107 [2013] 2 SCR 357 [37]–[50] (McLachlin CJ).
108 [1990] OJ No 2011 (Supreme Court of Ontario).
109 ibid 28.
110 [2007] 2 SCR 177.
111 ibid [111].

4. Conclusions and Connections

This chapter has considered a copyright licence implied by custom. For the establishment of the custom, the main criteria as recognised under contract law and more refined criteria as appropriate for copyright were identified.

Courts look at communities for the operation of customs—such as trade, business, or profession. Often, in modern times, it may not be possible to identify such communities, because their membership is too disparate. For example, if one were to consider a practice that applies to purchasers of machinery, the community to which such practice applies would be potentially very large. Instead of defining communities, a better approach may be for the courts to categorise certain types of contracts to which certain common incidences apply. In the above example, in all contracts for the sale of goods with limited life, the common incidence is that the goods will require repair at some point. To facilitate repair without infringing copyright in those goods, a licence may be implied. The justification for such implication is stronger for policy reasons than for custom. This leads us to the Chapter 7 below, which considers policy-based implied contractual licences.

In cases such as *Express Newspapers* or *Sanofi-Aventis*, the court was ready to imply a licence based on a custom not because of its consensual origin, but because of the copyright owner's non-objection alone. It has been argued by this author above that even if there was no positive act on the part of the copyright owner providing access to the work to a competitor, a custom can still come into existence when there is public interest to support it. The public interest can be in the free flow of news or of essential product information on which the assessment of safety and efficacy of therapeutic products depend. It is possible in rare circumstances that public interest alone is sufficient for a bare licence to be implied, without having to prove that such practice has also become a custom. These cases are discussed in Chapter 8 below.

The formation, maintenance, and even perishing of customs within a community is a constant and inevitable process. With the interaction between different stakeholders over time, different practices come to be acknowledged, adopted, repeated, and recognised as binding. It is possible that the existence of the digital environment over the last two decades has resulted in practices that meet the criteria for establishing a custom. Whether such customs might exist and how they may be used for implying a licence on the internet is discussed in Part III below.

7
Policy-based Implied Contractual Licences

This chapter focuses on the cases where there is a pre-existing contract, and a policy-based licence is implied into such contract. To the extent that a contract exists, there is a certain voluntariness on part of the copyright owner in entering into the contract. However, a term is implied regardless of the consent of the copyright owner. Therefore, instead of assessing the conduct and knowledge of the copyright owner, it is more appropriate in these cases to ascertain if the implication is attributable to the courts giving effect to policy objectives. In this sense, although the contract is entered into on a consensual basis, the implication of a licence departs from the consensual basis, moving towards a policy-based implication.

The methodology that the courts currently adopt for implying a term by law, as it is called in contract law, is to identify the type of contract based on the common incidents that all contracts of that type share; and imply the term into the contract if it is necessary to do so.[1] Despite the support for courts engaging in policy matters, the methodology for implying a term by law says nothing about policy, be it the need for identifying it or giving effect to it. This makes the methodology diluted to a degree that courts become blind to the distinction between cases that are amenable to implying a term in fact and those amenable to implying one by law. The discussion below analyses the methodology for implying a term by law to see how it may be made more transparent, so that we can go on to apply it for implying copyright licences specifically.

Among the scholars who support the courts' powers to imply a term by law in contract law, Peden foregrounds strong arguments for the courts to be more honest about the policy reasons that drive their decisions, rather than hide behind the vagueness of the methodology. She asserts that the list of policy reasons that the courts can consider is non-exhaustive.[2] She puts forward several policy considerations to which courts give effect without acknowledging them as policy—such as placing the burden of a term on the party best able to bear it, which may manifest itself in reallocating rights within the contract, insuring, or indemnifying a loss, and so on. Bringing about a balance in a standard form contract can also be one of the objectives that the courts pursue. She points out that considerations of the welfare

[1] Patrick Atiyah and Stephen Smith, *Atiyah's Introduction to the Law of Contract* (6th edn, Clarendon Press 2005) 160; see also Jack Beatson, Andrew Burrows, and John Cartwright, *Anson's Law of Contract* (30th edn, OUP 2016) 155.

[2] Elizabeth Peden, 'Policy Concerns Behind Implication of Terms in Law' (2000) 117 LQR 459, 475–76.

Implied Licences in Copyright Law. Poorna Mysoor, Oxford University Press (2021). © Poorna Mysoor.
DOI: 10.1093/oso/9780198858195.003.0008

of society underlie the policies that support implying of the term into the contract in these cases. She also postulates that implying a term is the court's way of granting a remedy in cases where no other remedy would be possible or appropriate.[3] Let us see how the existing methodology can find a place for policy considerations.

In the words of Lord Cross in *Liverpool City Council v Irwin*, while implying a term by law, the court lays down a 'general rule' that in all contracts of 'a certain type', some provision is to be implied, unless the parties have expressly excluded it.[4] In *Irwin*, the category was a tenancy agreement between the council and its tenants in a high-rise block of flats. The logic appears to be that if a court were to interfere with freedom of contract, then it should do so in a way that does not interfere with the certainty of the law. If courts were willing to imply a term into individual contracts that were not reflected in the joint intention of the parties, it would incentivise a party to a contract who finds herself in a bargain she no longer wants to exclude herself from her obligations with the court's help. Therefore, if courts are implying a term for reasons other than those reflected in the joint intention of the parties, courts try to ensure that such a term is implied into all contracts of that particular type. To this extent, the methodology makes sense as it brings greater certainty to the contracting parties.

However, it is not always clear how the courts go about defining the type of contract into which the term will be implied.[5] In *Reid v Rush and Tompkins Group Plc*,[6] an employee employed overseas to drive a vehicle was injured in an accident during his employment. The court was unwilling to imply a term that all employers must insure employees, on the basis that it would be too onerous on the employers.[7] However, the court can define a narrower type of contract within the larger category of employment contracts, which it did in *Scally v Southern Health and Social Services Board*.[8] Here, the employer had a pension scheme for its employees whose terms were complex, and the employees had to depend on the employer to explain its terms. The court implied into the contract of employment that the employer had an obligation to explain the terms to its employees. This did not apply to all employment contracts, but only to those where the employees did not have an opportunity to negotiate the contract individually, and where the employment contract had terms of value to employees which they might not be aware of, unless their attention was drawn to them.[9] In *Crossley v Faithful and Gould Holdings Ltd*,[10] the employee had retired early and could not benefit from the beneficial changes that

[3] ibid 471–75.
[4] [1977] AC 239, 257–58.
[5] Peden (n 2) 461–62; Andrew Phang, 'Implied Terms in English Law: Some Recent Developments' [1993] JBL 242, 247–48.
[6] [1990] 1 WLR 212 (CA).
[7] ibid 227–28.
[8] [1992] 1 AC 294 (HL).
[9] ibid 307.
[10] [2004] EWCA Civ 293.

were made to a pension scheme after his retirement. Even with the ability to classify the contracts narrowly, it was held that no term that the employer must advise the employee as to the economic benefits of pension schemes needed to be implied.

The reason for such anomalous treatment of different cases is not always clear. Focusing on the common incidents of a specific category of contracts that the term to be implied addresses can shed some light on the judicial thought process. However, if the methodology for implying does not address what influences the common incidents, one could classify a contract simply based on superficial incidents such as the commonality of the parties to the contract—say employer and employee. But we know from *Reid* and *Crossley* that not all employer and employee relationships could have the term at issue being implied into their contracts. Commentators identify sale of goods, hire purchase, agency, employment, tenancy, and the like as examples of well-recognised categories of contracts.[11] However, identifying the common incidents is not a mechanical exercise based merely on the parties involved or the subject matter of the contract. To make a meaningful classification, the common incidents should be identified based on the policy reasons that drive them. These policy reasons could include setting right the inequality in access to information, identifying who is better able to bear the risk, and so on.

To illustrate, in *Irwin* one of the terms sought to be implied into the lease was that, in a building with multiple occupants, the landlord owed a duty to take reasonable care to keep the common areas of the premises in reasonable repair and usability.[12] This was because the landlord was better placed than the tenant to bear such responsibility. Therefore, this is a case of efficient allocation of risk and resources, as it would have been expensive and time-consuming for the tenant to organise herself to maintain the common areas.[13] This policy reason informed the common incidents of all contracts of this type—meaning in all tenancy agreements of the multi-storeyed block of flats where the landlord was the council, this common incident was shared. Therefore, the class of contracts was identified as the lease agreements of a multi-storeyed building where the council was the common landlord, as opposed to all leases in general.

In *Reid*, on the one hand, a class of contracts could not be identified because the underlying policy objective sought to be achieved did not drive the common incident of all contracts of that type.[14] There is no policy that unites all employment contracts in relation to insuring the employees. Insuring or not insuring employees depends very much on the resources available to the employer and the particular

[11] Atiyah and Smith (n 1) 159.

[12] *Liverpool City Council v Irwin* (n 4) 254.

[13] Hugh Collins, *The Law of Contract* (4th edn, LexisNexis 2003) 245.

[14] Peden argues that a narrower type of contract addressing only overseas employees was put forward, but the court did not consider it perhaps because the category was too small or because the amount of time spent overseas could vary between employees, making it too disparate a group. See Peden (n 2) 461–62.

field of employment. In *Scally*, on the other hand, the policy that united employees who did not have an opportunity to negotiate individually was to balance the information asymmetry arising out of the inherently unequal relationship between the employer and employee. The employees need to be given information that they cannot or do not know that they should ask for. In *Crossley*, retiring early was a decision the employee took for his health reasons. There is no common incident that could unite all contracts of early retirees, given the diversity of reasons why employees retire early which impacts on the timing of their retirement. If there had been inequality of information inherent in the relationship, it may have been a uniting factor. But this was not the case. These examples drive home the point that articulating the policy reason that underlies the term to be implied and accordingly the common incident of the type of contracts is an essential step in the methodology.

A term should be implied only if it is 'necessary' to do so, as opposed to being 'reasonable' to do so. However, courts do not make it clear why it is necessary. In most cases, the terms are not necessary to make the contract work. The contracts are perfectly functional without the implied term, questioning how low the bar of necessity really is. In *Irwin*, providing and maintaining elevators was found by the House of Lords to be necessary in a multi-storeyed building with individual living quarters. However, commentators doubt whether, under the circumstances of that case, providing these facilities was strictly necessary, given that access through the staircases was always available. Likewise, in *Scally*, it was not strictly necessary for the employer to inform the employees about the pension scheme. The employees may have come to know of it from other sources. Commentators point out that the courts seem to be advocating implying a term when it is 'reasonably necessary'.[15] But 'reasonableness' also hides what exactly the courts are doing. There must be some other reason why it is necessary to imply the term. That reasin is that the policy objectives underlying these terms must be achieved; and, more importantly, that implying the term is the only way in which a court can achieve the policy objective. In other words, there is no other way to address policies such as inequality of risk allocation or information other than by interpolating it into the private ordering set by the parties. This is done by implying a policy-based term into the contract. Therefore, this book adopts the three-pronged approach as stated in Chapter 3, reframing methodology reflecting the role of the policy objectives being achieved. This chapter will demonstrate that the three-pronged methodology can provide a robust basis for implying a policy-based copyright licence.

Despite the recognition of separate manner of implication between implied in fact and implied by law, cases—especially those concerning architectural plans—continue to cause confusion in this area. While it is possible that the same term may

[15] Atiyah and Smith (n 1) 161.

be implied based both on consent and on policy, it is still essential to distinguish the reasons that support a consent-based implication from those that support a policy-based implication. Section 1 of this chapter deals with this discussion. Once the differences between the methodologies is firmly established, this chapter goes on to deal with different classes of contracts based on the policy objective that underlies the common incident of these types of contract. When a copyright owner sells or authorises the sale or otherwise transfers ownership of a product incorporating the copyright work (let us call this a Copyright Product), in general, the use made by the person acquiring the Copyright Product may not interfere with the copyright owner's exclusive rights. For example, a person reading a book she has purchased does not interfere with any rights of the copyright owner. However, there may be certain uses to which the owner of the Copyright Product wants to apply, which may interfere with the copyright owner's exclusive rights. Although these situations are now largely addressed in the statute, Sections 2 and 3 illustrate that if there had been no such provision, the courts would have implied a policy-based licence. Section 4 goes on to discuss the highly regulated industry of hazardous substances and the legal regulation surrounding material safety data sheets (MSDSs), and how the information flow in this sector can be explained using the framework proposed here for policy-based implied contractual licences.

1. Distinguishing between Consent-based and Policy-based Implications

In Chapter 5 it was seen that cases concerning architectural plans are better rationalised under consent-based implied contractual licences. However, Kirby and Crennan JJ have held in *Concrete Pty Ltd v Paramatta Designs* that cases on architectural plans form a class of contracts into which a court may imply a term by law,[16] based on the line of cases such as *Beck v Montana*[17] and *Blair v Osborne.*[18] However, the judges did not go on to explain how they arrived at this class of contracts, nor as to why it is necessary to imply a term. In *Devefi v Mateffy*[19] the possibility of implying a term by law permitting the use the plans by the subsequent purchaser of the commissioner was considered. But a term was not implied, not because implied by law was an incorrect approach, but because the court found that the parties had expressly excluded such an implied term. These examples need to be unpacked. It is not argued here that policy-based licences cannot be implied in architecture plans cases; rather, we need more clarity as to the aspects of

[16] (2006) 231 ALR 663 [59].
[17] [1963] FLR 298.
[18] [1971] 2 QB 78.
[19] (1993) 113 ALR 225.

architectural plans cases that are amenable to implying based on policy as opposed to consent. Simply stating that architectural plans cases form a class of contracts lending themselves for implication by law is not helpful. On the contrary, it serves only to confuse the methodology between licences implied based on consent and those implied based on policy.

Let us first discuss the implied term at issue. The term being considered for implication is the copyright licence in favour of the person who commissions the creation of a copyright work. As argued in Chapter 5 above, the implied licence that a commissioner enjoys to use the commissioned work is consent-based because the copyright owner knows that the purpose for which the work was commissioned was for it to be used by the commissioner and the fee agreed represents this.[20] The scope of licence is dependent on the level of knowledge or the reasonable expectation of the copyright owner as to the extent to which the commissioner will use the work. Additionally, a fact rich enquiry as to whether a development consent has been applied for or obtained or refused and so on, make this manner of implication attributable more to consent. The view taken in this monograph is that it is only when considerations other than those that concern the parties to the contract, such as welfare and societal considerations justify the term to be implied, can we speak of implication by law (or policy-based). If the considerations are only those of the parties to the contract such as the terms they negotiated and what was or ought reasonably to have been within their knowledge, then it must be a case of implied in fact (or consent-based).

Having said this, there may be a possibility to argue for policy basis for the implied assignability of this implied licence in favour of a successor in title of the land to which the plans relate, in addition to the consent-based arguments presented in Chapter 5 above. The assignability could be based on a policy if we can identify one and follow the rest of the methodology for implying this term based on policy. What could the policy be?

Concrete gives some clue. In *Concrete*, the court said that if the implied licence was not assignable, it would 'sterilise the land in terms of its usage, in conformity with that development consent, in the hands of successors in title . . '.. This was despite the fact that the 'development consent would remain otherwise in force and effect vis-à-vis the original grantee of that consent for the requisite statutory or regulatory period of time'.[21] One can argue that it is a matter of policy to not let an architect block the ability of a subsequent purchaser benefiting from the development consent, if the development consent has been granted based on the architect's plans. Further, if the development consent runs with the land, it will also be in force and effect vis-à-vis the successor in title. What is clear from this is that, in addition to the market consideration, there is also an argument of efficiency—it would be

20 See ch 5, sections 1(c)(ii) and (iii) above.

21 [2004] FCA 1312 [100], [133], as confirmed by the High Court in (2006) 231 ALR 663 [83].

inefficient in terms of the cost and effort required for the government authorities to approve another set of plans. These are certainly considerations that relate to the community as a whole and are not specific to the parties to the contract.

Having thus identified the policy, we now need to find the type of contract that shares a common incident arising out of this policy. The existence of development consent is what binds the contracts of this type, which makes the arguments of policy such as market and efficiency considerations relevant. Therefore, it is not sufficient to say that architectural plans cases form a class of contracts. We must go further and define the class of contracts as those contracts where a person commissions an architect to draw plans for the land she owns, to apply for and obtain development consent, in exchange for consideration (normally payment, but can be an equity share as in *Concrete*). This excludes cases where consideration was for drawing the plans only and not for applying for development consent, as in *Stovin-Bradford v Volpoint*[22] and *Muir Durran v The Shand Partnership*,[23] where the commissioner was not the owner of the land for which the plans were commissioned.

Finally, in addressing the necessity to imply this term, no other law assists the successor in title in being able to use the plans that were commissioned by her predecessor in title. The statutory provisions that enable a development consent to run with the land only relate to the development consent. While it can assist in laying down a background policy in relation to land development, it does not by itself negate the need for a copyright licence to use the plans. Implying a licence based on the policy explained above is the only way open to a court. A court can therefore imply a term making the implied licence assignable to achieve this policy objective.

2. Transfer of Ownership of Copyright Products—Exhaustion

Having thus clarified the distinction between consent-based and policy-based implication, we move on to specific policies that have required policy-based implication in a contractual setting. When a copyright owner sells or transfers the ownership of the Copyright Product, the person acquiring it might want to sell it further or otherwise transfer the ownership. If the exclusive rights of a copyright owner included an unrestricted right to issue copies to the public, then each time the purchaser of a Copyright Product wants to sell it, she will need a licence from the copyright owner. To depend on the copyright owner to grant a consent-based express licence would be cumbersome. Therefore, a licence permitting the further distribution of the Copyright Product needs to be implied. To imply a consent-based licence will not capture the basis appropriately because the purchaser's ability to resell the Copyright Product does not depend on the consent of the copyright

[22] [1971] 3 All ER 570.
[23] 2003 Scot (D) 21/12.

owner, but rather on the purchaser becoming the owner of a distinct piece of personal property. Although this area is now governed by statute, it makes sense to explore whether implying a policy-based licence to further distribute the Copyright Product would have been an option .

(a) Policy underlying the licence

One of the most important policy reasons lies within the justification for the protection of copyright or, for that matter, any intellectual property. The policy gives the owner a recompense for the time, effort, and money in actualising the invention or the work. The invention or the work may result in the production of a product, which may then become the subject of commerce. The compensation which the intellectual property owner can extract on the first sale of such product is regarded a just recompense, so long as the sale happens with her consent. Thereafter, in principle, the product can be freely sold, and the intellectual property owner cannot assert her exclusive rights to prevent such resale. In the terminology of continental jurisdictions, the copyright owner has 'exhausted' her rights by such authorised first sale.[24]

The second reason is that the Copyright Product becomes a distinct item of personal property in the hands of the acquirer. One of the most fundamental attributes of personal property is its transferability and the ownership control means that the acquirer be free to sell or further transfer the ownership of the Copyright Product. One of the earliest cases to address this was a patent case, *Betts v Willmott*.[25] At issue in this case was a patent for making metallic capsules for covering the corks and necks of bottles. The capsule had been patented in England and France, and manufactured in both these countries. Betts claimed that Willmott, a chemist, had been selling capsules in England similar to the patented capsule, in violation of the patent. Willmott claimed that he procured the capsules from suppliers in London, who may have been supplied by Betts' manufactory in France. Betts claimed that, even if that was true, the capsules could not be sold in England without his permission.[26] The question was whether there was an unauthorised use of the patent. Lord Hatherley held that if Betts had not supplied the capsules at all, there would have been unauthorised use. However, he went on to hold:

[24] Gillian Davies, Nicholas Caddick, and Gwilym Harbottle, *Copinger and Skone James on Copyright* (17th edn, Sweet & Maxwell 2016) para 24-18.

[25] (1871) LR 6 Ch App 239.

[26] ibid 240–42.

> When a man has purchased an article he expects to have the control of it, and there must be some clear and explicit agreement to the contrary to justify the vendor in saying that he has not given the purchaser his *license* to sell the article ...

This means that if a patentee wants to prevent the resale of her product after purchase, she must expressly say so at the time of the initial sale. If she did not, it is within the powers of the person who purchases the patent product to sell it further, as the owner of personal property.

A third policy reason is to facilitate trade in Copyright Products. If a purchaser had to seek permission of the copyright owner each time she wanted to sell Copyright Products, it would increase her transaction costs. To achieve the larger objective of facilitating uninterrupted trade in Copyright Products, the non-interference from the copyright owner in the market after she has disposed of her work for the first time (called the aftermarket) becomes important.

(b) Type of contract with the common incident

The common incident is that the owner of personal property should be free to transfer it further. A person acquires ownership over the Copyright Product either by a contract of sale and purchase or by way of a gift. It may be possible to adopt the definition of sale of goods as provided under the relevant sale of goods legislation in a jurisdiction.[27] This definition might only apply to tangible goods, which would be appropriate in jurisdictions such as Canada where the statute narrows down these contracts to exclude Copyright Products that are not in tangible form.[28]

Products including downloadable software which do not exist in a physical form may not be covered in this type of contracts. However, since transfer of ownership of the intangible Copyright Product is possible, there is no reason why these should not be included in contracts of this type. Digital exhaustion is a contentious issue which this author has discussed in detail elsewhere.[29] However, with the decision of the Court of Justice of the European Union (CJEU) in *Nederlands Uitgeversverbond v Tom Kabinet Internet BV*,[30] which is binding on the UK as it was decided before the Exit Day, digital exhaustion may not be possible for works other than software,[31] unless the Supreme Court decides to depart from it after the Exit Day.

[27] See eg Sale of Goods Act 1978 (SGA), s 2 read with s 61(1).

[28] Canadian Copyright Act 1985 (CCA), s 3(1)(j).

[29] Poorna Mysoor, 'Exhaustion, Non-exhaustion and Implied Licence' (2018) 49 IIC 656.

[30] Case C-263/18 *Nederlands Uitgeversverbond v Tom Kabinet Internet BV* ECLI:EU:C:2019:1111.

[31] Case C-128/11 *UsedSoft GmbH v Oracle International Corp* ECLI:EU:C:2012:407 permitted digital exhaustion for computer programs and will continue to be good law.

If the class of contracts is confined to contracts of sale and purchase, then a gift of the Copyright Product will be excluded. Since the common incident is triggered by any transfer of ownership, gifts should also be included. Since in English common law, a gift is not regarded as a contract unless it is by way of a deed, a deed of gift may also belong to the class of contracts of concern here. If no deed or no writing is used when effecting a gift of the Copyright Product, a bare licence to permit the resale of the Copyright Product could be implied.[32]

(c) Necessary to imply the licence

It would have been necessary to imply a policy-based licence if the statutory provision in the UK under section 18 of the Copyright, Designs and Patents Act 1988 (CDPA) had not been drafted in a way that captures within the statute the liberty to redistribute the Copyright Product. The effect of this statutory provision is that, although the first two prongs of the methodology are satisfied, it is still not necessary to imply a licence because of the existence of the statutory provision.

Section 18 introduced the exclusive right to issue copies to the public into the CDPA, which was not present in the previous statute. However, it also provides that the exclusive right to issue copies to the public is only infringed if a person puts into circulation copies of a work in the European Economic Area (EEA)[33] for the first time, without the consent of the copyright owner. Therefore, the right to issue copies to the public is not an unqualified right—but is confined to copies not already put into circulation within the EEA, by or with the consent of the copyright owner. This qualification liberates subsequent copies to be freely sold and resold to any purchaser anywhere in the world, if the first issuing within the EEA had been with the consent of the copyright owner. In the language of licence, into the contract of sale that puts the copies of the work in circulation for the first time into the EEA is implied a licence in favour of the purchaser to sell it further, and this licence is based on the policy objectives discussed above. One might argue that using the language of licence is no longer required because section 18(2) states that the exclusive right to issue copies to the public does not include any subsequent issue of copies of the work. Thus, one may argue that this right only grants the exclusive right of first sale of copies, and no overlap with what the subsequent purchasers might want to do with the copies they purchase. However, it helps to show that, had this provision not been drafted in this manner, a policy-based implied licence could have been pressed into service.

[32] For more on policy-based implied bare licences see ch 8 below.

[33] The territorial limit of first sale will continue to be the EEA until the expiration of the transitional period on 31 December 2020. After this date, the territorial boundary of the first sale will only be the UK https://www.gov.uk/guidance/exhaustion-of-ip-rights-and-parallel-trade-after-the-transition-period accessed 11 July 2020.

In Canada, until 2012 the copyright statute did not enumerate the right of issuing copies to the public as an exclusive right. But the amendment of 2012 included section 3(1)(j), which grants exclusive right of sale or otherwise transfer of the ownership of works in tangible form for the first time, meaning that the subsequent sale or transfer of ownership of works in tangible form is free of the exclusive right. If the work is not in tangible form, the licence of the copyright owner will still be required, and it might be possible to argue that such licence should be implied based on policy considerations as argued above.

In Australia, which is modelled on the UK 1956 Act,[34] the exclusive right granted is only to publish, which meant making public a work which had been previously unpublished.[35] Once the work is published, this right does not interfere with the ability of the purchaser of the Copyright Product to resell it, negating the need to imply any licence. Thus, purchasers of Copyright Products would have been free to purchase and resell those works. This would have meant that, once a work is published in Australia, the products incorporating such work can be subject to both export and import. However, the Australian Copyright Act 1968 (ACA) provides under section 37(1)(a) that importing infringing copies knowing that they are infringing is also an infringement. This provision is problematic because of the way it defines infringing copies—as copies that would have infringed copyright of its owner if it had been manufactured in Australia by the person importing. This meant that, even if an importer imports genuine copies from overseas, if she did not have domestic licence to make those copies, she would be regarded as importing infringing copies.

There are many cases that have been litigated in this context. These cases have a certain pattern to them, namely the importation of commercial quantities of the product incorporating a copyright work. In the Australian cases of *Interstate Parcel Express Co Pty Ltd v Time-Life International*,[36] it was certain cookbooks; in *Computermate Products (Aust) Pty Ltd v Oxi-Soft Pty Ltd*,[37] it was certain software; in *Lorenzo & Sons Pty Ltd v Roland Corporation*,[38] it was musical equipment, and in *R&A Bailey & Co Ltd v Boccaccio Pty Ltd*,[39] it was the copyright incorporated in the label of Bailey's Irish Cream. The respective copyright owner sued the defendants for copyright infringement, since the making of the products named above within Australia by the importer would have infringed copyright in them. The defence put forward in each of these cases was that, since the copyright owner did not place any restrictions on the purchase of commercial quantities of these products overseas

[34] Copyright Act 1956, s 2(5)(b) for literary works and s 3(5)(b) for artistic works.

[35] *Infabrics Ltd v Jaytex Ltd* [1981] 1 All ER 1057, 1067; see also John Phillips and Lionel Bently, 'Copyright Issues: the Mysteries of section 18' (1999) 21 EIPR 133.

[36] (1977) 138 CLR 534.

[37] (1988) 83 ALR 492.

[38] (1992) 23 IPR 376.

[39] (1986) 77 ALR 177.

or as to what could be done with them after purchase, it should be understood as implying a licence permitting the defendant to import these products. From this it is clear that the defendants relied on the conduct of the copyright owner amounting to consent, rather than a policy reason forming the basis for implying the licence. Starting from the High Court authority in *Time-Life*, the courts have consistently held that a mere lack of restriction does not amount to a licence.[40] This conforms to the analysis in this monograph that, for a consent-based licence to exist, there must be a positive act. A mere non-restriction or neutral act does not by itself amount to consent. If a licence must be implied based on consent, an overt act indicating consent must be shown.

A better approach might have been to put forward policy arguments stated in (a) above. The first sale overseas should have exhausted the copyright owner's ability to control the aftermarket, whether in the country where it was first sold or when it was exported to Australia.[41] These policies would have been able to unify the common incident of all contracts of this type, and it could have been argued that it is necessary to imply this licence to address these policy reasons. Further, unlike statutory provisions on exhaustion, there was no other statute or rule of law which could help, necessitating the courts implying a licence. Although the policy reasons were never raised before the court, they were found to be strong enough that subsequent committees recommended reforming the law in this area.[42] Accordingly, the ACA enacted ss 44A, 44C, 44D, 44E, and 44F, addressing specific type of works and excluding importation of copies of genuine products from becoming an infringement.

3. Transfer of Ownership of Copyright Product—Repair

The issue of repair can arise with Copyright Products that are tangible (for example, machinery) or intangible products (for example, software). Tangible products needing repair tend to be industrial goods (as opposed to say books or paintings), whose spare parts might incorporate copyright works (such as drawings), although

[40] *Interstate Parcel Express Co Pty Ltd v Time-Life International* (n 36) 543, 553–54, 557; *Computermate Products (Aust) Pty Ltd v Oxi-Soft Pty Ltd* (n 37) 494–96; *Lorenzo & Sons Pty Ltd v Roland Corporation* (n 38) 380–81; *R&A Bailey & Co Ltd v Boccaccio Pty Ltd & Pacific Wine Co Pty Ltd* (n 39) 186–87.

[41] In Canada, the situation is different because the infringing copies for secondary infringement under s 27(2) of the CCA makes importing of products infringing if they had infringed copyright where they were made. This issue was brought alive in *Euro-Excellence Inc v Kraft Canada Inc* [2007] 3 SCR 20, where the Supreme Court of Canada held that since Kraft Foods Switzerland and Kraft Foods Belgium made the relevant chocolates that were imported both in Europe and in Canada, the actions of the importer did not amount to importation of infringing goods. Although this is not an implied licence issue, it is interesting to see how the difference in the wording means that importing of genuine products is not caught by this provision.

[42] Andrew Stewart and others, *Intellectual Property in Australia* (6th edn, LexisNexis Butterworths 2018) paras 8.33–8.37.

much of the intellectual property in spare parts may be protected by design rights. To the extent that copyright protects spare parts, if the spare parts and consequential repair services are provided by the copyright owner or a person authorised by the copyright owner, then there is no problem. However, if the owner of the Copyright Product herself wants to produce spare parts to repair the Copyright Product or have a person not authorised by the copyright owner to produce the spare parts, then this could interfere with the exclusive right of reproduction of the copyright owner. Therefore, a question arises whether it is possible to imply into the contract of sale a licence to reproduce the work to enable production of spare parts for repair. Again, as for exhaustion, a consent-based licence is not appropriate because the ability of the owner of the Copyright Product to repair does not depend on the consent of the copyright owner, but rather on the policy that the owner of personal property such as the Copyright Product must have complete control over such product. Therefore, we must consider implying a policy-based licence. To do this, we need first to understand the underlying policy objectives behind repair.

(a) Policy objectives underlying the licence

The policy is that a person who purchases or otherwise acquires the ownership of a Copyright Product must be able to prolong its life by repairing it, as an incident of the ownership of the product. However, this does not mean that repair services should be made available to all purchasers of Copyright Products as of right. At the time of purchase, there are terms implied into the contract of sale that the goods purchased are of satisfactory quality and are fit for their purpose.[43] Beyond this, there is no general duty or liability placed on the person selling a product also to provide repairs that become necessary owing to the ordinary use of the Copyright Product.[44] Thus, the ability to repair is a privilege that the owner of personal property has, and the seller of goods has no right to interfere with such repair. But what if the only way a repair can be carried out is by reproducing one or more of the copyright works incorporated within the Copyright Product (typically in the form of a spare part)? The underlying policy of allowing the owner of personal property to have control over the goods she purchases should be sufficient to compel the copyright owner to permit reproduction of her copyright works should the need for repair arise.

This matter was first considered in the context of patents, given that Copyright Products needing repair are normally industrial goods incorporating patented

[43] See eg SGA, s 14.

[44] Under rare circumstances there may be a liability on the seller/manufacturer to provide repair services. Michael Bridge, *The Sale of Goods* (4th edn, OUP 2019) para [7-120].

inventions within them. A patent grants the patentee of a product the exclusive right to make, use, dispose off, and import the invention, among others.[45] A strict interpretation of this language leads to an absurd conclusion that a person who purchases a patented product infringes the patent if she uses the product. To avoid this absurdity, the courts had historically applied the doctrine of implied licence. Accordingly, one of the earliest cases to rule on this was *Betts*. The issue, as discussed above, was of resale of a patented product. In addition to holding that the purchaser had a licence to sell, Lord Hatherley held that the licence extends 'to use it wherever he pleases' and the sale 'has the power of conferring *a complete right* on him . . .'.[46] Lord Hatherley therefore found that there was no unauthorised use.

The significance of *Betts* lies in articulating the reasonable expectations of a personal property owner to exercise control over the product she purchases. *Betts*, as explained above, was a case of resale of patented products, and not specifically on repair. However, in the subsequent years, the courts have confirmed that a licence may be implied to enable repair.[47] An implied licence in favour of the purchaser of a patented product was necessary because the exclusive rights of a patentee included the right to 'use' the patented product. Since the statute did not further qualify the word 'use', the courts had to step in to imply a licence to permit the legitimate use of it by reselling it. The plain language of the judgment makes the scope of this licence broad and open to interpretation. For example, for products with limited life, 'use' could include 'repair', on the basis that if one cannot repair, one cannot use for a prolonged period of time. Accordingly, in *Sirdar Rubber Company Ltd v Wallington, Weston & Co*,[48] repair was held to be limited to prolonging the life of a product, but not to make a new product under the guise of a repair.[49]

However, the argument of an implied licence to repair lost favour with patent law in *United Wire Ltd v Screen Repair Services (Scotland) Ltd*.[50] Although the policy objective of enabling repair of the products purchased continues, Lord Hoffmann disapproved of the implied licence approach. He preferred to ask the question whether the defendant 'made' the patented product (which is an exclusive right of the patentee), rather than asking whether the defendant had an implied licence to repair. He stated that repair shares a boundary with making but does not trespass upon its territory.[51] This means that making a patented product has a higher threshold than repairing it, and so any person can undertake repair of a patented product without infringing the right to make it. Since this decision, the right to repair in patent law is a matter of interpretation of the patentee's exclusive right

45 Patents Act 1977, s 60(1)(a).
46 *Betts v Willmott* (n 25) 245 (emphasis added).
47 *Dunlop Pneumatic Tyre Co v Neal* (1899) 16 RPC 247.
48 (1907) 24 RPC 539.
49 ibid 543.
50 [2001] FSR 24.
51 ibid [19]–[20].

to make, rather than a matter of implied licence of the patentee's right to use.[52] Lord Hoffmann expressed no views on copyright in *United Wire Ltd*, as the facts did not warrant it. However, the same line of argument cannot be true of copyright, as the exclusive rights of copyright are different. The only way to legitimate reproduction for repair purposes is by a licence,[53] unlike in patent where repair sits ambiguously between making and using the patented product. Therefore, the implied licence argument should continue in relation to copyright. Additionally, the underlying policy of permitting repair of the goods purchased should be clarified.

The decision in *Solar Thomson Engineering Co Ltd v Barton*[54] made a decisive assertion of this policy in copyright scenarios. In *Solar*, the product at issue incorporated both a patented invention and a copyright work. If, as in *Betts*, the purchaser can do what she pleases with the product, does the purchaser acquire a licence also to reproduce the copyright work to effect repairs? In *Solar*, the plaintiff held a patent for certain pulleys and the copyright in the corresponding engineering drawings. The defendants were the providers of repair services and the manufacturers of replacement parts for machinery, made to order by the customers of the plaintiff. The replacement parts were manufactured by way of working drawings, which were held to be substantially similar to the patentee's working drawings, and therefore, a reproduction. The plaintiff claimed infringement of both patent rights and copyright.[55] The Court of Appeal held that such reproduction of copyright drawings was no more than repair of the patented machinery, permitted by an implied licence in favour of the owner of the patented machinery. To quote Buckley LJ:

> If I am right in the view I have expressed about the existence here of an implied licence under the patent to repair pulleys by replacing worn rubber rings, it must, I think, follow that purchasers of Polyrim pulleys are also impliedly licensed to infringe the plaintiffs' copyright in their drawings to the extent necessary to enable such repairs to be carried out. To hold otherwise would be to allow the copyright to stultify the implied licence under the patent.... [A]ny purchaser of a patented article might find himself deprived of his ostensible right to repair that article by the existence of a copyright of which he would probably be ignorant when he made the purchase.[56]

The language of Buckley LJ asserts that copyright protection cannot make the implied licence under patent law illusory. If there are reasons to prevent the rights

[52] *Schütz (UK) Ltd v Werit (UK) Ltd* [2011] EWCA Civ 303 [62].

[53] But see *British Leyland Motor Co Ltd v Armstrong Patent Co Ltd* [1986] 1 All ER 850, where the House of Lords applied the principle of non-derogation from grant to permit repair, rather than implied licence. See ch 8 below.

[54] [1977] RPC 537.

[55] ibid 560. The contract of sale of the machinery expressly reserved copyright in the drawings to the patentee. However, Buckley LJ held that this express term is not inconsistent with implying a term.

[56] ibid 560–61 (emphasis supplied added).

owner from asserting her patent rights, those reasons should likewise prevent the same rights owner from asserting her copyright. Although Buckley LJ mentioned business efficacy as the reason for implying the copyright licence,[57] it makes more sense to ascribe the implication to the policy objective of not interfering with the property rights of the purchasers of products incorporating patent rights and copyright works.

Although the policy of facilitating repair was confirmed in *Solar* in relation to copyright cases, some doubt was cast on it in the Singapore Court of Appeal decision in *Creative Technology Ltd v Aztech Systems Pte Ltd*.[58] Here, Aztech presumably purchased the sound card made by Creative Technology in the market and reverse engineered it. In that process, it copied Creative Technology's software. Relying on the principle in *Betts*, Aztech Systems claimed that the right to copy was a reasonable use, which emanates from Aztech Systems' purchase of Creative Technology's sound blaster card and the software that came with it. However, Aztech Systems was commercially producing sound cards in competition with Creative Technology's sound cards. The Court observed that, unlike a patented article, when a copyright article is sold, the economic interests in the copyright and moral rights still remain with the copyright owner. It held, therefore, that there was no place for the *Betts* principle in Singapore copyright law.[59] It is worth noting that *Solar*, which connects the *Betts* principle to copyright law, was not mentioned in this decision.

This decision is problematic. Implied licence is necessary *because* exclusive rights still remain with the copyright owner. The *Betts* principle did not negate the exclusive rights of the copyright owner. Indeed, it is the continued existence of the exclusive rights in the hands of the patent owner that made it necessary in *Betts* for the purchaser of the patented product to benefit from an implied licence to control the product he purchased as its owner. Further, *Betts* is more relevant to copyright law than patent law, given the reasons in *United Wire* for discarding the implied licence approach for patent cases. Rather than denying a place for an implied licence, the better reasoning for the court to adopt would have been to point out the lack of a genuine repair presented by the case. This is because the defendant had copied all of the claimant's technology including the sound card for sale in competition with the claimant, as opposed to enabling repair of a part that was not working. *Creative Technology* should therefore be treated with caution, as far as the policy underlying *Betts* and *Solar* is concerned.

57 ibid 561.
58 [1997] 1 SLR 621.
59 ibid [1]–[7], [83]–[84].

(b) Type of contract with the common incident

The common incident is that a person who receives the transfer of the Copyright Product expects to have control over the personal property she acquires, including the ability to repair it. As in Section 2 on exhaustion above, a person can become an owner of personal property by way of a contract of sale and purchase or by way of gift. Although circumstances where the Copyright Product is given as a gift may be rare, in principle it could be a class of contracts similar to the manner explained for exhaustion above.

Let us take the more common class of contracts, namely the contract of sale of tangibles as a class of contracts. A consequence of rationalising *Solar* based on the framework suggested in this chapter is that it must be taken as applying to all contracts of sale of tangibles. This means that contracts of the same class should have the benefit of the implied licence enabling repair. Accordingly, *Gardner & Sons Ltd v Paul Sykes Organisation Ltd*[60] was a case in relation to copyright in the design drawings of pistons of diesel engines. The claimant was the manufacturer of diesel engines and also provided spare parts like pistons. The defendant engaged in buying and reconditioning diesel engines—meaning extending the lifespan of a machine that was not performing well or enhancing it to serve some other purpose. The defendant did not always use spare parts manufactured by the claimant but depended on other suppliers. When the claimant's factory went on strike and pistons were in short supply, the defendant placed an order with a Hong Kong company and procured the required number of pistons. These pistons had been the subject of an Anton Piller order which was sought to be discharged by these proceedings. The claimant alleged copyright infringement and the defendant relied on implied licence to repair based on *Solar*. The issue before the court was whether the claimant grants an implied licence to repair in the most economical way when it sells its engines.[61] Foster J relied on *Solar* and held that a piston is not usually repaired, but always replaced. If no conditions have been placed by the claimant, the defendant is free to use pistons manufactured by other providers.[62]

Similarly, in *Weir Pumps Ltd v CML Pumps Ltd*,[63] the claimant was in the design, manufacture, and repair business of a wide variety of pumps. It had supplied pumps to an electricity generation board, which had contracted the repair of its pumps to the defendant. The defendant had manufactured some of the spare parts for the board based on certain confidential drawings and some spare parts by reverse engineering. The board had been brought in by way of third-party proceedings by the defendant claiming indemnity for the work it had done on behalf of the

[60] [1981] FSR 281.
[61] ibid 282–83.
[62] ibid 284.
[63] [1984] FSR 33.

board, to which the board had claimed by fourth party notice, a declaration of non-infringement owing to implied licence. The relevant issue for our discussion here is whether the board, upon the purchase of the pumps, had an implied licence to repair them. The court relied on *Solar* again and held that, although reverse engineering does amount to copyright infringement, the board and its agents did have the defence of implied licence to effect repairs and, in pursuance of this, to reproduce spare parts.

There may, however, be some difficulty in implying a licence to repair when the Copyright Product is software, and even if the type of contract is a commissioning contract. This is because removing defects from software generally requires access to the source code. But access to source code also enables further development of the program, which is far beyond what is required by way of removing defects. Courts have consistently held that access to source code is only possible if there is an express or an implied term to that effect. If it is an implied term, the implication is a matter of consent of the copyright owner, rather than the policy of repair, as explained in Chapter 5 above.[64] Therefore, unless the copyright owner has consented to the commissioner removing defects, a licence will not be implied into all commissioning contracts based on the policy of repair. If the software is purchased as a retail product as opposed to being commissioned, there is even less likelihood that the purchaser will obtain access to the object code to repair the software. This appears to tip the balance in favour of maintaining the rights of the copyright owner, rather than the owner of the Copyright Product in relation to software. However, we will see in subsection (c) below that some of these aspects are now covered by statutory provisions

Once the contract of sale of (tangible) goods is recognised as a class of contracts, then all contracts in the chain may be included in this class, whether the sale is made by a distributor or a retailer, and whether the purchaser is a trader or a consumer. This is because, in all of these contracts, the common incident still remains transfer of ownership of personal property. Into all of these contracts is implied a licence permitting the purchaser to reproduce copyright works in the spare parts to repair the Copyright Product, unless it is found not necessary, as explained below.

(c) Necessary to imply the licence

As discussed above, it would be necessary to imply the licence if it is the only way to achieve the policy objective. The High Court of Australia has held this to be the case in relation to survey plans where the existence of a statutory licence permitting their use rendered unnecessary the implication of a term.[65]

64 See ch 5, section 1(c)(ii) above.

65 *Copyright Agency Ltd v New South Wales* (2008) 233 CLR 279 [92]–[93] (Gleeson CJ, Gummow, Heydon, Crennan, and Kiefel JJ).

Let us examine the cases where it was found necessary to imply the licence. In *Gardner* above, when the defendant purchased the claimant's diesel engines, into that contract of sale and purchase was implied a licence from the claimant for the defendant to reproduce the copyright incorporated in its spare parts. When the defendant placed the order with the Hong Kong supplier, the implied licence to reproduce was sub-licensed to the supplier, enabling it to produce pistons without infringing the claimant's copyright. It can only be a sub-licence of the implied licence and not an assignment of the implied licence because the purchaser of the Copyright Product might want to use the implied licence to place multiple orders for the spare parts during the lifetime of the copyright product and might place the orders with different providers. This means that, in order to achieve the policy objective of repair, not only is it necessary to imply a term in favour of the purchaser of the Copyright Product, but also imply a term making the implied licence sub-licensable. *Weir* also confirms this in that the implied licence in favour of the board was held to be available to its agents. The defendant was not technically the board's agent, but an independent contractor who had produced the spare parts. Therefore, it would have made more sense to hold that the board can sub-license the implied licence in its favour to other third parties such as the defendant.

Even if the implied licence can be sub-licensed, its usefulness is limited in the market economy. The dispute is normally not with the purchaser of the Copyright Product, but with the person who carried out the repair, as in *Solar*. Cases like *Weir* are rare where the purchaser of the Copyright Product is brought in by way of third-party proceedings. But the point is that the licence is implied into the contract of purchase. This licence is in turn sub-licensed to the person carrying out the repair, upon being commissioned to do so by the purchaser. However, it is more common in the market economy for the person carrying out the repairs to produce spare parts in advance of receiving the orders from the purchaser, as in *United Wire*, building a stock of spare parts to service the demand efficiently. This prevents a devolution of the implied licence from the purchaser, as the spare parts which need reproduction of copyright works are manufactured not in response to, but in advance of receiving an order to repair from the purchaser.[66] Given that a majority of spare parts are produced in advance in the market economy, it is difficult to imply *Betts* or *Solar*-like licence to enable such manufacture, even if the need for repair is genuine.

This leaves a small class of sophisticated and perhaps expensive machinery, where the purchasers may have spare parts made to order, and not mass produced in advance. In these cases, the manufacturer is likely to exercise control over the spare parts market, and in reality, the purchasers themselves might prefer spare parts from the original manufacturer, given the sophisticated nature of the

[66] This was perhaps an unacknowledged reason why the implied licence approach to repair was rejected in *United Wire* .

machinery. However, in principle, if a purchaser does want a third-party repair service to be able to supply spare parts upon order, it should still be possible for the court to imply a licence to reproduce spare parts in furtherance of repair, based on *Solar*.

In situations where the statute addresses the policy objective, there will be no need to imply a licence. In the UK, certain amendments have been made in relation to industrial drawings to limit the number of cases where implied copyright licence would be necessary. Section 51 of the CDPA denies copyright protection for the design drawings. Instead, a separate regime of unregistered design protection has been introduced, under Part III of the CDPA, which is for a shorter duration than copyright, and with much less extensive rights than copyright.[67] The exceptions to design rights are embodied in section 213(3)(b)(i) for features of an article that enable one article to connect with another (must-fit exception), or section 213(3)(b)(ii) for features dependent upon the appearance of another article forming an integral part (must-match exception). These amendments were made to address the spare parts market, such that spare parts shaped in a way that makes them fit with a product would be exempted by the must-fit exception.[68]

Regarding software, section 50A(2) of the CDPA permits a person having a right to use the software under a licence or otherwise ('lawful user'), to make back-up copies under section 50A, decompile under section 50B, and observe, study or test the functioning of the software to determine the ideas and principles underlying it under section 50BA(1). These three provisions cannot be overridden by a contrary contractual provision. However, under section 50C, a lawful user can copy or adapt the software as necessary for lawful use or to correct errors, subject to any contractual term to the contrary. If there is no express or (consent-based) implied term denying the ability to correct errors, this provision enables the correction of errors.[69]

Merely because the number of contracts into which a policy-based licence may be implied is small does not mean that there is no legitimate basis to imply this kind of licence in appropriate cases. Despite the enactment of the statutory provisions enumerated above, it is essential to drive home the point that this does not take away from the courts' power to imply a policy-based licence in situations not covered by these provisions.

[67] CDPA, s 226–227. For the practical effect of these provisions see the discussion on *Lucasfilm* in ch 5 above.

[68] *Ultraframe UK Ltd v Clayton* [2002] EWHC 1964 (Ch) [73]; quoted with approval in *Dyson Ltd v Qualtex (UK) Ltd* [2004] EWHC 2981 [18]–[19], [33], although here Mann J insists that there is nothing in the provisions of Part III of the CDPA to restrict them to spare parts alone.

[69] *Saphena Computing v Allied Collection Agencies* [1995] FSR 616, 637 was a case where there was no implied term to the contrary. There are similar provisions in the ACA which eliminate the necessity of implying a licence. See ACA, ss 47D an 47E. No licence was implied in *Centrestage Management Pty Ltd v Riedle* [2007] FMCA 1147, (2008) 77 IPR 550 because of the existence of these provisions.

4. Hazardous Substances and the Use of Material Safety Data Sheets

Hazardous substances form a highly regulated market. In particular, it is important that the information regarding the risks posed by and the appropriate handling of these substances is made available to all parties who need to know. The Australian cases of *Acohs Pty Ltd v RA Bashford Consulting Pty Ltd*[70] and *Acohs Pty Ltd v Ucorp Pty Ltd*[71] are a good illustration. The parties in both cases were competitors in producing and compiling MSDSs to make them available to manufacturers, suppliers, and importers of hazardous substances. A MSDS, as the name suggests, is a summary of the information regarding the substance it relates to in the prescribed form and provides the most current information regarding the safe handling of the respective substance. The manufacturers, suppliers, or importers engage a service provider such as Acohs, Bashford, or Ucorp to produce for them the MSDSs for particular compounds they need to deal with. There were several ways in which the service providers create an MSDS. One of the ways relevant for our purposes is the process of transcription where a manufacturer, supplier, or importer provides a copy of an existing MSDS to a service provider at the time of commissioning for updating it with the most recent guidelines on safety. The existing MSDS may have been created by a competing service provider. Despite the low degree of originality and questionable authorship, the courts in both these cases held that MSDSs satisfy both the requirements, and thus the service providers who initially brought the MSDS into existence were regarded as owners of the copyright in the MSDSs.[72] In *Bashford*, Bashford claimed copyright infringement by Acohs of 43 of its MSDSs owing to their reproduction and adaptation, and in reply Acohs claimed that the implied licence granted to the respectivemanufacturer, supplier, or importer which commissioned the creation of these MSDSs extended to Acohs. Similarly, in *Ucorp*, Acohs claimed copyright infringement by Ucorp and Ucorp claimed that its actions were covered by implied licence.[73] The question for us here is whether this licence is implied based on policy. Accordingly, these cases must be rationalised under the three-factor framework, as follows.

(a) Policy objectives underlying the licence

The policy behind requiring the MSDS is to protect health and safety in the workplace of those who handle dangerous substances by providing information on the

[70] (1997) 144 ALR 528.
[71] (2012) 287 ALR 403.
[72] *Acohs Pty Ltd v RA Bashford Consulting Pty Ltd* (n 70) 540–43.
[73] ibid 531; *Acohs Pty Ltd v Ucorp Pty Ltd* (n 71) [6], [92].

characteristics and hazards of those substances to help respond to emergencies and to prevent occupational death, injuries, and disease. The objective is to have a ready access to the most updated information.[74] Accordingly, under the relevant statutes, regulations, and guidelines,[75] manufacturers, suppliers, and importers of hazardous substances are required to make sure that a current MSDS is provided with the first supply of hazardous substance to the purchaser and to each subsequent supplier on request. An employer must make such MSDS provided with the first supply are available to its employees with a potential for exposure to these substances. So, all employers must make sure that employees get a copy. Access could be given through a paper copy, microfiche copy, or computerised copy. The relevant public authorities and emergency services are also required to have access to MSDSs. Although retailers are not obliged to have the MSDS, if they wished to have a copy, they should be able to access it through upstream suppliers. While in *Bashford* the law had been adopted by most if not all states in Australia, in *Ucorp* the provision of MSDSs had been made mandatory.[76] In *Bashford*, the court noted that these requirements were important to set the standard of care when deciding the liability in negligence.

(b) Type of contracts with the common incident

In *Bashford*, Merkel J identified all commissioning contract as the type of contract into which a licence may be implied by law, relying on *Beck*.[77] He came to this conclusion based on the purpose for which a commissioning contract has been entered into. There are obvious difficulties with this view. Ascertaining the purpose of the contract is not on its own determinative of whether a term is to be implied in fact or by law. Even when implying a consent-based licence the purpose of commissioning is taken into account. Such purpose is set by the commissioner and the implied licence depends on the knowledge or reasonable expectation of the copyright owner of such purpose. For example, in *Ray*[78] the purpose of commissioning the catalogue was for Classic FM to use it for its programmes. But since it was not within Ray's knowledge or expectation that such purpose could extend outside the

[74] *Acohs Pty Ltd v RA Bashford Consulting Pty Ltd* (n 70) 532–33. *Acohs Pty Ltd v Ucorp Pty Ltd* (n 71) [94].

[75] Worksafe Australia Standard for Control of Workplace Hazardous Substances (1994) and National Code of Practice were declared under s 38(1) of the National Occupational Health and Safety Commission Act 1985. See *Acohs Pty Ltd v RA Bashford Consulting Pty Ltd* (n 70) 532, 548–49. The Occupational Health and Safety (Safety Standards) Regulations 1994 (Cth) was amended to provide that an MSDS must be prepared in accordance with the National Code of Practice. See *Acohs Pty Ltd v Ucorp Pty Ltd* (n 71) [12].

[76] *Acohs Pty Ltd v RA Bashford Consulting Pty Ltd* (n 70) 549; *Acohs Pty Ltd v Ucorp Pty Ltd* (n 71) [12].

[77] *Acohs Pty Ltd v RA Bashford Consulting Pty Ltd* (n 70) 547.

[78] [1998] EWHC Patents 333

UK, there was no implied licence for such overseas use. If it had been a policy that the engagement of a person for a fee to create a copyright work always results in an implied licence, the extent of knowledge or the reasonable expectation of the copyright owner as to the purpose of the contract would have had no impact on the licence implied. Although the appllate court in *Ucorp* draws a clearer distinction between implied in fact and implied by law cases, it does not make it clear whether *Beck v Montana* exemplified implied in fact or implied by law.[79]

There is certainly an identifiable purpose for commissioning contracts in the *Acohs* cases discussed here. However, such purpose is neither set by the commissioner nor is the knowledge of it by the copyright owner relevant for implying a licence. The purpose of the commissioning contract is regulated by law, as detailed above. Accordingly, the commissioning contracts where the law regulates the purpose to which the commissioned work can be put, should form the class of contracts. The policy behind such law should unify all contracts of this type. Contracts for commissioning MSDSs is perhaps not the only type of contracts that will form part of this class. One may think of disclosures in the financial industry whose purpose may be regulated by law, but such disclosures may be commissioned to be produced by an external contractor such as an auditor, as opposed to being produced internally. It is into this type of contracts that a licence may be implied based on the policy explained above, but only if it is necessary to do so.

(c) Necessary to imply the licence

The statutory framework stated above requires that, although it is the manufacturers, suppliers, or importers who commission the MSDSs, the MSDSs must be reproducible by and for the use of other suppliers, by employers for their employees, and by employees during the course of their handling of the substances. In order to achieve the policy of health and safety, it would be necessary to imply a licence into the commissioning contract in favour of the commissioning manufacturer, supplier, or importer. Such implied licence should be capable of being further sub-licenced to benefit all those whom the MIS is required by law to provide a copy, for them to further reproduce the MSDSs. This means that when the manufacturers, suppliers, and importers sell hazardous substance, a copy of the MSDS is provided to the purchaser, and into the contract of sale is implied a sub-licence to reproduce the relevant MSDS for the benefit of the purchaser's employees, as required by law. It is a sub-licence and not an assignment of implied licence by the relevant manufacturer, supplier, or importer to its customers because a manufacturer, supplier, or importer may need to reproduce the same MSDS for its own purpose or for

[79] *Acohs Pty Ltd v Ucorp Pty Ltd* (n 71) [147]–[148].

another customer who may also need the licence to reproduce the same MSDS. Therefore, it brings greater clarity to regard the manufacturer, supplier, or importer as the primary beneficiary of the implied licence from the copyright owner, with the ability to sub-license the reproduction of the MSDS as required by law.

As stated above, in *Bashford* Acohs was trying to establish itself as the beneficiary of this implied licence and in *Ucorp*, Ucorp was trying to do the same. Therefore, a question arises as to the beneficiaries of the sub-licence, and in particular, as to where the competing service providers Acohs and Ucorp fit into the statutory provisions. Clearly, the service providers do not themselves handle hazardous substances, nor are they mentioned by the statutes, although they do play a key role in compiling and updating the key information underlying the MSDSs. While the manufacturers, suppliers, and importers are required by law to provide the most up to date MSDSs, they are not obliged to commission updating by another person. While one can see the necessity of the manufacturer, supplier, or importer's implied licence being sub-licensable to its customers, the same argument of necessity may not hold good in extending the sub-licence to service providers like Acohs or Ucorp. This point is illustrated in *Bashford*, where the initial MSDSs at issue were created by Bashford upon being commissioned by a manufacturer, supplier, or importer, which they later took to a competitor of Bashford's, namely Acohs, to have them updated. On the one hand, it is difficult to argue that it was 'necessary' to let the relevant manufacturer, supplier, or importer sub-license the implied licence to reproduce the initial MSDS in favour of Acohs when the manufacturer, supplier, or importer entered into a contract with Acohs to update the MSDS. It was not necessary for Acohs as a competitor of Bashford to benefit from a free licence to reproduce the MSDS, much less a free licence to create an adaptation of it by updating it, especially when Acohs provided the updated MSDS back to the commissioning manufacturer, supplier, or importer for a fee. On the other hand, given Acohs' commercial motive, Acohs should have paid a licence fee to Bashford, as the maker of the initial MSDS, to reproduce and adapt it.

Merkel J took the view in *Bashford* that since the service providers were also engaged in a service that ultimately helped to achieve the health and safety objective, the competing service providers should also be able to benefit from the implied licence. Merkel J went on to say that if he was incorrect in his view that the implied licence itself extended to the service providers, then the implied licence could be transferred.[80] As noted above, what he meant here was that Bashford's implied licence could be sub-licensed to the service providers in the same way that it could be sub-licensed to the customers of Bashford. Not only did Acohs have the benefit of the implied licence (by way of sub-licence) to reproduce and adapt the MSDS when commissioned by the manufacturer, supplier, or importer to transcribe, but the

[80] *Acohs Pty Ltd v RA Bashford Consulting Pty Ltd* (n 70) 550.

implied licence also extended to what Merkel J called 'industrial use' and 'library use'. Industrial use entailed the use of all the transcribed MSDSs made available in an electronic database to those manufacturers, suppliers, and importers who had commissioned such transcription. This use by Acohs was held to be included within the implied licence. Library use was where all the transcribed MSDSs were held in a database and made available to the public emergency services and organisations for a fee. Merkel J held that providing such access to public emergency services fell within the 'safety related purpose' for which the MSDS are brought into existence.[81] This meant that Acohs could not only benefit from a free licence to reproduce and adapt MSDS, but could also make a profit from the transcribed MSDS through the industrial and library use.

One may argue that it is hard to support the decision based on necessity, especially for a licence of this wide a scope. Clearly, implying a licence of this nature is not the only way in which the policy could be achieved. Acohs being a profit-making entity could be made to take an express ongoing licence from Bashford, paying a licence fee for such use, in recognition of the commercial use made by Acohs. However, the unspoken logic here may have been that each service provider was creating adaptations of a competitor's MSDSs. Therefore, it was not Acohs alone who took from Bashford; it is possible that Bashford also took from Acohs and other competitors. The overriding logic may well have been that the licence fee owed by or to a service provider may have been cancelled out.

In *Ucorp*, while Acohs admitted that there was an implied licence in favour of the suppliers and employees of the manufacturer, supplier, or importer, it argued that such implied licence could not extend to benefit a commercial competitor at no cost and for the competitor's commercial benefit.[82] However, given that the decision in *Bashford* benefited Acohs, Acohs did not argue that no licence may be implied at all in favour of commercial competitors such as Ucorp. What it did argue before the primary judge was that the library use that Ucorp could make extended only to reproducing and adapting a competitor's MSDSs in response to a request by a manufacturer, supplier, or importer, and not in advance and in anticipation of such request being made at some point in future.[83] While the primary judge accepted that Acohs was reproducing and adapting work simply to build a collection for its commercial benefit, he held that such use was also covered by implied licence. This is because the ultimate use which Acohs made of the entries in the collection was still in keeping with the health and safety policy in assisting manufacturers, suppliers, importers, and employers. Further, building a collection of updated MSDS was a step towards the industrial use permitted in *Bashford*. The primary judge recognised that the scope of this implied licence is broader than that

[81] ibid 551.
[82] *Acohs Pty Ltd v Ucorp Pty Ltd* (n 71) [96].
[83] (2010) 86 IPR 492 [128].

found in *Basford*. He also noted that some state legislations required that a copy of the MSDS can be requested by any member of the public or any person who reasonably requires it, and therefore, such a member of the public could equally be Ucorp.[84] However, it is clear that accessing a copy of MSDS is different from making further copies of it for commercial use and adapting it by updating it, and it is difficult to equate the access to public with the implied licence extending to a commercial service provider like Ucorp. Therefore, appellate court disagreed with the primary judge. It held that in reproducing and adapting a competitor's MSDS in anticipation of it being requested by a manufacturer, supplier, or importer, Ucorp was relying on a licence it 'did not then have and might never have'. It further held that there is no reason of necessity for Ucorp to engage in such 'antecedent and anticipatory acts' and even if reasons of 'convenience and expediency' were provided, these were not sufficient.[85]

These cases drive home the point that what is necessary may be a function of the manner in which the particular industry is set up. Acohs copying Bashford-authored MSDSs and Ucorp copying Acohs-authored MSDSs show a mutually dependent industry. However, this does not mean unlimited copying of each other's databases should be regarded as necessary. The acts of copying must be mediated by a manufacturer, supplier, or importer requesting an MSDS to be updated and thereby giving access to an MSDS to a service provider that is authored by a competitor. In other words, the implied licence granted to a manufacturer, supplier, or importer by a service provider during the commissioning of a new MSDS will extend to a competitor when the manufacturer, supplier, or importer takes this MSDS for updating by the competitor, by way of a sub-licence of the initial implied licence. This is regarded by the courts as necessary, despite commercial motives, given mutually dependent industry serving the same policy of health and safety.

Although this anticipatory use was found by the full court to be not 'necessary', a better explanation is that there is no contract in existence in these situations into which a licence may be implied. In effect, the appellate court's decision follows the contract into which the implied licence can be further sub-licensed. Ucorp is only able to gain the benefit of the implied licence enjoyed by the manufacturer, supplier, or importer by way of a sublicence when the manufacturer, supplier, or importer requests the updating of an MSDS initially authored by Acohs. Even if Ucorp can access Acohs-authored MSDSs from other sources, such as online, it cannot simply copy from those sources and retain these MSDSs in its own collection, in anticipation of being requested by a manufacturer, supplier, or importer. When Ucorp or any service provider creates a collection of MSDSs on its own volition, there is no contract into which a licence may be implied that it is permitted to reproduce and

[84] ibid [96], [136], [139], [141].
[85] *Acohs Pty Ltd v Ucorp Pty Ltd* (n 71) [152]–[153].

update its collection. Such licence, if it were to exist, must exist as a bare licence, which brings us to the end of this chapter and connects it to the next chapter.

5. Conclusions and Connections

This chapter began by discussing why the existing methodology of implying a term by law is inadequate, and justified the framework put forward in Chapter 3. It went on to apply this framework, first, to address the issue of what distinguishes implied in fact cases from implied by law, especially since Australian authorities such as *Concrete* had noted that architectural plans cases lend themselves to terms implied by law. Having thus clarified this distinction, the chapter moved on to address specific policies driving implied contractual licences by examining how exhaustion can be explained as a policy-based implied contractual licence. This chapter also went on to apply the framework to the issue of spare parts and repair, where a policy-based licence was implied to reproduce the copyright work underlying a spare part to facilitate repair. And, finally, this chapter has discussed a specialised industry such as hazardous substances and how the information flow in this industry is regulated by policy-based implied contractual licences.

The discussion on the licence to repair raises a question—what happens if a member of the public wishes to provide spare parts in advance of receiving instructions from his customers to repair? As stated above, he cannot rely on a sublicence from the purchaser of the product incorporating copyright work. What if the production of spare parts by such third parties involves reproducing copyright work incorporated in the product? Since the third party is in a contractual relationship neither with the copyright owner nor with the owner of the the Copyright Product at the time of reproducing the copyright works to produce spare parts, there is no contract into which a licence can be implied. We reach the same conclusion while discussing the *Acohs* cases in relation to hazardous substances and MSDSs. The question then is can the third party still receive a bare licence based on the respective public policy—of facilitating the repair of the product in the most economical and efficient manner or providing ready access to the most updated MSDS? This is discussed in Chapter 8 below.

8
Policy-based Implied Bare Licences

Chapter 7 above considered situations where a licence is implied for policy reasons into a contract. We saw that the existence of a contract provides, to some extent, voluntariness on part of the copyright owner in dealing with the copyright work. Judges regard themselves justified in implying a licence within such a contract, even if the licence does not strictly emanate from the consent of the copyright owner, but is attributable to a public policy. This chapter considers whether the courts have power to imply a bare licence to give effect to a policy, even if no contract exists.

Chapter 3 above identified the common law rule preventing or restricting copyright enforcement in public interest. It was demonstrated that the refusal to enforce copyright against a particular use indirectly resulted in a licence to continue with that use of the copyright work, which was termed as policy-based implied licence.[1] It also raised the possibility of this power being exercisable in other common law jurisdictions. Given the breadth of discretion granted to the courts, Chapter 3 suggested the exercise of this power within the framework of the three-step test, or the fundamental rights regime in the alternative. In none of these jurisdictions has the court used the expression policy-based implied bare licence, nor the methodology used for implication, although in most cases it is referred to as a public interest defence. This chapter seeks to demonstrate how the jurisdiction of the court can be brought under this framework.

As far as the three-step test is concerned, this was also seen as a way of bringing the exercise of this power closer to the obligations under the Berne Convention (BC). This author has argued elsewhere that the power of the courts to restrict or prevent the enforcement of copyright is compatible with EU law,[2] to the extent it is relevant before the Exit Day. However, one may point to the three recent decisions of the Court of Justice of the European Union (CJEU) in *Spiegel Online v Volker Beck*,[3] *Funke Medien v Bundesrepublik*,[4] and *Pelham v Ralf Hütter*,[5] all three of which reiterated the exhaustive list of the statutory limitations or exceptions (SLEs)

[1] See ch 3, section 3 above.
[2] Poorna Mysoor, '"Capturing the Dynamism of Fairness": a Common Law Perspective' in Daniel Gervais (ed), *Fairness, Morality and Ordre Public in Intellectual Property* (Edward Elgar Publishing 2020) 14–16.
[3] Case C-516/17 ECLI:EU:C:2019:625.
[4] Case C-469/17 ECLI:EU:C:2019:623.
[5] Case C-476/17 ECLI:EU:C:2019:624.

Implied Licences in Copyright Law. Poorna Mysoor, Oxford University Press (2021). © Poorna Mysoor.
DOI: 10.1093/oso/9780198858195.003.0009

within the Infosoc Directive. Although these decisions held that a derogation of exclusive rights was not possible based on fundamental right to free speech under Article 11 of the Charter beyond those recognised under the SLEs, these decisions read the fundamental rights into the language of the exclusive right in issue or the SLE in issue. If an existing SLE does not cover a legitimate public interest pointing to the violation of a fundamental right, it would be difficult to argue that the courts should rather let the fundamental rights be violated than to let the formalism of exhaustive list of SLEs be exceeded. Further, as argued in Chapter 3, the nature of the power confirmed under section 171(3) is different in that it does not directly derogate from the rights guaranteed to the copyright owner; it only prevents or restricts the enforcement of copyright if there is an overwhelming public policy reason. The CJEU has also, in certain earlier decisions, exercised its jurisdiction to deny relief for copyright infringement choosing the rights of the users above the copyright owners'.[6] Moreover, the latter part of recital 3 declares 'public interest' as one of the fundamental principles of EU law with which the harmonisation achieved by the Infosoc Directive must comply. Further, recital 31 states that the existing exceptions should be 'defined harmoniously', which means that public interest is one of the fundamental principles to bear in mind in bringing about such harmonisation. The power of the court confirmed under section 171(3), even if regarded an SLE, existed before the enactment of the Infosoc Directive, and the public interest is central to interpreting this power. As such, it can scarcely be said that the exercise of this power went against harmonisation.

Assuming that the above three decisions have effectively nullified any power that may remain in the hands of the judges in the UK, after the Exit Day only the directives that have already been implemented within the domestic law on the Exit Day will remain part of the UK domestic law.[7] The UK has not transposed into its statutes that the list of SLEs is exhaustive; on the contrary, it made no changes to section 171(3) when implementing Infosoc Directive into the Copyright, Designs and Patents Act 1988 (CDPA). As for the CJEU decisions handed down before the Exit Day, the High Court and the Court of Appeal will be bound by these, but the Supreme Court can choose to depart from these, applying the same principles as it would for departing from its own decisions.[8] As stated in Chapter 3, Section 3(b) above, article IP.15 of the Trade and Cooperation Agreement negotiated between the EU and the UK only requires that any limitations or exceptions to copyright be in compliance with the three-step test. Further, the Agreement provides for no ongoing supervisory jurisdiction of the CJEU. As such, that the UK courts will not need to interpret domestic law compatibly with EU law on an ongoing basis,

[6] Case C-70/10 *Scarlet Extended SA v SABAM* ECLI:EU:C:2011:771 and Case C-275/06 *Promusicae v Telefonica* ECLI:EU:C:2008:54.

[7] See European Union (Withdrawal) Act 2018, ss 2–4.

[8] European Union (Withdrawal) Act 2018, s 6(4)(a) and (b), read with s 6(5).

beyond the provisions of the European Union (Withdrawal) Act 2018. Therefore, the courts in the UK could realise the full potential of the public interest. In addition, in combination with the Freedom of Information Act 2000, the public interest defence can be a powerful tool for users to press into service.

The exhaustive list of SLEs is a feature of EU law, not necessarily shared by common law jurisdictions. The BC does not prescribe an exhaustive list of SLEs. Indeed, when the test was first introduced under Article 9(2), the objective was to unify the existing SLEs and guide future ones.[9] Article 9(2) opens with the words: 'It shall be a matter for legislation in the countries of the Union ...'. This indicates that the Union members continued to enjoy a level of freedom in adopting the SLEs of their choice.[10] Over the years, the test has been adopted by many subsequent international treaties, in relation to a wider array of rights, all of which regard the test as enabling the legislature of the respective contracting parties to design their SLEs.[11] While adopting the test in the WIPO Copyright Treaty, the agreed statement under Article 10 reiterated that the test is meant to be used to balance the competing interests, especially when a high level of protection is granted.[12] Therefore, in jurisdictions such as Australia and Canada the statutes do not dictate that the list of SLEs in their statute is exhaustive.

However, in the Australian context, one may note Gummow J's observations obiter in *Collier Constructions Pty Ltd v Foskett Pty Ltd*,[13] that there was no public interest defence in the Australian context, but admitting that the discretion to refuse an equitable relief was transposed into the Australian statute. However, subsequently in *Acohs Pty Ltd v RA Bashford Consulting Pty Ltd*, Merkel J held that the public interest defence does exist and that the underlying principle was premised on the court's discretion more so than a defence disentitling a copyright owner from relief.[14] He drew support from cases where the court in Australia refused to enforce copyright.[15] Referring to sections 115 and 116 of the Australian Copyright Act 1968 (ACA), Merkel J noted that the grant of equitable remedies also continues to be discretionary under the ACA. In relation to damages, he held that, although the grant of damages is normally non-discretionary, there may be situations where considerations of public policy such as illegality, dishonesty, or

[9] Martin Senftleben, *Copyright, Limitations and the Three-Step Test* (Kluwer Law 2004) 43–82; Sam Ricketson and Jane Ginsburg, *International Copyright and Neighbouring Rights, vol 1* (OUP 2005) paras [13.03]–[13.09].

[10] Mary Vitoria and others, *Laddie, Prescott and Vitoria: The Modern Law of Copyright* (5th edn, LexisNexis 2018) para [21.4].

[11] WTO Agreement on Trade-Related Aspects of Intellectual Property Rights, art 13; WIPO Copyright Treaty, art 10; WIPO Performances and Phonograms Treaty, art 16.

[12] See WIPO Doc CRNR/DC/4, para 12.09.

[13] (1990) 97 ALR 460, 471.

[14] (1997) 144 ALR 528, 553.

[15] Chief among them being *A-One Accessory Imports v Off Road Imports* (1996) 34 IPR 332, 334.

unconscionability may result in a court refusing to enforce a legal right, including a right to damages.[16]

Courts might still do well to respect the three-step test as a guideline to bear in mind while exercising this power, even if the international obligations do not have direct application in the countries of the Union. However, some commentators argue that the historical origins required the test to be vague, making it unsuitable as a guideline for the courts.[17] What may appear vague from one perspective may appear flexible from the other. As the courts are in the forefront dealing with the current challenges, arming the courts with the application of the test to meet these challenges may be a more pragmatic option.[18] In some jurisdictions like the EU, it is arguable that the addressees of the test are not only national legislatures, but also national courts.[19]

Indeed, the courts are in a good position to be the addressees of the three-step test, as they can make the best use of its open-ended abstract criteria, on a case by case basis. As this author has also argued elsewhere,[20] it is in the very nature of a judicial process to identify with precision the certain special cases within the limits of which the use of the work in public interest is to operate. As the extant literature reveals, the most controversial is the second step—whether the use of the work being permitted conflicts with the normal exploitation of the work. This is because, on the one hand, the WTO Panel decision on the three-step test appears to envisage that only economic and market considerations inform the assessment of 'normal'.[21] Scholars, on the other hand, insist that normative aspects such as education and research should also inform the assessment of normal.[22] If these broader considerations are not made way for, certain legitimate uses might not even pass muster beyond the second step. Accordingly, in this chapter, Section 1 groups the cases based on the potential for exploitation of the works. The first part deals with cases where the work had no market for its exploitation because of their low originality and low commercial value; the second part deals with works that have a significant market for exploitation owing to their high commercial value, but the work is of low originality; and the third part deal with works that have a significant market for exploitation owing to the high commercial value of the works and their high originality. It will be seen from the discussion below that in most cases the courts have

[16] He relied on *Kalamazoo (Aust) Pty Ltd v Compact Business Systems Pty Ltd* (1985) 5 IPR 213, 84 FLR 101 at 127–8(Thomas J).

[17] Jonathan Griffiths, 'The "Three-step Test" in European Copyright Law: Problems and Solutions' (2009) 4 IPQ 428, 429–30.

[18] Huaiwen He, 'Seeking a Balanced Interpretation of the Three-step Test' (2009) 40 IIC 274, 306.

[19] Christophe Geiger, 'From Berne to National Law, via the Copyright Directive: The Dangerous Mutations of the Three-Step Test' (2007) 29 EIPR 486, 488–90.

[20] Mysoor (n 2) 16–18.

[21] Panel Report of 15 June 2000, United States—Article 110(5) of the US Copyright Act WT/DS160/R [6.166], [6.178], and it just so happened that in that case only economic considerations were relevant.

[22] Ricketson and Ginsburg (n 9) paras 13.20–13.22.

exercised restraint in reading public interest, even when the three-step test would have permitted a broader reading.

It may so happen in certain cases that it makes more sense to apply the fundamental rights discourse to a situation than the three-step test. Although fundamental rights can also be read into the second and the third steps of the three-step test, it has an independent and well-established methodology of its own, which could be pressed into service. Since each jurisdiction has its own constitutional culture, this chapter takes the example of the UK as one such jurisdiction. This is dealt with in Section 2 below.

1. Three-step Test as the Framework

Scholars regard public interest to be a justifiable ground to deny copyright enforcement only in the interest of morality, *ordre public*, prevention of abuse of the process, and disclosure of confidential information. However, as this Section will demonstrate, the cases to which public interest methodology can be applied are much more diverse.

(a) Low originality and low commercial value copyright works

Some of the cases discussed here arose in the context of confidential information. Indeed, it is said that copyright law 'filched' the public interest defence from the law of confidentiality.[23] This is not entirely accurate as public interest has been used also in cases where there was no confidentiality. However, it must be acknowledged that cases requiring disclosure of information in the public interest arose first in the context of confidentiality. If confidentiality only extended to information, no copyright would subsist in it. With the continued lowering of the threshold for originality, the same information in which confidentiality is claimed could also be protected by copyright. In most cases, the existence of copyright is purely incidental. There is little or no prospect of the copyright work in question being exploited independently, either because the copyright owner values its confidentiality or because the copyright owner does not market products derived from the copyright works. Given the low commercial value of the copyright work and no market for its exploitation, it should be relatively straightforward that the second step of the three-step test is satisfied. The assessment then is whether permitting the use at issue prejudices some other legitimate interest of the copyright owner and balancing the public interest with such interest. One will see that in most cases

[23] Alexandra Sims, 'The Public Interest Defence in Copyright Law: Myth or Reality?' (2006) 28 EIPR 335.

the user is a publisher, newspaper, or a television channel that may have benefited from the fair dealing defence. However, what the user seeks is a verbatim reproduction of either the entire work or a large part of the work beyond that permitted by fair dealing. Under these circumstances, even when there was no other legitimate interest of the copyright owner that needed protection, a court still has not permitted the use sought because the public interest did not reach the threshold beyond that of fair dealing.

In this vein, the meeting minutes and memoranda that concern government operations are a good starting point. In *Beloff v Pressdram Ltd*,[24] an internal memorandum written by the plaintiff, a correspondent of a newspaper, was reproduced and published by the defendant magazine. The memorandum contained discussions with cabinet ministers as to who should succeed the prime minister in the event of his accidental death.[25] The plaintiff claimed both breach of confidence and copyright infringement. The defendant raised the public interest as a defence both to confidentiality and copyright infringement, apart from fair dealing. Given the minimal literary quality of the memorandum, the court acknowledged that it was not a genuine case of copyright infringement. The confidential nature of the memorandum appeared stronger since it named the cabinet ministers as the source of the plaintiff's information. The court treated the case as concerning confidentiality, couched in terms of copyright infringement. The court referred to earlier cases on confidentiality in concluding that the public interest would come into play only if there was a 'disclosure of iniquity'.[26] Since the memorandum did not disclose any iniquity or misdeed on anyone's part that needed to be covered up, the court held that no public interest would be served in its disclosure. As the public interest defence was unsuccessful in relation to confidentiality, the court did not consider whether it was a defence to copyright infringement. Nevertheless, it drives home the point that copyright could come in the way of a public interest defence to breach of confidence if a similar defence were not recognised against copyright infringement.

It is outside the scope of this work to critique the public interest defence to confidentiality. However, *Beloff* may have held a particularly generous view of the government's claim to confidentiality. The Australian case of *Commonwealth v John Fairfax & Sons Ltd*[27] sheds light on this. Here, certain authors and publishers published a book entitled *Documents on Australian Foreign Policy and Defence 1968-75*, which contained a small part of the authors' own commentary, but a majority of the book reproduced hitherto unpublished government documents, the copyright

24 [1973] FSR 33.

25 ibid 35, 54–55.

26 ibid 55–58. The cases referred to were *Initial Services Ltd v Putterill* [1968] 1 QB 396, 403–405, and *Hubbard v Vosper* [1972] 2 QB 84, 92, 95, which had held that the disclosure was necessary in the public interest where there is a crime, fraud, or a misdeed committed or contemplated.

27 (1980) 147 CLR 39.

in which was owned by the claimant. The plaintiff had obtained an ex parte interim injunction restraining certain newspapers from publishing a serialised version of the book and against the publishers of the book from distributing the book. However, the claimant was too late to obtain the injunction in both cases, as some copies of both the newspaper and the book were already in circulation. The plaintiff claimed copyright infringement and the commission of a crime by breach of confidentiality, as it claimed that the documents had been classified as confidential and their disclosure would prejudice Australia's foreign affairs. The defendants denied that the documents disclosed were confidential and that, in any event, it was too late to stop the distribution of the work.[28] Mason J held that a democratic society must enable the public to discuss, review, and criticise government action. Accordingly, the court held that when a government claims confidentiality, '[u]nless the disclosure is likely to injure the public interest, it will not be protected'.[29] He found that the documents disclosed did not contain technical information of military significance or information of material value to a hostile power. Although it may have caused embarrassment to Australian foreign relations, the court found that it was not sufficient to restrain the book's publication. Therefore, instead of preventing disclosure, public interest would have enabled disclosure in this case, if not for the copyright infringement claim.

In relation to copyright, the court held that the use was not covered by fair dealing. Referring to *Beloff*, Mason J did acknowledge the public interest defence to copyright infringement and held that it makes legitimate the publication of material in which copyright subsists so as to protect the community from destruction, damage, or harm. He went on to observe that the defence applies to disclosures of things done in breach of national security or through fraud. He held that there was no precedent of the public interest defence being used in a case like this where none of these considerations existed and that to apply the defence to such a situation would break new ground. In granting the injunction, Mason J observed that, although a plaintiff does not ordinarily exploit copyright in its documents for commercial advantage,, this does not give defendants title to infringe that copyright. He went on to add that the essence of copyright in an unpublished work is that it enables the owner to prevent others from publishing the work. Although he recognised that the injunction would protect the information contained in the documents, he held that nothing stopped the defendants from publishing the information, so long as they did not reproduce the manner in which the information was expressed.[30]

One may argue that this case is a missed opportunity. As the court recognises, there was no prospect of the work being exploited by the government. The court

[28] ibid 44–46, 48–49.
[29] ibid 52.
[30] ibid 57–58.

had also recognised that it was in the public interest to publish the documents to encourage discussion. The only interest of the copyright owner that may have been prejudiced is that the documents were unpublished. But this will be the case in all information over which the government wants to claim confidentiality. Someone must publish them if a democratic debate is to be encouraged. Clearly, the same expectation of freedom to publish or not publish does not apply to governments, and therefore, it is not a good excuse to say that the information contained in the documents could be published without having to reproduce the whole document verbatim. Especially when one deals with the government, the information is as important as how it is framed, the turn of phrase used, and so on, necessitating the reproduction of the whole document. Instead of regarding breach of confidence as having no relationship with copyright infringement, the court should have weighed against the interests of the copyright owner the same public interest considerations that informed the disclosure of confidential information, in assessing the third step of the three-step test. Surely, a new public interest need not be established to defend against copyright infringement.

A somewhat different situation arose in *Ashdown v Telegraph Group Ltd*,[31] in that the author of the copyright work was an individual who had personal interest in publishing it. The claimant was a leader of the political party and had authored the minutes of a confidential meeting with the then prime minister of the UK regarding a possible coalition of the ruling party with the claimant's party. The claimant was in the habit of keeping diaries of his political career, which he later wanted to publish as a book, and he wanted to reproduce these minutes therein. He had disclosed the minutes to a small group of journalists and publishers in strict confidence, informing them about his intentions. The minutes were somehow leaked, and the defendant newspaper carried a feature, quoting extensively from the minutes. The claimant sued for breach of confidence and copyright infringement, claiming an injunction and damages. The claimant also filed an application for summary judgment on the copyright issue. The defendant claimed the defence of fair dealing and public interest.[32]

The High Court granted summary judgment on the copyright issue, stating that neither defence was made out. The court did not give a finding on whether the public interest defence was made out in relation to confidentiality. It held that there was no justification for the defendant to have used the exact words of the minutes, and that it could have used its own words to describe the contents of the minutes, especially since there were other newspapers which reported the same event without copying extensively from the minutes.[33] Upon the defendant's appeal, the

[31] [2001] Ch 685. The application of the Human Right Act 1998 raised in this case is discussed later in this chapter.
[32] ibid [1]–[5].
[33] ibid [79]–[81].

Court of Appeal endorsed this view. It held that the fair dealing defence under section 30 of the CDPA would 'normally afford the court all the scope' it needs to reflect the public interest in freedom of expression, and therefore, there would be no need to consider separately the public interest defence under section 171(3).[34] The court went on to recognise, however, that there may be cases where one may need to demonstrate the authenticity of a source requiring a journalist to quote the source verbatim. But it regarded these to be very rare cases and that, in the current case, the threshold of public interest did not reach the required level for such verbatim reproduction.[35]

It must be acknowledged here that, unlike *John Fairfax* above, the claimant did want to exploit the minutes he had drafted commercially. Seeking its confidentiality was only to ensure that his upcoming book was the only source of it. The claimant here wanting to maintain the freedom of when he wishes to publish a work that he has authored is distinguishable from a government department authoring a memorandum, as in *John Fairfax*. Therefore, one might argue that, to this extent, the second step was not satisfied, since permitting the verbatim disclosure of the minutes would have interfered with its normal exploitation by its author. One may also argue here that, if normal means acting according to a standard, then normative considerations should inform such standard to determine what is normal exploitation under these circumstances—the normative consideration being quoting verbatim promotes the authenticity when the matter concerned the public life of politicians whose actions had implications for the public. However, it may well be difficult to argue in this case that the minutes in question were not such that a person would only believe the words if they were quoted verbatim, given that other newspapers had reported the minutes without quoting verbatim. Nevertheless, *Ashdown* is important because it arose after the Infosoc Directive was transposed into the CDPA. Although it did not apply the public interest defence, it acknowledged its existence.

To appreciate the manner in which the public interest defence operates outside the context of the government, one may look to the celebrated case of *Lion Laboratories Ltd v Evans*.[36] The unequivocal exposition of the public interest defence for copyright by Stephenson LJ made it worthy of mention in the parliamentary debates in the run up to the enactment of the CDPA in the context of the public interest defence.[37] In this case, the plaintiff carried on the business of selling intoximeters, which were instruments used by the police for measuring intoxication from alcohol for road safety. Two of the defendants who were employees of the plaintiff resigned from their positions and, while leaving, took with them certain

[34] [2001] EWCACiv 1142, [2002] Ch 149 [66].
[35] ibid [31], [44]–[46].
[36] [1985] QB 526, 550.
[37] HL Deb 8 December 1987 vol 491, col 76.

internal correspondence indicating the faulty calibration of intoximeters giving incorrect results. The ex-employees gave the correspondence to the defendant newspapers for publication. The plaintiff sued them for breach of confidence and copyright infringement. There was no dispute as to the confidentiality of the correspondence nor as to the plaintiff's ownership of copyright in it. The trial judge granted an interim injunction restraining the defendant newspapers from publishing, against which the defendants appealed.[38]

The Court of Appeal held that there was no requirement of iniquity, misdeed, or criminality before a public interest defence could be established in relation to confidentiality, since it was inconclusive whether the plaintiff had tried to cover up the faults with intoximeters. Given the plaintiff's monopoly in supplying these instruments and the evidentiary value of their readings in criminal convictions, Stephenson LJ found that the public had a genuine interest in knowing the fallibility of these instruments. Having thus found the public interest, he went on to hold that the courts 'will restrain breaches of confidence and breaches of copyright unless there is a just cause or excuse for breaking the confidence or infringing copyright'.[39] Thus, he expressly recognised that the enforcement of copyright is subject to the same public interest defence as confidential information. Griffiths LJ and O'Connor LJ concurred with Stephenson LJ, although cautiously, to hold that the defence extended also to copyright infringement under exceptional circumstances.[40]

By this, the scope of the public interest defence in relation to confidentiality was expanded along similar lines as in *John Fairfax*, but beyond the specific context of the government. In terms of the three-step test, these internal documents did not have any prospect for independent exploitation. Therefore, one could move to the balancing of any other legitimate interest the copyright owner might have with considerations of public interest. It is clear in this case that the public interest was so overwhelming that no interest of the copyright owner in a work not amenable for economic exploitation, however legitimate, would have outweighed it. Admittedly, there was a need to reproduce extensively from the internal communications (beyond the limits permitted by fair dealing) to make the story believable. In the language of licence, the court implied a bare licence in the defendants' favour, to reproduce and communicate the internal correspondence to the defendant newspapers (who benefited from an implied sub-licence from the defendant employees), based on the public interest in the disclosure of the discrepancies in the intoximeters.

In the cases above, the breach of confidence provided the context to determine the extent of the public interest defence also for copyright infringement. There

[38] *Lion Laboratories Ltd v Evans* (n 36) 532–35.
[39] ibid 536–39, 550.
[40] ibid 548, 551.

are equally cases where the cause of action did not disclose any breach of confidence, but only copyright infringement. An important case in this regard is *Service Corporation International Plc v Channel Four Television Corporation*. Here, an employee of a funeral services home conducted an undercover operation for the defendant television channel and had made film footage to disclose to the public the disrespectful and abusive treatment of corpses carried out by the claimant.[41] The plaintiff (SCI) sought a temporary injunction on the basis of defamation, trespass, breach of confidence, and copyright infringement. The defendant raised the defence of justification against defamation and public interest against copyright infringement, denying that it had used any confidential information.[42]

Lightman J held that the primary objective of SCI was to protect its reputation, but the law prohibited the grant of an injunction against a defamatory statement when the defence was justification, leaving only damages as a possible remedy for a claimant to pursue. Lightman J observed that if the other causes of action were merely an attempt to overcome this prohibition, the court would give effect to freedom of speech which was the overwhelming factor to be considered in this case. He went on to rule that even if the defendant had trespassed upon SCI's land, this could not be the reason to prevent the showing of the film. He also found that the film had been made without the use of any confidential material. As for copyright ownership, he held that SCI did not have an arguable case on copyright ownership, since the employee had produced the film outside the course of his employment, without breaching his fiduciary duty.[43] However, even if SCI could show its entitlement to copyright, he held that the defendants had an arguable case that the broadcast of the programme was in public interest. He held that the defendant's film revealed 'a scandalous state of affairs and supports the defendants' case that the funeral home industry should be regulated as a matter of "substantial public interest"'. Although he mentioned neither section 171(3) nor any case law to support this conclusion, he factored in the public interest in the balancing exercise to refuse the injunction.[44]

In terms of the three-step test, even if one were to accept that SCI had acquired copyright in the film footage owing to the employee's breach of fiduciary duty, SCI would have seen no prospect of exploiting the footage. Indeed, it would be in its best interest to destroy the footage. There would have been no other legitimate interest of SCI as a copyright owner that could have weighed against the public interest in broadcasting the footage. *Service Corporation International* represents

41 [1999] EMLR 83.

42 ibid 86–88.

43 ibid 89–91. In *Australian Broadcasting Corporation v Lenah Game Meats* (2001) 185 ALR 1, where the operations of a slaughterhouse were covertly captured on camera, the claimant made no claim to copyright but sought an injunction against the ABC based on various grounds, including confidentiality and breach of privacy. However, the High Court of Australia held by a majority that no injunction could be granted as the balance of convenience tipped in the ABC's favour.

44 *Service Corporation International Plc v Channel Four Television Corporation* (n 41) 91–92.

the classic application of the public interest defence in the weighing and balancing act that a court must engage in when granting an injunction. Using the language of licence, assuming that SCI was the copyright owner in the footage, by refusing an injunction the court implied in favour of the defendant a licence to broadcast the footage on the basis of the public interest in its disclosure.

The question of copyright infringement without questions of confidentiality were raised again in *Hyde Park Residence Ltd v Yelland*.[45] Here, the plaintiff managed the security of Villa Windsor, a place visited by Princess Diana and Dodi Fyed on the day before their deaths in a car accident. Certain still photographs of the Princess and Fyed taken from the claimant's security cameras during their visit to the villa had been given away by the claimant's employee to the defendant newspaper, without permission, allegedly to expose the falsehood surrounding their deaths. The plaintiff alleged copyright infringement, but not breach of confidentiality.[46] The defendant raised the defence of fair dealing and public interest.

Jacob J upheld the claim of fair dealing, but also dealt with the public interest defence anyway. He disagreed with the claim that no defence of public interest exists. While recognising the close connection the defence has with confidentiality cases, he clarified that the defence is narrow and applies only in cases where no right-thinking person would conclude otherwise, and that the disclosure must be proportionate to the public interest.[47] On the facts, Jacob J held that the public interest defence had been made out for the same reasons as the fair dealing defence. Even if the outcome is laudable, this finding is problematic. For the public interest defence to be successfully claimed, if it takes the same or similar facts as the fair dealing defence, then there is no independent utility of the public interest defence. A more nuanced analysis of the circumstances in which the public interest defence would be successful independently of any other defence would have been helpful.

On the plaintiff's appeal, the Court of Appeal began by delineating the public interest defence for copyright infringement in the absence of a breach of confidence. To Aldous LJ, the difference lay in the fact that if confidential information is disclosed in the public interest, the very foundation of the action disappears. But the disclosure of a copyright work does not destroy the foundation of an action in copyright infringement. In this sense, he held that the breadth of the public interest defence for confidentiality is not comparable with that for copyright infringement.[48] For Mance LJ, public interest as a defence to confidential information was borne out of freedom of expression and information; and copyright did not 'lie on the same continuum as, nor was it the antithesis of, freedom of expression', and

[45] [1999] EWHC 247 (Pat); [1999] EMLR 654.

[46] ibid [1]–[8].

[47] ibid [30], [40]. Jacob J relied on the Australian decisions in *Commonwealth v John Fairfax & Sons* Ltd (n 27) discussed above and *Acohs Pty Ltd v RA Bashford Consulting Pty Ltd* (n 14), discussed below.

[48] [2000] EWCA Civ 37, [2001] Ch 143 [64].

therefore the protection of copyright could not be 'weighed in the same direct way against a public interest in knowing the truth'.[49]

Aldous LJ was stating the obvious distinction between the two causes of action. But this does not mean that the considerations that go into a defence for one are necessarily different for the other. It is in the very nature of public interest that overriding considerations of persons other than the parties to the litigation are considered, whether it is against breach of confidence or copyright infringement. In cases where both causes of action of breach of confidence and copyright infringement exist, the same considerations that inform the public interest defence against breach of confidence can also inform the public interest defence against copyright infringement, as *Lion* demonstrates. In cases where the only cause of action is copyright infringement, it is likewise conceivable that there would be public interest considerations that could prevent or restrict copyright enforcement. Mance LJ's observation that enforcement of copyright does not directly affect freedom of expression is also problematic because copyright can be an antithesis to freedom of expression and information, as will be discussed in the next section below.

Aldous LJ acknowledged the existence of the defence of public interest to copyright infringement, but held it to be limited to cases where enforcement of copyright would 'offend against the policy of the law'.[50] However, while admitting that the circumstances under which the public interest defence would come into play are not capable of definition, Aldous LJ still went on to enumerate these circumstances thus: where the copyright work is immoral, scandalous, or contrary to family life, or is injurious to public life, public health and safety, or the administration of justice. Mance LJ disagreed and held that the public interest defence is not capable of precise categorisation. Stuart-Smith LJ gave a one line judgment agreeing with Aldous LJ. On the facts, the Court was unanimous in holding that no defence of public interest (nor of fair dealing) was established.[51]

There are several points to be noted here. First, the categorisation of public interest is unjustified. There is a reason why section 171(3) is broadly worded—to give the courts maximum flexibility in assessing each case on its own facts. The legislative history also supports this.[52] Secondly, and substantively, the categories are clearly quite narrow. They represent only the line of cases where copyright enforcement is refused because the content of the work is objectionable, and not because the public should benefit from its disclosure. This suggests that there is no public interest defence that extends to copyright infringement if the objective is disclosure in public interest. Thirdly, it paid no heed to the High Court decisions

49 ibid [76].
50 ibid [64].
51 ibid [66], [77]–[79], [83].
52 Mysoor (n 2) 10–12.

that had already recognised the public interest defence, independent of a claim in confidentiality, such as *Service Corporation International*.[53]

Viewing from the prism of the three-step test, the plaintiff's only claim to copyright in the CCTV images was that it had installed the camera. It has questionable originality in the minimal effort and skill it takes to install the CCTV. Even if the photographs satisfy the minimum level of originality, the possibility of the plaintiff exploiting these images would have been non-existent. These considerations should have been weighed against the public interest in publishing the photographs. Scholars have claimed that the public interest in exposing the lies surrounding the death of 'a future sovereign's mother' outweighed the copyright protection in the photographs, which, in any event, were captured owing to no exercise of human creativity.[54] With the second step satisfied, in the third step there were no other legitimate interests of the copyright owner that the court could have regarded as weighing above the public interest in publishing the photographs.

Aldous LJ's enumeration in *Yelland* of circumstances in which the public interest defence could be exercised was regarded by the High Court in *Ashdown* as the majority view and a view binding on the High Court. It held that the facts of the case did not fall within any of those categories.[55] Denying the defendants a defence in both fair dealing and public interest, the High Court granted the plaintiff summary judgment. Fortunately, the Court of Appeal held that the High Court's strict adherence to the list of circumstances enumerated by Aldous LJ was unjustified, as Mance LJ had disagreed with him and Stuart-Smith LJ had not expressed a specific opinion. As such, the Court went on to regard *Lion* as the authority on the point. Upon analysing the judgment, it held that two of the three judges in *Lion* had recognised a defence of public interest even when there was no moral turpitude. The Court, therefore, endorsed Mance LJ's views that the circumstances in which the public interest defence can be claimed are not capable of precise enumeration.[56] *Ashdown* brought back, to some extent, the flexibility and breadth of the public interest defence.

The cases above demonstrate that low originality and a low prospect of exploitation does not necessarily make it easier for the public interest defence to be established. On its own, the public interest should be so grave that it far outweighs any prejudice that may be caused to any other legitimate interest of the copyright owner. The purpose of the public interest defence is not to dilute the fair dealing defence, but to address cases that pose far graver threats to the public interest than fair dealing can address.

53 Robert Burrell, 'Defending the Public Interest' (2000) 22 EIPR 394, 402.
54 Sims (n 23) 338.
55 [2001] Ch 685 [32].
56 [2001] EWCA Civ 1142, [2002] Ch 149 [51]–[58].

(b) Low originality and high commercial value copyright works

The reigning theme in the above cases is the disclosure of copyright work in the public interest. By no means is the public interest confined to this theme. The line of cases below on spare parts and other works of low originality but high commercial value demonstrates how broad the application of the public interest can be. In these cases, because of the dominant commercial argument, normal exploitation under the second step on its face appears to go against recognition of the public interest defence. However, normative considerations that inform normal exploitation and the balancing exercise under the third step might still result in the public interest defence being upheld and copyright not being enforced. The result of not enforcing copyright is that a competitor of the copyright owner benefits indirectly from a licence to do what he could not otherwise have done, because of an overarching public interest.

Chapter 7 above addressed, inter alia, licence to repair a product that incorporates a copyright work. If repair involves reproduction of the work, implied into the contract of purchase of the product is a licence permitting the reproduction of the copyright work to enable repairs. We saw that if the person repairing is a third party rather than the purchaser of the product, the licence to repair could be sublicensed, so that the purchaser of the product can authorise someone else to repair. However, economic efficiency requires the person repairing the product to manufacture spare parts in advance of receiving an order. Here, there is no contract into which a licence permitting copying of the work can be implied before the manufacture of such spare parts. In these circumstances, it might be possible to imply a bare licence in favour of the spare parts provider, bypassing the purchaser of the product, to achieve the policy objective that the purchaser of the product should have access to the most economical and efficient way to repair the product.

This situation first arose in *British Leyland Motor Company Ltd v Armstrong Patent Company Ltd*, where the plaintiff (BL), a car manufacturer, had asserted its claim to copyright in the design of spare parts, and had compelled many spare parts manufacturers to become licensees and pay royalties on sales of spare parts. However, the defendant (Armstrong) had always resisted becoming a licensee. In this action, BL claimed that Armstrong had reverse engineered and copied BL's exhaust pipes, thereby infringing its copyright in the design of the exhaust pipe.[57] The question was whether there was anything in the law to prevent BL from asserting its copyright to prevent Armstrong from reproducing the exhaust pipe design.

Solar Thomson Engineering Co Ltd v Barton was distinguished on many grounds, including that in this case the exhaust pipes were not patentable. In addition, at issue in *Solar* was expensive machinery to which spare parts would be

[57] [1986] 1 All ER 850, 854.

manufactured in response to a specific order of a purchaser of the machine, and not in advance in anticipation of the need.[58] In the Court of Appeal, Oliver LJ was prepared to accept that the purchaser of a BL car might herself copy, or commission another to copy the original exhaust pipe to provide replacements. He was willing to accept also that the implied licence could extend if the purchaser wanted two or three spare parts made in anticipation of future breakdowns. However, he found it impossible to derive from this a blanket licence in favour of any member of the public to copy the design of the exhaust pipe, in the absence of a specific order. Therefore, Oliver LJ rejected the possibility of an implied licence resting on a contractual basis.[59]

Lord Bridge in the House of Lords articulated two policy considerations, the first of which was that the owner of a car must be entitled to do whatever is necessary to keep it in running order and to effect whatever repairs may be necessary in the most economical way possible. He found that 'it is a right inherent in the ownership of the car itself' and 'to curtail or restrict the owner's right to repair in any way may diminish the value of the car'.[60] Secondly, he observed that BL had already enjoyed the primary benefit which its copyright protected when they sold cars fitted with exhausts based on its copyright drawings. To allow BL to enforce its copyright to maintain a monopoly for itself and its licensees in the supply and replacement of exhausts detracted from the car owners' rights and, at least potentially, the value of their cars.[61] But how does the entitlement to repair inherent in the ownership of a car translate to a general privilege of any member of the public to produce spare parts in advance and not in response to an order? Both Lord Bridge and Lord Templeman found their answer in the doctrine of non-derogation from grant, whereby the sale of the car was the grant, and to assert copyright over its spare parts was to derogate from that grant,[62] because it makes the repair more expensive, thereby diminishing the value of the grant. This went on to be known as the spare parts exception in subsequent cases.

However, this still does not translate to any member of the public being able to produce spare parts in advance, for several reasons. Non-derogation is for the benefit of the purchaser of the car. In Hohfeldian terms, if the grant is of the car together with a right against derogation, and a corresponding duty on BL not to derogate, it still does not explain why this right acquired by each car owner translates generally to any member of the public having a privilege to produce spare parts in advance. Even if one regards the non-derogation as being in rem, the duty not to derogate or the no-right to derogate will only arise once there is a grant, and not in advance of the grant. A plausible explanation is that the policy objectives identified

58 See ch 7, section 3 above.
59 [1984] FSR 591, 611–12.
60 [1986] 1 All ER 850, 861.
61 ibid 862.
62 ibid 873.

by Lord Bridge justify the implication of a bare licence in favour of any member of the public to produce spare parts in advance, to provide the most economical and efficient repair services possible. On this view, the doctrine of non-derogation from grant is irrelevant under these circumstances. As discussed below, that *British Leyland* was grounded in policy was recognised also by the subsequent decisions.

The effect of *British Leyland* was to permit Armstrong to continue to use BL's designs for the exhaust pipes without having to pay any compensation, although BL was exploiting these designs. Therefore, this decision would have interfered with the second step of the three-step test. However, it is arguable that the normative need for the owners of chattels to have access to economical and efficient supply of spare parts for repair can be regarded as much higher than the need for economic exploitation of copyright in the design. As regards the third step, on balance, it may be possible to argue that the copyright owner's legitimate interest extends to getting the value for the product she sells, namely the car. Her legitimate interest in copyright does not extend to the aftermarket for spare parts. Therefore, in particular, since these spare parts are normally of low originality, copyright ownership over the spare parts cannot be used to stifle the aftermarket. One may counterargue that even if the court was unwilling to grant an injunction to stop Armstrong from producing the exhaust pipes, it could have awarded damages which would have taken care of BL's legitimate interest. However, the entire purpose of the litigation was that Armstrong did not wish to pay a licence fee, which would have made the spare parts expensive, taking away their competitiveness in the aftermarket. Despite all the criticism of this case, the public interest identified in this case stands vindicated because some of the provisions of the CDPA were introduced because of the decision in *British Leyland*—in particular, section 51 and the unregistered design rights regime with shorter duration of protection to address the spare part industry.

The decision in *British Leyland* came into sharp focus again in *Canon Kabushiki Kaisha v Green Cartridge Co (Hong Kong) Ltd*,[63] a case dealing with the application of UK Copyright Act 1956, as it applied to Hong Kong before 1997. In this case, the plaintiff was the owner of copyright in the cartridges of the printers it manufactured. Its business model was such that it sold the printer at a relatively low price, with a significant part of the profits arising from the running cost of the printers, including in the sale of the cartridges. The defendant manufactured cartridges for the plaintiff's printers having reverse engineered the technology behind it (over which the plaintiff had a patent) and copied the drawings.[64] The question was whether the defendant's actions were covered by the spare parts exception carved out by *British Leyland*. Having been litigated before the High Court of Hong Kong and the Court of Appeal, the matter finally reached the Privy Council.

63 [1997] AC 728.
64 ibid 733–35.

Speaking for the board, Lord Hoffmann observed that *British Leyland* was founded neither on property nor on contract, but on an overriding principle of public policy, namely the need to prevent a manufacturer from using copyright to control the market in spare parts. He urged that courts must exercise caution in applying a judicially declared public policy in relation to protected statutory right. He found that the need for replacing cartridges was not a genuine repair since it is only required when the toner runs out, not because it needs repair owing to a malfunction, wear and tear, or breakdown. Therefore, he held that this case was not comparable to *British Leyland*. He also held that the unfairness that was seen by the House of Lords in permitting a manufacturer to control the aftermarket could not be found in this case.[65]

While one may accept Lord Hoffmann's efforts to emphasise the exceptionality of *British Leyland*, one should not read his opinion as denying any jurisdiction for courts to engage in policy. Although Lord Hoffmann was applying the 1956 Act, surely by the time of his judgment in 1997, the public interest defence had been established sufficiently for it to be raised and retained after the passing of the CDPA. In any event, the lack of genuine repair was sufficient on its own to negate any normativity in the normal exploitation of the plaintiff's copyright in the designs. It was clear that any public interest argument would interfere with the economic returns of the plaintiff. The lack of genuine repair would have made the need for public interest not to override the legitimate interests of the copyright owner.

The lack of genuine repair was again at issue in *Mars UK Ltd v Teknowledge Ltd*.[66] Here, the machine at issue was a coin discriminator operated electronically by way of sensors and software. In order to allow the machines to be able to discriminate newer coins, Mars introduced a new machine with a new discriminator program and database called Cashflow, which the defendant managed to reverse engineer and recalibrate when new coins were introduced.[67] Mars sued the defendant for infringement of copyright in the computer program and of database rights. It was held that the defendant could not use the spare parts exception because recalibration to accept new coins could amount to updating, but not to 'repair' of a part that is malfunctioning, worn out, or broken.[68] Further, the buyers of coin discriminators are not ordinary consumers but are buyers of sophisticated machinery, who expect the machinery to be recalibrated by the original supplier. As such, it was held that the analogy of these consumers to a consumer of an automobile does not work. In addition, he also believed that economic indicators such as pricing do not suggest that this layer of the market should be protected against Mars' monopoly.[69]

65 ibid 737, 739–40.
66 [1999] EWHC 226 (Pat).
67 ibid [1]–[8], [12].
68 ibid [9], [27]. Jacob J gave this finding as an alternative, assuming his findings that spare parts exception did not survive the CDPA was incorrect.
69 ibid [25]–[27].

It was argued in *Mars* that the spare parts exception did not survive the passing of the CDPA since it provided for the new unregistered designs regime and its own exceptions (must fit and must match exceptions under section 213(3)(b) of the CDPA). Jacob J held that this exception covered some, if not all, cases of spare parts and that, in relation to unregistered designs, no spare parts exception outside that which is expressly recognised can survive. However, *Mars* concerned software and database rights, and not rights in unregistered designs, and therefore he went on to consider whether the spare parts exception exists in relation to these rights. Jacob J stated that neither the exceptions specific to computer programs nor the Directive on Legal Protection of Databases provide for a repair exception and, thereforethe judge-made law cannot override them.[70] Since these are derived from EU directives, to him this meant that EU Member States could not recognise new exceptions beyond those recognised under the directives.[71] The problem with this statement is that it is exactly in these situations when other exceptions do not respond to the case at hand that the public interest defence is pressed into service. As addressed above and elsewhere, the public interest defence from which the spare parts exception is derived would have been compatible with EU law when used under exceptional circumstances. Similar to the arguments in Chapter 7 above, the codification does not take away the powers of the courts under exceptional circumstances to imply a policy-based bare licence in circumstances not covered by the statutes.

Jacob J, however, was willing to accept that there is a public interest defence that applies to cases of repair, and he held on the facts that it did not meet the test of 'no-right thinking member of society would quarrel with the result'.[72] It may well be that he saw the lack of genuine repair as a sufficient reason not to bring this case within the purview of the public interest defence. Indeed, as in *Canon*, the lack of genuine repair eliminates any possibility of bringing normative arguments into the interpretation of normal exploitation in the second step of the three-step test. On balance, recognising the spare parts exception in this case would have caused prejudice to the legitimate interests of the copyright owner.

The idea of a third party benefiting from an implied licence bypassing the person in a contractual relationship with the copyright owner was considered in the Australian cases of *Bashford* and *Ucorp*. These cases were discussed in relation to policy-based contractual licences in Chapter 7 above. From Chapter 7, one may gather that manufacturers, suppliers, or importers may commission the initial creation of material safety data sheets (MSDSs) from a service provider such as Acohs,

[70] ibid [14], [18]–[19]. Sections 50A–50C of the CDPA enumerate exceptions in relation to computer programs. Article 6(2)(d) of Directive 96/9/EC on the legal protection of databases deals with exceptions to database protection.

[71] Commentators continue to argue that the spare parts exception may no longer exist under UK copyright law. See Gavin Llewellyn, 'Does Copyright Recognise a Right to Repair?' (1999) 21 EIPR 596, 599.

[72] *Mars UK Ltd v Teknowledge Ltd* (n 66) [23], relying on his own ruling in *Hyde Park Residence Ltd v Yelland* (n 45) 247.

Bashford, or Ucorp, on completion of which the commissioning manufacturer, supplier, or importer receives a licence implied into the commissioning contract to reproduce it and to have it updated (adapted) as required by law. Therefore, all service providers benefit from this implied licence, which is sub-licensed to them when the manufacturer, supplier, or importer gives them access to the initial MSDS for its updating. However, if the service providers want to develop a collection of MSDSs and update all the MSDSs in their collection in the absence of, but in anticipation of, any such request being made by a manufacturer, supplier, or importer, then we will have to ascertain whether it is possible to resort to implying a policy-based bare licence. Therefore, the point for consideration for our purposes is whether a bare licence can be implied in favour of all providers of MSDSs permitting them to update an MSDS originally compiled by a competitor.

Merkel J in *Bashford* specifically addressed the public interest defence being applicable under these circumstances, taking authority from *Beloff* and *Lion*, in addition to citing section 171(3) of the CDPA. In the Australian context, he referred to *John Fairfax* as acknowledging the existence of the public interest defence. Merkel J noted that the main remedy sought in *Bashford* was injunction and the claim for damages had been withdrawn. In denying injunction, Merkel J articulated two reasons. First, if the information contained in an MSDS was required for safety related reasons by any user or emergency services, a court should not prevent its supply by the grant of injunctive or other similar relief for copyright infringement. Secondly, the grant of the relief sought is likely to affect the interests of the manufacturers, suppliers, and importers which commissioned the MSDSs, who are under a duty to ensure ready availability or access to the safety related information contained in the MSDSs. Since the manufacturers, suppliers, and importers are not parties to these proceedings, a court must exercise caution in granting injunctive relief.[73]

Merkel J adopted the above reasoning as an alternative to the implied licence reasoning he had given earlier in his judgment. This meant that he was using the technique of refusing injunctive relief to enable Acohs to adapt, update, and reproduce MSDSs authored by Bashford, in order not to interfere with the achievement of the health and safety related policy objectives behind the requirement of MSDSs. This reasoning only enabled the industrial and library use. *Ucorp* proceeded on the basis that *Bashford* was correct but was unwilling to extend the implied licence to anticipatory adaptation and updating of a competitor's MSDS. Ucorp, however, did not apply the public interest defence. Given that the public interest considerations remain the same in both *Bashford* and *Ucorp*, and perhaps more defined by the time *Ucorp* was litigated, it is possible to argue that the public interest defence should extend also to anticipatory use in *Ucorp*. Accordingly, in order not to

[73] *Acohs Pty Ltd v RA Bashford Consulting Pty Ltd* (n 14) 555–56.

interfere with health and safety policies and to ensure that the most current MSDSs are maintained in the databases of all service providers at all times, the court could have refused the grant of injunction to Acohs against the anticipatory use of the MSDSs by Ucorp. This would have resulted in all service providers benefiting from a policy-based implied bare licence that enables them to maintain a database of MSDSs with the most current information at all times, and not only in response to an order for an MSDS made by a manufacturer, supplier, or importer.

A competitor benefiting from the copyright work of another in the same industry was in focus in *Sanofi-Aventis*,[74] with the copyright work at issue being the product information documentation concerning a pharmaceutical product. This case was also discussed in much detail in Chapter 6 as the case also raised important issues of usages in the industry. Apotex had developed a generic version of a drug over which Sanofi had obtained a patent. Apotex had submitted product information in support of its application to make and distribute the generic drug, which had copied substantial parts of the Sanofi product information for the original product. The question was whether there were policy reasons why Apotex should be allowed to use Sanofi's product information.

In this regard, the court accepted that there is a public interest in product information for the same or bioequivalent drugs also being the same. However, the court saw this as an issue that may explain the relevant regulator's perspective, that 'it does not establish the existence of an implied licence for one drug company to copy the product information of another drug company'.[75] Interestingly, the ACA had already been amended recognising an SLE under section 44BA permitting copying from one drug to another. However, this SLE only had prospective application and, therefore, did not apply to the facts of this case, which had arisen prior to the relevant date. The court saw this as the legislature having spoken by recognising the public policy and chose to defer to it.[76] The court could equally have taken strength and vindication from the fact that there was already an acknowledged public interest in the copying of product information and, therefore, the court giving recognition to it would not have been out of line with what the legislature would have done in similar circumstances.

These cases indicate that the low originality of the works may have had some impact on the courts weighing the public interest higher in the balance. The high potential for exploitation of these works is only by their association with some other product having that characteristic—such as a car, a printer, a chemical, or a drug. The public interest manifests itself in the welfare of the consumers in having a competitive market or in protecting their health and safety and so on, which are of such grave importance that copyright enforcement had to give way.

74 (2011) 281 ALR 705.
75 ibid [375].
76 On appeal, the full court agreed with this finding. See [2012] FCAFC 102 [82].

(c) High originality and high commercial value copyright works

We move to cases where the copyright work has high originality and does have a significant market for exploitation. Unlike cases discussed in Section 1(a) above, the copyright owner wants to publish the work and make a profit out of its exploitation, and a market does exist for the copyright work. A court may refuse to enforce copyright because the content of the work violates a law or because the content of the work must be disclosed in the public interest. When the enforcement of copyright in these works is refused, depending on the terms of the order, it may mean that anyone can copy the work and distribute it. However, the considerations of public interest must be so overwhelming that a court regards it as justifiable that the copyright enforcement is refused.

In the past, courts have refused copyright enforcement on the basis that the content of the copyright work is immoral. An example is *Glyn v Western Feature Films*, where the author of a novel, Glyn, complained of unauthorised use of her work by the defendant in its film. The novel was called *Three Weeks*, which recounted the clandestine affair of the queen of a fictitious country.[77] Although the court held that there was no unauthorised use, it held (obiter) that 'copyright cannot exist in a work of a tendency so grossly immoral'.[78] In this case, the court rejected the very subsistence of copyright in Glyn's work. To be sure, this is not the type of case of concern in modern times. The concern here is only refusing the enforcement of copyright once the copyright subsists. Moreover, the power of the court ought only to be confined to refusing enforcement of copyright once copyright subsists. Glyn is cited with approval in recent times not to support rejection of copyright subsistence, but to hold copyright unenforceable if the content of the work is opposed to the public interest.

Attorney General v Guardian Newspapers (*Spycatcher*)[79] was one such case where an ex-employee of the British Secret Service (MI5), Peter Wright, wrote a book called *Spycatcher*, about the alleged irregularities at MI5, after his retirement from the service, for publication in Australia. The Attorney General had obtained an injunction preventing its publication in Australia, but it did not prevent *Spycatcher*'s publication outside Australia. Before the Attorney General could obtain an injunction, *Spycatcher* was published in the United States. Two other defendant newspapers published reports of the content of this book and the Attorney General had sought to obtain injunctions against their publication. Additionally, *The Sunday Times*, another defendant, obtained serialisation rights from Wright's Australian publisher and published the first extract of the book in the UK. The Attorney General again moved the courts in the UK to obtain an injunction against

77 [1916] 1 Ch 261.
78 ibid 269.
79 [1990] 1 AC 109.

the defendant newspapers on the grounds of national security and Wright's breach of confidentiality.[80]

There was no cause of action for copyright infringement since the Attorney General was seeking to stop publication of the book, rather than copy or distribute the book. The issue of copyright arose rather indirectly. It must also be noted that neither the copyright owner nor his original publisher was a party to the dispute, although *The Sunday Times* was a licensee in that it had contracted the serialisation rights. The core of the decision of the trial judge was that *Spycatcher* violated the Official Secrets Act 1911 and, therefore, if Wright or his original publisher tried to publish *Spycatcher* in the UK, and its publication was opposed by the Attorney General, an injunction would most likely be granted against them. But in the current dispute, the injunction was sought against the newspapers, only one of whom was a licensee, on the same basis that the publication violated the Official Secrets Act 1911. The trial judge refused to grant a permanent injunction against any of the newspapers, since the secrecy in the book had been destroyed by the publication of the book in the US. He also refused an injunction against further serialisation of the book in *The Sunday Times*. He went on to observe that the consequence of the denial of a permanent injunction is that the defendant newspapers and indeed any member of the public could publish, copy, and distribute *Spycatcher* in the UK, and neither Wright nor his original publisher could take issue with this because their rights would not be enforced before the UK courts. He also awarded an account of profits against *The Sunday Times*.[81] The Court of Appeal agreed with the trial judge.

The Attorney General appealed to the House of Lords, where a majority again affirmed the decision at the trial. Their Lordships did not want Wright to profit from his own wrongdoing. Relying on *Glyn*, Lord Griffiths observed that he would 'expect a judge to say that the disgraceful circumstances in which he wrote and published *Spycatcher* disentitled him to seek the assistance of the court to obtain any redress'. Similarly, Lord Jauncey noted that Wright's action 'reeked of turpitude' and it was 'inconceivable' that a court in the UK would protect his or his publisher's rights. He further noted that 'anyone can copy *Spycatcher* in whole or in part without fear of effective restraint by Wright or those claiming to derive title from him'.[82]

In terms of the three-step test, clearly the economic aspect of normal exploitation in the second step was not satisfied. The work was of high exploitable value. However, the normative aspect of public interest that one may not write a book giving away official secrets and expect to gain copyright protection was so grave that it was sufficient to override any interest of the copyright owner, economic or

[80] ibid 116, 120–23.
[81] ibid 173.
[82] ibid 275–76, 294. In *Hyde Park Residence Ltd v Yelland and Others* (n 45), Jacob J quoted with approval Lord Jauncey's approach to non-enforcement of copyright in certain cases. See [1999] EWHC 247 [24] (Pat); see also [2000] EWCA Civ 37 [62]–[63] (Aldous LJ).

otherwise. Indeed, the judicial view was to refuse the enforcement of copyright almost as a punishment, preventing Wright from profiting from his wrongdoing. This would have encouraged the reverse of what a secret should have achieved. This might have made his work popular, but court expected him not to gain economically from the popularity. This, in the court's view, was the achievement of public interest which drove the refusal of enforcement of copyright. In the language of licence, by this ruling, the rest of the world gained a policy-based implied bare licence to copy and distribute *Spycatcher*.

While in *Spycatcher* the refusal of copyright enforcement was to prevent the copyright owner from earning a profit by publishing objectionable content in the copyright work, in *Beggars Banquet Records Ltd v Carlton Television Ltd*, the refusal was in recognition of the significant educational value of the content. Here, the plaintiff was a record company, which had provided music for an all-night dance party, colloquially called a 'rave'. The plaintiff entered into an agreement with the second defendant, Spidercom, a film production company, to create a film about the rave. Spidercom filmed about 32 hours of footage using five camera crews. During the event, a teenage boy died owing to his consumption of the prohibited drug Ecstasy.[83] The film was never completed, and Spidercom was not paid in full for its services. Spidercom collaborated with the first defendant, Carlton, a television channel, and produced a documentary on the dangers of drug use and the death of the teenager. When the documentary was broadcast, the plaintiff discovered that the footage it had engaged Spidercom to film had been used to produce it. The plaintiff approached the court for an interim injunction to restrain Carlton from further broadcasting the documentary and Spidercom from using the footage for any other purpose in the future and the delivery up of the footage, on the grounds of copyright infringement.[84] The defendants raised public interest as one of the defences to the plaintiff's assertion of copyright.

Although a significant issue was the ownership of the footage shot by Spidercom, Warren J concluded that there was an arguable case that the plaintiff was the sole owner of the footage based on the agreement with Spidercom, or a better claim for joint ownership with Spidercom for being the one who made the arrangements to film the event. As this was the interlocutory stage, no final finding needed to be made. In any event, this meant that Spidercom needed the plaintiff's licence to be able to use the footage to produce the documentary, which could be sublicensed to Carlton. Since the plaintiff had granted no such licence, there was a prima facie case for copyright infringement. As regards the injunction restraining Carlton from further broadcasting the documentary, Warren J acknowledged the defence of public interest, relying on *Lion* and *Hubbard*, among others, as pointing to an 'emerging jurisdiction'. He refused the injunction against Carlton owing to

[83] [1993] EMLR 349, 353–36.
[84] ibid 359–60.

the public interest in conveying with 'vivid and telling' images the dangerous effects of Ecstasy and the goings on at rave parties.[85] He did this by reading public interest into the balancing exercise required for the grant of an interim injunction. He noted that any harm to the plaintiff is likely to be outweighed by the harm to the public interest if the broadcast is prevented. Warren J, however, granted the injunction restraining Spidercom from further using the footage for any other purpose and ordered it to provide access to the footage to the plaintiff.[86]

These orders need unpacking. From the perspective of the three-step test, the footage was such that the plaintiff could have extracted its full commercial value. Spidercom's production of the documentary and Carlton's broadcast of it interfered with the plaintiff's normal exploitation of the footage. However, the court found a powerful normative element in educating and warning the public of the dangers of using prohibited drugs, which could be read into normal exploitation. In the balancing exercise, the court was able to demarcate the public interest that would be served by the documentary being further broadcast and the legitimate interest of the plaintiff in the footage for its further exploitation. This explains why the court not only restrained Spidercom from further use of the footage, but also ordered it to provide access to it to the plaintiff. The court's refusal to restrain Carlton from broadcasting the documentary meant that Carlton was free to broadcast the documentary. In the language of licences, Carlton had a licence implied by policy of educating the public. This should also mean that Spidercom had a licence implied by policy to adapt and reproduce the footage to produce the documentary in the first place. However, the court restraining Spidercom from further using the footage and ordering it to provide the plaintiff access to it meant that Spidercom did not benefit from an ongoing licence to use the footage and that the licence was non-exclusive.

When a court refuses an interim injunction, it leaves only a remedy in damages for the copyright owner.[87] Copyright owners whose works have high original content and a high potential for exploitation are more likely to pursue damages at trial. By pursuing a claim in damages, the copyright owner could have obtained the economic value of the very use that was allowed by the refusal of the injunction. In this sense, the licence that the user gains by the refusal of an injunction may not entirely be a bare licence, but a licence that is paid for through the damages. Although courts support this view, in no case thus far where the public interest defence has succeeded after trial has there been an order for damages. In *Spycatcher* above, *The Sunday Times* did have to account for profits for publishing the first episode of the serialisation, although the subsequent publications were not subject

[85] ibid 364, 371–72.

[86] ibid 372–73. Public interest was read into the test in *American Cyanamid v Ethicon Ltd* [1975] UKHL 1.

[87] An approach supported in *Ashdown v Telegraph Group* (n 34) [46] and *HRH Prince of Wales v Associated Press* [2006] EWHC 522 (Ch) [186]–[187].

to this. However, this amount did not go to the copyright owner, but to the government because it represented damages for the breach of official secrecy, rather than copyright infringement.

2. Fundamental Rights Regime as the Framework

Even before the European Convention on Human Rights (ECHR) had been transposed into domestic law, some cases discussed in Section 1 above had relied on Article 10 of the ECHR, typically where the defendant was a newspaper or a broadcaster asserting its press freedom arising from freedom of speech. The earliest among these is *Lion Laboratories Ltd v Evans*, where Stephenson LJ made references to the ECHR in support of the 'countervailing interest of the public in being kept informed of matters which are of real public concern'.[88] In *Spycatcher*, although Scott J recognised that the ECHR had not yet become part of the domestic law, he accepted that he must pay attention to the authorities before the European Court of Human Rights (ECtHR).[89] The Court of Appeal was similarly willing to take into account ECtHR decisions, and in doing so the Court found no inconsistency with the domestic law.[90] This view was also confirmed by the House of Lords.[91] A few months before the Human Rights Act 1998 (HRA) was passed, *Service Corpration International* also made references to the provisions of the ECHR.[92]

While it is commendable that these cases took into account the constitutional values, since the passing of the HRA in 1998 the obligations on the court have attained greater certainty. Of particular note is section 12, which refers to the considerations a court must take into account when granting relief that might affect a person's freedom of expression. These considerations must now be part of the balancing act that a court is required to perform when granting interim relief.[93] There has been a developing jurisprudence, both domestic and by the ECtHR, which one can tap into for the methodology of applying the fundamental rights regime. The Charter of Fundamental Rights of the European Union (CFREU) will cease to apply to the UK after the Exit Day.[94] However, those CJEU decisions which have taken into account the provisions of the CFREU in interpreting the directives will still be part of the UK domestic law, unless and until the Supreme Court decides to depart from those decisions.

[88] *Lion Laboratories Ltd v Evans* (n 36) 536.
[89] *Attorney General v Guardian Newspaper* [1990] 1 AC 109, 156–59.
[90] ibid 178–79, 203, 219–20.
[91] ibid 256 (Lord Keith), 283–84 (Lord Goff).
[92] *Service Corporation International Plc v Channel Four Television Corporation* (n 41) 89.
[93] See generally *Cream Holdings v Banerjee* [2005] AC 253.
[94] European Union (Withdrawal) Act 2018, s 5(4).

To begin with, one must know the kinds of dispute to which the fundamental rights regime will apply. This stage of assessment is called 'applicability'. Once we have a dispute to which the fundamental rights regime will apply, the next question is whether the state action is compatible with the fundamental rights regime.[95] As far as applicability is concerned, scholars have identified two broad kinds of disputes: vertical, where the state is a party to the proceeding against a private person and a state action is challenged as being incompatible with the fundamental rights; and horizontal, where the dispute is between private parties, but the validity or the interpretation of the law applicable to them is challenged. The disputes of concern here are horizontal. The dispute arises because the interpretation of the SLEs does not extend to the situation at hand. The user therefore asks the court to interpret the public interest defence, i.e., to prevent or restrict the enforcement of copyright in order to uphold the fundamental rights of the user. This indirectly amounts to implying a licence in favour of the user, based on the policy considerations of those fundamental rights.

In the UK, the horizontal applicability of the ECHR and the CFREU have been controversial in other areas of law.[96] This is despite the clear provision that a court is obligated under section 6(1) read with section 6(3)(a) as a public authority to act in a manner compatible with the Convention right. In relation to copyright disputes, however, there appears to be less resistance to horizontal application. The cases before the UK courts which considered the ECHR through the HRA provisions have typically been disputes with newspapers involving issues of freedom of expression and press freedom, perhaps making it easier to permit horizontal applicability in these cases. The applicability of the CFREU to intellectual property disputes is well established within the CJEU's jurisdiction. Indeed, there is a growing number of cases, such as *UPC Telekabel v Constantin Film*,[97] *Deckmyn v Vandersteen*,[98] and *McFadden v Sony Music*,[99] to name but a few, where the CJEU has held that in interpreting and applying EU directives, the national courts must comply with the CFREU. The UK courts have also applied the CFREU rights to horizontal disputes, following the CJEU decisions.[100]

Once a dispute is found to be of the kind to which the fundamental rights regime applies, one must then assess compatibility. This assessment deals with the manner in which the ECtHR and the CJEU have interpreted copyright law in a fundamental rights-compatible manner. The ECtHR, being a specialised court for

[95] See generally Amy Goymour, 'Property and Housing' in David Hoffman, *The Impact of the UK Human Rights Act on Private Law* (CUP 2013) 251.

[96] Alison Young, 'Mapping Horizontal Effect' in David Hoffman, *The Impact of the UK Human Rights Act on Private Law* (CUP 2013) 16–22.

[97] Cases C-314/12 ECLI:EU:C:2014:192.

[98] C-201/13 ECLI:EU:C:2014:2132.

[99] C-484/14 ECLI:EU:C:2016:689.

[100] See eg *Twentieth Century Fox Film Corporation v British Telecommunications Plc* [2011] EWHC 1981 [163[–[177] (Ch).

human rights with longer history, has its own way of approaching the issue of compatibility of a law with the ECHR. Scholars identify three main questions:

- is/are a fundamental rights/s engaged in the dispute?
- is there an interference with the fundamental right/s?
- is the interference justified?[101]

Let us unpack this methodology. Identifying the fundamental rights engaged is a relatively less controversial exercise. In horizontal disputes the interference with the relevant fundamental rights is caused by the court's interpretation of the relevant law or the exercise of discretion in failing to uphold fundamental rights. In this context, the ECtHR adopts a deferential approach in allowing the national courts a wide margin of appreciation in their interpretation and exercise of discretion. For example, in *Dima v Romania*, where the issue was whether national symbols attract copyright protection, the ECtHR held that there was no interference with Dima's fundamental rights because the Romanian courts had a margin of appreciation in interpreting Romanian law, which was unclear on the copyright protection extended to national symbols.[102] An interference will be justified if it can be shown that the means employed by the state is proportionate to the objectives it seeks to achieve.[103] Scholars regard proportionality not as a simple formula but as a complex matter requiring a thorough analysis. In general, proportionality can be achieved in three ways: where the interference is suitable, necessary, or strikes a fair balance among competing interests. [104] Thus far, in relation to copyright cases the ECtHR has only applied the second and the third means. An interference is necessary if there is no other measure which is less onerous. For example, in *Balan v Moldova*, where the state had used a photograph which Balan had taken without compensation, the ECtHR held this to be an unjustified and disproportionate interference with Balan's fundamental rights under Article 1 of the First Protocol (A1P1) in his photograph and that Moldova could have used a less invasive option.[105] Scholars believe that the ECtHR generally prefers the method of striking a fair balance to achieve proportionality.[106]

With the methodology thus explained, albeit briefly, let us analyse the kind of disputes of concern here in the light of this methodology. Since the dispute is

[101] Laurence Helfer, 'How Intellectual Property and Human Rights Can Live Together' in Paul Torremans (ed), *Intellectual Property Law and Human Rights* (3rd edn, Wolters Kluwer 2015) 39; see also Goymour (n 95) 274.

[102] *Dima v Romania*, App no 58472/00 (ECtHR, 26 May 2005) para [78].

[103] Helfer (n 101) 37–38.

[104] Jonas Christoffersen, 'Human Rights and Balancing: The Principle of Proportionality' in Christophe Geiger, *Research Handbook on Human Rights and Intellectual Property* (Edward Elgar Publishing 2015) 19–20.

[105] App no 19247/03 (ECtHR, 29 January 2008) paras [7]–[18].

[106] Christoffersen (n 104) 35–36; Helfer (n 101) 37–38.

against enforcement of copyright protection, A1P1 will be engaged because the ECtHR has held that copyright (and indeed other forms of intellectual property) are protectable as possessions under A1P1.[107] The effort is to establish the public interest defence to copyright infringement. To ascertain whether this amounts to an interference, one must look at the second and the third sentences of A1P1, which respectively refer to deprivation of property and control of use as the forms of interference. Deprivation includes expropriation and is more invasive. Control of use encompasses lesser restrictions. The concern here is control of use by way of licences (directly or indirectly), and not deprivation by extinguishing copyright interest altogether. An interference by way of control of use can only be justified by a law in the 'general interest', as opposed to deprivation which is only justified in the 'public interest'. While it might depend on the context how public interest is different from general interest, in our context the effort will be either to establish a countervailing public interest or assert fundamental rights against the copyright owner's A1P1 right to justify the refusal of copyright enforcement.

One of the most common competing rights put forward is the right to freedom of expression and information under Article 10(1). Like all other fundamental rights, there are grounds on which an interference with this right will be justified if prescribed by law and are necessary in a democratic society. Article 10(2) sets out a variety of circumstances that justify interference with the freedom of speech, including those that are in the interests of national security, territorial integrity, or public safety, protection of reputation or rights of others, protection of confidentiality or impartiality of judiciary, and so on. The following cases illustrate how fair balance is approached when there are conflicting rights.

Ashby Donald v France[108] and *Frederik Neij v Sweden*[109] both concern criminal convictions for copyright infringement. When the convicted infringers claimed their right to freedom of expression under Article 10, in both cases the ECtHR held that the interference was justified since it was prescribed by law and pursued the legitimate aim of protecting the property rights of copyright holders and can be considered necessary in a democratic society. In both cases, the ECtHR held that the domestic courts have a wide margin of appreciation in balancing between the right to freedom of expression and right to property, in securing these convictions.[110] Copyright in all cases of concern to us will qualify as 'the rights of others' whose protection is necessary in a democratic society. This might convey that in all cases depriving a person's free speech when pitted against copyright will be justified.

[107] *Dima v Romania* (n 102) on copyright and *Anheuser-Busch Inc v Portugal* (2007) 45 EHRR 36 on trademarks.

[108] App no 36769/08 (ECtHR, 10 January 2013).

[109] App no 40397/12 (ECtHR, 19 February 2013).

[110] Henning Grosse Ruse-Khan, 'Overlaps and Conflict Norms in Human Rights Law' in Christophe Geiger, *Research Handbook on Human Rights and Intellectual Property* (Edward Elgar Publishing 2015) 86–87.

However, the ECtHR in other contexts has affirmed that the Member States have a positive obligation to protect Article 10 against interferences by private persons or corporate organisations.[111] Further, Article 10 protects not only the freedom to hold opinions, but also to 'receive and impart information and ideas without interference by public authority and regardless of frontiers'. As such, the right takes on an additional dimension on the internet. Indeed, the ECtHR recognises the importance of the internet in enhancing the public's access to and dissemination of information, and as 'the principal means by which individuals exercise their right to freedom of expression and information'.[112] Therefore, Article 10 can act as a constraint on the scope of copyright protection and a powerful tool in the hands of users of copyright content in both online and off-line contexts. Since the ECtHR gives a wide margin of appreciation to the domestic courts in striking a fair balance between competing rights, the onus is on the domestic courts to use Article 10 to its fullest potential.

Article 52(3) of the CFREU states that the substantive content of the rights in the CFREU correspond to those in the ECHR. The CFREU guarantees protection specifically for intellectual property under Article 17(2), in a seemingly absolute way.[113] However, Article 52(1) acknowledges that the rights guaranteed in the CFREU also have limits, and any such limitations should be provided for by law, must respect the principle of proportionality, and must be in the general interest or protect the rights of others. Unlike the ECtHR, the CJEU has adopted only the method of striking a 'fair balance' in furthering proportionality. Article 53 of the CFREU requires that the provisions of the CFREU shall not be interpreted in a manner restricting or adversely affecting the fundamental rights recognised by the Member States as the signatories to the ECHR. Therefore, read with Article 52(3), the interpretation of the CFREU cannot result in a different scope of the rights under the CFREU than under the ECHR. The cases below provide a brief summary of the approach of the CJEU, which may appear wanting in consistency. Although consistency is important, given the diversity of circumstances as the cases below demonstrate, a degree of flexibility is also necessary for the court to weigh competing interests.

The idea of fair balance in the copyright context is enshrined in recital 31 of the Infosoc Directive. In addition, recital 3 of the Infosoc Directive identifies the protection of intellectual property, freedom of expression, and public interest as the fundamental principles of law, pointing to the main interests that need to be balanced in a specific case. However, as confirmed by the CJEU in *Funke Medien*, *Spiegel Online*, and *Pelham*, striking a fair balance does not mean that fundamental

[111] *Wojtas-Kaleta v Poland*, App no 20436/02 (ECtHR, 16 July 2009).

[112] *Times Newspapers Ltd v UK (Nos 1 and 2)*, App nos 3002/03 and 23676/03 (ECtHR, 10 March 2009); *Ahmet Yildirim v Turkey*, App no 3111/10 (ECtHR, 18 December 2012).

[113] Christophe Geiger, 'Intellectual Property Shall be Protected!? Article 17(2) of the Charter of Fundamental Rights of the European Union' (2009) 31 EIPR 113.

rights can be the basis for a new SLE beyond the exhaustive list enumerated in the Infosoc Directive. Having said that, the CJEU has read fundamental rights into the interpretation of exclusive rights and SLEs to protect the rights of the users. In *GS Media BV v Sanoma Media Netherlands BV*, the CJEU gave a restrictive interpretation of the right of communication to the public by holding that a person who does not know or cannot reasonably know of the non-infringing nature of the content, and does not seek profit for such hyperlinking, does not communicate the copyright work to the public. Given the importance of hyperlinking in making access to information efficient, the CJEU observed that recitals 3 and 31 of the Infosoc Directive require that a fair balance be struck between the right to property under Article 17 of the CFREU and the right to freedom of expression under Article 11 of the CFREU.[114] Similarly, the CJEU has read the free speech requirements to interpret the parody exception more broadly in *Deckmyn*.[115]

It is significant to note in our context that the CJEU has also required fair balancing among conflicting fundamental rights in assessing the grant of remedies to counter online copyright infringement. While in *Promusicae*, the issue was whether an internet service provider (ISP) could be required to reveal the identity of the infringers,[116] in *Scarlet* the issue was whether an ISP could be required to place filtering mechanisms to identify and block infringing content.[117] In *Telekabel*, the issue was the validity of blocking injunctions issued against the ISPs,[118] and *McFadden* addressed measures that a trader providing free WiFi could be required to take in order to prevent online copyright infringement using his network.[119] In all of these cases, the right to protection of intellectual property under Article 17(2) of the respective content owners was in conflict with the right to conduct business of the ISPs under Article 16 and the right to freedom of information of the internet users under Article 11. While categorically stating that the right to property protected under Article 17(2) is by no means absolute or inviolable, the CJEU refused the grant of relief in *Promusicae* and *Scarlet*.[120] In *Telekabel*, the CJEU outlined the measures that may be taken which will not violate the ISPs rights under Article 16 and the user's rights under Article 11.[121] In *McFadden*, the Court held that requiring the trader to protect his network by a password balanced his rights under Article 16 with those of the copyright owners.[122] Regarding the CJEU's decisions, the UK courts have followed the CJEU's rulings in *Promusicae*, *Scarlet*, and *Telekabel*, while considering the issue of granting injunctions against ISPs to block

114 Case C-160/5 ECLI:EU:C:2016:644 [44]–[47].
115 *Deckmyn v Vandersteen* (n 98) [18], [25]–[26].
116 *Promusicae v Telefonica* (n 6) [29]–[33].
117 *Scarlet Extended v SABAM* (n 6) [19]–[20].
118 *UPC Telekabel v Constantin Film* (n 97) [42].
119 *McFadden v Sony Music* (n 99) [90].
120 *Scarlet Extended v SABAM* (n 6) [43].
121 *UPC Telekabel v Constantin Film* (n 97) [52]–[53], [56]–[57].
122 *McFadden v Sony Music* (n 99) [90].

websites containing infringing content.[123] Therefore, even if a court cannot formulate a new SLE by relying on the fundamental rights, it is entirely legitimate for it to deny remedies if the grant violates the fundamental rights of the users.

With this background, we move to the domestic law where the courts in the UK have considered applying the fundamental rights regime of the ECHR through the HRA in copyright infringement disputes. In *Ashdown*, as discussed in Section 1 above, the publication of certain minutes of a confidential meeting authored by the plaintiff had been published with extensive quotations by the defendant newspaper. The issue was whether the right to freedom of expression of the newspaper to report it in public interest overrode the A1P1 right of the author of the minutes. The High Court followed the ECtHR methodology in first considering whether any fundamental right has been engaged. Having held that Article 10, ECHR is engaged, the court proceeded to consider whether there was an interference with this right. The court observed that it had a margin of appreciation in balancing between A1P1 and Article 10, and that the provisions of the CDPA already provide sufficient balance between these rights. The court held that since the legislature has already struck this balance, one cannot create new exceptions outside the CDPA by reading public interest with Article 10.[124] The trouble with this interpretation is that if the existing SLEs were sufficient and the list was immutable, then the CDPA would not have incorporated an additional public interest defence.

However, the Court of Appeal held that copyright only protects expression and not the information. Therefore, protecting copyright still enables the free circulation of information, except in cases where the expression of the information per se might be relevant. In this sense, the Court held that copyright could be antithetical to freedom of expression in some cases.[125] As discussed above, the Court recognised that it is possible to conceive of a situation where the public interest is so grave as to warrant verbatim reproduction of a copyright work. Under these circumstances, a court might find the existing SLEs inadequate. Under these exceptional circumstances, a court can read the free speech arguments into the public interest without the risk of opening the floodgates. The first step to do so is to deny an injunction. However, a court might go on to award damages or an account of profits for such use after trial, because freedom of information should not carry with it the right to make free use of another's work.[126] In relation to section 171(3), the Court held that:

> Now that the Human Rights Act 1998 is in force, there is the clearest public interest in giving effect to the right of freedom of expression in those rare cases

[123] See eg *Twentieth Century Fox Film Corporation and Others v British Telecommunications Plc* (n 100) [163]–[177]; *EMI Records Ltd v British Sky Broadcasting Ltd* [2013] EWHC 379 [91]–[95] (Ch).

[124] [2001] Ch 685 [12]–[14], [20].

[125] [2001] EWCA Civ 1142 [30]–[31], [43].

[126] ibid [44]–[46].

> where this right trumps the rights conferred by the 1988 Act. In such circumstances, we consider that section 171(3) of the Act permits the defence of public interest to be raised.[127]

Whilst the Court of Appeal's approach was an improvement over the High Court's reading of section 171(3), the above extract should not be read as conveying that the enforcement of free speech under the HRA is the only situation where section 171(3) could be pressed into service. This is not the case. As the discussion in Section 1 above demonstrates, the public interest defence can be asserted in much more diverse circumstances. In *British Leyland*, for example, the A1P1 right of BL in its copyright would be in conflict with the A1P1 right of the car purchasers in their cars. Although on the facts section 171(3) was not enforced in *Ashdown*, it is conceivable that, in an appropriate case, a court can interpret section 171(3) in the light of the fundamental rights regime in such a way that it creates a policy-based implied licence in favour of the users.

The decision in *Ashdown* was followed in *HRH Prince of Wales*, where the Prince of Wales had maintained a journal of his travels, copies of extracts of which were sent to certain members of his staff strictly in confidence. A member of his staff allegedly gave an extract of the Prince's journal to the defendant newspaper, which published articles incorporating extracts from the journal. The Prince sued for breach of confidentiality and infringement of copyright. The defendant raised the defence of fair dealing and public interest.[128] The court relied on *Ashdown* to hold that the public interest consideration must be 'over and above those available under fair dealing defences' to justify the denial of copyright enforcement.[129]

One may wonder what an appropriate case may be for a court to hold that public interest outweighs copyright enforcement. In a pandemic situation like the one during 2020, if a library is unable to afford e-books and wishes to provide a scanning service that makes its physical collection accessible online without the consent of the copyright owner, over and above what is permitted by the educational exceptions, will this be covered by the public interest defence? Some scholars have taken the view that it may be very difficult to make a case, based on current case law in the UK.[130] However, if the public interest is formulated using the fundamental rights as described here, one may have a better chance of success. If copyright owners bring an action for copyright infringement, a court can consider whether the fundamental rights of the users outweigh the rights of copyright owners. And in balancing these rights, a court might decide not to enforce the copyright in

127 ibid [58].

128 *HRH Prince of Wales v Associated Press* [2006] EWHC 522 [1]–[6], [162], [178] (Ch).

129 ibid [179]–[180].

130 Emily Hudson and Paul Wragg, 'Proposals for Copyright Law and Education During the Covid-19 Pandemic' 13–18 https://ssrn.com/abstract=3617720 accessed 3 July 2020.

recognition of the overwhelming public interest in uninterrupted access to educational materials during a pandemic of unprecedented proportions.

3. Conclusions and Connections

This chapter has examined the case law that denied copyright enforcement in the public interest in the light of the three-step test and the fundamental rights regime. Examining the case law from the perspective of the three-step test, it classified cases based on the level of originality and the potential for normal exploitation of the work to ascertain what may be at the heart of a court's decision in enforcing or not enforcing copyright. It was found that, even if one successfully passes the second step, the gravity of public interest is one of the most important ingredients one must demonstrate in the balancing act in the third step, so that it weighs above copyright enforcement. Despite the paucity of cases applying the HRA in the copyright context, this chapter indicated how fundamental rights may be pressed into service in future cases.

The courts' powers to enforce the public interest from an open-ended list is useful in permitting certain basic functionalities on the internet, especially when the copyright content is placed without the consent of the copyright owner, which leads us to Part III below.

PART III

APPLICATION OF IMPLIED COPYRIGHT LICENCES TO THE INTERNET

This Part tests and illustrates the analyses of implied licence in the foregoing chapters, in relation to the internet, and in particular, the three basic capabilities at the heart of the internet's technological prowess, namely browsing, hyperlinking, and indexing. Although users engage in other activities on the internet such as downloading and peer-to-peer sharing, this Part only deals with these three activities. This is because these activities benefit not only the internet users, but also the copyright owners who can make their works accessible to an unprecedented number of recipients. However, the technological processes underlying these activities may engage exclusive rights of reproduction and acts of communication to the public. To deny any of these functions by asserting these exclusive rights reduces the benefits of the internet. One way to permit these functions is to explore if the exclusive rights they engage can be impliedly licensed.

Courts have dealt with the challenges posed by browsing, hyperlinking, and indexing by applying legal reasoning other than implied licence or with a limited role for implied licence. This Part argues for a bigger role for implied licences and, indeed implied licences as the preferred alternative to address these challenges. Some of the questions addressed here may not be litigated. But this does not mean that that they are settled. Further, some stakeholders like end users may never vindicate their rights. However, these rights do need a reasoned confirmation. Moreover, given the reality of Brexit and a possibility of the UK charting a new path in relation to copyright law, implied licences have significant potential to offer an alternative solution.

This Part takes the UK law, and pivotal Court of Justice of the European Union (CJEU) decisions that are part of UK law as an illustration to demonstrate how these might respond to applying implied licences to the internet. To the extent that no illustrative cases exist in the UK or the EU, this Part relies on certain specific cases from the United States and Germany. Although the court's reasoning is discussed briefly, these cases are relied on more for their facts, which are analysed in

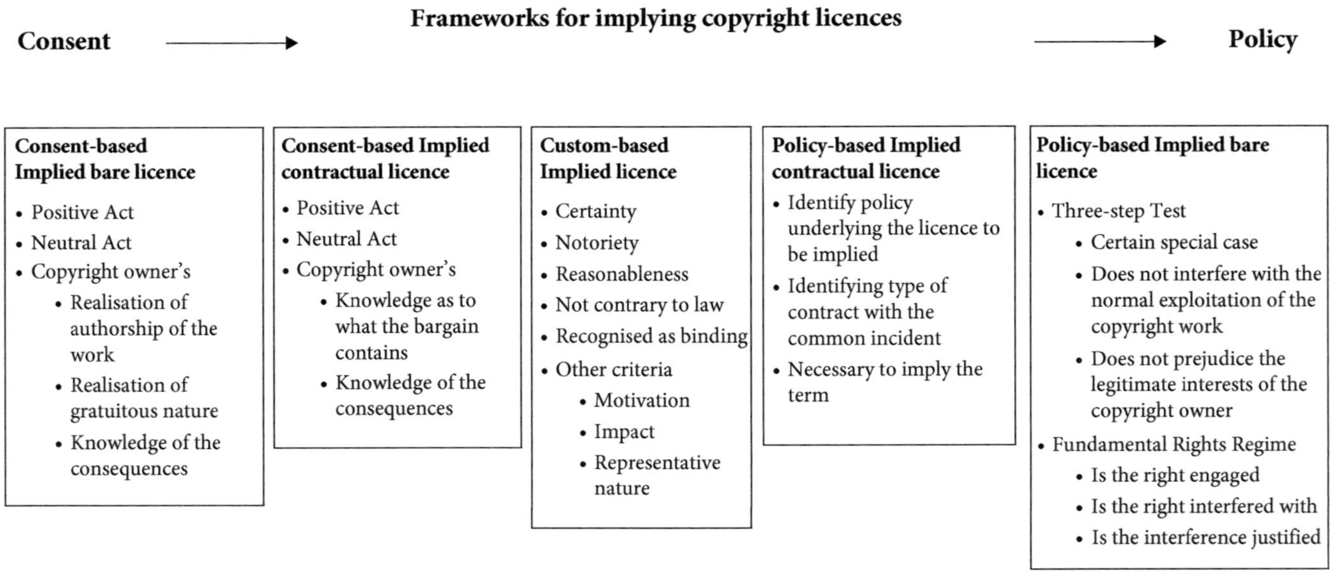

Figure 2 Frameworks for implying copyright licences

the light of the relevant framework proposed in this monograph for implying a copyright licence.

This Part begins with Chapter 9 setting the stage for the application of the learnings from the previous chapters to specific actions on the internet. This chapter discusses certain fundamentals and preliminary matters that are common to each of Chapters 10, 11, and 12. This chapter acts as the essential connection among the discussions in Part I, Part II, and this Part. Figure 2 above shows a consolidation of the frameworks proposed.

Arguably, the most basic of all actions that a user can engage in on the internet is browsing—meaning simply reading, viewing, listening, or watching the content on the internet. This is often the first point of contact for users to receive and interact with the content on the internet. Browsing is dealt with in Chapter 10. A user is able to browse the content because someone has communicated the content on the web in the first place. A user can access such content either because the user knows the web address (or the uniform resource locator (URL)) of the site or because the user has clicked a hyperlink that takes her to the relevant content. Hyperlinking is discussed in Chapter 11. For the user to be able to access content through a link, there is normally an internet service provider who has made it possible for a link to the content that a user is looking for, to appear on their monitor when she searches for it. This leads us to the discussion on indexing in Chapter 12. Although courts engage in overlapping discussions on hyperlinking and indexing, this Part deals with them as separate actions, potentially capable of giving rise to liability on their own.

9
Implied Licences on the Internet—Fundamentals

Technological advancements have always had an impact on copyright laws, starting from the mother of all copyright-generative innovations, the printing press. From its inception, copyright law has had to deal with a level of abstraction because of the intangibility of the protected subject matter. With the technological innovation of the last few decades, the work, its expression, and its exploitation have all required the law to deal with even higher levels of abstraction, because of the works taking on a digital form and being exploited on the internet. While the exclusive rights of communication and making available to the public are a direct result of technological advancements, a concern arises as to whether the balance that copyright law tried to achieve in the offline world could be upset if sufficient attention is not paid to the interests of the other stakeholders. This is where the idea of 'prescriptive parallelism' becomes relevant.[1] It conveys the notion that the traditional copyright balance of rights and exceptions should be preserved also in the digital environment. It was conceived in the context of the danger of technological protection measures placed on copyright works denying copyright users the benefit of the statutory limitations or exceptions (SLEs). But it can also be relevant in informing the scope of exclusive rights—what is not covered by an exclusive right in the offline world, such as reading a book, should not be covered by an exclusive right also in the online world.

It was stated at the outset in this monograph that implied licences occupy the spectrum between an express licence of the copyright owner and the SLE. Implied licences deal with cases that fall between the cracks and aim to achieve a balanced outcome. Accordingly, prescriptive parallelism may also demand that the frameworks for implying copyright licences and the dynamics of their operation in the offline world should remain the same in the online world. The multi-factor frameworks proposed in Part I for implying copyright licences have been developed with a distance from the specificities of the cases sufficient to make them applicable as much to the offline scenarios in Part II as to the online scenarios in Part III. Moreover, rationalising the case law in Part II in the light of the frameworks

[1] Jerome Reichman, Graeme Dinwoodie, and Pamela Samuelson, 'A Reverse Notice and Takedown Regime to Enable Public Interest Uses of Technologically Protected Copyrighted Works' (2007) 22 Berkeley Tech LJ 981, 1042.

Implied Licences in Copyright Law. Poorna Mysoor, Oxford University Press (2021). © Poorna Mysoor.
DOI: 10.1093/oso/9780198858195.003.0010

proposed in Part I demonstrates the robustness of the methodology ready for it to be cross-applied to the online world.

This chapter divides the content on the internet between, on the one hand, that which is placed by or with the consent of the copyright owner and, on the other hand, that which is placed on the internet without the copyright owner's consent.[2] This facilitates an orderly analysis since the bases on which a licence may be implied, and the arguments presented, changes between these two categories. This chapter goes on to lay down the parallels that exist in the online world for the application of the frameworks for implying copyright licences under different bases. The effort in this chapter will be to lay a common foundation for browsing, hyperlinking, and indexing dealt with in each of the successive chapters below.

1. Content Placed on the Internet with the Copyright Owner's Consent

A copyright owner placing their content on the internet or consenting for someone else to do so is a voluntary act. This might signal the copyright owner's consent to benefit from the advantages of the internet, namely browsing, hyperlinking, and indexing. Therefore, one may first explore whether a consent-based licence can be implied. The framework for consent-based implied licences discussed in Chapters 4 and 5 above may be applied to these situations. To imply a consent-based licence (bare or contractual), one needs a positive act, a neutral act, and the circumstances within the knowledge of the copyright owner.

The act of placing the content on the internet can be regarded as the positive act and can potentially become the first step towards implying a licence. To be sure, the copyright owner placing or consenting to place their content on the internet does not mean that there is an implied licence to use the content in every manner possible. Owing to the free accessibility of information on the internet, internet users may believe that all the content available on the internet is free for whatever use they wish to make of it. Further, lay persons may wish to believe that, by placing copyright content on the internet, copyright owners have relinquished their rights. Although it is practically possible for the users to use the content on the internet in whatever manner they please,[3] and it is very difficult for the content owners to police such uses, there is still no legal basis for the assertion that the content on the internet is 'free for all'. In legal terms, this would have meant the copyright owners assigning their rights and essentially gifting away their rights in the content by

[2] A similar division was adopted in *Warner Music UK Ltd v TuneIn Inc* [2019] EWHC 2923 para 109(iii) (Ch).

[3] In Case C-161/17 *Land Nordrhein-Westfalen v Renckhoff* ECLI:EU:C:2018:634 the CJEU held that downloading of a copyright work on the internet (a photograph) from its location and reposting it on another location infringes the communication right.

simply placing it on the internet. As a matter of personal property law, the intention to gift the copyright work is missing. As discussed in Chapter 4, Section 1(c)(iii) above, giving lyrics of a poem in *Tumber v Independent Television News Ltd* or the draft opening script in *Brighton v Jones* were all treated as giving rise to a licence, and not as outright assignment.[4] Therefore, the mere act of placing content on the internet does not amount to anything more than pointing to a possibility of implying a licence, depending on the existence of the other factors.

The positive act of placing content on the internet must be coupled with the inaction of leaving the content there. There are three possible ways of leaving the content on the internet. First, the copyright owner does not place any terms of use for the works she places on the internet. This does not mean that users can make unrestricted use of copyright works. Even if there are no terms of use, the scope of a consent-based implied licence depends on what is within the copyright owner's knowledge or expectation. Secondly, the copyright owner does place terms of use in relation to the works they place on the internet. In general, all rights are reserved, unless specifically permitted. Terms of use can affirm expressly what is not permitted and permit actions which are otherwise prohibited. This makes the neutral act partial. Thirdly, the copyright owner can deny access to all content placed on the internet by placing technological protection measures or placing the content behind a paywall. Here, the neutral act is conditional in that, unless the condition is satisfied (e.g., payment being made or a password obtained), the effect of the positive act cannot be realised.

Neither the positive act nor the neutral act can occur in a vacuum. They must be accompanied by the knowledge of the copyright owner. Copyright owners placing their content on the internet can be of different levels of sophistication—starting from a person writing a short piece on social media or a blog, to a person having a bespoke website built to showcase their work or to promote a business. Content placed on social media or blogging platforms will normally be subject to the terms and conditions of the platform. In most other cases, the copyright owner places their content on the internet with the help of web designers. This can have an impact on their knowledge in that the technological process may or may not be sufficiently articulated and, in certain circumstances, the knowledge must be imputed.

Although copyright owners are increasingly becoming more savvy about incorporating terms of use, there is still a sizeable content on the internet that is unaccompanied by any terms of use. In the absence of the terms of use, the licence, if implied, will be a bare licence. Therefore, the components of the knowledge of the copyright owner will include the realisation of authorship, the realisation of the gratuitous nature of her actions, and the knowledge of the circumstances, as set out in Chapter 4, Section 1(c)(i), (ii), and (iii) above. The absence of the terms

[4] [2017] EWHC 3093 [2] (IPEC); *Brighton v Jones* [2004] EWHC 1157 [21] (Ch).

of use might be because the copyright owner does not realise that their work attracts copyright protection. As discussed in Chapter 4, Section 1(c)(i), this component of the knowledge must be assessed, even if a court sets a low threshold for its assessment. The conduct of not incorporating any terms of use nor a paywall conveys that the copyright owner is aware that there is no bargain and no consideration that flows back to them according to Chapter 4, Section 1(c)(i). This leaves us with the last component, namely the knowledge of the circumstances. Placing no terms of use still does not mean unrestricted use of copyright works. The scope of the licence is determined by the actions of the users that are reasonably within the copyright owner's knowledge. On the internet, the knowledge of the circumstances of relevance for the discussion here are the possibility of the users of the internet engaging in browsing, hyperlinking, and indexing. The knowledge of the copyright owner in relation to these actions must be assessed to the extent that these functions engage the exclusive rights of reproduction and communication to the public.

If for any reason the knowledge of the copyright owner as to the technology involved cannot be established, then one may look to whether these user actions on the internet can be established as customs on the internet, based on the framework discussed in Chapter 6. On the one hand, one may argue that the internet is too vast an environment to be regarded as a location, and its users too disparate to be regarded as a community. On the other hand, one may argue that anyone with internet connectivity can be regarded as being part of the internet community. One may also point out that the internet as a location does have distinct characteristics, and the actions that the users engage in on the internet are consistent across this community, and indeed across the globe. The global pandemic of 2020 has only increased our dependence on the internet and has potentially increased the number and regularity of access to the internet, of both creators and consumers of copyright works. Therefore, depending on the context, it is possible to speak of an internet community. If a custom can be established, then, as discussed in Chapter 6, Section 1(a)(ii), the notoriety of the practice will mean that the knowledge of the copyright owner as to these practices can be presumed. This approach is more useful in relation to hyperlinking and indexing than browsing.

Terms of use being incorporated has become increasingly common in recent times. These terms of use normally concern not only the use of copyright works such as text, images, and software, but also the use of a website as a whole. In most cases, the website terms of use amount to an express bare licence. The terms of use of a website providing information are more likely to amount to a bare licence.[5] The terms of use of an interactive website such as a newspaper providing for readers' contributions are also likely only to amount to an express bare licence, rather than

[5] See eg London Stock Exchange disclaimer https://www.londonstockexchange.com/disclaimer accessed 13 July 2020.

a contract.[6] In the case of social media platforms,[7] it is arguable that there is some mutuality in the relationship between the user and the platform, although the enforceability of the provision of the services and facilities to the user is questionable. In *Ryanair Ltd v PR Aviation BV*[8] the Court of Justice of the European Union (CJEU) has held that Ryanair's terms of use amount to a contract (although in English law they might only be a bare licence[9]) and enforceable.

It is a controversial question whether terms of use amount to a contract. However, as far as the discussion on how the framework for implying a consent-based licence applies, it does not matter if the terms of use amount to a contract or a bare licence, for the following reasons. For a consent-based express bare licence, the components of the knowledge that are relevant are the knowledge of the terms of use and other surrounding circumstances (Chapter 4 (1)(c)(iii)). If the website terms of use amount to a contractual licence, these terms of use are likely to be more in the nature of copyright exploitation contracts or consumer contracts, but not commissioning contracts. Therefore, the components of knowledge to be considered are the knowledge of the terms of use and of the surrounding circumstances (Chapter 5(2)(c) and 3). Effectively, the terms can be assessed under the same components of knowledge, regardless of whether the terms of use amount to an express bare licence or a contractual licence. Therefore, in Chapters 10, 11, and 12, this distinction is not further discussed. The effort will be to ascertain how a licence may be implied into these terms enabling browsing, hyperlinking, and indexing.

Terms of use vary in content. At one end of the spectrum, a copyright owner might simply provide the © sign, with or without the words 'All rights reserved'. These words convey no more than the fact that copyright is claimed. Since copyright is an automatic right, even without such symbol or the words, copyright in the content on the website is protected. Therefore, the situations where this expression is used is not different from a situation where no terms of use are incorporated. It would be reasonable to conclude that the copyright owner's objective is to benefit from browsing, hyperlinking, and indexing.

More commonly, websites may provide that only private and non-commercial use of the content is permitted, and that any commercial use must be authorised by an express licence. Even in the absence of this term, it is arguable that a user cannot use the content on the internet for commercial gain. For example, no person can download content from the internet, print, and sell copies of it, regardless of whether there are terms of use prohibiting such commercial use. Even if this may be technologically possible, it is not within the knowledge or expectation

6 See eg https://www.theguardian.com/help/terms-of-service accessed 29 July 2020.

7 See eg https://www.facebook.com/legal/terms accessed 29 July 2015.

8 Case C-30/14 ECLI:EU:C:2015:10.

9 However, the Irish High Court held in *Ryanair Ltd v Billigfluege.de GmbH* [2010] IEHC 47, that Ryanair's terms of use amount to a contract.

of the copyright owner that such use of their content will be made. To the extent that the copyright owner has willingly placed their content on the internet (positive act) and stood back with terms of use (partial neutral act), it may be a matter of interpreting 'commercial use' to explore the uses it prohibits, in addition to exploring whether a consent-based licence may be implied to permit browsing, hyperlinking, and indexing.

At the other end of the spectrum are terms of use where a copyright owner might specifically prohibit acts such as linking, scraping, crawling, and indexing, without the copyright owner's consent. Under these circumstances, it will be difficult to imply a consent-based licence. Even if these functions are established as customs, such customs cannot override these express terms. As such, implying a policy-based licence must be considered. If these terms of use amount to a contract, the methodology in Chapter 7 will apply. Even if the terms of use do not amount to a contract, but are express bare licences, since there is a certain voluntariness to the copyright owner's actions in placing the content on the internet, the methodology in Chapter 7 can apply by analogy. As required by the methodology, first, the underlying policy of browsing, hyperlinking, and indexing must be identified. The website terms of use, being more in the nature of copyright exploitation contracts or consumer contracts, are a sufficiently discrete class of contracts. Finally, the necessity for such implication may be established based on the fact that no SLE or other legal provision addresses the situation at hand. Therefore, based on the respective policy considerations for permitting linking and indexing, a policy-based licence can be implied.

As stated above, even if a content owner places their content on the internet indicating a positive act, if they do not leave the content freely available on the internet, but instead incorporate the technological protection measures (TPMs) (including paywalls), it becomes a conditional neutral act. When the TPMs are in place, browsing, linking, and indexing the content are all restricted. Browsing will only be possible if the user obtains authorisation to go beyond the TPM. As for linking, even if a person lawfully gains authorisation and finds the web address, the web address is unlikely to work as a hyperlink, unless the TPM has been circumvented. A person who clicks on a link of content protected by the TPMs may only gain access up to the page before the TPM, requesting them to take the necessary action (such as payment) to gain further access. Circumventing TPMs amounts to an infringement under section 296ZA of the Copyright, Designs and Patents Act 1988 (CDPA). If a person breaks a TPM and places the content back on the internet without access restrictions, then they infringe the copyright owner's making available right. Whether users can still engage in browsing, hyperlinking, and indexing in relation to infringing content is discussed in the section below.

2. Content Placed on the Internet without the Copyright Owner's Consent

Content might find its way onto the internet without the consent of the copyright owner either because the content had never been placed on the internet by or on behalf of the copyright owner or because it was previously behind a paywall and the paywall has been tampered with. Both cases infringe the copyright owner's exclusive right of making available to the public. In the former scenario, the first step that signals a consent-based implied licence, namely the copyright owner's positive act of placing the content on the internet, is absent. In the latter, the removal of the TPM changes the copyright owner's conditional neutral act into an absolute neutral act. Since the resulting absolute neutral act is not the copyright owner's conduct, it cannot be considered towards the copyright owner's consent. In the absence of the positive and/or the neutral acts in these scenarios, there is no point in assessing the knowledge of the copyright owner. Therefore, no consent-based licence may be implied. Other bases may be pressed into service for a very limited licence.

As stated in Chapter 6 above, a custom can be born out of non-objection. Even if the copyright owner has not consented for their content to be placed on the internet, their non-objection to continued actions of the users in hyperlinking and indexing may have gone on to become a custom. It is, therefore, arguable that internet customs of this nature exist, based on which licences permitting hyperlinking and indexing may be implied. The reasonableness of this custom will have to be informed by the universal utility of these actions on the internet.

The framework proposed in Chapter 7 of implying a policy-based contractual licence will not apply because the content was placed on the internet without the copyright owner's consent and one can speak of no terms of use standing in as a contract between the copyright owner and the user. The framework to consider when there is no voluntariness on the part of the copyright owner at all is that for a policy-based bare licence, as discussed in Chapter 8. One must assess whether the exercise of the court's powers to restrict or prevent copyright enforcement in the public interest complies with the three-step test; or, alternatively, whether it complies with the fundamental rights regime. A limited licence permitting browsing, linking, and indexing of infringing content may be implied to give effect to the public interest inherent in engaging in these actions on the internet.

3. Conclusions and Connections

This chapter has addressed certain fundamental aspects of applying implied licences to the internet. To begin with, it divided the content on the internet between that placed by or with the copyright owner's consent and the content placed without such consent. This division is so fundamental in clarifying the relevant bases of implication that Chapters 10, 11, and 12 also adopt this structure. This chapter then went on to address the parallels in the online world for the criteria in the proposed frameworks that have been discussed only in relation to the offline world in Part II. This discussion is not only foundational for the upcoming chapters, but it is also an efficient way of addressing these aspects without having to repeat them in relation to each of browsing, hyperlinking, and indexing.

The discussions in the next three chapters will reveal that the courts have not applied implied licence reasoning to deal with browsing and hyperlinking, while courts have relied on implied licences to a limited degree in relation to indexing. The upcoming chapters will demonstrate that implied licence can provide a better response to the challenges presented by browsing, hyperlinking, and indexing, owing to their ability to provide a flexible and targeted solution. In doing so, connections and cross-references will be made not only to the discussion in this chapter, but also to the frameworks discussed in Part I and the discussion of the offline case law in Part II.

10
Browsing and Streaming

Users of the internet must be able to benefit from the vast resources on the internet by viewing or 'browsing' on their computer monitors. When a user types the address of a webpage, several temporary copies of the content are made while transmitting the webpage from its server, and on the user's monitor. Additionally, even if the user does not download the content, copies are made within the viewer's computer temporarily for easy access to the pages in future and to reduce network traffic, which are called cached copies. Cached copies may be deleted by the user or automatically after some time, depending on the configuration of the relevant computer.[1] While the term browsing applies to text and images, in relation to audio and video content, the process is more appropriately described as streaming. Again, in this process, in addition to copies made on screen and in transmission, copies are made in the buffer of the computer in order to facilitate uninterrupted streaming, even if the content is not downloaded. If each copy made in this process needs permission from the copyright owner, then it would significantly impede the functioning of the internet. If browsing is not authorised, it would make infringers out of millions of users for simply viewing websites.[2]

The response in the UK has been to subsume this process into the statutory limitations or exceptions (SLEs) under section 28A of the Copyright, Designs and Patents Act 1988 (CDPA), which was transposed from Article 5(1) of the Infosoc Directive. This provision exempts from infringement temporary copies that are transient or incidental, and are an integral and essential part of a technological process, if the sole purpose of these copies is to enable a transmission of the work by an intermediary, or a lawful use of the work, so long as it does not have an independent economic significance. Recital 33 of the Infosoc Directive defines lawful use as a use authorised by the copyright owner or not restricted by law. Over the years, the Court of Justice of the European Union (CJEU) has added rich case law interpreting different aspects of this provision. But the interpretation of this provision suffers from inadequacies owing to the inherent inflexibility with the language used.[3]

[1] *Public Relations Consultants Association Ltd v The Newspaper Licensing Agency Ltd* [2013] UKSC 18 [2].

[2] ibid [36].

[3] Case C-5/08 *Infopaq v Danske* ECLI:EU:C:2009:465 [54].

Implied Licences in Copyright Law. Poorna Mysoor, Oxford University Press (2021). © Poorna Mysoor.
DOI: 10.1093/oso/9780198858195.003.0011

However, implied licences can offer a flexible response to this issue. Since the inception of the internet, scholars have written about whether these temporary copies made either during transmission, display, or in the computer's cache, infringe the reproduction right and, if they do, whether such reproduction can be impliedly licensed.[4] These writings focus mostly on consent-based licences. This chapter demonstrates that depending on whether the content was placed on the internet with the consent of the copyright owner or without, licences implied on different bases could be pressed into service to address different scenarios. It examines whether implied licences provide a better solution than the SLE approach. Since streaming involves a technologically similar process to browsing in terms of making temporary copies, the arguments presented here apply equally to streaming.

1. Content Placed on the Internet with the Copyright Owner's Consent

As stated above, browsing and streaming are simply the act of viewing content online. An analogy can be drawn with the physical world to explain this. Suppose P, an artist, creates a pamphlet regarding her upcoming art exhibition, incorporating certain photographs she has taken of her art. She places copies of the pamphlet on a display stand dedicated for promoting upcoming events at the city's major public exhibition venue. The display stand in the public place can be likened to the internet as a platform. The printed pamphlets can similarly exist on a website. Just as people come to this stand to look at the pamphlets, people visit websites for a similar purpose. It is in the very nature of the location of the stand that it is publicly accessible. Similarly, it is in the very nature of the internet that it is publicly accessible. Whoever places content on this stand knows its public nature, just as whoever places content on the internet knows its public nature. Just as placing a pamphlet signals a possible consent for the pamphlet to be used in some way, placing content on the internet signals a possible consent for such content to be used in some way. P not only knows that members of the public will see the pamphlet; indeed, it is the objective she wants to achieve. Similarly, one of the most obvious consequences of placing or consenting to place one's work on the internet is that it can be viewed by millions of users. In many cases, this may not only be within the copyright owner's knowledge, but indeed their objective.

On the one hand, from the perspective of the public, the public viewing the pamphlet violates no right of the copyright owner's.[5] Therefore, they do not need

[4] Lisa Anne Katz Jones, 'Is Viewing a Web Page Copyright Infringement?' (1998) 4 Appeal 60 para [8]; Richard S Vermut, 'File Caching on the Internet: Technological Infringement or Safeguard for Efficient Network Operation?' (1997) 4 J Intell Prop L 273, 315–27; Graham Smith and others, *Internet Law and Regulation* (Sweet & Maxwell 2007) 23–25.

[5] *Public Relations Consultants Association Ltd v The Newspaper Licensing Agency Ltd* (n 1) [1] (Lord Sumption).

the copyright owner's licence for this purpose. On the other hand, in the internet context the public views the content on the internet using a computer monitor or some other electronic display machine. However, the technology behind it generates many copies in the process—in transmission, onscreen, and in the computer's cache, thereby engaging the right of reproduction, although the copies are only temporary. The question is whether a consent-based bare licence may be implied in this scenario.

Continuing on from the discussion in Chapter 9, if placing of the content on the internet amounts to a positive act and standing back when the content is seen by the users amounts to a neutral act, we need to explore the knowledge of the copyright owner of the circumstances. It is important to bear in mind that all else remains comparable to the analogue world, including the fact that a copyright owner places her work in a public place for it to be seen. The copyright owner must know that at least one copy of her work is made when it is displayed on one user's monitor. Even if the copyright owner does not know the exact technological process regarding the copies made in transmission and the cached copies, she will know that by putting it on the internet she exposes her work to innumerable copies being made by innumerable users accessing the work on their monitors. Further, given the length of time the internet has been in existence and the increasingly indispensable role the internet plays in peoples' lives, it is more likely than not that the copyright owners are aware of the copies generated during browsing. Based on such knowledge, it must be possible for a consent-based bare licence to be implied.

The above argument holds good when the copyright owner places no terms of use in relation to the display of her work. The copyright owner might equally choose to place terms of use indicating what is permitted in relation to the work. One of the most common clauses a copyright owner normally places in these terms is to prohibit 'commercial use'. The question is whether it is still possible to imply into these terms a consent-based licence permitting browsing?

It might help again to go back to the offline example of P's art exhibition. If P incorporates a sentence at the bottom of the pamphlet that any commercial use of the pamphlet is prohibited, does it mean that it prohibits the public also from simply *viewing* the pamphlet? The very objective of P placing the pamphlet in a public place is to maximise its noticeability. Even if Q, a commercial art collector, benefits from the pamphlet, Q's viewing of the pamphlet alone cannot be regarded as a commercial use. In any event, viewing a copyright work is not a restricted act. Thus,, when a copyright owner places her works on the internet, even with a term of use prohibiting commercial use, such term cannot mean that the mere viewing is prohibited, even if a person commercially benefits from viewing or reading the work. Although such viewing itself makes onscreen, cached, and transmission copies of the work owing to the technological process behind browsing, such copying cannot be regarded as being for commercial use when the reason for such copies coming into existence, namely viewing of the website, itself cannot be regarded a commercial use. Therefore, when the copyright owner places the content on the internet knowing that copies of the work will be created, even if the terms of use prohibit commercial use, it is possible to imply a consent-based licence to permit browsing.

In the internet context, if the only copies made are those that enable viewing of the webpage, then such viewing alone cannot be for commercial purposes. Where there may be a commercial use of the work on the internet is when a person makes a profit from further communicating the work to other users. It happens generally with news aggregators who take copyright content from newspaper/magazine websites and offer a service to their own clients for a fee, to receive and view only the content of relevance to them. If the clients of the news aggregators are commercial entities who want to further send it to their clients, the profits made are attributable more to hyperlinking and indexing than browsing. This is addressed in Chapters 11 and 12 below on hyperlinking.

Since browsing simply amounts to viewing the content on the internet, it would be artificial to explore whether the practice of users viewing content on the internet has become a custom. As for temporary copies, since these are created following the technological process, it would also be difficult to regard such copying as a practice that may have become a custom. Therefore, a custom-based implied licence is not viable for browsing.

However, there is a clear public policy in permitting browsing as one of the chief modes of connection between the copyright owner and the user. Even if the terms of use bar commercial use, a licence may be implied also based on policy to permit browsing. Following on from the arguments in relation to policy-based implied contractual licence, an analogy could be drawn from the decision in *Solar Thomson Engineering Co Ltd v Barton* which was discussed in Chapter 7 above. Here, the copyright owner voluntarily sold a chattel incorporating copyright work. The owner of a chattel being able to prolong the life of the chattel by making repairs is a matter of public policy. However, to effect repairs, copies of the copyright work must be made. Therefore, to give effect to the public policy, a licence to copy the drawings is implied from the owner in favour of the user/purchaser of the chattel.[6] Similarly, here the copyright owner voluntarily places her content on the internet. The information placed on the internet without technological protection must be available to be freely viewed and read by the users, as a matter of public policy. However, viewing creates copies of the work. Therefore, to give effect to this policy, a licence may be implied into the terms of use to permit making copies of the content on the internet to enable browsing.

[6] [1977] RPC 537, 560–61.

As stated above, the courts in the UK have not adopted the implied licence approach, but rather the SLE approach. This was applied in *Newspaper Licensing Agency v Meltwater Holdings*.[7] Here, the plaintiff (the NLA) was a licensing body, of which the publishers of many national newspapers are members. The first defendant (Meltwater), a news aggregator, used crawling robots to scrape content from the newspapers and prepared its own index. It provided a commercial news aggregating service called *Meltwater News*, which is an online periodic newsletter for its clients, with headlines as links, opening words and a summary of all articles published within that period containing the search term that their clients had chosen, for a fee. The second defendant, the Public Relations Consultants Association (the PRCA), represented the interests of public relations consultants, many of whom were clients of Meltwater's. The issue, among others, was whether the members of the PRCA required a web end user licence from the NLA to receive and view *Meltwater News*, in addition to Meltwater requiring its own licence from the NLA. Although Meltwater had also contested that it required a licence from the NLA, it had agreed to enter into a licence on such terms as the Copyright Tribunal would find reasonable. The NLA also contended that some of the public relations consultants use *Meltwater News* to send to their own external clients, which required public relations consultants to obtain a web end user licence.[8] The terms of use of all newspapers prohibited the use of their content for commercial purposes. Some newspapers had specifically stated that commercially operated news aggregators and their end users both require a licence to use their content. The NLA contended, on the one hand, that by 'receiving and viewing' *Meltwater News*, the public relations consultants would be making copies of the copyright content, infringing the newspaper publishers' copyright. The PRCA, on the other hand, contended that the licence to Meltwater to provide *Meltwater News* implies a licence for its clients to receive and view it on their screens.[9]

Proudman J was willing to accept that Meltwater's licence to provide *Meltwater News* meant an implied licence in favour of the public relations consultants to receive *Meltwater News*. But she did not accept that this licence extended to viewing *Meltwater News*, as viewing (browsing) generated copies whether they received it as a newsletter or visited Meltwater's website. Such copying, Proudman J opined, was not covered by implied licence. As such, she held that there is prima facie infringement, unless an exception applied. In relation to Article 5(1) of the Infosoc Directive, she held it to be not applicable because the cached copies were not authorised and, therefore, not a lawful use; that the onscreen and cached copies

[7] [2010] EWHC 3099 (Ch).
[8] ibid [1]–[6], [8], [13], [22]–[26].
[9] ibid [45], [48], [95].

were not an integral and essential part of technological process, because there was human volition involved in creating those copies; and the onscreen copies had an independent economic significance because those copies were the very product for which the public relations consultants paid Meltwater.[10] The Court of Appeal confirmed Proudman J's decision,[11] and did not consider implied licence at all.

The Supreme Court reversed the High Court and the Court of Appeal's decisions, but only as to the interpretation of Article 5(1), with no reference to implied licence. The Supreme Court held that viewing of a website was a lawful use, since viewing of an infringing website, just like reading an infringing book, is not a restricted act. Thus, a person who merely views or reads an infringing copy of a work on the internet infringes no copyright in such work.[12] The Supreme Court further clarified that the economic significance of a copy required under Article 5(1) is the kind of significance which is independent of its value as a display copy. Since onscreen copies only had value as display copies, they lacked independent economic significance.[13] Although the Supreme Court also held that browsing is covered by the temporary copying exception under Article 5(1), it referred the matter to the CJEU for reconfirmation on the impact of human volition on Article 5(1). The concern was that, since cached copies are generated as a result of the volition of the person browsing, whether they were an integral part of the technological process.[14] The CJEU held that the copies produced during browsing do not lose their incidental nature merely because there is human intervention in initiating and terminating their production, as these copies exist only so long as the technological process of browsing continues.[15]

Let us examine how implied licence could have been of assistance. Meltwater agreed to take a licence from the NLA not because Meltwater's browsing of the newspapers needed a licence, but because Meltwater was scraping the newspapers' websites and providing hyperlinks to its clients for a fee (more on this in Chapters 11 and 12 below). The profit made by Meltwater was attributable to these activities rather than the fact that Meltwater was able to browse the newspapers. As far as browsing was concerned, the moment the newspapers were placed on the internet with the consent of the copyright owners, a consent-based bare licence could be implied in favour of all those who wished to view

[10] ibid [49]–[55], [101]–[109].

[11] [2011] EWCA Civ 890.

[12] *Public Relations Consultants Association Ltd v The Newspaper Licensing Agency Ltd* (n 1) [1] (Lord Sumption).

[13] ibid [27], relying on Case C-403/08 *FAPL v QC Leisure* ECLI:EU:C:2011:631 [179]. The Court noted that this requirement should be read in such a way as to encourage new technologies and not to impede them.

[14] *Public Relations Consultants Association Ltd v The Newspaper Licensing Agency Ltd* (n 1) [29]–[33].

[15] Case C-360/13 *Public Relations Consultants Association v Newspaper Licensing Agency* ECLI:EU:C:2014:1195 [63].

the newspapers, whether they were a media monitoring service like Meltwater or a public relations consultant or any member of the public, so long as the copies made facilitated browsing. No enquiry into whether these copies were initiated because of the intervention by the users is necessary. A licence is implied based on the conduct of the copyright owner and not based on the conduct of the users. And the conduct of relevance here is that of the copyright owner in placing the content on the internet with the knowledge of the consequences.

An additional reason why public relations consultants do not need a licence is because a licence in their favour can be implied also based on Meltwater's licence with the NLA. The particular facts of this case were that Meltwater had agreed to take a licence from the NLA to continue providing its services. This meant that the NLA's licence to Meltwater to provide *Meltwater News* consented to the whole activity of providing such news, i.e., news that can actually be read by Meltwater's clients. There would be no point in Meltwater providing the news if its clients could receive it but could not view it without an additional licence. Surely, the fee Meltwater charged its clients covered not only the links delivered, but also the content displayed on the clients' monitors. That the NLA's licence to Meltwater authorised Meltwater to provide *Meltwater News* to its customers must have been within the knowledge of the newspapers concerned who were, in any event, members of the NLA. The fact that viewing of *Meltwater News* creates onscreen and cached copies of the copyright works is also well within the knowledge of both the NLA, as a collecting society, and its member newspapers. Therefore, such knowledge should have been sufficient to imply a consent-based licence in favour of the public relations consultants, enabling them to browse *Meltwater News*. Therefore, even if the courts found the SLE route was unable to cover the use in issue, implied licence arguments could have been pressed into service.

Further, the difficulty with the SLE approach is that it defines the exception based on the technicalities of the process to the exclusion of all other factors. Ironically, the certainty that the SLE route is meant to bring about as opposed to implied licence, did not materialise in this case. While Article 5(1) made it clear that the copies made during transmission are exempt from copyright infringement, it was unclear what happens to all the other copies that are made not in transmission, but onscreen or in cache. The role of human volition was also unclear, although one can argue that even copies made during transmission do not arise on their own and that there will be some human activity that causes the transmission. In theory, 'lawful use' is a helpful concept. Its interpretation as 'not restricted by law' appears to have been intended to address the primary use—i.e., viewing/reading. However, it can be incorrectly applied to the secondary use—i.e., the incidental copies made. This will be evident when one considers the issue of browsing of infringing content on the internet, discussed below.

2. Content Placed on the Internet without the Copyright Owner's Consent

The inadequacies of Article 5(1) of the Infosoc Directive is best demonstrated in *Stichting Brein v Jack Frederik Wullems*. Here, Mr Wullems sold a multimedia device called 'Filmspeler', which acted as a medium between copyright content on one hand and a television monitor on the other. The device incorporated hyperlinks of websites that enabled streaming of infringing content. Mr Wullems advertised it as a device that enabled viewing of infringing content.[16] Stichting Brein, a collecting society, sued Mr Wullems for copyright infringement. Several issues arose in relation to Mr Wullems' liability, which were referred to the CJEU. However, the issue of relevance to us here is the liability of the end users for receiving the stream of infringing content. More precisely, the question was whether the copies made as a result of the end users streaming the infringing content on to their devices can be regarded 'lawful use' in order to bring it under the temporary copying exception under Article 5(1) of the Infosoc Directive.[17]

The CJEU noted that 'lawful use' in accordance with recital 33 of the directive occurs where a use is authorised by the copyright owner or is not restricted by the applicable legislation. It is clear that the use in this case was not authorised by the copyright owner. The question is whether it is restricted by the applicable legislation. The CJEU regarded the three-step test incorporated in Article 5(5) to be the appropriate yardstick to assess whether the use made during streaming was lawful use. It went on to hold that the temporary copies produced during streaming of infringing content interfered with the normal exploitation of the work because it resulted in the 'diminution of lawful transactions' in the works and prejudiced the legitimate interests of the copyright owner.[18] The CJEU did not go into the normative aspects of the normal use. It therefore, held that the copies made during streaming did not benefit from the temporary copying exception. This meant that end users were liable for infringement owing to the temporary copies produced when they streamed infringing content on their devices. This effectively interpreted 'lawful use' to mean 'use of lawful copies'. If interpreted this way, this approach is likely to raise problems also in relation to the need for independent economic significance of the temporary copies under Article 5(1). This is because, the very copies that appear on-screen and in the cache have economic value which the subscribers pay to a streaming service.

To unpack this, one needs to take a step back and understand what copyright protects in the offline world and the policy behind it. As Lord Sumption stated

[16] Case C-527/15 *Stichting Brein v Jack Frederik Wullems* ECLI:EU:C:2017:300 [15]–[18].

[17] ibid [22]. This assumed that the other requirements of art 5(1) had been satisfied.

[18] ibid [65]–[66], [70]. The CJEU followed the Advocate General's opinion. See the Opinion of AG Sanchez-Bordona ECLI:EU:C:2016:938 paras [71]–[72], [77].

in *Public Relations Consultants Association*, a person does not violate any exclusive rights if she sees or reads or listens to a copyright work.[19] If a person needed the copyright owner's permission each time she saw, read, or listened to a work, then it would not only be counterproductive to the copyright owner's ability to exploit her work, but also this would place an unreasonable hindrance on the access to knowledge and information. If the copy that the user sees, reads, or listens to is infringing, even then it does not amount to an infringement in the offline world.[20] The only possible infringement here is for secondary liability of possession of infringing copies, but such liability only attaches for possession in the course of business.[21] In effect, even if the act of end users purchasing and experiencing an infringing copy dilutes the market for lawful copies and interferes with the normal exploitation of the work, only those who deal in infringing copies are liable and not the end users who purchase a copy in the offline world. The logic here is that a person is able to purchase an infringing copy because someone has sold it to her and it would serve the copyright owners' interests far better if the law targeted the source of supply of such infringing copy, rather than individual purchasers of the copy. In this sense, lawful use is a much broader concept than use of lawful copies and therefore, confining the concept to the lawfulness of the copies would be short-sighted.

The normative question is whether the same policy should apply to the online scenario. Prescriptive parallelism discussed in Chapter 9 above means that the temporary copying exception must be interpreted to achieve the same goal. This means that, since the primary use viewing the work is not restricted by law even if it is an infringing copy, then the secondary use of it (which makes incidental copies) should also be exempted from infringement. However, the CJEU failed to appreciate that the primary use of an infringing work by an end user is lawful in that it violates no rights of the copyright owner. As noted in relation to the offline example, the law takes a broader view of who should be pursued for infringement.

The problem is exacerbated when one considers what may happen if the end user does not know and has no way of knowing whether a particular content is placed on the internet by or with the consent of the copyright owner. If the lawfulness of the temporary copies is assessed based on their compliance with the three-step test like the CJEU did in *Wullems* taking purely economic considerations of the copyright owner into account, then it would be irrelevant whether the end users know of the infringing nature of the copies or not. It so happened in *Wullems* that the end

[19] Michael Hart, 'The Legality of Internet Browsing in the Digital Age' (2014) 36 EIPR 630, 633. See also Caroline Herbert, 'The Vexed Issue of Streaming, Sports and Set-top Boxes in New Zealand' (2019) 30(8) Ent LR 242, 243.

[20] *Public Relations Consultants Association Ltd v The Newspaper Licensing Agency Ltd* (n 1) [1]. One may note in this case that, to the extent that Meltwater was not authorised to scrape newspaper content, the content was infringing.

[21] Copyright, Designs and Patents Act 1988 (CDPA), s 23.

users knew that the copies were infringing. But there may be any number of cases where the content on the internet may be infringing and an end user has no knowledge of it. This results in making infringers out of millions of users of the internet. This does not achieve any of the copyright owner's purposes, as no copyright owner would want to sue millions of end users and struggle to obtain any meaningful relief. Indeed, this would be counterproductive in that the impact of copyright infringement will be diluted, making end users complacent about respecting copyright law. Therefore, it would make more sense if the online scenario mirrored the offline scenario in this regard. When content is placed on the internet without the consent of the copyright owner, there is an initial act of infringement of the right of making available to the public. If there is infringing content on the internet, the rights of copyright owners can be protected by pressing into service the provisions of the CDPA that hold liable the person who created the infringing copy by either circumventing the technological protection measures (TPMs),[22] or by making a business out of infringing copies,[23] rather than the person who browses infringing copies. Dealing with the issue of liability in this manner goes to the root of the infringement, rather than addressing the relatively innocuous and hard to police temporary copies.

Regardless of whether a person knows that the content they are viewing is infringing, they must be permitted browsing. Post-Exit Day, if a matter arises in the UK on the issue of browsing or streaming infringing content and the liability of the end users,[24] and if the matter reaches the Supreme Court, the Supreme Court can depart from *Wullems*. It can revert to the observations of Lord Sumption in *Public Relations Consultants Association* that viewing infringing content is not an infringement. This might set right the interpretation of 'lawful use' in section 28A of the CDPA.

If the courts are unwilling to read these policy arguments into the interpretation of lawful use under section 28A, then these arguments can be presented as the basis for implying a policy-based licence using public interest defence. This will be in tune with the exceptionality of the public interest defence that it only applies when no SLE can be pressed into service. In addition to the above arguments, since browsing is the way in which internet users can perceive the content on the internet, it is fundamentally important to enable browsing unhindered, thereby promoting public interest. Based on this, a court can restrict copyright enforcement in relation to such onscreen and cached copies. This will pass the three-step if

[22] ibid s 296ZA.

[23] ibid s 23 and the tortious liability of authorising infringement as crystallised in *Twentieth Century Fox Film Corporation v Newzbin Ltd* [2010] EWHC 608 [90] (Ch).

[24] This question has arisen in at least one other common law jurisdiction, New Zealand, in the High Court's decision in *Sky Network Television Ltd v My Box NZ Ltd* [2019] 2 NZLR 411, where it held that end users cannot benefit from the temporary copying exception for streaming infringing content.

unlike in *Wullems*, the normative and non-economic considerations are also considered to interpret normal exploitation.

Alternatively, one may explore whether the fundamental rights regime can assist. Since browsing opens up the vast repository of information to internet users, browsing plays a vital role in protecting the right to freedom of information, engaging Article 10 of the European Convention on Human Rights (ECHR). If users can be held liable for infringement for browsing the content on the internet, it interferes with their Article 10 right. This right can only be interfered with for considerations such as protecting the rights of others in a democratic society, among others (under Article 10(2) ECHR). This engages the copyright owners' right under Protocol 1, Article 1 (A1P1) of the ECHR, which can only be interfered with in the general interest. On the one hand, interference with a fundamental right is justified only if it is proportionate or strikes a fair balance.[25] On the other hand, allowing internet users to browse its content freely promotes their Article 10 right. If the browsing is held legal only in relation to viewing of lawful content, then the onus will be on the end users to ascertain the legality of the content they view. If browsing is held infringing only when a person knowingly views infringing content, then this is not an effective way to enforce the copyright owners' A1P1 right. This is because holding end users liable for copyright infringement through browsing gives no effective remedy to copyright owners to protect their A1P1 right, given the expense and effort involved in securing an injunction against each of them and, worse still, getting them to pay damages. Therefore, Article 10 trumps the A1P1 right, thereby permitting browsing regardless of the lawfulness of the content.

3. Conclusions and Connections

This chapter has examined the application of implied licences to browsing as an activity on the internet. Although browsing has been subsumed under the temporary copying exception under section 28A of the CDPA, this chapter has examined the inadequacies of this formalistic approach. Drawing analogy with offline scenarios, this chapter established that it is possible to defend browsing regardless of whether the content is lawful or infringing. Since Article 5(1) of the Infosoc Directive has been transposed into UK law in the form of section 28A, unless there is an amendment to the CDPA, this provision will continue after the Exit Day. With *Meltwater Holdings* and *Public Relations Consultants Association* being UK decisions and the CJEU only providing clarification on the application of temporary copying exception, browsing will continue to be dealt with under section 28A. However, where there is an opportunity for the UK to depart from EU law is in relation to browsing

[25] See ch 8, section 2 above.

or streaming of infringing content. This chapter has explored the arguments that may be put forward in this connection.

Users are able to view and interact with the content on the internet more often than not because they clicked on a hyperlink and that hyperlink was brought to their monitor by a search engine. Therefore, in addition to browsing, one must also consider hyperlinking and indexing, to appreciate the challenges posed by the internet. This is dealt with in the next two chapters, respectively.

11
Hyperlinking

The internet infrastructure enables a person to 'hyperlink' directly to the web page containing the required information without having to remember or type the website address or uniform resource locator (URL), making the accessibility of information more efficient. Given the enormity of the content on the internet, the ready accessibility and cross-connections enhance the value of the internet exponentially. If linking amounts to an act of communication to the public requiring the consent of the copyright owner, each time a person wishes to link to a website, the consent of the copyright owner must be obtained. This will dramatically reduce the efficiency of the internet.

Some scholars believe that hyperlinking does not involve an act of communication to the public.[1] Although it is not the purpose of this monograph to provide a detailed discussion of what amounts to the exercise of the right of communication to the public, it may be briefly addressed here. Scholars argue that an act of communication must involve transmission, and hyperlinking does not involve such transmission; and even if it does, such transmission is not of a 'work' as required under Article 3(1) of the Infosoc Directive.[2] If this argument is taken to its extreme, placing content on the web also does not involve transmission until a person uses the URL to summon the page on her monitor. Nevertheless, the mere placing of the content on the web is regarded as communicating the work to the public because the very reason a person places content on the web is for it to be seen by web users. While some argue that making available is a different right from a communication right, section 20 of the Copyright, Designs and Patents Act 1988 (CDPA) is clear that communication includes making available. Similarly, until the hyperlink is clicked, the page that it corresponds to is not transmitted. Once clicked, the linked page is summoned from its hosting server and the digital bits of the page are transmitted to the user's monitor for display. Although there is transmission only

[1] Interestingly, there are decisions of the Supreme Court of Canada in *Wayne Crookes v Jon Newton* [2011] 3 SCR 269 and the Supreme Court of Victoria in *George Defteros v Google LLC* [2020] VSC 219, where the court has considered whether hyperlinking amounts to publishing for the purposes of the law of defamation and have come to opposite conclusions.

[2] European Copyright Society, 'The Reference to the CJEU in Case C-466/12 *Svensson*' Paper No 6/2013 (February 2013) para 6 http://ssrn.com/abstract=2220326 accessed 22 July 2020.

Implied Licences in Copyright Law. Poorna Mysoor, Oxford University Press (2021). © Poorna Mysoor.
DOI: 10.1093/oso/9780198858195.003.0012

once the hyperlink is clicked, the only purpose of a link is for it to be used to reach the webpage it relates to, thereby encompassing transmission in the very reason for a hyperlink's existence. Hyperlinks create active links to the page being linked to and are more than the characters that appear in the URL. Therefore, it is arguable that hyperlinks are more than a mere facility for communicating the work and are a sufficient intervention for communication.

There are different types of linking. Linking to an internal page by passing the home page is deep linking. Linking can also take place in such a way that when clicked, it opens while being surrounded or framed by another webpage, which is called framing. It is also possible for the framed content to display automatically without the user having to click it, which makes the process even more likely to amount to communication. Although framing and deep linking may give rise to different issues such as passing off or loss of advertising revenue, as far as an act of communication to the public is concerned, these are technologically comparable.[3] Therefore, the arguments in relation to hyperlinking also generally hold good for framing and deep linking, unless stated otherwise.

Hyperlinks communicate works that are already communicated on the internet. However, Article 3(3) of the Infosoc Directive says that the communication right 'shall not be exhausted'. This provision has not been transposed into the CDPA, on the basis that rights that are not expressly provided to exhaust do not exhaust. In any event, on the internet, this means that the copyright owner placing her content on the internet does not exhaust the communication right; every subsequent act of communication which any member of the public engages in must still be licensed. If an express licence does not exist, one can ascertain if there is an implied licence. Therefore, implied licence is particularly helpful in understanding the right of communicating to the public.

Depending on whether the Court of Justice of the European Union (CJEU) wishes to permit or not permit hyperlinking in a given situation, the CJEU has interpreted the right of communication to the public to suit the ends, by adding incrementally to the ingredients that need to be established, even if such ingredients have little bearing on the language of the provision. Rather than straining the language of the provision, this chapter asks if it makes sense to regard hyperlinking as amounting to the exercise of the right of communication to the public based on a consistent interpretation, but go on to argue that such exercise does not infringe the right because of the licence implied on different bases.

[3] See *Christopher Wheat v Google* [2020] EWHC 27 (Ch), where framing (also called inline linking) was analysed as communication to the public. Cf Peter Mezei, 'Enter the Matrix: the Effects of CJEU Case Law on Linking and Streaming Technologies' (2016) 11 JIPLP 778, 779.

1. Content Placed on the Internet with the Copyright Owner's Consent

When content is placed on the internet by or with copyright owner's consent, following on from Chapter 9 above (which discussed the positive and the neutral acts), whether a copyright owner consents to communication by way of linking depends on the knowledge of the copyright owner as to the possibility of internet users linking to her work.[4] Going back to the example of P's pamphlets on the public shelves, suppose that a member of the public, Q, picks up a copy of the pamphlet and places it on the notice board of his housing estate. Suppose also that the pamphlet is surrounded by other information such as other events (i.e., framed by other content). P's placing of the pamphlets on the shelf was with the objective of bringing them to the attention of as many members of the public as he could. Q doing more to expose the information on the event to even more members of the public will still be within the copyright owner's knowledge or expectation, as her objective is to maximise the exposure. It will not matter if the notice is provided as stand-alone information or is surrounded by other information as well.

A similar logic applies to linking, with the copy on the notice board being likened to a link and the placing of it on the notice board amounting to an act of communication to the public. However, it is not an infringing exercise of this right because the copyright owner consented to such linking. The content originally placed on the internet with the copyright owner's consent is potentially open to any user of the internet, indicating that the copyright owner wishes to take advantage of all the benefits of the internet as a public platform. Since this objective is achieved by providing the link, it can be regarded as being within the copyright owner's knowledge, thereby completing the requirements for consent. It will not make a difference if the link is provided by way of framing or deep linking, since all pages are potentially exposed to the public. What is within the copyright owner's knowledge is a function of several factors, including any terms of use placed, as will be discussed below. But even if there are no terms of use placed, a person linking to content originally placed on the internet with the copyright owner's consent, benefits from a bare licence to communicate the work through linking, implied based on the copyright owner's consent.[5]

If for any reason, the knowledge of the copyright owner as to the possibility of internet users hyperlinking to their content cannot be established, but must be

[4] See ch 4 above for the framework and discussion on consent-based implied bare licences.

[5] To the extent that it is argued here that linking is a matter of implied licence, the views expressed here may seem similar to those of Association Litteraire et Artistique Internationale (ALAI) in its 'Report on the making available and communication to the public in the internet environment: focus on linking techniques on the internet' (15 September 2013) http://www.alai.org/en/assets/files/resolutions/making-available-right-report-opinion.pdf accessed 15 July 2020. However, the bases for implying a licence explored in this monograph go beyond the consent of the copyright owner.

presumed, then one can explore if the conduct of placing internet links can be established as a custom. It has been argued that there are numerous practices that have emerged in the online world that can be regarded as internet customs and that, in particular, linking as a practice has become an internet custom. As such, one may argue that internet users do not need the copyright owner's authorisation.[6] However, the threshold for a practice to become a custom in common law jurisdictions is very high, as discussed in Chapter 6 above.[7] It must therefore be explored whether linking has become a custom according to the criteria identified in that chapter.

If the content is on the internet with the consent of the copyright owner, a custom on this consensual basis may be established. Linking as a practice is consistent, and therefore 'certain'; it is 'notorious' given its widespread use; it is not only 'reasonable', but it achieves the objective for which the internet exists; it is not contrary to any law because the copyright owner's content is already on the internet with his consent; and one may argue that the practice is recognised as binding because it enhances the efficacy of the internet. As regards the refined criteria,[8] the internet community can be taken to be representative of the copyright owner, since the copyright owner has utilised the internet to reach her audience. The motivation underlying linking is to enhance the efficacy of the internet, and not mere convenience. Given the objectives that hyperlinking achieves on the internet, its impact can be regarded as balanced. Thus, once the custom is established, it is possible to imply a bare licence based on it to enable internet users to hyperlink to the content on the internet.

However, as stated above, the CJEU followed a different line of reasoning. In *Svensson v Retriever Sverige AB*, the applicants were journalists who wrote articles in a certain newspaper. The defendants operated a media monitoring service providing a list of clickable links to articles published by other websites chosen based on a search word agreed with their client. It was common ground that these articles were freely accessible on their website.[9] The decision does not state specifically that these websites did not carry any terms of use. The question was whether linking amounts to an act of communication to the public, requiring the copyright owner's consent before one could link. And whether it made any difference if the act of linking amounted to framing.[10]

The CJEU held that a clickable link makes copyright works available to the public at a time and from a place chosen by them, and therefore is an act of communicating them to the public. In order to be regarded as communication under

[6] Paul Polański, *Customary Law of the Internet: in the Search for a Supranational Cyberspace Law* (University of Melbourne 2007) 305, 307–11 (based on the author's thesis).

[7] See ch 6, section 1 above.

[8] See ch 6, section 2 above.

[9] Case C-466/12 ECLI:EU:C:2014:76 [8].

[10] ibid [13], [14].

Article 3(1) of the Infosoc Directive, the communication of the works using the same technical means must be to a 'new public'. The content which was linked was in any event freely available to the users, as there were no restrictions for its access. Since a clickable link only provided direct access to the content to which the same public already had access, the CJEU held that this did not amount to an act of communication to a 'new public'. As such, the CJEU held that there was no need for the act of linking to freely accessible content to be authorised by the content owners.[11] The CJEU further held that a new public comes into existence when the hyperlink makes it possible for users to access works by circumventing restrictions, because such public was not within the copyright owner's contemplation during the original authorisation. The CJEU also held that its decision would not alter if the link was provided as a frame.[12] Although the outcome is not necessarily incorrect, this discussion focuses on three issues with this reasoning and demonstrates how implied licence would have led to a more coherent approach to the decision.

First, *Svensson* does not make it clear how one is to ascertain the extent of public taken into account by the copyright owner with the initial act of communication. *Svensson* does not state specifically that it is a matter of consent, although it is arguable that the CJEU's reasoning had the undertones of a consent-based implied licence. A subsequent CJEU decision in another context also confirmed the implied consent reasoning underlying *Svensson*.[13] The reason why the exercise of the right of communication must be considered in relation only to the members of the public who were not taken into account by the copyright owner during the initial communication is because the members of the public who were exposed to the initial communication had the benefit of the copyright owner's consent-based implied licence.[14] Applying the framework proposed in Chapter 4, the consent depends on the extent of the copyright owner's knowledge, objectively assessed. Although it is within a copyright owner's powers to grant licences territorially, when she makes her work available on the internet knowing the extent of exposure her works receeive, the members of the public that she takes into account ought reasonably to be all of the users of the internet. This appears to be how *Svensson* understood the members of the public exposed to the original act of communication, but implied licence argument makes this reasoning transparent.

However, in *Warner Music UK Ltd v TuneIn Inc*, a territorial reading was given to the public. This case concerned hyperlinks to music streams communicated by internet radio stations across the globe. The claimants own or hold exclusive

[11] ibid [19]–[20], [25]–[28].

[12] ibid [30]–[31].

[13] Case C-301/15 *Soulier v Premier Ministre* ECLI:EU:C:2016:878 [36]–[37].

[14] For a more detailed discussion see Poorna Mysoor, 'Exhaustion, Non-exhaustion and Implied Licence' (2018) 49 IIC 656, 680–81. For an analysis of *Svensson* from a German law perspective see Stavroula Karapapa, 'The Requirement for a "New Public" in EU Copyright Law' (2017) 42 European L Rev 63, 73–76.

licences to copyright in sound recordings of music and represent about 43 per cent of global digital sales of recorded music. TuneIn, the defendant, is an aggregator of these hyperlinks providing a service whereby users can access any stream an internet radio station communicates at a given point in time.[15] While the consequences of aggregation and indexing are discussed in the next chapter, the relevant question here is whether hyperlinking to the streams amounted to an infringement of the right of communication to the public. If the internet radio stations wish to communicate recorded music, they need a licence from the relevant collecting society, of which the claimants are typically a significant member. Such licence would provide the authorisation for the initial act of communication by the internet radio station that gets the content over to the internet. This must mean that the collecting society, as the representative of the copyright owners, knows or ought reasonably to know that the content communicated by the internet radio station reaches potentially any user on the internet globally.

Birss J divided the internet radio stations into four categories: those that were (i) licensed in the UK to stream on the internet; (ii) not licensed anywhere; (iii) licensed in a country outside the UK; and (iv) part of a premium service. The court held that category (i) did not infringe any copyright as the members of the public that TuneIn communicated to were already those members of the public who had been taken into account by the original authorisation. The court held TuneIn to be liable in relation to all other categories.[16] Of relevance is category (iii), where the internet radio stations were licensed in a country outside the UK to communicate over the internet. Birss J held that even if the internet radio stations were licensed outside the UK, since TuneIn's services targeted UK users, it needed a UK specific copyright licence. He held that the grant of the licence by the collecting society should be deemed to have authorised the users of the respective internet radio station's website or at most the 'users in the locality'.[17] This places an artificial territorial limit to the internet in that, instead of the original communication being addressed to all users of the internet, it limits the exposure to the public of a particular territory. This reading of the initial act of communication risks making a mockery of internet communications. The collecting societies granting licences to their content to internet radio stations to communicate the content over the internet should be taken to have priced their licence to encompass users accessing the internet radio station's streams from anywhere in the world. It must be within the collecting society's knowledge or expectation that hyperlinks to the radio streams may be provided by any internet user anywhere in the world, and not necessarily only in the area where the licence was granted. This knowledge may also be gathered from the licence agreements between the collecting societies and the internet

15 [2019] EWHC 2923 (Ch) [3]–[6].
16 ibid [113], [141], [160], [161].
17 ibid [137].

radio stations, which is always an express licence. But having noted the oddity of *Svensson* not requiring a court to consider the terms of initial authorisation, Birss J still went on to ignore them.[18]

The second issue with *Svensson* is that the concept of a 'new public' only addresses the question of who is authorised to communicate, and not how she is authorised to communicate. The concept of a 'new public' assumes that, so long as it is the same members of the public to whom the copyright owner directed her original communication, and the means remains the same (internet), it does not matter how such members of the public further communicate. What if a user downloads a work from a website which has no access restrictions, and uploads the work on another website? When posting the work on the initial website, the copyright owner is taken to have all internet users in mind. When a user downloads a work and uses it again on the internet, the user also exposes the work to the same people. But surely, this still amounts to an infringement.

This issue arose in *Renckhoff*, where a pupil had downloaded a photograph from the website of its author where it was posted with his consent and had used it in a school assignment. The school had placed the pupil's work on its website.[19] Although the CJEU was correct to distinguish *Svensson* and to hold that it amounted to infringement, it still justified it based on the concept of a 'new public'. It held that the members of the public of concern for the school's website was a 'new public' because the initial posting of the photograph only took into account the users of that website.[20] This is undoing the power of the internet's seamlessness. This happened because a 'new public'—simply saying who the communication is directed to—is insufficient; it must also include how it is communicated—i.e., by downloading, reposting, and, indeed, any act which is not within the copyright owner's contemplation. Not making this clear had the consequence in this case that a 'new public' will be given an artificially restrictive meaning. This is demonstrated also by the reasoning of Birss J in *TuneIn* which gave an artificially restrictive and territorial reading of the 'public' who are authorised by the initial communication.[21]

Applying the framework proposed for consent-based implied licence, this can be analysed as a component of the knowledge of the copyright owner. As stated in Chapter 9, Section 1 above, when a copyright owner places her work on the internet, while it is possible that her work can be downloaded, printed, adapted, reposted, and so on, these are not within her reasonable expectation that the users would do. What is within her reasonable expectation, however, is that the work may be linked, which is why the implied licence extends to hyperlinking and not

[18] ibid [56]–[59], [107].
[19] Case C-161/17 *Land Nordrhein-Westfalen v Renckhoff* [2019] ECDR 3 [6]–[8].
[20] ibid [35]–[39].
[21] *Warner Music UK Ltd v TuneIn Inc* (n 15) [109(iv)].

to any other act. The knowledge of the copyright owner is a complex assessment of circumstances encompassing not only who the copyright owner knows will be able to access her work on the internet, but also how those members of the public may use it. Assessing different components of this knowledge provides a truer picture of the copyright owner's consent.

What if the users make commercial use of the content through linking? In particular, if there are terms of use which say, for example, that the works cannot be used for commercial purposes, the issue is not to whom the users are authorised to communicate, but how they can communicate—namely, only for non-commercial purposes. On the one hand, members of the public engaging in commercial use of the work may be the same members of the public to whom the original communication was available, but they are still not authorised to communicate the works for commercial purposes. In such cases, the CJEU's binary definition of whether 'a public' is 'new' does not assist. Indeed, it conflates the assessment and risks leading to unfair results.

On the other hand, the implied licence approach can accommodate this nuance more coherently. To illustrate commercial use, although linking was not specifically at issue in *Meltwater*, it is a good example to demonstrate the commercial value of linking as a content delivery mechanism. In *Meltwater*, the newspapers had published their content on the internet free of charge and free of access restrictions, but with terms of use prohibiting commercial use of the content. However, Meltwater charged its clients a fee to receive the same content through the delivery mechanism of linking. Linking for private and non-commercial purposes would have been within the knowledge of the newspaper publishers as normal use of their content. A use like that of Meltwater's charging a fee to provide links to freely available newspaper content will not be within the newspaper publishers' knowledge or contemplation as normal use of their content. It is arguable that the absence of knowledge or expectation that the users will use the content for commercial purposes negates consent, even in the absence of the terms of use, although the existence of terms of use helps to make a stronger argument in support of the lack of consent.

Meltwater might argue that it did not make commercial use of the content itself but charged its clients a fee only to deliver the content relevant to them. However, Meltwater's clients' only interest in the links is to click through and get to the content to which the hyperlinks point. Even if Meltwater built the infrastructure to scrape relevant content and to connect its clients to the content, ultimately it is the content which Meltwater's clients are interested in. While scraping is separately addressed in Chapter 12 below, if the newspapers did not provide content, there would be nothing that Meltwater could provide in its *Meltwater News*. Owing to the direct relationship between linking and the content, as a matter of interpretation of the terms of use, commercial use of the content will include delivering the content through linking for a fee. Therefore, particularly when the terms of use exclude commercial use of the content, it is difficult to imply a consent-based licence to permit hyperlinking by those who profit from linking as part of their business model to deliver content. Even if there are no terms of use, based on what is within the knowledge or reasonable expectation of the copyright owner, it is arguable that commercial use of copyright works through linking will not benefit from a consent-based implied bare licence.

Whether a work is used for commercial purposes through linking is not always a straightforward question. For example, Google provides its search results also as a hyperlink. No one can deny that Google is a profit-making entity. However, Google does not collect a fee from the end users for the search results, as Meltwater does, but derives its revenues predominantly from advertising. To assess if Google makes commercial use of the works, is the fact that the end user can access the links free of charge to be taken into account or the fact that Google makes a profit from other sources? And importantly, which of these would be within the knowledge or reasonable expectation of the copyright owners to assess their consent to this manner of use? Perhaps a question to ask is how closely connected copyright works are to the profits made. One may argue that services that make their revenue from advertising are only indirectly interested in the content. They offer search services and serve up the content that a user is looking for only to target such a user with advertisements from its own clients that may be of interest to the user. It is arguable that their interest in the content is only to the extent that it helps them understand the user, so that they can target their advertisements more precisely. When the enquiry is what is within a copyright owner's reasonable expectation as a commercial use of her content, caution must be exercised in holding linking services that are based on advertising revenue, for the lack of close connection between the copyright works and profit derived.

This was illustrated in *Warner Music*, although a direct question was not raised in this regard. TuneIn has two categories of service—a free service where TuneIn makes a profit from advertising and a subscription-based service which is free of advertisements. TuneIn tried to argue that its services are exactly like search engines, but in relation to specialised content, namely internet radio stations which communicate music.[22] In relation to the free services where TuneIn generates its revenue from advertisements, it does not derive a profit directly from the content it links to. The court did not ask the question whether such use ought reasonably to be within the collecting society's knowledge. However, if Google displaying the same links was not commercial use, then TuneIn displaying them should not be commercial use either. Commentators suggest multiple factors to be considered before linking is permitted, such as whether the user who utilises linking does so systematically or occasionally, and whether the material being linked to is chosen

22 *Warner Music UK Ltd v TuneIn Inc* (n 15) [120].

predominantly by the service provider or by the users and so on,[23] which may also be helpful in this assessment.

If establishing the copyright owner's knowledge is not an option, one may explore if a custom-based licence may be implied to permit hyperlinking in this context. Even if linking as a conduct is a custom,[24] it does not follow that the person so allowed to link can make a profit out of linking. In other words, even if hyperlinking as a practice satisfies most criteria discussed in Chapter 6, hyperlinking for commercial purposes might not satisfy the criterion of reasonableness and a balanced allocation of rights. A custom that enables the conduct of linking to freely accessible content without having to seek the copyright owner's consent denies a copyright owner the opportunity to make a profit out of linking. Having denied the copyright owner the profit from linking, it is unlikely that there will be a custom that enables the internet users to make a profit from linking. Therefore, it is unlikely that linking for commercial purposes will be regarded a custom for it to become the basis for implying a licence in favour of users like Meltwater.

One may also explore if a policy-based licence can be implied. Just as a custom recognising the practice of internet users linking for profit cannot be established for the lack of reasonableness, a policy cannot be recognised for the same reasons. Even if there is a policy that internet users' ability to link to freely available content on the internet is essential for the efficient functioning of the internet, this presupposes that copyright owners will not make a profit from such linking. However, to let the internet users in turn make a profit from content which they accessed free of charge is unlikely to be recognised as a policy for the purposes of Chapter 7. Nor will it pass the three-step test, or the fundamental rights regime discussed in Chapter 8. Therefore, if the terms of use prohibit commercial use, then it will be difficult to imply a policy-based licence to permit hyperlinking. But on the contrary, there may be website operators whose terms of use prohibit all linking, whether for commercial or non-commercial purposes. Ryanair is a significant example.[25] In this case, it may be argued that a substantial public policy does exist that recognises the utility of linking for non-commercial purposes for internet efficiency, based on which a licence may be implied to permit non-commercial linking, despite prohibition on all linking.

The above discussion demonstrates that if the users make commercial use of the content through linking, it will be difficult to imply a consent-based, a custom-based, or a policy-based licence to permit hyperlinking. However, the *Svensson* approach may not necessarily lead to the same result. This shows that the implied

[23] Tanya Pihlajarinne, 'Setting the Limits for the Implied License in Copyright and Linking Discourse: the European Perspective' (2012) 43(6) IIC 700, 709–710.

[24] Polánski (n 6) 307–11.

[25] Terms of Use cl 7 says: 'You may not establish and/or operate links to this website without the prior written consent of Ryanair.' See https://www.ryanair.com/en/terms-of-use/ accessed 15 July 2020.

licence approach is more receptive to the nuances of the case, presenting a lower risk of conflation and higher chances of reaching a fair conclusion.

The third issue with *Svensson* is that the concept of new public hinges on the 'access' to the works on the internet. According to *Svensson*, if the works linked to are freely accessible, then there is no 'new public' with linking. If the works are not freely accessible, i.e., they are behind a paywall, then there is a 'new public' if the link circumvents such access restrictions.[26] If a person, P, breaks the paywall and places the content on the internet and makes it available to a subsequent user on the internet, Q, then such content is then freely available, as Q can access it without restrictions. With the 'access' definition of a 'new public', Q will not be a 'new public', and Q's linking to the freely accessible (infringing) content will still not amount to an act of communication to the public under the *Svensson* approach.[27] This is an unsatisfactory result, especially if Q knows of the infringing nature of the content and still goes on to communicate to the public. The CJEU's simplistic approach to how a 'new public' comes into existence will not work if a person links to infringing content. Again, implied licence is a better approach, which takes us to the section below.

2. Content Placed on the Internet without the Copyright Owner's Consent

The question of linking to infringing content came up in *GS Media BV v Sanoma Media Netherlands BV*. In this case, certain copyright protected photographs had been uploaded to the internet by a third party without the consent of the defendant, the copyright owner. An online magazine, *GS Media*, provided a link to these photographs on its website, knowing that the photographs infringed Sanoma's copyright. The CJEU again dealt with it as a matter of interpretation of the right of communication to the public by giving it a restrictive interpretation. It held that for the *Svensson* rule of exempting linking from communication to the public to apply, the content on the internet must have been placed with the copyright owner's consent.[28] Although in *Svensson* the CJEU had used free accessibility of the content as the determining factor, in this case it changed it to the copyright owner's consent.

The CJEU realised that there is a problem if the copyright owner's consent is the sole determining factor. This is because, if the initial placing of the content on the internet lacks the copyright owner's consent, then not only the initial placing but

[26] This was confirmed in Case C-279/13 *C More Entertainment AB v Linus Sandberg* ECLI:EU:C:2015:199.

[27] This problem had been highlighted by Case C-348/13 *BestWater International v Michael Mebes* ECLI:EU:C:2014:2315, as pointed out by other commentators. See eg Mezei (n 3) 782–83.

[28] Case C-160/15 *GS Media BV v Sanoma Media Netherlands BV and Others* ECLI:EU:C:2016:221 [41]–[43].

all subsequent linking will amount to an infringement. The CJEU recognised that this could cause undue hardship in making all users ensure that the content they link to is not infringing. Abandoning its adherence to the concept of a 'new public', the CJEU read the fundamental rights and the notion of public interest into the interpretation of the right of communication to the public. The CJEU cited the importance of the internet in promoting free speech under Article 11 of the Charter of Fundamental Rights of the European Union. Accordingly, the CJEU held that if a person linking to certain content does not pursue a profit, and does not or cannot reasonably know of the infringing nature of the content, then the act of linking does not amount to an act of communication to the public. [29] However, if a person posts link for profit, she will be expected to ascertain whether the content she links to is infringing. The Court went a step further in holding that, if a person links for profit, there will be a rebuttable presumption against such person that she has posted the link with full knowledge of the infringing nature of the work. If she is unable to rebut such presumption, she will be held to have violated the right of communication to the public.[30]

There are two groups that the CJEU decision addresses—the end users who do not communicate and all others who might. As regards the end users, what would otherwise have been an act of communication to the public does not cease to become so merely because the person communicating had no knowledge of the infringing nature of the content and did not pursue a profit. Clearly, the knowledge and the profit-making motive are external to the act of communication. Neither the language nor the spirit of the right of communication to the public warrant this reading. The CJEU relied on considerations such as the fundamental rights and the public interest to inform the interpretation of the provisions, which is not wrong in principle. However, it is unclear which of the words used in Article 3(1) of the Infosoc Directive this approach tries to interpret. As regards all others who are not end users, the liability is based on a combination of pursuit of profit and knowledge of the infringing nature of the content. Scholars have criticised this decision for imposing the requirement of knowledge on the part of the internet users as to the infringing nature of the content being communicated, as they argue that it blurs the distinction between primary and secondary infringement.[31] Since users link to content that has already been subjected to primary infringement, this argument does have merit. After the Exit Day, if linking to infringing content is brought before the Supreme Court, the Supreme Court may depart from *GS Media*.

One can see the slippery slope in being able to ascertain what amounts to posting a link for profit. Revisiting *Warner Music*, the internet radio stations in category (ii) were not licensed anywhere in the world to offer internet radio services. The

[29] ibid [45]–[47].
[30] ibid [51].
[31] Joshua Colby, 'It's the End of the (Online) World as We Know It?' (2017) 28 Ent LR 161, 165–66.

issue was if these internet radio stations did stream the claimants' music on their internet services which TuneIn hyperlinked to, whether this amounted to communicating infringing content. Birss J held that TuneIn operates for profit and linking is at the core of such business. He dismissed the arguments that TuneIn is like a conventional search engine, holding that the number of internet radio stations that TuneIn needs to check is not so significant as to make the process of checking if they have the required licences 'unduly troublesome'.[32] The trouble is that TuneIn's business model is more comparable to Google than Meltwater, meaning it does not derive its profits directly from the end users use of the content in the links, as far as its free services are concerned, as discussed above. It is unclear if any extent of profit-making is sufficient to trigger the knowledge presumption. If the distinction from Google was being made on the basis that the volume of links handled by TuneIn would not cause undue hardship to investigate the lawfulness of the content, then it is also unclear how much effort must be shown to rebut the presumption of knowledge of the infringing nature of the content. While these factors turn on the facts, it still does not justify why this enquiry is necessary to establish liability for primary infringement.

Let us consider the implied licence approach. It would be much more coherent to accept that the solution to this problem must exist outside the exclusive right. And the way one could do that is to accept that the right is exercised but hold that it was not an infringing exercise of the right because it was impliedly licensed, saving certain users from the liability of infringement. This means that the knowledge and the profit element is not read into the exercise of the right; rather, the exercise of right is taken as a given, but the knowledge and profit elements are considered to support implied licence. Although end users are a clear beneficiary also of this approach, this approach does not rule out the eligibility of other profit-making entities if there is an overriding policy reason why they should still be permitted to continue with linking.

Since the content was not placed on the internet with the copyright owner's consent, the conduct necessary for a consent-based implication (i.e., the positive and the neutral acts) is absent. With the relevant conduct absent, there is no point in going on to assess the copyright owner's knowledge. Therefore, one will have to rule out consent as the basis. However, even if the initial act of placing the content on the internet was not consensual, one may ascertain whether internet customs exist because of the repeated conduct of non-objection or inaction, based on

32 *Warner Music UK Ltd v TuneIn Inc* (n 15) [148]. It appears that Birss J relied on the decision of the German Federal Supreme Court in *Vorschaubilder III* (Case No I ZR 11/16) in recognising that, although search engines are profit-making entities, their automated nature does not trigger the knowledge requirement. Cited from Thumbnails III (*Vorschaubilder III*) Decision of the Federal Supreme Court (Bundesgerichtshof) (2018) 49 IIC 357, 365.

which a licence may be implied.[33] It is a matter of evidence whether the copyright owners have consistently, uniformly and notoriously been not objecting to linking to infringing content. In order to argue that the custom is reasonable, one will have to consider whether there is a policy that justifies continued recognition of this inaction. Given the enormity of the content on the internet, access to information becomes more efficient with the ability to link freely, and this can be the policy that supports reasonableness of this custom.

The CJEU was not incorrect in recognising the significance of hyperlinking to free speech and the associated public interest in maintaining the network of connections within the internet through hyperlinking. However, unlike the CJEU, what one needs to do is to recognise these as external policy considerations that can be taken as the basis for implying a policy-based bare licence. In the language of the CDPA, this translates to establishing the public interest defence in favour of the end users. To ascertain whether this is possible, let us apply the three-step test or alternatively, the fundamental rights regime, as proposed in Chapter 8 above.

Let us examine the compliance with the three-step test. First, hyperlinking is a sufficiently specific case. The second requirement that such hyperlinking not interfere with the normal exploitation of the work requires a more detailed consideration. When the content is already infringing, its very existence on the internet already interferes with the normal exploitation of the works. Linking to such content further aggravates the interference with the normal exploitation of the work, unless one can demonstrate overriding normative reasons why the normal exploitation must be pegged to a different standard. These normative considerations are easier in relation to end users who link for non-commercial purposes and who have no wherewithal to ascertain the infringing nature of the content they link. It would place an unreasonable burden on them if they are required to check the lawfulness of the content before they link, which eventually reduces the efficacy of the internet. Therefore, what is normal under these circumstances should be defined by excluding end users who link for non-commercial purposes and have no knowledge of the infringing nature. In the third step of balancing the legitimate interests of the copyright owner, the interests of the end users might outweigh those of the copyright owner because of the importance of hyperlinking to sharing and access to information.

In the implied licence analysis, as stated above, knowledge and commercial use are only considered as factors weakening normative argument for the three-step test. This means that if one of these factors is absent, then it would weaken the normative argument, unless another overriding policy consideration exists. Thus, if a user links for commercial purposes, depending on the nature of the commercial

[33] The origin of a custom does not need to be a consensual act. See ch 3, section 2 above; see also the discussion on *Express Newspapers Plc v News (UK) Ltd and Others* [1990] 3 All ER 376 in ch 6, section 3(a) above.

use, if it can be argued that the user ought reasonably to have known the infringing nature of the content,[34] it reduces the normative element. Therefore, it may be held to interfere with normal exploitation of the work. However, if a search engine links, although it operates for profit, it is arguable that it does not derive profit directly from the content. Moreover, given the automated processes used to generate links in the search results, it is also arguable that, despite making a profit, search engines do not have the knowledge of the infringing nature of the content. If a person does not link for commercial purposes, but knows of the infringing nature of the content, the normative argument is again likely to be reduced, depending on the impact and scale of such linking. Such users might still interfere with the normal exploitation of the work.[35] Finally, if a person knowingly links to infringing content and makes a profit from it, then there is clearly no normative argument and therefore it interferes with normal exploitation. In the third step, the balance might tip in favour of the legitimate interests of the copyright owners.

As an alternative, the fundamental rights regime may also be considered. A copyright owner's Protocol 1, Article 1 (A1P1) right is engaged, which can only be deprived in general interest. Since there is a direct relationship between access to information and hyperlinking, hyperlinking plays a vital role in furthering internet users' right to freedom of expression and information, and therefore Article 10 of the ECHR is engaged. In an assessment of proportionality and fair balance, the outcome may be similar to the balancing in the third step in the three-step test. A person who links for a non-commercial purpose not knowing of the infringing nature of the content may have her free speech more readily protected over and above the copyright owner's interests. A search engine may similarly be able to argue the significant role it plays in fostering free speech and delivery of information under Article 10. Even if it pursues a profit, it is possible that a court might not hold its activities infringing in order to balance free speech with the copyright owner's A1P1 right. In all other cases, a court is unlikely to be persuaded by an argument that the copyright owner's rights should be interfered with by permitting internet users to link knowingly to infringing content.[36] Therefore, even under the fundamental rights regime, a person who knowingly links to infringing content is unlikely to benefit from a policy-based implied bare licence to link. In the absence of an implied licence, the exercise of the right amounts to infringement.

[34] In this connection, the presumption of knowledge held to be necessary in all cases of commercial use, putting the onus on the user to rebut it, does not appear to be necessary. It is the copyright owner who must establish infringement and must bear the onus of proving that the user ought reasonably to have known that the content was infringing.

[35] Drawing analogy with the offline world, CDPA, s 23(d) only recognises distribution of infringing copies otherwise than in the course of business if it prejudicially affects the copyright owner.

[36] Connecting this argument with ch 10 above, a person who browses infringing content is able to access such content because someone communicated it to them, likely through linking and likely knowing of its infringing nature. Therefore, it makes sense to hold the person who communicates, including by linking, liable for infringement, rather than the person who browses it.

3. Conclusions and Connections

This chapter has dealt with hyperlinking and how implied licence can help better understand it both when the content was placed by or with the copyright owner's consent and without, and has put forward the appropriate bases for implying licences in different circumstances. It has pointed to the problems that exist with the kind of reasoning adopted by the CJEU in *Svensson* and *GS Media* and demonstrated that, under the implied licence approach, not only can the court's reasoning be more coherently explained, but it can also provide a more nuanced reasoning under this approach.

Hyperlinking is used as a content delivery mechanism in the business model of not only media monitoring services like Meltwater, but also by search engines. In relation to these operators, in addition to dealing with hyperlinking, the technology that gathers content and makes hyperlinking possible, namely indexing, should also be analysed for the exclusive rights that it engages and how implied licence plays a role in that regard. Courts do not always make a distinction between acts of linking and acts of indexing; nor do they attribute liability separately for these actions. To demonstrate the importance of drawing this distinction, this author deals with indexing separately in Chapter 12 below.

12
Indexing

The growth of the content on the internet has been exponential since its inception. This has been made possible by applications facilitating free and ready searches to access relevant information. Without such applications, the labyrinth of information on the internet could become inaccessible if the exact address of the page is unknown. The function of these applications is broadly termed in this chapter as 'indexing', but these applications have varied capabilities. Normally, they have the ability to crawl websites or scrape content. Crawling software or spiders (as they are commonly called) 'visit' or 'discover' the website and render a copy of it to understand what is on it.[1] Scraping is a process by which specific information accessible on a website is extracted.[2] The information extracted is analysed and categorised to prepare a searchable index of almost every bit of information that appears on the website—whether textual or non-textual content.[3] The technology also allows for making a cached copy, which the search provider can display if the main website is unavailable. Each of these functions creates copies of the copyright works on these webpages. While making of the cached copies may be exempt from liability for damages and criminal enforcement under regulation 18 of the Electronic Commerce (EC Directive) Regulations 2002, hosting services, i.e., storage of information, are exempt from liability under regulation 19 under certain conditions.[4] Despite these provisions, it has been argued that if the service provider actively provides indexing services which facilitate intuitive, efficient, and easy access to stored information, it communicates the underlying works to the public. If the search provider must seek permission from the copyright owner each time it crawls, scrapes, and indexes a website or makes the results available, the efficacy of the internet will be dramatically reduced.

The results of a search are delivered as a list of hyperlinks to the specific webpages matching the search criteria. Hyperlinking, as discussed in the previous chapter, engages the communication right. However, if indexing as the first act can be halted by the copyright owner, a webpage will not be in the relevant search provider's index, and therefore, it will not be hyperlinked in the search results. To the extent

[1] https://moz.com/beginners-guide-to-seo/how-search-engines-operate accessed 21 July 2020.

[2] https://owasp.org/www-project-automated-threats-to-web-applications/assets/oats/EN/OAT-011_Scraping.ht ml accessed 17 July 2020.

[3] https://support.google.com/webmasters/answer/70897?hl=en accessed 17 July 2020.

[4] What amounts to hosting service is also hotly contested. See Lionel Bently and others, *Intellectual Property Law* (5th edn, OUP 2018) 1292.

Implied Licences in Copyright Law. Poorna Mysoor, Oxford University Press (2021). © Poorna Mysoor.
DOI: 10.1093/oso/9780198858195.003.0013

that hyperlinking as such infringes the copyright owner's rights, the discussion can be found in Chapter 11 above. This chapter only addresses the actions that are encompassed within indexing. It is hotly contested whether indexing by itself engages the right of communication to the public. Unlike hyperlinking, which can involve transmission as argued in Chapter 11, it is difficult to argue that creating an index and enabling an intuitive search in themselves involve transmission. However, as explained in the introduction to this monograph and in Chapter 11 above, implied licences trigger once the right is exercised. Since this monograph is about licences rather than exclusive rights, it does not undertake a detailed discussion of what amounts to the exercise of the right of communication to the public. Nevertheless, a brief summary of the arguments is given in Section 2 below, when discussing the content placed on the internet without the copyright owner's consent.

Based on the cases that have been litigated, the entities that carry out indexing can be broadly classified based on the searching capability they have and the rights they engage, although they may have overlapping features. One may consider first those that organise the information on the entire World Wide Web. These are search engines like Google, Yahoo!, Bing, and so on, who invest in their own crawling software that visits every page on the web and creates an index, posing a challenge to the right of reproduction. The indexing architecture is normally simple with features that are relatively less intuitive and, therefore, search engines may not engage the right of communication beyond linking. In this chapter, these are together referred to as search engines. Secondly, we consider those that are social media platforms, such as YouTube, Facebook, and Instagram, which have millions of users uploading their content on these platforms. These have software that crawl their own platforms and index the content to make it easily searchable, normally in addition to providing many other features for more incisive searches. These additional features in the indexing architecture may engage the right of communication to the public. In this chapter, these are together referred to as content sharing platforms. Thirdly, there are aggregators who scrape certain type of websites for certain type of content to provide services such as price comparison, weather reports, flight information, news summaries, and so on. While many aggregators only extract information not eligible for copyright protection, news aggregators are a significant example for scraping copyright content. This chapter therefore, makes a further distinction between news aggregators and other content aggregators. The indexing architecture of the news aggregators may not have features that engage the communication right, which other content aggregators might do. But the fact that they deliver relevant content through hyperlinks may still engage the communication right in both cases.

Courts in jurisdictions such as the United States and Germany have had an opportunity to address the liability of search engines like Google against a copyright owner. The Court of Justice of the European Union (CJEU) has had an opportunity to decide cases on content sharing platforms such as *Ziggo* and a few references are pending before the CJEU against YouTube and others. At the time of writing, the Advocate General's opinion had been given in relation to two of them. News aggregators have been sued before the UK courts (*Meltwater*) more prominently in relation to browsing, but licensing issues in relation to scraping of newspaper websites have been considered before the Copyright Tribunal. Other content aggregators have also been drawn into litigation in the UK (*see Warner Music UK Ltd v TuneIn Inc* below). This chapter explores the extent to which implied licences can assist in addressing infringement in relation to these types of search providers.

1. Content Placed on the Internet with the Copyright Owner's Consent

Continuing on from Chapter 9 above, to imply a consent-based licence enabling indexing, one must show that the actions involved in indexing are within the copyright owner's knowledge, to the extent that such processes engage exclusive rights. Going back to the example above of P's pamphlet of her art exhibition, the very reason for P to choose the public location is to enhance the visibility of her event. Additionally, if the venue where she leaves her pamphlets organises the shelving spaces in such a way that certain shelves are dedicated to art, the pamphlet on the shelves organised in alphabetical order of the exhibition venue or genre of art and so on, these factors only assist P in having her pamphlets attain the most relevant visibility and may well be the reason why she chose this venue for the display of her pamphlets in the first place. If the venue made further copies of the pamphlet in the process of organising it, then P's knowledge of it would be a question of fact. However, since her primary objective was to reach a relevant audience, it might be possible to argue that it is within her expectation that such copies will be made. Similarly, on the internet, search providers are driven by making the information on the internet reach the most relevant audience.

To have a more granular analysis of the knowledge, let us deal with each type of search provider identified above. Among the search providers, the content sharing platforms are easier to explain in relation to the content on their platform that has been uploaded by or with the consent of the copyright owner. Users must open an account with these platforms, which enables the platform to get the users to agree to their terms and conditions, which give the platforms a non-exclusive worldwide licence to reproduce and communicate such content.[5] Therefore, a user posting her content on such platforms cannot complain of copies of her work being made during crawling, scraping, and indexing by the respective online content sharing platform and of her works being communicated to the public (to the extent that this

[5] https://help.instagram.com/581066165581870 accessed 17 July 2020.

right is engaged). Users are taken to know that this helps achieve their objective of reaching the relevant audience to whom the platform is exposed. Content sharing platforms which also offer services of social networking permit users to control their own privacy settings,[6] which prevents information shared within their network from being indexed and made available in the search results outside such network. This could also prevent a general search engine from crawling and indexing such information. Owing to the existence of these express terms, implying a licence to enable indexing may not be required.

Let us now turn to search engines. These can potentially index most webpages that exist on the World Wide Web. Crawling, scraping, and indexing are all processes automated with the use of software. Given the impossibility of individually seeking consent from each website owner before engaging in these activities, there are widely recognised and well-publicised industry standards which allow website owners to let the crawling software know whether they consent for their webpages to be crawled. These take the form of meta-tags within the software code of the website, which the search applications are equipped to read and follow.[7] Alternatively, the insertion of a 'robots.txt' file on the website with an indication of 'allow' or 'disallow' can also instruct the crawling software whether the website can be crawled. A robots.txt file set to disallow means that such website or its cached copy should not be shown in the search results.[8] If the website is not displayed in the search results, then no question of the search engine communicating the work to the public arises, thereby addressing both the rights engaged. For simplicity, in this chapter, these technological measures are referred to as the 'code'. If the code is not used in designing a website at all, the crawling software still goes ahead to index the website.

Copyright owners must not only know the possibility of their websites being indexed, but also of their ability to put in place the codes to convey their indexing preferences. The conduct of the copyright owner in relation to the code settings can be regarded a continuation of the neutral act. Once the content is left on the website, the copyright owner can go on to set the code to send a signal to the crawling software whether it can crawl or not. Copyright owners have their websites built most likely with the intention that they can showcase their work to the millions of users on the World Wide Web. They are therefore likely to want search engines to display their websites in the search results, given the ubiquity of the use of search engines by internet users. This may be so even if they are unlikely to know the technological processes of crawling, scraping, and indexing. Most copyright owners will engage a person skilled in building websites who is likely to have the

[6] See eg https://www.facebook.com/about/basics/ accessed 17 July 2020.

[7] https://developers.google.com/webmasters/control-crawl-index/docs/robots_meta_tag accessed 17 July 2020; see also *Field v Google*, 412 F Supp 2d 1106, 1112–13.

[8] https://support.google.com/webmasters/answer/79812?hl=en accessed 17 July 2020; *Field v Google Inc* (n 7) 1113.

knowledge of incorporating the code while building the website. The website is likely to be built in discussion with the copyright owner, including as to the code settings. Therefore, copyright owners who have their websites built are more likely to be aware through their web designer of the use of the code. If they use the code in the design of their website, then this will most likely convey their knowledge of both the possibility of indexing taking place and of the code which enables them to signal to the crawling software. If they then set the code to allow indexing, they cannot then argue that they were unaware of the functionality of the code, to negate their consent.

It is sometimes possible that the copyright owner consents for her work to be used on someone else's website, in which case it is possible that the knowledge that can be gained vicariously through building one's website is not acquired. However, the copyright owner's awareness that the website on which her work appears will want to maximise its relevant audience and therefore will be shown in search results could be sufficient basis for her consent for her work being indexed. Drawing analogy from *Banks v CBS Songs Ltd*, Banks knowing that the lyrics of her song would be sung by Khan for UB40 was sufficient also conclude on that basis that she would have consented to the lyrics being adapted to make it suitable for the band.[9] Similarly, a copyright owner knowing that the visibility of her work will be maximised is sufficient basis to conclude that she would have consented to the work being indexed.

If a copyright owner's knowledge of the code is difficult to establish, one may explore if such knowledge can be imputed to the copyright owner. For this, one may explore if it is possible to establish a custom recognising the practice of the search engines taking the code used on the websites as an instruction for their crawling software. Applying the criteria discussed in Chapter 6 above, the practice is consistently followed (including the commands necessary to implement it for each major search engine), and therefore, 'certain'. Major search engines publicise detailed information on their websites on the meanings of different codes and how to use them.[10] These are also widely known to the web designers who are most likely to be employed when a copyright owner wishes to place her content on the internet. Therefore, notoriety is likely to be established. The practice is also 'reasonable' because it makes the automated process of scraping more responsive to the instructions of the copyright owner. It is not against the law, but indeed, its incorporation could help avert infringement. There may be an issue with recognising these as binding, because some commentators believe that these codes are followed only as a social norm, and not as a binding duty.[11] However, over the years,

[9] *Banks v CBS Songs Ltd* [1996] EMLR 440. See ch 4, section 1(c)(iii) above for discussion.

[10] See generally https://support.google.com/webmasters/answer/6062608?hl=en and https://support.google. com/webmasters/answer/79812?hl=en both accessed 21 July 2020.

[11] Monika Isia Jasiewicz, 'Copyright Protection in an Opt-out World: Implied License Doctrine and News Aggregators' (2012) 122 Yale LJ 837, 844, 848. Cf John Seiman, 'Using the Implied Licence to Inject Common Sense into Digital Copyright' (2007) 85 NCL Rev 885, 915–16.

in view of the increased importance of search engines, these may have moved towards becoming binding duties. If challenged before a court, given the difficulty in communicating the copyright owner's consent to a search engine in any other meaningful way, a court is more likely to regard the code settings as placing an obligation on the search engine to follow instructions. As regards the remaining criteria in Chapter 6, the practice of using the code is motivated by enhancing the technological efficacy of indexing, which is essential for organising and accessing the enormous content on the internet. The practice is not burdensome to copyright owners, and hence its impact is balanced. The internet community would be representative of the copyright owner since the copyright owner has authorised her website to be communicated on the internet. Thus, it may be possible to establish that the practice of copyright owners placing these codes on their website to communicate with the search engines and the search engines in turn recognising the codes has become a custom. It will then be possible to imply a licence in favour of the search engines based on such custom to permit indexing of these websites.

A good example of a court taking note of the code settings is the US case of *Field v Google Inc*, although in this case only the caching function of search engines was at issue. Here, the claimant, Field, an author, had placed his poems on his personal website. Field claimed that the defendant, Google, was liable for copyright infringement for copying and distributing his work by making cached copy of Field's work and providing a link to the cached copy.[12] Google stated that, in view of the enormity of the content on the internet, Google uses an automated means called the Googlebot to crawl across the internet and index webpages. As part of this process, Google makes a copy of each web page and stores it temporarily as 'cache' for archival purposes, which a website owner can prevent by incorporating the relevant code. In the search results, Google provides a link to the cached copy, so that it may be accessed if the main website is inaccessible for some reason.[13] In his evidence, Field admitted that he knew about the use of codes relating to caching function and had set it to 'allow' search engines to cache his website. The court held that, since Field knew that Google would interpret Field's website code settings as a permission to cache his website, he had impliedly licensed Google to carry out these activities.[14]

Caching as such is unlikely to be raised as an issue in the UK in view of the Electronic Commerce Regulations 2002, as discussed above. In any event, it is noteworthy that in *Field*, conveniently, Field admitted to actual knowledge of the controlling function of the code and had indeed used it to allow caching. Therefore, it was possible for a consent-based bare licence to be implied. What if the copyright owner places no code on her website even for crawling? In the German case

[12] *Field v Google Inc* (n 7) 1110, 1114.
[13] ibid 1110–12.
[14] ibid 1113–14, 1116. The court also ruled on the basis of estoppel and fair use. See ibid 1116–17.

of Google Image Search (*Vorschaubilder I*),[15] an artist had maintained a website on which she had displayed images of her work. The artist had placed no codes in building her website. Google crawled her website and indexed these images as thumbnail images, and provided them as search results whenever anyone searched the claimant's name.[16] The German Federal Supreme Court held that the making available of these images without the code settings that indicate whether the contents of the website can be scraped, amounts to implied consent to crawl, scrape, and index the content. The Court went a step further to hold that, even if a copyright owner incorporated terms of use on its website (which it refers to as individual notification), if the codes have not been set to disallow crawling, it conveys an implied consent to scrape.[17] The Court also emphasised the organising function of search engines and that copyright owners ought to know the existence and the use of the codes.

The Court's decision did not consider whether the claimant had the knowledge of the existence of such codes in the first place, to instruct Google's crawling software, although it referred to an implied consent from the copyright owner. In the framework proposed by this author, consent must turn on the knowledge of the copyright owner, even if such knowledge is objectively assessed. If a website owner does not place any code in building their website, there may be some possibility that they were unaware of it. *Vorschaubilder I* was decided in 2010, but it may well be that the knowledge of these codes has increased since then to a point that it might not be incorrect for a court to conclude that a copyright owner ought reasonably to know that search engines index their websites according to the code. While this may still be the knowledge of the copyright owner objectively assessed, if the one wants to pursue an argument of presumed knowledge, one may regard this practice of search engines as a custom, as argued above. It is also open to a court to give effect to the policy behind the organising function of the search engines and make that a basis to permit search engines carry on their activities. However, within the frameworks discussed in this monograph this will not be called 'implied consent', but implied by policy. A note of caution here would be that if the code is set to disallow, then the policy of organising the web should not allow the search engines to ignore the code and still benefit from a policy-based implied licence. In the methodology used here, this will not pass the three-step test. Having invested in educating website builders to use the code, search engines should not be allowed to ignore it, giving their role of organising the web a disproportionately larger significance.

[15] Federal Supreme Court, 2010 GRUR 628, cited from Matthias Leistner, 'The German Federal Supreme Court's Judgment on Google's Image Search' (2011) 42 IIC 417, 423–30. See also Birgit Clark, 'Google Image Search Does not Infringe Copyright, says Bundesgerichtshof' (2010) 5 JIPLP 553.

[16] *Vorschaubilder I* Federal Supreme Court, 2010 GRUR 628 para 16.

[17] ibid paras 37–39.

In neither *Field* nor *Vorschaubilder I* had the copyright owner placed any terms of use on their websites. But if the terms of use are incorporated and generally exclude commercial use, is it possible to imply a consent-based licence into those terms to permit indexing? Search engines profit from the advertising revenue derived from driving user traffic to the relevant sites. Even if they do not directly profit from the copyright content on these websites, if there was no content on the internet, search engines would not exist. To this extent, they are dependent on content being placed on the internet. So, indexing websites may be regarded as commercial use prohibited by the terms of use. However, it may still be preferable to regard the conduct of the copyright owner in setting the code as the expression of consent for indexing, rather than through terms of use. The basis for this interpretation is the simplicity of the use of the code and its ability to effectively communicate with an automated process, without reducing the efficacy of this process by requiring it to read the terms of use and understand that no scraping is permitted.[18] Even if the terms of use specifically prohibit all crawling,[19] but the copyright owner sets the code to allow crawling or sets no code at all, crawling software will go ahead and index such websites. Therefore, using the code to allow crawling can be the basis for implying a consent-based, custom-based, or even policy-based licence as discussed above.

So, the onus will be on the copyright owner who wishes to stop search engines from indexing also to place the appropriate code in its website, regardless of what the website says in the terms of use. By the same token, if the terms of use do not prohibit generally or specifically indexing by search engines, but the code is set to disallow indexing, then the search engine must be obliged to follow those instructions. As argued above, the policy of allowing search engines to organise the web should not permit them to ignore the code settings and still imply a policy-based licence, regardless of what the terms of use say.

Let us now discuss the news aggregators. Unlike search engines, news aggregators are less likely to invest in a crawling software that crawls all of the web, and more likely to use scraping software that extract data from defined websites, although search engines like Google may also engage in news aggregation offering Google News. Generally, news aggregators' business model is such that they focus on a particular set of websites, rather than the whole web. News aggregators derive profit from the content they scrape, whereas search engines derive a significant part of their profit from advertising revenue associated with driving traffic to relevant websites. Although news aggregators also implement an automated process, the scale of their processing ability is nearly not as voluminous as a search

[18] Although it may be possible in future to make search engines invest in artificial intelligence (AI) driven crawlers which are also capable of comprehending and responding to terms of use.

[19] See eg *Telegraph* terms of use cl 6(6) http://www.telegraph.co.uk/topics/about-us/3692012/Terms-and-Conditions.html accessed 19 July 2020.

engine's. The scraping software that the news aggregators deploy are unlikely to respond to the codes that communicate with crawling software. Experts speak of certain other technological measures that can be put in place to prevent websites being scraped.[20] The question is what is the role of these technological measures in indicating consent?

Let us begin with a scenario where a copyright owner has not placed any technological measures on their website against scraping, nor have they placed any terms of use. Unlike search engines where absence of code can still form the basis for implying a licence for search engines to crawl, the absence of technological measures against scraping does not form the basis for implying a licence in favour of news aggregators. This is because the enormity of data handled by search engines is not shared by news aggregators. News aggregators do not promote the use of technological measures in the same way that search engines promote the use of the code. These measures are not universally known, nor are they deployed as extensively as the code. As argued in Chapters 9, 10, and 11 above, copyright owners placing their content on internet without access restrictions does not mean that they consent to their works being exploited for commercial purposes, even if they do not incorporate terms of use on their websites. Therefore, news aggregators will not be able to benefit from an implied licence and will be liable for copyright infringement even in the absence of terms of use and absence of technological measures on the websites they scrape.

What if copyright owners insert terms of use prohibiting commercial use generally or scraping of their content specifically, but do not incorporate the technological measures? If it had been a search engine, the enormity of the process involved would have enabled them to escape having to read and honour the terms of use and take the absence of code as consent to crawl. However, news aggregators cannot escape from reading and respecting the terms of use, nor can they interpret the absence of technological measures as implying consent to scrape. Since news aggregators have control over the list of websites they scrape, it is reasonable to expect them to go through the terms of use of each website they scrape.

It has become common for newspaper websites to incorporate terms of use that specifically prohibit scraping. A perusal of the Newspaper Licensing Agency Ltd's website on standard web database licence terms indicates that scraping of newspaper websites is only allowed in accordance with the licence.[21] There is a push towards making news aggregators honour the terms of use, rather than take comfort in the code settings. However, some commentators believe that placing the terms of use alone may still not be sufficient. Although copyright owners may be able to vindicate their rights, it may be only after protracted litigation, as vividly

[20] See eg Shaumik Daityari, 'Protect Your Site Against Web Scraping' *Jscrambler* (21 March 2017) https://blog.jscrambler.com/protect-your-site-against-web-scraping/ accessed 19 July 2020.

[21] https://www.nlamediaaccess.com/web-database-licence/ accessed 19 July 2020.

demonstrated by the *Meltwater* saga. Therefore, they recommend that copyright owners implement technological measures in addition to the terms of use, to prevent news aggregators from scraping.[22] Depending on the technological measure applied, it either makes it technologically cumbersome or expensive (if not impossible) for news aggregators to scrape websites.

The discussion above drives home the point that news aggregators must be regarded differently from search engines.[23] Although their activities can be broadly classified together as indexing, market, and policy considerations are distinct. While code alone can be an effective response in relation to search engines, technological measures do not play a similar role in relation to news aggregators. Even from a practical perspective, it may be preferable to discriminate between search engines and news aggregators through the respective technological response to communicate with each of them in accordance with the copyright owner's preferences. Thus, copyright owners may let search engines crawl their content and disallow all scraping software. This was seen in *Meltwater*, where the newspaper websites were available for search engines to crawl and index,[24] but some newspaper publishers only objected to the news aggregators scraping their websites, as indicated by the terms of use of some of their websites.

The dispute with news aggregators has become so acrimonious generally within Europe that under Article 15 of the new Directive on Copyright in the Digital Single Market (2019/790) (the DSM directive) a new right has been recognised, granting publishers of press publications the right to reproduce and communicate their works to the public for a period of two years. It appears to be an effort to enable press publishers to take on news aggregators directly to negotiate terms for scraping. However, the empirical basis for its effectiveness is questionable.[25] In any event, the UK has confirmed that it will not implement this Directive into its domestic law, as the deadline for doing so is beyond the Exit Day.[26]

This leads us to the other content aggregators. *Warner Music UK Ltd v TuneIn Inc* is a good illustration, although it must be noted at the outset that the internet radio stations whose streams TuneIn indexed were not the defendants in the proceedings,

[22] Neil Hawley, 'Can the Small Print help? Can Terms and Conditions be Used to Prevent Scrapers?' (February 2011) https://www.taylorwessing.com/download/article_smallprint.html accessed 19 July 2020.

[23] The proceedings between the Newspaper Licensing Agency Ltd and Meltwater before the Copyright Tribunal (CT114/09) proceeded on the basis that Meltwater needed a licence from the Newspaper Licensing Agency Ltd to conduct its activities and focused only on the reasonableness of the terms of the licence.

[24] The High Court noted in the decision in *Meltwater* that the newspaper publishers had 'arrangements or understandings' with certain 'free' news aggregating services such as Google News and Google Alerts, whereby those services were 'licensed or otherwise permitted'. See [2010] EWHC 3099 [20] (Ch).

[25] https://www.create.ac.uk/policy-responses/eu-copyright-reform/article-11-research/ accessed 21 July 2020.

[26] https://www.parliament.uk/business/publications/written-questions-answers-statements/written-question/Commons/2020-01-16/4371 accessed 19 July 2020.

unlike the newspapers which were indexed by Meltwater. The claimant was the copyright owner of a significant number of the sound recordings in these streams who complained that TuneIn's services infringed its right of communication to the public. Birss J stated that TuneIn's services are more like search engines and not like conventional linking as in *Svensson* and *GS Media*.[27] However, he went on to apply the case law that applies to conventional linking, namely *Svensson* and *GS Media*, to decide the liability. And then he took pains to explain how TuneIn's aggregation and indexing set it apart also from conventional linking, but he did not apply any principles of communication to the public that apply to aggregation and indexing as separate actions from hyperlinking. He nevertheless held TuneIn liable for infringing the communication right. Birss J perhaps wished to treat TuneIn the same way as a news aggregator, but significant differences exist.

At the outset, it may be noted that TuneIn's features do not appear to engage the reproduction right. This is because, TuneIn scrapes only the metadata of the music streams of the internet radio stations, such as artist, track, and album names, and uses it to create its own index. It does not scrape the music itself, nor does it store it on its servers.[28] Since TuneIn does not scrape, store, or otherwise make copies of any copyright works, but only metadata which are unprotected, no liability can arise from scraping, as it does in the case of Meltwater, for example. One must, therefore, focus on indexing features to ascertain whether these amount to communication.

Although the purpose of this monograph is not to examine what amounts to the exercise of the communication right, let us briefly examine whether the features of TuneIn could have amounted to an act of communication to the public. TuneIn operates a search engine that gives users the ability to search the streams based on different categories or search terms, such as station names and artists. With the latter, the search will produce a collection of stations which are playing music from that artist at the time and Birss J believed that this feature is not present in conventional search engines. On the one hand, this can be argued as simply a result of the metadata of the streams that TuneIn scrapes and indexes, rather than URLs that search engines index. But, on the other hand, it may be argued that TuneIn's indexing has made the streams accessible which would otherwise not have been, unless one visited the relevant internet radio station's website. TuneIn's provision of recommendations of streams based on user listening history and of specific internet radio stations curated by it are but illustrations of search optimisation. Birss J noted that, unlike a search engine which aggregates all kinds of information, TuneIn only aggregates hyperlinks to music streams, frames the hyperlink when the stream is

27 *Warner Music UK Ltd v TuneIn Inc* [2019] EWHC 2923 (Ch) [124], [130]. See also Case C-466/12 *Svensson v Retriever Sverige AB* ECLI:EU:C:2014:76 and Case C-160/15 *GS Media BV v Sanoma Media Netherlands BV* ECLI:EU:C:2016:644.

28 See *Warner Music UK Ltd v TuneIn Inc* (n 27) [7].

playing, such that the user interfaces with TuneIn's site and sees TuneIn's visual advertisements.[29] Although nothing much turns on framing as far as the indexing function goes, the fact that it enables searches of a particular kind of content and not all types of content, might point to the fact that the extent of TuneIn's aggregation is not as enormous as a search engine's.

Given the focus of this monograph, assuming that TuneIn's indexing architecture engages the right of communication to the public, the question is whether such exercise can still be held to be impliedly licensed. As noted in Chapter 11 above, in relation to internet radio stations in category (iii) which had a licence from the relevant collecting society to operate in a country other than the UK, such licence, being one granted to operate radio services on the internet specifically, should be taken to have permitted the internet radio station to communicate to the listeners on the internet from all over the world, and not simply the listeners in the locality, as found by Birss J. Since the indexing services only enable the licensed content to reach more listeners on the internet, these may be held to be impliedly licensed based on the express consent of the collecting society.

2. Content Placed on the Internet without the Copyright Owner's Consent

Indexing infringing content results in making copies of the infringing content through crawling and scraping. Some may argue that it also results in communicating to the public depending on the manner of indexing and the features supplied. This section deals with each type of indexing entity to ascertain the circumstances in which implied licence may be of assistance.

Let us first consider whether the right of communication to the public is engaged in relation to the content sharing platforms because users of these platforms uploading infringing content is a significant problem and the platforms themselves indexing such content amplifies the problem. On the one hand, the CJEU held in *Ziggo* that the Pirate Bay website—providing a searchable index and categorising the content, thus making it easily accessible—amounted to a communication to the public.[30] However, on the other hand, this decision has been distinguished in the Advocate General Saugmandsgaard Øe's recent opinion delivered on 16 July 2020 in *Frank Peterson v Google* and *Elsevier v Cyando*.[31] The Advocate General opined that the findings of *Ziggo* cannot be separated from its context that the Pirate Bay, a platform notorious for sharing infringing content, had created and manged the platform deliberately to make infringing content more accessible. The Advocate

[29] ibid [8]–[9], [128].
[30] Case C-610/15 *Stichting Brein v Ziggo BV and Another* ECLI:EU:C:2017:456 [36]–[38].
[31] Joined Cases C-682/18 and C-683/18 ECLI:EU:C:2020:586.

General believed that deriving a general statement from *Ziggo* that merely creating an index is communicating to the public would be incorrect. He went on to explain in his opinion that it is the users who place infringing content on the platform who communicate and not the platform concerned because the latter does not decide on its own initiative to transmit the content. Therefore it does not play an indispensable role in communicating, but only provides physical facilities to enable communication.[32] The fact that a content sharing platform has some degree of sophistication, whose purpose is to facilitate the use of that platform, is therefore unimportant, and in any event does not amount to active intervention in communicating it to the public. Even if platforms offer additional services such as recommended videos, these do not amount to communication to the public, despite their influences the content viewed by the users, because these are generated automatically based on the videos previously viewed by the user and they do not reflect the platform's decision to communicate a given work to a public.[33] On the contrary, the Advocate General opined that content sharing platforms would be eligible for immunity as a hosting service under Article 14 of the Ecommerce Directive.[34]

This author agrees with the Advocate General in that it is more appropriate to not regard indexing as giving rise to primary liability for communication to the public but consider indexing for liability for authorising infringement on a case by case basis. It is uncertain if the CJEU will follow the Advocate General's opinion and if the CJEU's decision will be delivered before the Exit Day. In any event, since the concern of this monograph is implied licence and not an analysis of the exercise of the right, one may explore what happens even if one assumes that the right of communication to the public is exercised. It is arguable that such exercise may still not amount to primary or secondary infringement because of a licence implied by policy. Further, this author also agrees with the Advocate General that, in principle, content sharing platforms must be eligible for immunity for hosting. However, the immunity is only against damages and criminal liability, and not against injunctions. It is technically possible in an appropriate case that a copyright owner can seek an injunction against a content sharing platform continuing to offer indexing, even if the service otherwise satisfies hosting requirements. The arguments below also address this situation.

Clearly, no question of consent arises since the positive act of placing the content on the internet is missing. We will have to consider one of the other two bases. If a copyright owner alleges that indexing is an act of communication to the public,

32 ibid [73]–[75], [80].

33 ibid [82]–[84]. The Advocate General goes on to hold that knowingly facilitating communication to the public, as in *GS Media*, *Wullems*, and *Ziggo*, amounts to secondary liability, according to the civil laws of EU Member States. See ibid [102]. See also Case C-160/15 *GS Media BV v Sanoma Media Netherlands BV* (n 27); Case C-527/15 *Stichting Brein v Wullems* ECLI:EU:C:2017:300; and Case C-610/15 *Stichting Brein v Ziggo BV and Another* (n 30).

34 *Frank Peterson v Google* and *Elsevier v Cyando* (n 31) [168].

then for a content sharing platform it may be a weak argument to ask the court to imply a custom-based licence based on the non-objection of the copyright owner to the platform's indexing infringing content. A custom of this kind may be of questionable consistency, notoriety and reasonableness. A better alternative is the public interest defence and, consequently, a licence implied based on policy considerations. It may be argued that the policy of permitting the content sharing platforms to continue indexing satisfies the three-step test. From an objective standpoint, platforms build their infrastructure for indexing to assist lawful content being indexed. The fact that it can also be used by users who upload infringing content should not take away from the positive outcome for a substantial number of legal users. This may be read into the understanding of normal exploitation as a standard that at a normative level should not affect lawful users from benefiting from sophisticated features of indexing. On balance, it can be argued that the prejudice caused to copyright owners is far outweighed by considerations of the lawful use of indexing services. In the alternative, the fundamental rights regime helps argue for the promotion of free speech of users through a robust indexing service for lawful users. A content sharing platform being geared up for lawful users to take advantage of it to further their right to information cannot be sidestepped by the copyright owners' Article 1 Protocol 1 (A1P1) rights. It would not be a fair balance to require the content sharing platforms to eliminate features that add value to lawful users only because it also helps infringers. It would achieve a fair balance to place the onus on the copyright owners to be more vigilant in bringing infringing content to the attention of the content sharing platform, rather than having the platforms take away valuable features of indexing.

Peterson only dealt with the law as it exists in the EU before the DSM directive is implemented by the Member States. Article 17(1) of the DSM directive, however, proceeds on the basis that content sharing platforms communicate to the public potentially by their mere operation, as the liability seems to arise by the platforms merely providing access to the protected works uploaded by their users. It goes on to require content sharing platforms to take blanket licences from copyright owners, failing which, to make best efforts to prevent infringement under Article 17(4). The UK government, as stated above, will not implement the DSM directive.[35] However, the efficacy of this provision to deal with infringing content being accessible on content sharing platforms is to be seen.

Turning to the aggregators, news aggregators are likely to have more control over the websites they index, as they target only the sites that are of interest to their clients, although it is still possible for their scraping software to scrape and index infringing content. For example, a news aggregator might scrape a newspaper article hosted on a newspaper website which has infringing photographs. Under these

[35] https://www.parliament.uk/business/publications/written-questions-answers-statements/written-question/Commons/2020-01-16/4371 accessed 22 July 2020.

circumstances, rules similar to linking could apply. If the news aggregator was unaware or could not reasonably ascertain the infringing nature of the content, even if it pursued a profit, indexing of such content may pass the three-step test. If the news aggregator was aware of the infringing nature of the content or targets websites for the infringing content, then no policy can assist on the basis of which to imply a licence.

Moving on to the other content aggregators, in *TuneIn*, the internet radio stations in category (ii) are of concern here—which are the stations which had not been licensed to operate an internet radio station anywhere in the world by a collecting society or other authorised persons. Many of the features of TuneIn described in Section 1 above are comparable to the features discussed by the Advocate General in relation to YouTube and may not amount to an act of communication to the public. However, unlike YouTube, TuneIn's users do not upload music on its website for it to claim that it indexes whatever is uploaded; like news aggregators, TuneIn has some control over the internet radio stations' streams it indexes. In any event, even if TuneIn's activity amounts to an act of communication to the public, we may still consider whether such exercise of the right does not amount to infringement because of a policy-based implied licence.

Applying the three-step test, TuneIn's streaming of unlicensed works will interfere with the normal exploitation. If TuneIn can show that its services are predominantly lawful and it has a robust system in place to minimise interference with the normal exploitation of copyright works, then it may be possible to argue that such interference is minimal. Birss J noted that the number of internet radio stations indexed was not so high (as that of a search engine) and, therefore, one can expect greater involvement by TuneIn in ensuring that its streams were licensed. TuneIn argued that the internet radio stations sign a warranty before their streams are indexed by TuneIn, confirming that their streams are licensed. Although Birss J had questioned its efficacy, one can see from the decision that, to the extent possible, TuneIn indexes only lawful streams. Elsewhere, Birss J noted it to be true that 'a large share of the internet radio stations provided by TuneIn do not involve infringement of the claimants' rights', but he still held this to be irrelevant.[36] If this is taken into account together with TuneIn's efforts of obtaining a warranty from the internet radio stations it indexes, then one may argue that TuneIn does not interfere with normal exploitation of the work. The third step of balancing interest of different stakeholders can also be argued to rest with the users given the value addition TuneIn brings to both radio stations and end users. Alternatively, it is arguable that internet radio stations themselves have an important role to play in promoting free speech under Article 10 of the ECHR and TuneIn assists in achieving this end by connecting users to the internet radio stations' streams. In balancing this right

[36] *Warner Music UK Ltd v TuneIn Inc* (n 27) [200(v)].

against the claimants' A1P1 rights, one may argue that a predominantly lawful service with an otherwise robust mechanism to exclude infringing content should not be constrained in its delivery of lawful speech. In any event, permission has been given to both parties to appeal the High Court decision. This author has been informed that TuneIn has filed an appeal.

Finally, we turn to search engines. Search engines provide an important service of bringing order to the vastness of content on the internet, and in making the content readily accessible. This has a bearing on the rights of free speech and right to information of internet users under Article 10 of the ECHR. Search engines aim to index all content on the internet, both lawful and infringing. Crawling software does not yet have the ability clearly and fully to discriminate between lawful and infringing content while crawling. Even if the features on the search engines engage the right of communication to the public, it must be possible to recognise public interest in search engines being able to index the internet freely.

Let us assess it against the three-step test. Indexing is a sufficiently special case. Since the search engines make access to infringing content easier, copyright owners may claim that this interferes with the normal exploitation of their work. However, the inevitability of the search engines having to index both lawful and infringing content can support an argument of normativity in the normal exploitation. It may also not prejudice the legitimate interests of the copyright owner, as the balance may tip in favour of allowing search engines, given their role in free speech and access to information. However, if a search engine is made aware of the infringing nature of certain content it has indexed, continued indexing can interfere with both the normal exploitation and the copyright owner's legitimate interests. If the search engine provides a mechanism for reporting, which some do,[37] and promptly takes down such content from its index, then it can continue to benefit from a policy based implied licence. Considering the fundamental rights regime in the alternative, in assessing the proportionality and a fair balance between free speech of the users and the A1P1 rights of the copyright owners, it is possible to argue that the efficacy of the search engines may be reduced if they are required constantly to watch what they crawl and investigate its legality. On the contrary, the copyright owner's A1P1 right will be served more effectively by pursuing the person who brought the infringing content to the internet in the first place.

Applying an implied licence argument as above means that it does not matter how the copyright content reaches the internet. It may have been freely available on one website, which is downloaded and reposted on another site without permission, as in *Vorschaubilder II*;[38] or it may have been placed behind a paywall by the

[37] https://support.google.com/legal/troubleshooter/1114905?hl=en accessed 21 July 2020.

[38] The German Federal Supreme Court's decision in I ZR 140/10 of 19 October 2011, cited from Birgit Clark, 'Google Image Search Still Does not Infringe Copyright, Reaffirms Bundesgerichtshof' (2012) 7 JIPLP 788.

copyright owner, which is downloaded and reposted without access restrictions and without permission, as in *Vorschaubilder III*.[39] Or, indeed, the work may never have been placed on the internet by the copyright owner at all. The policy-based arguments above do not turn on what the copyright owner did, but on an overriding policy reason why her copyright should not be enforced, which results in the search engine continuing to index the site.

While the Federal Supreme Court in *Vorschaubilder III* resolved the issue based on linking the principles of *GS Media*, as stated in Chapter 11 above, in *Vorschaubilder II*, the court reasoned based on implied consent. The copyright content in *Vorschaubilder II* was not expressly authorised to be exploited on the defendant's website but was otherwise available on other websites with the copyright owner's consent. Google indexing the content on the defendant's website and displaying it as thumbnail images was regarded not to be an infringement by the Federal Supreme Court of Germany, on the basis that the copyright owner had otherwise made his works available to the public on another website. The Court observed that the other websites had not implemented the code preventing Google from indexing it, which implied consent in favour of Google to index the images.[40] This appears to be a contrived understanding of consent viewed from the framework for consent adopted in this monograph, although German scholars point out that this is consistent with the German conception of implied consent.[41] The fact is that Google did not index the website where the images were lawfully uploaded. Even if that website did not prevent indexing, that action cannot be read as consent to index another website where the image may be found unlawfully. If the court was going to disregard consent, it would have made the court's reasoning more transparent if it attributed it to policy reasons. The role of a search engine in organising the content on the internet can be argued to be a sound policy based on which one may imply a licence in favour of search engines to index, as argued above.

In relation to a case where the copyright owner never uploaded her content on the internet, it appears that German courts may apply hosting immunity to search engines. In *Vorschaubilder I*, in the context of crawling lawful content, the Court had held obiter that search engines may be eligible for hosting immunity under the e-Commerce Directive and that their liability arises only if they have actual knowledge of the infringement.[42] Although commentators argue that the services provided by search engines cannot be strictly regarded as hosting services, and the services of search engines may not be sufficiently neutral,[43] the recent opinion of the Advocate General in *Peterson* discussed above notes in relation to content

[39] *Vorschaubilder III* (Case No I ZR 11/16).

[40] *Vorschaubilder II* I ZR 140/10 of 19 October 2011.

[41] S Karapapa, 'The Requirement for a "New Public" in EU Copyright Law' (2017) 42 European L Rev 63, 74–75.

[42] *Vorschaubilder I* (n 16) para 39.

[43] Leistner (n 15) 433–34.

sharing platforms that they are eligible for immunity as a hosting service. This opinion may equally apply to the search engines. As stated above, since it is uncertain if the CJEU will follow the Advocate General's opinion and decide this issue before the Exit Day, and since immunity does not extend to injunctions, it is worth considering this issue under a policy-based implication as discussed above.

3. Conclusions and Connections

This chapter has addressed the actions that may be covered by indexing as a process distinct from hyperlinking and the way it may infringe exclusive rights. It has addressed the specific cases of search engines, news aggregators, data aggregators, and content sharing platforms to show how different considerations inform implying licences both when the content is on the internet with the consent of the copyright owner and without. It has also showed how implied licence arguments can be made more nuanced by classifying the actors in the market based on their search capabilities.

The conclusions of this chapter enable search engines and certain online content sharing platforms to benefit from a policy-based implied bare licence, saving them from liability for indexing infringing content under certain circumstances. The sheer size of their operation, on the one hand, enables them to offer valuable services that have almost become 'a utility' in our daily lives, qualifying them for a different treatment under the law. But, on the other hand, these operators have over time grown to become monopolistic, posing risks of market distortion and high barriers for new entrants. The connection that one can make from this chapter is to competition law and the extent to which one can place one's faith in it to address macroeconomic issues that arise from the activities of these operators.

Final Remarks

It all begins with the definition of infringement—the doing of a restricted act without 'the licence of the owner of copyright'. This can be refined to define infringement as the doing of a restricted act without the express or implied licence of the copyright owner, as the idea of implication is no stranger to English private law. Implied licence 'of the owner of copyright' intuitively points to the copyright owner's consent as being the basis for implying such a licence. But 'licence' as such is a much broader concept in the law of property. Whenever a person is permitted to make limited use of another person's property, a licence arises. Copyright being personal property, if a person is permitted to make limited use of another person's copyright work, a licence arises in her favour. An analysis of copyright law reveals that such permission can arise not only because the copyright owner consents to the use of her work, but also if a custom permits the use of a work and if there are policy reasons why the use of the work should be permitted. Therefore, consent, custom, and policy can become the basis for implying a copyright licence. These bases are analogous to the bases for implying a term into a contract, thereby reconfirming their legitimacy. These, in a nutshell, are the reasons why this monograph takes a justifiably broad view of implied licences in copyright law.

Some may believe that the concept of licence adopted by this monograph is too broad and artificial. This author, however, believes that there is jurisprudential basis for the conceptualisation of licence adopted here. Aside from the justification in analytical jurisprudence, land law has always maintained a residuary view of licences in defining them as what remains after all other estates and interests have been defined. Since in copyright law, arguably estates and interests have not been recognised, in every situation where a non-owner of a copyright work has permission to use a work, a licence arises. This means that statutory limitations or exceptions are also fundamentally licences, but because of the reasons explained in Chapter 2, Section 1(c), they are treated differently in this monograph. In this sense, licences in relation to any property including copyright arise much more frequently and are much more ubiquitous than one may imagine. This monograph brings these permissions within the parlance of copyright law so that they benefit from a systematic study. Most notable illustrations of this are policy-based implied bare licences, which are not acknowledged by courts or commentators as licences at all. But this author views them as licences because when a court restricts or prevents enforcement of copyright in the public interest against a person engaging in a restricted act, it effectively allows the person to continue to engage in that

Implied Licences in Copyright Law. Poorna Mysoor, Oxford University Press (2021). © Poorna Mysoor.
DOI: 10.1093/oso/9780198858195.003.0014

restricted act. Since such continued use is justified by public interest, this author regards them as policy-based implied bare licences. If not for the language of licence, this would otherwise remain unexplained, unfamiliar, and unexplored by judicial reasoning. If the language of licence can bring transparency to the underlying concepts and make them familiar, then that supplies a valid reason why this should be brought within the study of licences.

Some may also regard the idea of 'implied' licences adopted in this book too broad—becoming 'imputed' in case of custom-based and 'imposed' in case of policy-based licences. Even if the ordinary meaning of 'implied' may extend only to those that are 'inferred', either from conduct or circumstances, the legal meaning of implied is broader. The principles of implying a term in a contract are a good example to show how even when a custom or a policy is relied on as the basis, the process is still called 'implying'. Even if one argues that inroads into freedom of contract are more readily justifiable than inroads into a property right such as copyright, the copyright statute itself recognises the authority of the state to interfere with copyright to achieve policy objectives in the form of compulsory and statutory licences. One cannot ignore or stop the practices in various copyright industries going on to become customs. A good way to legitimise them is to provide objective standards for their recognition, always with an eye towards reasonableness. All these arguments drive home the point that copyright licences may be implied on bases other than consent, such as custom and policy, and this process can still be justifiably called 'implying' a licence.

Having thus justified its approach to 'licences' and 'implying', the next challenge this book has addressed is the absence of principles guiding the implication of copyright licences. While the principles of implying a term into a contract and those of implying easements have provided an inspiration, licences do not always exist within a contract, nor are licences the same as easements. The effort in this book, therefore, has been to propose frameworks for implying copyright licences to make the process of implication methodical and transparent. These frameworks have been proposed more as guidelines rather than rigid rules depriving implied licences of their flexibility. The objective of making the process of implication methodical and transparent assists the users as much as the copyright owners in being able to put forward arguments that enable or resist implying copyright licences.

Bare licences are a powerful legal tool for granting permission. A bare licence can arise as much in favour of one person (Mr Khan) when the copyright owner (Ms Banks) hands her copyright work (lyrics of a song) to that person,[1] as in favour of the millions of internet users when a copyright owner places her work on the internet. The framework for consent-based implied bare licences discussed in Chapter 4 might appear intuitive, and therefore unnecessary or superfluous. But if

[1] *Banks v CBS Songs Ltd* [1996] EMLR 440, 448.

what it takes to imply a consent-based bare licence was so intuitive, then it should have been equally intuitive what happens when a copyright owner places her work on the internet. It should have been especially convenient to explain hyperlinking if the consent-based bare licence approach had been used, as explained in Chapter 11. Instead, this topic has given rise to a complex and, often, barely intelligible case law.

One may have expected this author to have simply applied the contractual principles of implying a term in fact in Chapter 5 and a term by law in Chapter 7. There are several reasons for not adopting these principle in their entirety. The idea of necessity dominates the contract principles of implication. But, on the face of it, the need for necessity appears tautologous. If one asks when a term is necessary to be implied, the answer is simply when it is necessary to be implied! In case of implied in fact, one might break the tautology by answering when it is necessary to achieve business efficacy. However, as demonstrated in Chapter 5, business efficacy is a nebulous concept, the application of which throws little light on how a court comes to a particular conclusion. Instead, the framework proposed here helps marshal the facts and circumstances of the case, revealing the factors responsible for the court's conclusions. Business efficacy is such a broad concept that even decisions that are otherwise more appropriately classified as implied by law are justified based on business efficacy (as discussed in Chapter 7, Section 1). The idea of necessity has no such foothold for implied by law cases, and the tautology is starker. This author argues that the foothold must be the policy that underlies the implication, so that one can break the circularity and make some progress towards understanding why and how licences are implied. Accordingly, the framework discussed in Chapter 7 adds the essential element of identifying the underlying policy, although it draws other elements from the existing methodology in contract law for implying a term by law. This also helps to demarcate the distinction between consent-based and policy-based implications.

The custom-based implied licences discussed in Chapter 6 open up the basis for implication for community participation, beyond the individual conduct of the copyright owner and without the need for the sanction of a court or a statute. Including this basis for implying copyright licences can provide a more participative and inclusive response to copyright infringement. Internet customs have a significant potential for inclusiveness. Further, by demonstrating that in appropriate cases a continued non-objection by the copyright owner can equally give rise to a custom based on which a licence may be implied, Chapter 6 recognises the potential that customs have in creating an efficient ordering within the respective communities. For customs of this kind, the caveat of reasonableness and that a custom cannot go against the law can bring in policy considerations, thereby not making these customs too onerous for nor too favourable to one party.

Perhaps the most controversial are policy-based implied bare licences. These take advantage of both the power of bare licences in permitting the use of copyright works without the need for a contract, and the power of policy which can operate regardless of the consent of the copyright owner. Consequently, this becomes potentially quite a powerful way of implying copyright licences. Therefore, the framework proposed incorporates the three-step test, which is the same test that all statutory limitations and exceptions must pass before they find a place in the statute; and the fundamental rights regime which lays down a high threshold to be crossed because of the copyright owners' Article 1, Protocol 1 rights, before a licence can be successfully implied.

Implied licences rely on the simple truth that, for copyright infringement to take place, two ingredients need to be satisfied: an exclusive right must have been exercised; and such exercise of the right must have been without a licence, express or implied. Nowhere is this formulation of copyright infringement more useful than on the internet, particularly in relation to hyperlinking (Chapter 11) and indexing (Chapter 12) as they relate to the right of communication to the public. Being able to deny that the right was exercised is certainly a powerful response to infringement. However, for exclusive rights like the right of communication to the public which have disputed boundaries, this approach could make the interpretation unpredictable. The approach of the courts in this regard is to hold that the exclusive right is or is not exercised, depending on the desired outcome. The problem with this approach is that, in its eagerness to reach a particular conclusion, the court often ignores how the exclusive right is defined. Since it is still a work in progress to determine what does and does not amount to an act of communication to the public, courts have been trying to find reasons to incorporate requirements that are not borne out in the language of the exclusive right, to reach the desired ends. A continued reliance on this technique erodes the law of certainty and coherence.

Instead, implied licence arguments enable a consistent interpretation of the exclusive right to be maintained. Admitting to the exercise of a right is not tantamount to an admission of infringement; rather, it is the exercise of the right without a licence which is infringement. As such, a court will not be forced to change the criteria necessary for the exercise of the right to meet the desired outcome. A court can follow a consistent and coherent interpretation of the exclusive right and can then rest assured that if the court still believes that there are considerations that point to liability for infringement not being attached, then it can take up these considerations under implied licences. In other words, the considerations not directly addressed by the exercise of the exclusive right which otherwise have a bearing on the infringement can all be considered in deciding whether a licence should be implied to defeat a claim of infringement. Given the breadth of considerations that can go into implying copyright licences as demonstrated in this monograph, it should be possible to slot these considerations within the relevant bases and meaningful criteraia laid out by the proposed frameworks. This can bring clarity to the interpretation of the exclusive right and will also make transparent the rationale for the line of reasoning adopted by the court.

This brings us to a practical issue—when faced with a case of infringement, while assessing the facts and circumstances, how is one to know which framework must apply to a new case? Just as the frameworks are not proposed as rigid rules for the courts to apply, they are also not proposed as independent and unconnected sets of criteria. The way in which the facts and circumstances of the case may flow through the frameworks is represented with a basic flow chart provided in Figure 3 at the end of this chapter. It can be elaborated as follows.

The assessment of the facts and circumstances to ascertain whether the copyright owner has engaged in the positive act is a good starting point (Chapter 4, Section 1(a)). This is because if the copyright owner did not even engage with the copyright work so that it could be used by the defendant, the most important requirement of consent is absent. If no consent can be established, then the only possibility is to assess whether a custom or a policy-based bare licence may be implied. If, however, there is a positive act, then ascertaining at the outset whether it is absolute or conditional can give an initial clue as to whether the licence, if implied, will be contractual. Even if the positive act is not conditional, the neutral act being conditional could point to the licence being contractual. If there is a contract, it would help to ascertain the type of contract (Chapter 5, Sections 1, 2 and 3).

Once the conduct of the copyright owner is assessed, one can move on to the assessment of the knowledge of the copyright owner. The existence and the scope of the implied licence depends on the extent of the copyright owner's knowledge of the circumstances or her reasonable expectations, objectively assessed. Depending on whether there is mutuality to the undertakings, a consent-based bare or contractual licence may be implied. If the copyright owner claims not to know of the circumstances, and the positive and the neutral acts were performed in furtherance of a practice which can be established as a custom, then the knowledge of the custom may be imputed to the copyright owner. A custom-based licence can then be implied. If a contract with the copyright owner exists, but it is more apt to attribute the implication to achieving a public policy goal, then a policy-based contractual licence may be implied.

If there is no positive act, no other aspect of consent-based implied licence needs to be assessed. It may be worth ascertaining whether a custom exists based on the non-objection of the copyright owner to the act complained of. If the criteria for establishing a custom are all satisfied, including the requirement of reasonableness and not being contrary to law, then a custom-based licence may be implied. If no such custom can be established, the assessment will then be whether there is a public policy worth enforcing under the public interest defence to restrict copyright enforcement. If yes, then it must be assessed whether doing so will be in compliance with the three-step test or, in the alternative, the fundamental rights regime. If yes, then a policy-based bare licence may be implied. If no, then no copyright licence may be implied under the circumstances.

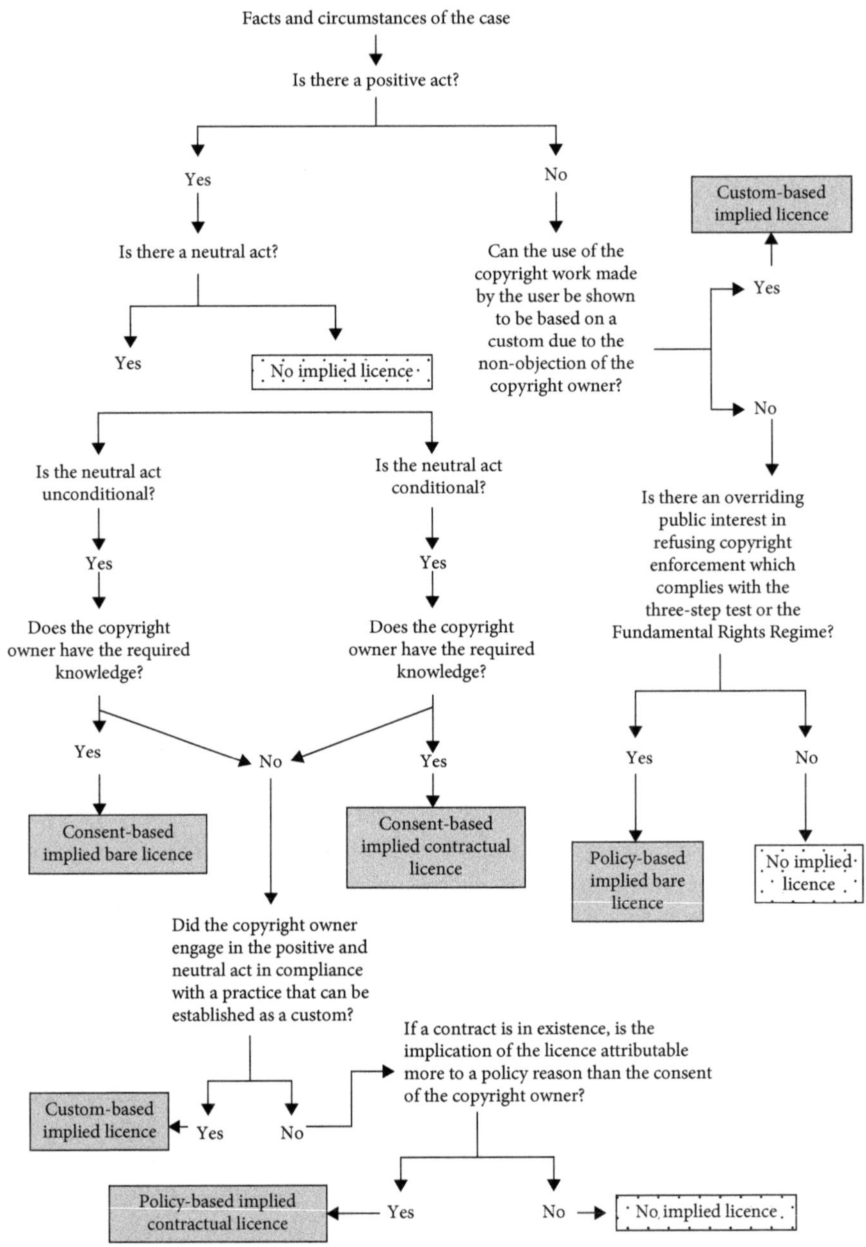

Figure 3 Flow chart on implied licences

The consent of the copyright owner reduces in significance as we move from Chapter 4 to the next chapters. While consent forms the basis of implication in Chapters 4 and 5, its relevance in custom-based implied licences in Chapter 6 is only to the extent that the underlying practice is consent-based. For customs that have a non-consensual origin, based only in non-objection to a practice engaging a copyright work, consent will be absent. But such custom will struggle to exist without some policy element, bringing reasonableness into it and making it not contrary to law. In policy-based contractual licences discussed in Chapter 7, consent is not taken into account. However, to the extent that the copyright owner has entered into a contract in relation to the copyright work, some voluntariness on her part still exists. In Chapter 8, the consent of the copyright owner is immaterial, because a court decides in the public interest whether to enforce a person's copyright. Thus, as we move from Chapter 4 towards Chapter 8, considerations beyond the copyright owner's conduct and the circumstances relating to the community and welfare become more relevant.

This is bound to have an impact on the burden of proof. As stated in the introduction to this monograph, a licence is not regarded as a defence, but as an ingredient of the tort of infringement, based on an analogy with the tort of trespass. But as the basis of the licence moves further away from consent, it begins to acquire the nature more of a defence. This means that the more the user depends on considerations outside the copyright owner's conduct and the circumstances surrounding the copyright owner, the more likely it is that the evidential burden of proving those circumstances will have to be discharged by the user.[2] Therefore, if a user wants to assert a custom-based or a policy-based implied licence, the evidential burden of doing so rests on him, although the copyright owner bears the overall burden of proving the case of infringement on the balance of probabilities. It is perhaps not a coincidence that the policy-based implied bare licence, which is at the end of the spectrum of implied licences abutting the statutory limitations or exceptions, flows from the public interest defence.

Scholars point out that the most significant weakness of implied licences is that express words override those that one may seek to imply. For express words to override, they need to be in existence before the situation necessitating implying a licence arises (ex ante) and be expressed in some writing. Therefore, this criticism applies more readily to contractual licences. These normally take the form of 'entire agreement clauses', which in effect state that what is stated in the contract represents the whole of the understanding between the parties, and no considerations external to the agreement may be considered. Since consent-based implied licences are borne out by the words used in the contract and the surrounding circumstances, these cannot normally be excluded by entire agreement clauses. In any event, since consent-based implications, be it of a licence or any other term in the contract, address unforeseen circumstances, it would be in the interest of neither party to exclude this kind of implication by confining their relationship rigidly to the words used in the contract.

[2] See *Acohs Pty Ltd v Ucorp Pty Ltd* (2012) 287 ALR 403 [170]–[175] for a good discussion on this aspect.

Entire agreement clauses can be effective to override an implication based on custom or policy into the contract. In relation to the instances of policy-based licences discussed in Chapter 7, such as exhaustion, it is difficult to envisage a term in a contract that tries to override it, since exhaustion is built into the exclusive right of distribution itself and the copyright owner is not granted an exclusive right to distribute beyond the first sale. As for the right to repair, in *Solar Thomson Engineering Co Ltd v Barton*, Buckley LJ held that, although there was an express reservation of copyright, it was not inconsistent with the existence of an implied licence to reproduce the work for the purposes of repairing the article embodying the work.[3] In *Acohs Pty Ltd v RA Bashford Consulting Pty Ltd*, although there was a copyright note that required the written permission of the copyright owner before reproducing the material safety data sheets, the court still went on to imply a licence to copy the sheets without such written permission in view of the underlying policy of health and safety.[4] Although a clear decision has not yet been given, these decisions indicate that broad assertions of copyright are not sufficient to exclude the possibility of implying licences. Clearer and more precisely drafted terms are necessary to be able to override the possibility of implying policy-based contractual licences.

Entire agreement clauses may exist in a consent-based express bare licence. This assumes that the copyright owner knows to whom she may grant a bare licence. It may be possible in the internet context with the terms of use behaving similarly to browse-wrap agreements. However, Chapters 10, 11, and 12 demonstrate how implying a licence is still possible if there are terms of use of a particular kind (commercial use clauses). Further, as we saw in Chapter 4, bare licences that arise in informal settings are often not in express terms. Thus, in the absence of any express terms, if a consent-based bare licence can be implied based on the copyright owner's conduct and the surrounding circumstances, it can hardly be said that such implied licences can be overridden by express words. It is also difficult to argue that express words may override a policy-based implied bare licence. To begin with, the parties who are in dispute in which a policy-based bare licence may be considered, are not in contractual relationship. Indeed, the copyright owner might not know in whose favour a court might imply a policy-based implied bare licence, for the copyright owner to plan ex ante to override a possible implied licence with express terms. Indeed, there is no relationship into which a term may be inserted to override the possibility of an implied licence. Moreover, if the policy that forms the basis of implication is driven by the fundamental rights regime in that not implying the licence will violate a person's fundamental rights, again it can hardly be said that it is possible to override such an implied licence.

3 [1977] RPC 537, 560.
4 (1997) 144 ALR 528, 551–52.

The need for implying copyright licences will not disappear. The growing body of case law on implying a term into a contract is a testament to the fact that there are never going to be complete or comprehensive contracts. There will always be the need to fill in gaps, by way of implying licences based on the conduct of the copyright owner, or to give effect to a custom or a policy. Bare licence contexts are always possible, regardless of how carefully a copyright owner conducts herself in relation to her work. Despite the codification of licences that could otherwise have been implied by policy (such as those in the right to repair context), there will still be circumstances where courts are called upon to imply a copyright licence.

A final point—the UK has left the EU and it is unlikely that the implementation period will be extended. After the Exit Day it would be possible for the UK Supreme Court (and any court designated by a minister of the crown)[5] to depart from the decisions of the Court of Justice of the European Union (CJEU) delivered before the Exit Day. Despite the protracted negotiations and delays due to the pandemic, the Trade and Cooperation Agreement was concluded between the UK and the EU days before the Exit Day. And under the Agreement, there is no ongoing jurisdiction of the CJEU to ensure compliance of the UK domestic law with EU law. What this means to the UK is that the constraints that limit the reasoning of the CJEU, such as the exhaustive list of statutory limitations and exceptions, no longer limit the UK Supreme Court, to the extent that this is borne out by the CJEU's case law. UK courts in general could also become freer to choose approaches derived entirely from common law, without the risk of being inconsistent with EU law that has not been retained under the European Union (Withdrawal) Act 2018. In this regard, implied copyright licences, being a distinctly common law response, armed with a transparent methodology for implying copyright licences proposed in this book, can render apt and timely assistance.

[5] European Union (Withdrawal) Act 2018, s 6(5A).

Bibliography

— — https://www.create.ac.uk/policy-responses/eu-copyright-reform/article-11-research/
— — https://creativecommons.org/licenses/
— — https://developers.google.com/webmasters/control-crawl-index/docs/robots_meta_tag
— — https://www.facebook.com/about/basics/
— — https://www.facebook.com/legal/terms
— — https://www.gov.uk/guidance/exhaustion-of-ip-rights-and-parallel-trade-after-the-transition-period
— — https://help.instagram.com/581066165581870
— — https://www.lexico.com/definition/licence
— — https://www.londonstockexchange.com/disclaimer
— — https://www.nlamediaaccess.com/web-database-licence/
— —https://www.parliament.uk/business/publications/written-questions-answers-statements/written-question/Commons/2020-01-16/4371
— — https://www.penguin.co.uk/company/work-with-us/authors.html
— — https://www.ryanair.com/en/terms-of-use/
— — https://support.google.com/legal/troubleshooter/1114905?hl=en
— — https://support.google.com/webmasters/answer/70897?hl=en
— — https://support.google. com/webmasters/answer/79812?hl=en
— — https://support.google.com/webmasters/answer/6062608?hl=en
— — https://support.google.com/websearch/answer/1687222?hl=en
— — https://www.theguardian.com/help/terms-of-service
— — http://www.telegraph.co.uk/topics/about-us/3692012/Terms-and-Conditions.html

Afori O, 'Implied Licence: An Emerging New Standard in Copyright Law' (2009) 25 Santa Clara Computer & High Tech LJ 275

Arnold R, 'Reflections on The Triumph of Music: Copyrights and Performers' Rights in Music' (2010) 2 IPQ 153

Association Litteraire et Artistique Internationale (ALAI) Report on the making available and communication to the public in the internet environment: focus on linking techniques on the internet (15 September 2013) http://www.alai.org/en/assets/files/resolutions/making-available-right-report-opinion.pdf

Atiyah P and Smith S, *Atiyah's Introduction to the Law of Contract* (6th edn, Clarendon Press 2005)

Aufderheide P and Jaszi P, *Reclaiming Fair Use: How to Put Balance Back in Copyright* (University of Chicago Press 2011)

Austen-Baker R, *Implied Terms in English Contract Law* (2nd edn, Edward Elgar Publishing 2017)

Baines R, 'Copyright in Commissioned Works: a Cause for Uncertainty' (2005) 27 EIPR 122

Beatson J, Burrows A, and Cartwright J, *Anson's Law of Contract* (30th edn, OUP 2016)

Bell J, 'Sources of Law' in Burrows A (ed), *English Private Law* (3rd edn, OUP 2013)

Bently L and others, *Intellectual Property Law* (5th edn, OUP 2018)

Birks P, 'Before We Begin: Five Keys to Land Law' in Bright S and Dewar J (eds), *Land Law Themes and Perspectives* (OUP 1998)
Black's Law Dictionary (11th edn, Thomson Reuters 2019)
Breaky H, 'Properties of Copyright' in Howe H and Griffiths J (eds), *Concepts of Property in Intellectual Property Law* (CUP 2013)
Bridge M, *Personal Property Law* (OUP 2015)
— — et al, *The Law of Personal Property* (2nd edn, Sweet & Maxwell 2018)
— — *The Sale of Goods* (4th edn, OUP 2019)
Bridge S, Cooke E, and Dixon M, *Megarry and Wade: The Law of Real Property* (9th edn, Sweet & Maxwell 2019)
Burrell R, 'Defending the Public Interest' (2000) 22 EIPR 394
Chapdelaine P, *Copyright User Rights* (OUP 2017)
Christoffersen J, 'Human Rights and Balancing: The Principle of Proportionality' in Geiger C (ed), *Research Handbook on Human Rights and Intellectual Property* (Edward Elgar Publishing 2015)
Clark B, 'Google Image Search Does not Infringe Copyright, says Bundesgerichtshof' (2010) 5 JIPLP 553
— — 'Google Image Search Still Does not Infringe Copyright, Reaffirms Bundesgerichtshof' (2012) 7 JIPLP 788
Clark C, 'Licences in Real Property Law' (1921) 21 Colum L Rev 757
Cohen F, 'Dialogue on Private Property' (1954) 9(2) Rutgers L Rev 357
Colby J, 'It's the End of the (Online) World as We Know It?' (2017) 28 Ent LR 161
Collins H, *The Law of Contract* (4th edn, LexisNexis 2003)
Cooke E, *The Modern Law of Estoppel* (OUP 2000)
Cornish W, Llewelyn D, and Aplin T, *Intellectual Property: Patents, Copyright, Trademarks and Allied Rights* (9th edn, Sweet & Maxwell 2019)
Craig P, *UK, EU and Global Administrative Law: Foundations and Challenges* (CUP 2015)
Daityari S, 'Protect Your Site Against Web Scraping' *Jscrambler* (21 March 2017) https://blog.jscrambler.com/protect-your-site-against-web-scraping/
Davison M, Monotti A L, and Wiseman L, *Australian Intellectual Property Law* (3rd edn, CUP 2016)
Davies G, Caddick N, and Harbottle G, *Copinger and Skone James on Copyright* (17th edn, Sweet & Maxwell 2016)
Dixon M, *Modern Land Law* (11th edn, Routledge 2018)
Douglas S, 'Kuwait Airways Corporation v Iraqi Airways Company' in Douglas S, Hickey R, and Waring E (eds), *Landmark Cases in Property Law* (Hart Publishing 2013)
— — and McFarlane B, 'Defining Property Rights' in Penner J and Smith H (eds), *Philosophical Foundations of Property Law* (OUP 2013)
Epstein R, 'International News Service v Associated Press: Custom and Law as Sources of Property Rights in News' (1992) 78 Va L Rev 85
— — 'Some Reflections on Custom in the IP Universe' (2007) 93 Va L Rev Brief 223
European Copyright Society, 'The Reference to the CJEU in Case C-466/12 *Svensson*' Paper No 6/2013 (February 2013) para 6 http://ssrn.com/abstract=2220326
Feltham P and others, *Spencer Bower: Reliance-Based Estoppel* (5th edn, Bloomsbury 2017)
Gardner S and McKenzie E, *An Introduction to Land Law* (4th edn, Hart Publishing 2015)
Geiger C, 'From Berne to National Law, via the Copyright Directive: the Dangerous Mutations of the Three-step Test' (2007) 29 EIPR 486
— — 'Intellectual Property Shall be Protected!? Article 17(2) of the Charter of Fundamental Rights of the European Union' (2009) 31 EIPR 113

— — Gervais D, and Senftleben M, 'The Three-step Test Revisited: How to Use the Test's Flexibility in National Copyright Law' (2013) PIJIP Research Paper no 2013-04
Goymour A, 'Property and Housing' in Hoffman D, *The Impact of the UK Human Rights Act on Private Law* (CUP 2013)
Gray K and Gray S, *Elements of Land Law* (5th edn, OUP 2009)
Griffiths J, 'The "Three-step Test" in European Copyright Law: Problems and Solutions' (2009) 4 IPQ 428, 429–30
Halsbury's Laws, vol 32 (5th edn, LexisNexis 2019) para 5
— — para 51
Harno A, 'The Revocability of Licences as Applied to Property in Land' (1919) 7 Ky LJ 1
Harris J W, *Property and Justice* (OUP 2002)
Hart M, 'The Legality of Internet Browsing in the Digital Age' (2014) 36 EIPR 630
Hawley N, 'Can the Small Print help? Can Terms and Conditions be Used to Prevent Scrapers?' (TaylorWessing February 2011) https://www.taylorwessing.com/download/article_smallprint.html
He H, 'Seeking a Balanced Interpretation of the Three-step Test' (2009) 40 IIC 274
Helfer L, 'How Intellectual Property and Human Rights Can Live Together' in Torremans P (ed), *Intellectual Property Law and Human Rights* (3rd edn, Wolters Kluwer 2015)
Herbert C, 'The Vexed Issue of Streaming, Sports and Set-top Boxes in New Zealand' (2019) 30(8) Ent LR 242
Hill J, 'Termination of Bare Licences' [2001] CLJ 89
Hilty R, ' "Exhaustion" in the Digital Age' in Calboli I and Lee E (eds), *Research Handbook on Intellectual Property Exhaustion and Parallel Imports* (Edward Elgar Publishing 2016)
HL Deb 8 December 1987 vol 491, col 76
Hohfeld W, 'Some Fundamental Legal Conceptions as Applied in Judicial Reasoning' (1913–14) 23 Yale LJ 16
— — 'Fundamental Legal Conceptions as Applied in Judicial Reasoning' (1916–17) 26 Yale LJ 710
— — 'Faulty Analysis in Easement and Licence Cases' (1917) 27 Yale LJ 66
Honoré A M, 'Ownership' in Anthony Gordon Guest (ed), *Oxford Essays in Jurisprudence* (Clarendon Press 1961)
Hudson E and Wragg P, 'Proposals for Copyright Law and Education During the Covid-19 Pandemic' https://ssrn.com/abstract=3617720
Jasiewicz M I, 'Copyright Protection in an Opt-out World: Implied License Doctrine and News Aggregators' (2012) 122 Yale LJ 837
Jones L A K, 'Is Viewing a Web Page Copyright Infringement?' (1998) 4 Appeal 60
Karapapa S, 'The Requirement for a "New Public" in EU Copyright Law' (2017) 42 European L Rev 63
Lee S, 'Towards a Jurisprudence of Consent' in Eekelaar J and Bell J (eds), *Oxford Essays in Jurisprudence* (3rd Series, Clarendon Press 1987)
Leistner M, 'The German Federal Supreme Court's Judgment on Google's Image Search' (2011) 42 IIC 417
Llewellyn G, 'Does Copyright Recognise a Right to Repair?' (1999) 21 EIPR 596
McFarlane B, *The Structure of Property Law* (Hart Publishing 2008)
— — *The Law of Proprietary Estoppel* (OUP 2014)
— — Hopkins N and Nield S, *Land Law Text, Cases and Materials* (3rd edn, OUP 2015)
McMeel G, *The Construction of Contracts: Interpretation, Implication, and Rectification* (3rd edn, OUP 2017)
Merrill T, 'Property and the Right to Exclude' (1998) 77 Neb L Rev 730

Mezei P, 'Enter the Matrix: the Effects of CJEU Case Law on Linking and Streaming Technologies' (2016) 11 JIPLP 778
Muller B, 'How Search Engines Work' (Moz Pro) https://moz.com/beginners-guide-to-seo/how-search-engines-operate
Mysoor P, 'Proprietary Estoppel and Copyright Law' (2018) 29 King's LJ 470
— — 'Exhaustion, Non-exhaustion and Implied Licence' (2018) 49 IIC 656
— — 'Capturing the Dynamism of Fairness: a Common Law Perspective' in Gervais D (ed), *Fairness, Morality and Ordre Public in Intellectual Property* (Edward Elgar Publishing 2020)
Newman C, 'A License Is not a "Contract not to Sue": Disentangling Property and Contract in the Law of Copyright Licenses' (2013) 98 Iowa L Rev 1101
— — '"What Exactly are you Implying?": the Elusive Nature of the Implied Copyright Licence' (2013-14) 32 Cardozo Arts & Ent LJ 501
Peden E, 'Policy Concerns Behind Implication of Terms in Law' (2000) 117 LQR 459
Goudkamp J and Nolan D, *Winfield and Jolowicz on Tort* (20th edn, Sweet & Maxwell 2020)
Phang A, 'Implied Terms Revisited' [1990] JBL 394
— — 'Implied Terms in English Law: Some Recent Developments' [1993] JBL 242
Phillips J and Bently L, 'Copyright Issues: the Mysteries of section 18' (1999) 21 EIPR 133
Pihlajarinne T, 'Setting the Limits for the Implied License in Copyright and Linking Discourse: the European Perspective' (2012) 43(6) IIC 700
Pila J, *The Subject Matter of Intellectual Property* (OUP 2017)
Polański P, *Customary Law of the Internet: in the Search for a Supranational Cyberspace Law* (University of Melbourne 2007)
Rahmatian A, *Copyright and Creativity* (Edward Elgar Publishing 2011)
Reichman J, Dinwoodie G and Samuelson P, 'A Reverse Notice and Takedown Regime to Enable Public Interest Uses of Technologically Protected Copyrighted Works' (2007) 22 Berkeley Tech LJ 981
Ricketson S and Ginsburg J, *International Copyright and Neighbouring Rights* (Vol 1. 2nd edn, OUP 2005)
— — et al, *Intellectual Property: Cases, Materials and Commentary* (6th edn, LexisNexis Butterworths 2019)
Robertson A, 'Constraints on Policy-based Reasoning in Private Law' in Robertson A and Hang Wu T (eds), *The Goals of Private Law* (Hart Publishing 2009)
Rothman J, 'Copyright, Custom and Lessons from the Common Law' in Balganesh S (ed), *Intellectual Property and Common Law* (CUP 2013)
— — 'The Questionable Use of Custom in Intellectual Property' (2007) 93 Va L Rev 1899
— — 'Why Custom Cannot Save Copyright's Fair Use Defense' (2008) 93 Va L Rev In Brief 243
Ruse-Khan H, 'Overlaps and Conflict Norms in Human Rights Law' in Geiger C, *Research Handbook on Human Rights and Intellectual Property* (Edward Elgar Publishing 2015)
Seiman J, 'Using the Implied Licence to Inject Common Sense into Digital Copyright' (2007) 85 NCL Rev 885
Senftleben M, *Copyright, Limitations and the Three-Step Test* (Kluwer Law 2004)
— — 'The International Three-step Test: A Model Provision for EC Fair Use Legislation' (2010) 1 JIPITEC 67
Simone D, *Copyright and Collective Authorship* (CUP 2019)
Sims A, 'The Public Interest Defence in Copyright Law: Myth or Reality?' (2006) 28 EIPR 335
Steyn Sir J, 'Written Contracts: To What Extent May Evidence Control Language?' (1988) 41 CLP 23

Smith G and others, *Internet Law and Regulation* (Sweet & Maxwell 2007)
Smith H, 'Property as the Law of Things' (2012) 125 Harv L Rev 1691
Smith R, *Property Law* (9th edn, Pearson 2017)
Spence M, *Intellectual Property* (OUP 2007)
Stephens R, *Torts and Rights* (OUP 2007)
Stewart A and others, *Intellectual Property in Australia* (6th edn, LexisNexis Butterworths 2018)
Steyn Sir J, 'Written Contracts: To What Extent May Evidence Control Language?' (1988) 41 CLP 23
Steyn J, 'Contract Law: Fulfilling the Reasonable Expectations of Honest Men' (1997) 113 LQR 433
Swadling W, 'Property' in Andrew Burrows (ed), *English Private Law* (3rd edn, OUP 2013)
'Thumbnails III (Vorschaubilder III) – Decision of the Federal Supreme Court (Bundesgerichtshof)' (2018) 49 IIC 357
Vaver D, *Intellectual Property Law: Copyright, Patents, Trade-Marks* (2nd edn, Irwin Law 2011)
Vermut R, 'File Caching on the Internet: Technological Infringement or Safeguard for Efficient Network Operation?' (1997) 4 J Intell Prop L 273
Vitoria M and others, *Laddie, Prescott and Vitoria: The Modern Law of Copyright* (5th edn, LexisNexis 2018)
Young A, 'Mapping Horizontal Effect' in Hoffman D, *The Impact of the UK Human Rights Act on Private Law* (CUP 2013)

Index

For the benefit of digital users, indexed terms that span two pages (e.g., 52–53) may, on occasion, appear on only one of those pages.

Figures are indicated by *f* following the page number